Communications
in Computer and Information Science 477

Antanas Mitasiunas   Terry Rout
Rory V. O'Connor   Alec Dorling (Eds.)

Software Process Improvement and Capability Determination

14th International Conference, SPICE 2014
Vilnius, Lithuania, November 4-6, 2014
Proceedings

 Springer

Volume Editors

Antanas Mitasiunas
Vilnius University, Lithuania
E-mail: antanas.mitasiunas@mif.vu.lt

Terry Rout
Griffith University, Brisbane, QLD, Australia
E-mail: t.rout@griffith.edu.au

Rory V. O'Connor
Dublin City University, Ireland
E-mail: roconnor@computing.dcu.ie

Alec Dorling
InterSPICE Ltd, Cambridge, UK
E-mail: alec.dorling@interspice.uk.com

ISSN 1865-0929   e-ISSN 1865-0937
ISBN 978-3-319-13035-4   e-ISBN 978-3-319-13036-1
DOI 10.1007/978-3-319-13036-1
Springer Cham Heidelberg New York Dordrecht London

Library of Congress Control Number: 2014953337

Typesetting: Camera-ready by author, data conversion by Scientific Publishing Services, Chennai, India

Printed on acid-free paper

Springer is part of Springer Science+Business Media (www.springer.com)

Preface

On behalf of the SPICE Organizing Committee we are proud to present the proceedings of the 14th International Conference on Software Process Improvement and Capability dEtermination (SPICE 2014), held in Vilnius, Lithuania, during November 4–6, 2014.

The SPICE Project was formed in 1993 to support the development of an international standard for software process assessment. The work of the project has led to the finalization of the ISO/IEC 15504 – Process Assessment, and its complete publication represented a climax for the work of the project. The standardization effort continues, with the publication this year of the first documents in the new ISO/IEC 330xx family of standards on process assessment.

As part of its charter to provide ongoing publicity and transition support for the emerging standard, the project organized a number of SPICE Workshops and Seminars, with invited speakers drawn from project participants. These have now evolved to a sustaining set of international conferences with broad participation from academia and industry with a common interest in model-based process improvement. This was the 14th in the series of conferences organized by the SPICE User Group to increase knowledge and understanding of the International Standard and of the technique of process assessment.

The conference program featured invited keynote talks, research papers, and industry experience reports on the most relevant topics related to software process assessment and improvement; a significant focus this year was the transition to the new ISO/IEC 330xx framework, and the expansion in the range of applicable domains of interest. The technical research papers were selected for presentation following peer review by members of the Program Committee. In addition, a number of tutorials were hosted.

SPICE conferences have a long history of attracting attendees from industry and academia. This confirms that the conference covers topics that are up to date, important, and interesting. SPICE 2014 offered a unique forum for industry and academic professionals to discuss their needs and ideas in the area of process assessment and improvement, and related aspects of quality management.

On behalf of the SPICE 2014 Organizing Committee, we would like to thank all participants. Firstly all the authors, whose quality work is the essence of the conference, and the members of the Program Committee, who helped us with their expertise and diligence in reviewing all of the submissions. As we all know, organizing a conference requires the effort of many individuals. We wish to thank also all the members of our Organizing Committee, whose work and commitment were invaluable.

The local organizers acknowledge the support of Vilnius University and especially the Pro-Rector for Research Prof. Habil. Dr. Eugenijus Butkus, Director of the Directorate for Science and Innovation Ms. Vida Lapinskaite, Director of the

Directorate of General Affairs Mr. Lionginas Striganavicius, Dean of the Faculty of Mathematics and Informatics Prof. Habil. Dr. Gediminas Stepanauskas. In addition, we acknowledge the support of the Lithuanian Science Council.

The conference organizers wish to acknowledge the assistance and support of the SPICE User Group, SPICE 2014 Program Committee, and reviewers in contributing to a successful conference.

November 2014   Antanas Mitasiunas
                                                                    Terry Rout
                                                             Rory V. O'Connor
                                                                  Alec Dorling

Organization

General Chair

Alec Dorling   InterSPICE, UK

Program Chair

Terry Rout   Griffith University, Australia

Local Organizing Chair

Antanas Mitasiunas   Vilnius University, Lithuania

Industry Chair

Saulius Ragaisis   Vilnius University, Lithuania

Proceedings Chair

Rory V. O'Connor   Lero, Dublin City University, Ireland

Program Committee

Beatrix Barafort, Luxembourg
Luigi Buglione, Italy
Aileen Cater-Steel, Australia
Melanie Cheong, Australia
Francois Coallier, Canada
Gerhard Chroust, Austria
Antonio Coletta, Italy
Fabrizzio Fabbrini, Italy
Dennis Goldenson, USA
Christiane Gresse von
    Wangenheim, Brazil
Victoria Hailey, Canada
Linda Ibrahim, USA
Jørn Johansen, Denmark
Ravindra Joshi, India

Ho-Won Jung, South Korea
Bharathi V. Kumar, India
Giuseppe Lami, Italy
Marion Lepmets, Ireland
Catriona Mackie, UK
Antonia Mas, Spain
Tom McBride, Australia
Fergal McCaffery, Ireland
Takeshige Miyoshi, Japan
Risto Nevalainen, Finland
Rory O'Connor, Ireland
Mark Paulk, USA
Saulius Ragaisis, Lithuania
Alain Renault, Luxembourg
Patricia Rodriguez Dapena, Spain

Clenio Salviano, Brazil

Jean Martin Simon, France

Fritz Stallinger, Austria

Timo Varkoi, Finland

Local Organizing Committee

Romas Baronas   Vilnius University, Lithuania

Antanas Mitasiunas   Vilnius University, Lithuania

Saulius Ragaisis   Vilnius University, Lithuania

Table of Contents

Developing Process Models for Assessment

Constructing Process Measurement Scales Using the ISO/IEC 330xx
Family of Standards 1
    Ho-Won Jung, Timo Varkoi, and Tom McBride

Evolving a Method Framework for Engineering Process Assessment
Models 12
    Adriana M.C.M. Figueiredo and Clenio F. Salviano

Towards Methodological Support for the Engineering of Process
Reference Models for Product Software 24
    Fritz Stallinger and Reinhold Plösch

Software Process and Models 1

Towards a Process Assessment Model for Management System
Standards 36
    Stéphane Cortina, Nicolas Mayer, Alain Renault,
    and Béatrix Barafort

CERTICS - An ISO/IEC 15504 Conformance Model for Software
Technological Development and Innovation 48
    Clenio F. Salviano, Angela M. Alves, Giancarlo N. Stefanuto,
    Sonia T. Maintinguer, Carolina V. Mattos, and Camila Zeitoum

Development of the Project Management SPICE (PMSPICE)
Framework 60
    Antoni-Lluís Mesquida, Antònia Mas, Marion Lepmets,
    and Alain Renault

Software Process and Models 2

The Development and Validation of a Traceability Assessment Model ... 72
    Gilbert Regan, Fergal McCaffery, Kevin McDaid, and Derek Flood

Test Process Models: Systematic Literature Review 84
    Cecilia Garcia, Abraham Dávila, and Marcelo Pessoa

Government Process Capability Model: An Exploratory Case Study 94
    Ebru Gökalp and Onur Demirörs

Software Models and Product Lines

Tool for Usage of Multiple Process Assessment Models 106
   Stasys Peldzius and Saulius Ragaisis

Software Process Lines: A Systematic Literature Review 118
   Daniel Dias de Carvalho, Larissa Fernandes Chagas,
   Adailton Magalhães Lima, and Carla Alessandra Lima Reis

Assessment-Based Innovation System Customization for Software
Product Line Organizations 131
   Fritz Stallinger, Robert Neumann, and Robert Schossleitner

Assessment

A Lightweight Assessment Method for Medical Device Software
Processes 144
   Fergal McCaffery, Paul Clarke, and Marion Lepmets

A Safety-Critical Assessment Process 157
   Risto Nevalainen and Timo Varkoi

Towards Transparent and Efficient Process Assessments for IT Service
Management 165
   Anup Shrestha, Aileen Cater-Steel, Mark Toleman, and Terry Rout

Agile Processes

Systematic Literature Review on the Characteristics of Agile Project
Management in the Context of Maturity Models 177
   Larissa Fernandes Chagas, Daniel Dias de Carvalho,
   Adailton Magalhães Lima, and Carla Alessandra Lima Reis

An Agile Implementation within a Medical Device Software
Organisation 190
   Martin McHugh, Fergal McCaffery, and Garret Coady

Assessing Software Agility: An Exploratory Case Study 202
   Özden Özcan Top and Onur Demirörs

Processes Improvement and VSE

Modeling SPI Sustainment in Software-Developing Organizations:
A Research Framework 214
   Nazrina Khurshid and Paul L. Bannerman

Early Stage Adoption of ISO/IEC 29110 Software Project Management
Practices: A Case Study 226
    Rory V. O'Connor

Issues in Applying Model Based Process Improvement in the Cloud
Computing Domain 238
    Jeremy Cade, Lian Wen, and Terry Rout

Short Papers

An Assessment Framework for Engineering Education Systems 250
    Siegfried Rouvrais and Claire Lassudrie

Improving the Hardware/Software Culture 256
    Joanne Schell and Paul Schwann

Learning Process Maturity Model 261
    Justinas Marcinka, Oleg Mirzianov, and Antanas Mitasiunas

Designing Systems Engineering Profiles for Very Small Entities 268
    Claude Y. Laporte and Rory V. O'Connor

MDevSPICE - A Comprehensive Solution for Manufacturers and
Assessors of Safety-Critical Medical Device Software.................. 274
    Paul Clarke, Marion Lepmets, Fergal McCaffery, Anita Finnegan,
    Alec Dorling, and Derek Flood

Enterprise SPICE Export Extension 279
    Jeremy Besson, Antanas Mitasiunas, and Saulius Ragaisis

Author Index 283

Constructing Process Measurement Scales Using the ISO/IEC 330xx Family of Standards

Ho-Won Jung[1], Timo Varkoi[2], and Tom McBride[3]

[1] Korea University Business School, 145, Anam-ro, Seongbuk-gu,
Seoul, 136-701, Korea
hwjung@korea.ac.kr
[2] Finnish Software Measurement Association – FiSMA, Espoo, Finland
timo.varkoi@fisma.fi
[3] University of Technology, Sydney, Australia
Tom.McBride@uts.edu.au

Abstract. The emerging International Standard ISO/IEC 330xx family can be utilized to assess process quality characteristics, i.e., properties of processes such as process safety, efficiency, effectiveness, security, integrity and sustainability as well as capability like in ISO/IEC 15504. For development of scientific and consistent measurement framework for process quality characteristics, ISO/IEC 33003 defines requirements for a measurement framework in accordance to composite measure development steps. This study addresses some important principles of composite measures, identifies aggregation locales for process quality level (e.g., capability level in ISO/IEC 33020), and defines two types of aggregation methods. The aim is to improve understandability of process measurement frameworks of process quality characteristics.

Keywords: Aggregation, composite measure, multidimensional constructs, formative and reflective measurement models, measurement scale.

1 Introduction

Achieving acceptable levels of overall software quality seems now to be both reasonably well understood and insufficient for emerging interest in achieving higher levels of specific software qualities. There is ongoing interest in safety and in security, and potentially interest in sustainability as specific qualities of software products. An underlying principle of quality management has been that the quality of a product reflects the processes used to create it. That principle has underpinned efforts to establish and improve software development processes for at least 25 years. But now there is interest in how software and systems development processes can support the achievement of specific qualities such as security or safety. Part of that interest encourages development of processes and measurement scales for specific process quality characteristics [1].

Emerging process assessment International Standards within the ISO/IEC 330xx family [2] can be utilized to assess process quality characteristics, i.e., properties of processes such as process safety, efficiency, effectiveness, security, integrity and

A. Mitasiunas et al. (Eds.): SPICE 2014, CCIS 477, pp. 1–11, 2014.

sustainability as well as capability that was defined in the preceding standard ISO/IEC 15504 [3]. While preserving flexibility of measurement frameworks, the ISO/IEC 330xx family seeks consistency of all process measurement frameworks in principles and follows a scientific method of their development steps. For those purposes, ISO/IEC 33003 defines requirements for process measurement frameworks that derive composite measures (composite scaling and composite index) as process quality levels. Note, that in this study "scientific" implies rigorous steps, e.g., theory building and theory testing based in inductive and deductive cycles [4] and [5].

Furthermore, ambiguous measurement framework can be a source of problems or issues in providing reliable assessment results that "can be applied for improving process performance, benchmarking, or for identifying and addressing risks associated with application of processes" [2, page v]. However, there are few studies on the issues on measurement scale, aggregation, rating, etc. A study [6] provided a guide of standardization directions by following a scientific method. It describes issues associated with a foundation of ISO/IEC 33003. ISO/IEC 33020 [7] asserts that it meets the requirements of ISO/IEC 33003.

This study addresses some important principles of the requirements in ISO/IEC 33003 and associated ISO/IEC 33020 Clauses such as reflective and formative measurement models, their aggregation, etc. This study also identifies aggregation locales and addresses two types of aggregation methods to develop composite measures (scaling and index) based on reflective and formative measurement models. This would improve understandability of process measurement frameworks for process characteristic assessment.

2   Background

2.1   Composite Measures

ISO/IEC JTC1 SC7/WG10 developed a standard, numbered ISO/IEC 33003 [1], of requirements for process measurement frameworks. Since process quality characteristics to be measured in the framework are constructs/concepts, they are measured by using process (attribute) outcomes to generate a composite measure (e.g., process capability levels of ordinal scale in ISO/IEC 33003. Composite measure is a variable or value derived by aggregating a set of measures of a concept to a number or index such as ranking. It is based on an underlying/theoretical model of the multidimensional (i.e., higher order) construct that represents several distinct dimensions as a single theoretical concept [8].

In other than process domains, well-known composite measures include Organisation for Economic Co-operation and Development (OECD) ones including over 450 composite indicators (OECD term) across all domains (http://www.oecd.org/statistics/). UNDP (United Nations Development Programme) also presents over 200 ones [9]. OECD developed a guide to develop composite measures [10]. Main difference between composite measures developed by OECD/UNDP and process communities is ranking and process quality level, respectively.

2.2   Measurement Model Specification

The relationship (link) between a construct (or the latent variable representing the construct) and its indirect measures can be specified as reflective measurement or formative measurement model [11] and [12], depending on the point of view of the construct either as underlying factors of or indices produced by observed measures, respectively. ISO/IEC 33003 summarizes the characteristics of reflective and formative measurement models as shown in Table 1.

Table 1. Characteristics of reflective and formative (cited from [1])

Decision rule	Reflective measurement model	Formative measurement model
Characteristics of measures	• Measures are manifestations of the construct.	• Measures are defining characteristics of the construct.
	• Measures share a common theme.	• Measures need not share a common theme.
	• Measures should be interchangeable.	• Measures need not be interchangeable.
	• Measures should have the same or similar content.	• Measures need not have the same or similar content.
	• Excluding a measure should not alter the conceptual domain of the construct.	• Excluding a measure may alter the conceptual domain of the construct.
	• Measures are expected to co-vary with one another.	• Measures need not co-vary with one another.
Direction of causality between construct and measures	• The direction of causality is from the construct to its multi-item measures.	• Construct is a combination of its measures.
	• Changes in a measure should not cause changes in the construct.	• Changes in the construct should not cause changes in the measures.

A construct as an underlying factor is referred to as a reflective construct or a reflective (measurement) model (specification) as shown in Fig. 1a, whereas a construct as an index produced by observed measures is called a formative construct in Fig. 1b. In the figures, constructs are represented as ovals, observed measures as rectangles, causal paths as single-headed arrows, and correlations as double-headed arrows. Formative without disturbance term in Fig. 1c implies perfect measurement without missing measures. (Formative) Composite measures assume Fig. 1c, where aggregation utilizes multiple criteria (attribute) decision-making (MCDM/MADM). Fig. 1a and Fig. 1b are used in process model validation.

Correct specification of the measurement model should be empathized in the construct (theoretical) definition of process quality characteristics or attributes, because concepts and methods to aggregate outcomes depend on measurement model specification of constructs [1].

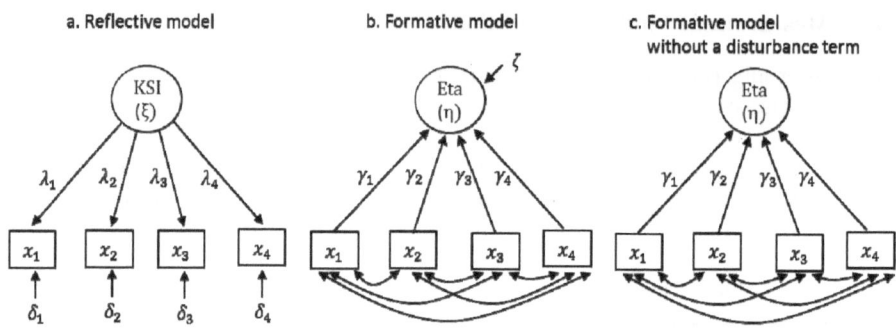

Fig. 1. Relationship between a construct and its measures [1]

3   Representing Process Outcomes with Measurement Models

Based on the requirements of ISO/IEC 33003 Clause 4.5 (Rating process attributes) and Clause 4.6 (Aggregation), ISO/IEC 33020 provides three types of rating methods. This section analyzes the first rating method in Table 2.

Table 2. Rating method R1 in ISO/IEC 33020 Clause 5.4.1

The approach to process attribute rating shall satisfy the following conditions:
a)   Each process outcome of each process within the scope of the assessment shall be characterized for each process instance, based on validated data;
b)   Each process attribute outcome of each process attribute for each process within the scope of the assessment shall be characterized for each process instance, based on validated data;
c)   Process outcome characterizations for all assessed process instances shall be aggregated to provide a process performance attribute achievement rating;
d)   Process attribute outcome characterizations for all assessed process instances shall be aggregated to provide a process attribute achievement rating.

3.1   Measurement Scale

ISO/IEC 33020 does not provide a measurement scale for process attribute outcome characterizations. Instead, ISO/IEC 33003 (4.5 Rating process attributes) requires a measurement scale of process attributes, i.e., nominal, ordinal, interval, or ratio [1]. This implies that if a process attribute (PA) is rated with a ratio scale, a process (attribute) outcome should be measured with ratio scale. Furthermore, if PA is rated with an ordinal scale, a process (attribute) outcome can be measured with an ordinal, interval, or ratio scale.

3.2   Rating Method R1

Rating method R1 in Table 2 requires the characterization (i.e. a) and b)) and aggregation (i.e. c) and d)) of process (attribute) outcomes across all process instances. The characterization requirements implicitly mean that process (attribute) outcomes are base measures. Base measure implies that they are functionally independent of other measures [13]. Process (attribute) outcomes as base measures meet the characteristics of the formative model in Table 1. For example, they are not interchangeable and do not share a common theme.

In order to avoid critics of formative models that measure cause construct, Edwards [14] presents an alternative representation (e.g., Fig. 2a) by replacing each formative measure with a single-measure reflective construct (e.g., Fig. 2b). This approach was also recommended in clinical studies [15]. In Fig. 2a, PA 2.2 (work product process attribute defined in ISO/IEC 33020) in oval is a formative construct of four process attribute outcomes as base measures denoted OC 2.2a, ..., OC 2.2d in rectangles. In Fig. 2b, each of four measures is depicted with a reflective construct with a single measure. Suppose error free measures of x s (i.e., var(δ_i)=0) and loadings of 1 (i.e., λ =0 for all i). Then Fig. 2b is reduced to Fig. 2a [14] . Thus, we can say that Fig. 2a is a special case of Fig. 2b. "Reflective" in ISO/IEC 33020 Figure A.1 represents the arrows between constructs and their measures OC 2.2a, ..., OC 2.2d in Fig. 2b.

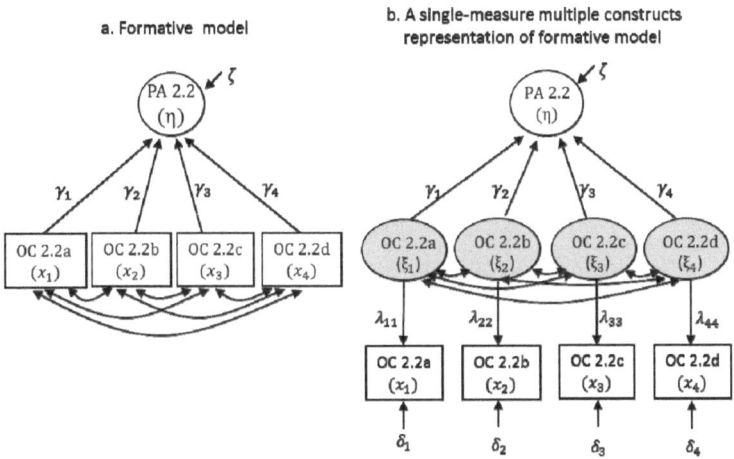

Fig. 2. Two ways of formative model representations (single process instance)

ISO/IEC 33002 (Clause 4.6.2) defines Class 1 assessment so that it requires a minimum of four process instances. This requirement assumes to measure the true value of process characteristic with precision. This is the same concept that increasing sample size reduces the standard error [6]. Note that measuring all process instances in an organizational unit (OU) implies to get a true value. Thus, increasing process instances should not be interpreted to measure organizational maturity. As a reference, organizational maturity is related to a scope of processes under assessment.

The reflective rationale is that n outcome scores of process instances at implementation-level can be considered as a random sample from all possible scores of corresponding outcomes in an assessed OU, i.e., a domain sampling [16]. They can be also considered as repeated measurement of an outcome defined. This is called repeatability in measurement reliability in the next section. A domain sampling is the same concept as reflective measurement.

PA rating in the process capability of multiple process instances can be depicted as a multidimensional construct shown in Fig. 3 (PA 2.2 example), where outcomes of each process instance is named as "implementation-level" outcomes. Aggregation across outcomes of all process instances for a specific outcome becomes "process-level" outcome as a composite measure [6]. Multiple observed outcomes would be expected to result in more reliable and less prone to random error than a single instance outcome. Then, each composite measure in process-level outcome (e.g., four composite measures in oval in Fig. 3 should be aggregated to a PA rating defined in ISO/IEC 33020 Clause 5.3 (Process attribute rating scale).

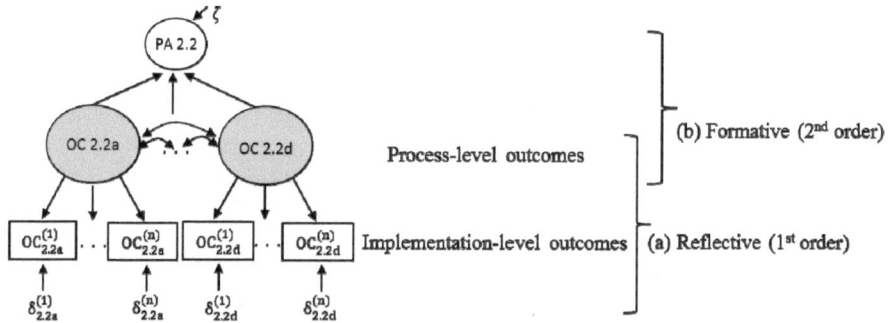

Fig. 3. A multidimensional construct of multiple process instances [6]

4   Aggregating Process Outcomes to a PA Rating

4.1   Aggregation Locales

Aggregating a set of measures to create a composite measure depends on the construct specification, i.e., reflective or formative constructs [4], [17], [18], and [19]. A composite measure of a reflective construct is sometimes called a composite scale(ing), whereas that of a formative construct is named as a composite index [4]. As measurement scales should be developed "sensible" to academia as well as practitioners, aggregate scales should also be developed to provide "sensible" meaning as well.

This study maps ISO/IEC 33020 Clause 5.5 (Aggregation method) shown in Table 3 to Fig. 2 and Fig. 3 as follows:

- In Table 3, the first bullet addresses the aggregation of process (attribute) outcomes of a single process instance in Fig. 2. This is implementation-level aggregation of formative measurement model. Process level equals to implementation level.
- The second bullet addresses implementation-level aggregation of reflective measurement model in the first order shown in Fig. 3 (a).
- The third bullet implies the reflective first-order (implementation-level) and formative second-order (process-level) in Fig. 3 (b).

Table 3. Aggregation method in ISO/IEC 33020 Clause 5.5

When rating a
• process attribute for a given process, one may aggregate ratings of the associated process (attribute) outcomes — such an aggregation will be performed as a vertical aggregation (one dimension). • process (attribute) outcome for a given process attribute across multiple process instances, one may aggregate the ratings of the associated process instances for the given process (attribute) outcome — such an aggregation will be performed as a horizontal aggregation (one dimension) • process attribute for a given process, one may aggregate the ratings of all the process (attribute) outcomes for all the processes instances such an aggregation will be performed as a matrix aggregation across the full scope of ratings (two dimensions)

In ISO/IEC 33020 (Table 1. Process capability level ratings), the heuristic transformation from a set of PAs to a capability level rating is also a kind of algorithmic/heuristic aggregation. In summary, there are three aggregation locales in SPICE assessments: Locale 1: (1st order part) – reflective; Locale 2: Fig. 3 (a) and Fig. 3 (b) (2nd order part) - formative, and Locale 3: from a set of PAs to a capability level rating. Locale 3 is not addressed in this study.

4.2   Aggregation Methods for Reflective

Aggregation of reflective measures corresponds to Fig. 3 (a) (1st order part, Locale 1) of multiple process instances. Characteristics of reflective measures in Table 1 illustrate that aggregation utilizes the concept of average. In traditional psychological studies, unweighted (equal weight) summated scores are efficient [16]. Fayers [20] cites that many other studies also confirmed its usefulness. Gerbing and Anderson [21] also computed a composite score which is calculated as the unweighted sum of item scores and is then used as an estimate of the corresponding construct under unidimensionality.

When using a ratio scale in the measurement of process (attributes) outcome, average may be an aggregation method. If measured values of process (attribute) outcomes include outliers or highly skewed values, median may be an alternative aggregation method. Mathematical concept of average aggregation can be found in Jung [6]. If an ordinal scale is used in process (attributes) outcome measurement, median may become a prospective method.

4.3   Aggregation Methods for Formative

Formative can have a linear combination form of measures, where weights are assigned by the importance or priority of those measures. This is called simple additive weighting (SAW) method in multiple attribute decision-making (MADM) [22]. Jung [6] suggests two more aggregation methods, called weighted product (WP) method and conjugate method, after reviewing 13 MADM methods described by Yoon and Hwang [22]. Depending on process quality characteristics, measurement scale, and/or assessment policy, appropriate aggregation methods can be employed for aggregation of formative specification.

SAW and WP aggregation methods require weight assignment to process (attribute) outcomes. This study recommends the analytic hierarchy process (AHP) [23]. AHP was successfully utilized in a SAW method for aggregating process practice (i.e., outcome) achievement [24]. A study [25] shows that AHP can be also employed to detect inconsistency in weight assignment among assessors. However, after analyzing a variety of medical datasets, Fayers [20] concludes that "usually a simple summation remains adequate and little is gained by other methods .... Because most items are considered to have important impact to a patient's HRQOL (Health-Related Quality-Of-Life) ... Patients who are weak are likely to suffer from multiple symptoms" (p. 173). This is a case that both formative and reflective specifications can utilize unweighted average as a composite measure.

5   Qualities of Outcomes

What are the desirable qualities of process (attribute) outcomes as measures of a construct? They are reliability and validity [26] that are defined in ISO/IEC 33003 Clause 5. Examples of their concepts are presented in Fig. 4. They can be applied to implementation-level outcomes in Fig. 3(a). Given evidence of unidimensionality among item measures, factor reliabilities and discriminant validity can now be assessed [21].

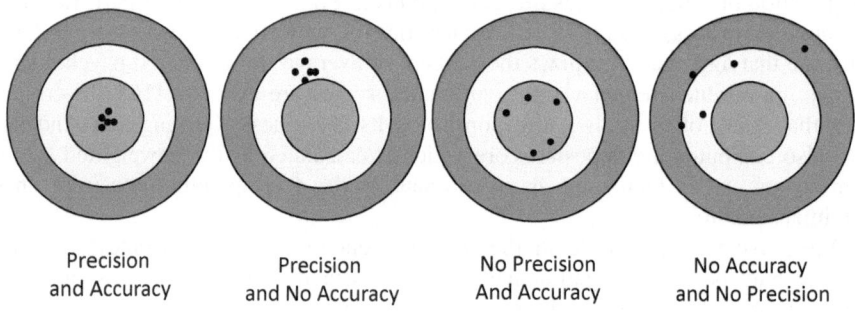

| Precision and Accuracy | Precision and No Accuracy | No Precision And Accuracy | No Accuracy and No Precision |

Fig. 4. Precision (Reliability) and Accuracy (Validity)

In statistical perspective, reliability implies precision that is the dispersion of the measurements around their average, whereas validity means accuracy, i.e., if repetitive measurements of the same object yield an average equal to its true value.

5.1   Reliability

The term reliability has sometimes been confused (e.g., "To improve the reliability and repeatability of the assessment" in ISO/IEC 15504-5, p. 14), because it includes two distinct aspects: (1) repeatability (stability) and (2) consistency (equivalence) [26]. Repeatability means that a measure (outcome) is considered reliable if it would give you the same result over and over again (assuming that what you are measuring is not changing). It can be estimated by using test-retests or alternative-form. On the other hand, consistency implies that any measuring instrument is relatively reliable if it is minimally affected by random measurement error. It is estimated by using split-half or internal consistency (Cronbach's alpha) with multiple outcomes' measurement at a single point in time [26].

Cronbach's alpha that denotes correlations among implementation-level outcomes is the most common method used in process studies [27] because it can be used to examine standard's ambiguities in wording and inconsistencies in its interpretation by assessors [27]. Outcomes in a unidimensional construct have a high value of Cronbach's alpha. Cronbach's coefficient can be also used to calculate the potential gain of adding extra outcomes to a scale because it increases as the number of outcomes in the scale increases.

In the context of 330xx family of standards, the more the process instances, the higher the Cronbach's alpha. Previous process studies followed their acceptable minimum Cronbach's alpha of 0.9 because assessment results can be used in important decisions [16]. A reliability of 0.9 means that about 90% of the variance of the observed score is attributable to truth and 10% is attributable to error.

5.2   Validity

ISO/IEC 33003 describes construct validity that denotes the degree to which operationalization accurately reflects its construct, i.e., any measuring instrument measures what it is intended to measure [26] as shown in Fig. 4. The standard describes construct validities such as face, content, predictive, concurrent, convergent, and discriminant.

Face and content validities are generally applicable to all hierarchies in a multidimensional construct. The remaining validities can be only applied to reflective models. Johnson, et al. [28] provides a guideline to improve validity of multidimensional construct. This guide can be consulted in case of developing and validating multidimensional construct.

In validity studies utilizing structural equation modeling (e.g., predictive validity), since formative construct cannot be identified [11], it cannot be estimated without two reflective indicators. Detail is described in [6].

6   Final Remarks

A plethora of process capability/maturity models has been developed and are under development. However, most of them do not show any rationale of their development steps or methods. ISO/IEC JTC1 SC7/WG10 develops ISO/IEC 33003 (Requirements for process measurement frameworks) based on measurement theories. We expect that ISO/IEC 33003 can contribute to the methods when establishing scientific process measurement frameworks within ISO process standardization groups.

This study provides a rationale of composite measures in ISO/IEC 33003 requirements and related clauses in ISO/IEC 33020. Specifically, three potential aggregation locates are identified and, wherein aggregation methods depend on measurement model, specifications are explained. We also address reliability and validity of process quality level. These methods can increase the confidence in assessment results of process quality levels including process capability. However, a simplified method may be considered according to class of assessment (ISO/IEC 33020 Clause 4.6) and/or categories of independence (ISO/IEC 33020 Annex A).

Measurement theories are relatively new in software (information technology) process communities including ISO process standardization groups. Thus, the next work should be to develop a formal, easy-to-use process quality-level determination guide with minimum amount of theories and statistical formula.

Acknowledgements. The authors would like to thank ISO/IEC JTC1 SC7/WG10 delegates who participated in the development of the 330xx family of International Standards. The research was supported by Korea University Business School (2013). This support is gratefully acknowledged.

References

1. ISO/IEC 33003: Information Technology — Process Assessment — Requirements for Process Measurement Frameworks. ISO/IEC JTC1/SC 7 WG10 (2014)
2. ISO/IEC 33001: Information Technology — Process Assessment — Concepts and Terminology. ISO/IEC JTC1/SC 7 WG10 (2014)
3. ISO/IEC 15504-5: Information Technology — Process Assessment — Part 5: An Exemplar Process Assessment Model. Geneva, Switzerland, ISO (2012)
4. Trochim, W.M.K., Donnelly, J.P.: The Research Methods Knowledge Base. Thomson Custom Pub. (2007)
5. Cooper, D.R., Schindle, P.S.: Business Research Methods, 11th edn. McGraw-Hill, Singapore (2011)
6. Jung, H.-W.: Investigating Measurement Scales and Aggregation Methods in SPICE Assessment Method. Information and Software Technology 55(8), 1450–1461 (2013)
7. ISO/IEC 33020: Information Technology — Process Assessment — Process Measurement Framework for Assessment of Process Capability and Organizational Process Maturity. ISO/IEC JTC1/SC 7 WG10 (2014)
8. Edwards, J.R.: Multidimensional Constructs in Organizational Behavior Research: An Integrative Analytical Framework. Organizational Research Methods 4(2), 144–192 (2001)
9. Bandura, R.: A Survey of Composite Indices Measuring Country Performance, Update. A UNDP/ODS Working Paper (2008), http://goo.gl/4se8yY
10. Nardo, M., Saisana, M., Saltelli, A., Tarantola, S., Hoffman, A., Giovannini, E.: Handbook on Constructing Composite Indicators: Methodology and User Guide. OECD publishing, http://www.oecd.org/std/42495745.pdf
11. Bollen, K.A., Lennox, R.: Conventional Wisdom on Measurement: A Structural Equation Perspective. Psychological Bulletin 110(2), 305–314 (1991)
12. Diamantopoulos, A., Siguaw, J.A.: Formative Versus Reflective Indicators in Organizational Measure Development: A Comparison and Empirical Illustration. British Journal of Management 17(4), 263–282 (2006)
13. ISO/IEC 15939: Information Technology — Process Assessment — Part 10: Safety Extension. Geneva, Switzerland, ISO (2007)

14. Edwards, J.R.: The Fallacy of Formative Measurement. Organizational Research Methods 14(2), 370–388 (2011)
15. Fayers, P.M., Hand, D.J.: Causal Variables, Indicator Variables and Measurement Scales: An Example from Quality of Life. Journal of the Royal Statistical Society: Series A (Statistics in Society) 165(2), 233–253 (2002)
16. Nunnally, J.C., Bernstein, H.H.: Psychometric Theory. McGraw-Hill, New York (2004)
17. Nardo, M., Saisana, M., Saltelli, A., Tarantola, S.: Tools for Composite Indicators Building. European Commission-Joint Research Centre, EUR 21682 (2005)
18. Bollen, K.A.: Indicator: Methodology. International Encyclopedia of the Social and Behavioral Sciences, 7282–7287 (2001)
19. Rijsdijk, S.A., Hultink, E.J., Diamantopoulos, A.: Product Intelligence: Its Conceptualization, Measurement and Impact on Consumer Satisfaction. Journal of the Academy of Marketing Science 35(3), 340–356 (2007)
20. Fayers, P.: Quality-of-Life Measurement in Clinical Trials: The Impact of Causal Variables. Journal of Biopharmaceutical Statistics 14(1), 155–176 (2004)
21. Gerbing, D.W., Anderson, J.C.: An Updated Paradigm for Scale Development Incorporating Unidimensionality and Its Assessment. Journal of Marketing Research 25(2) (1988)
22. Yoon, K.P., Hwang, C.-L.: Multiple Attribute Decision Making: An Introduction. Sage University Paper Series on Quantitative Applications in Social Sciences Thousand Oaks, CA (1995)
23. Saaty, T.L.: How to Make a Decision: The Analytic Hierarchy Process. European Journal of Operational Research 48(1), 9–26 (1990)
24. Jung, H.W.: Rating the Process Attribute Utilizing Ahp in SPICE-Based Process Assessments. Software Process: Improvement and Practice 6(2), 111–122 (2001)
25. Yoon, M.-S., Jung, H.-W.: A Study on the Utilization of Compatibility Metric in the Ahp: Applying to Software Process Assessments. In International Symposium on the Analytic Hierarchy Process (ISAHP 2005), Honolulu, Hawaii (2005), http://goo.gl/JUhMEc
26. Carmines, E., Zeller, R.: Reliability and Validity Assessment. Sage University Paper Series on Quantitative Applications in Social Sciences Thousand Oaks, CA (1979)

Evolving a Method Framework for Engineering Process Assessment Models

Adriana M.C.M. Figueiredo and Clenio F. Salviano

Centro de Tecnologia da Informação Renato Archer
Rodovia D. Pedro I, km 143.6, CEP 13069-901
Campinas, SP, Brazil
{Adriana.Figueiredo,Clenio.Salviano}@cti.gov.br

Abstract. In 2009 a research team analyzed how Process Assessment Models (PAM) had been produced. As a consequence, MFMOD was developed as a Method Framework for engineering Process Assessment Models (MFMOD). Producing PAMs using an engineering approach is a desirable research topic in Software Process Improvement due to the need for distinct and more specialized PAMs and the publication of ISO/IEC 15504 International Standard that includes requirements for PAMs. Lately MFMOD has been used as reference for defining processes for engineering three different PAMs and for defining a specific method for customizing PAMs. An analysis of how MFMOD was used confirmed its usefulness and indicated improvement opportunities for evolving it. This article introduces a work in progress to evolve it towards an improved version.

Keywords: Process Assessment Model (PAM), ISO/IEC 15504, SPICE, Software Process Improvement (SPI), Method Framework.

1   Introduction

A Reference Model with good practices is an important element in Process Assessment and Improvement. These practices are organized in specific processes and generic capability levels. These practices can be further organized in maturity levels. The most disseminate models are the Software Capability Maturity Model (SW-CMM), its successor the Capability Maturity Model Integration for Development (CMMI-DEV) [1], and an ISO/IEC 15504 conformance models, as, for example, the Enterprise SPICE integrated model for enterprise-wide improvement [2] and the Automotive SPICE Process Assessment Model [3].

A relevant reference is the ISO/IEC 15504 Standard for Process Assessment [4], also known as SPICE (Software Process Improvement and Capability dEtermination). The current version of ISO/IEC 15504 defines requirements, a measurement framework, examples and guidance for models and processes for process assessment. It defines three related types of models: Process Reference Model (PRM), Process Assessment Model (PAM) and Organizational Maturity Model (OMM). ISO/IEC 15504 is being revised and renamed to the ISO/IEC 33000 Series.

A. Mitasiunas et al. (Eds.): SPICE 2014, CCIS 477, pp. 12–23, 2014.

A wide range of these models have been developed, evolved and adapted over the past years. A systematic literature review has been performed to identify these models [5]. The authors examined all English-language articles on PAMs available from digital libraries and databases, published between January 1990 and April 2009. The authors limited the articles to peer reviewed work, including only papers published in journals or conference proceedings. The results identified 53 PAMs (and OMMs) distributed into 39 different domains. The results recognized that most of those models are concentrated around the CMM model, CMMI framework and ISO/IEC 15504. The results show that there exist a large variety of models with a trend to the specialization of those models for specific domains.

Meanwhile a methodology to evolve current software process improvement technologies from a model-based approach to a modeling driven approach has been developed: The PRO2PI Methodology (Process Modeling Profile to Process Improvement) [6].   PRO2PI Methodology guides process improvement driven by a dynamic Process Modeling Profile with elements from multiple models. PRO2PI also includes methodological support for engineering more specific models.

In 2009, as part of PRO2PI evolution, we analyzed how PAMs had been created. The objective of these analyses was to support the emergence of a method to guide the creation of new model. We concluded that although there was enough knowledge to design guidance to create new models, that knowledge was not sufficient to produce a method. Then we identified the concept of Method Framework. Method Framework was defined and used by Firesmith for a Method Framework for Engineering System Architectures [7]. A Method Framework is composed by an ontology of reusable concepts and terminology, a metamodel of reusable method components, a repository of reusable method components: work units, work products and workers, and a metamethod for generating appropriate project-specific engineering methods. Firesmith concluded: "No single system architecture engineering method is sufficiently general and tailorable to meet the needs of all endeavors". A similar conclusion was reached for a PAM engineering method. An alternative interpretation of Method Framework, with different types of components, was defined and used for a Method Framework for Engineering Process Assessment Models (MFMOD) [8] [9] as part of PRO2PI Methodology.

The constructing of PAMs using an engineering approach is a new research topic in Software Process Improvement due to the need for new and more specialized PAMs and the dissemination of ISO/IEC 15504.

During 2009-2010, a draft version of MFMOD was developed. It was validated in the engineering of two distinct models: one model for software development in a cooperative way and another model for confidence in software services [9]. These utilizations provided confidence about the usefulness of MFMOD. After minor adjustments, the first version of MFMOD was published in 2010. MFMOD is a methodological component of PRO2PI Methodology. In this context it is also identified as PRO2PI-MFMOD. The Method Framework can also be used independently of PRO2PI Methodology. It is described in this way in this article.

This article introduces a work in progress to evolve the current version of MFMOD.

2   Method Framework MFMOD Version 1.0

The current version of MFMOD is composed of five components: Sequential practices, Customization rules, Guidelines for using the framework, Repository for examples of utilizations and Repository for examples of techniques [9]. Figure 1 depicts the seven sequential practices.

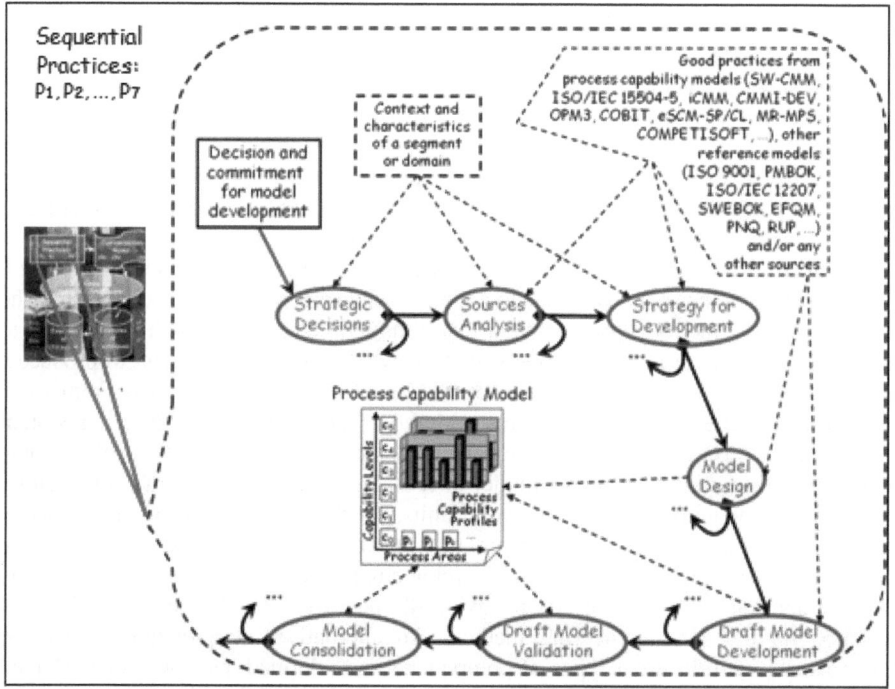

Fig. 1. Seven sequential practices of MFMOD [9]

There are seven sequential practices to guide the development of a method or process to engineer a model:

P1: Strategic decisions;

P2: Sources analysis;

P3: Strategy for development;

P4: Design;

P5: Draft development;

P6: Draft validation; and

P7: Consolidation.

The first practice of MFMOD is related to strategic decisions after a decision and commitment for model development. Two key strategic decisions are about the domain and context of the model and how the community of interest will be involved. The ISO/IEC 15504´s requirements for models include documenting the community of interest of the model and the actions taken to achieve consensus within that community of interest.

In the second practice (Sources analysis) we identified, gathered and analyzed sources for good practices. These sources can include other models, literature review, surveys, and others. These sources are based on the context and characteristics of a segment or domain. The third practice (Strategy for development) is related with the definition of the strategy to be used to develop the model. One key issue is how the community of interest will be involved in this development. Another issue is using selected good practices from process capability models, other types of reference models and/or any other sources.

The fourth practice (Model design) is related to the design of the model. ISO/IEC 15504 defines as general structure for a model as PRM, PAM or OMM. The fifth practice is the draft model development. The sixth practice is the validation of the draft model. The seventh practice is the consolidation of the model.

These sequential practices can be customized as activities of a method or process. This customization is oriented by combinations of eight simple rules (CR1 to CR8). These customization rules are described as follows, in terms of the relationship between one or more method framework´s practice and one or more method or process's activity:

- CR1: A practice corresponds to an activity (one practice to one activity);

- CR2: There is no activity that corresponds to a practice, because the results to be produced by the practice execution are already predefined by the method or process (one practice to zero activity);

- CR3: There are no activities that correspond to one or more consecutives final practices, because the life cycle of the method or process ends before those final practices (many final practices to zero activity);

- CR4: Two or more activities correspond to one practice, because the activities are more detailed customization of the practice (one practice to many activities);

- CR5: An activity corresponds to two or more consecutive practices, because the activity is a more general and simplified customization of the practices (many practices to one activity);

- CR6: There are consecutive activities that correspond to an activity followed by a previous activity, allowing cycles (go back pointer);

- CR7: In case of parallel activities, the other customization rules apply for each parallel sequence of activities and for the fork and joint connections; and

- CR8: There is one or more technique that is specified for one or more activities.

The Guidelines provides recommendations to understand and use the framework. There are two repositories: one for examples of utilizations and another for examples of techniques.

3   Analysis of Method Framework MFMOD Version 1.0

In the last four years, MFMOD has been used as reference for a process to develop a significant novel PAM (CERTICS Model) [10] [11], a process to develop a measurement reference for a future PAM (Systemic Maturity Model) [12] [13] and a specific method for knowledge acquisition to customize PAMs (KAcq Method) [14]. As a process to develop another new PAM (SaaS Reference Model) used KAcq Method, we considered that it indirectly used MFMOD. In order to guide the analysis of MFMOD, its objectives are defined using a revised GQM's template [16] [Table 1].

Table 1. Objectives

Revised GQM template	Objectives
Analyze	*MFMOD*
by means of	*the correspondence of practices and activities*
for the purpose of	*evaluate*
with respect to	*Usefulness*
in order to	*confirm its usefulness and identify improvement opportunities*
from the viewpoint of	*MFMOD specialist*
in the context of	*a research project to evolve MFMOD*

The basis for MFMOD development was the identification and generalization of the activities performed to construct a PAM. The sequential practices are a generalization of these activities. This analysis is following the same basis. With the mapping between the actual activities and the practices, the usefulness of MFMOD can be confirmed and improvement opportunities can be identified. The next four subsections describe utilizations of MFMOD with an overview about each one of them and a table with the correspondence between the phases and activities and the Practices (P1 to P7). When no correspondence is identified the term NC is used.

3.1   CERTICS Assessment Reference Model

CERTICS is the name of a methodology for assessment and certification of software resulting from technological development and innovation carried out in Brazil. Therefore the assessment examines the process performed to develop and commercialize the software. There are two key components of CERTICS methodology: the CERTICS Assessment Reference Model (CERTICS Model) and CERTICS Assessment Method.

The CERTICS Model is an ISO/IEC 15504 conformity PRM, PAM and OMM. This PAM has been developed by a multidisciplinary team from September 2011 to May 2012 (version 1.0) [10] and from July 2012 to June 2013 (version 1.1) [11] [Table 2].

Table 2. Correspondence for CERTICS

Phases and Activities	Practice
Phase 1 – Version 1.0 Development	
A1.1: Establish the project and project team	P1
A1.2: Study the context	P1
A1.3: Analyze general references	P2
A1.4: Define the concept for assessment	P1
A.1.5: Confirm development of a process assessment model	P1
A1.6: Analyze references and define development strategy	P2, P3
A1.7: Design the model	P4
A1.8: 1st develop and validate draft model cycle	P5, P6
A1.9: 2nd develop and validate draft model cycle	P5, P6
A1.10: 3rd develop and validate draft model cycle	P5, P6
A1.11: Consolidate model (version 1.0)	P7
Phase 2 – Version 1.1 Development	
A2.1: Revision from a public consultancy	P6
A2.2: Survey on usage for SME	P6
A2.3: Analysis and design decisions	P3, P4
A2.4: New cycle of develop and validate model	P5, P6
A2.5: Consolidate and release of version 1.1	P7

3.2   Systemic Maturity Model

Systemic Maturity Model is a term we created to mean a Measurement Framework for Quality of software production in the Digital Ecosystem Domain. The Systemic Maturity Model was developed for the Brazilian Public Software as an example of a Digital Ecosystem [12] [13]. The theoretical references ranged from ISO/IEC 15504 and MFMOD to concepts of complex systems, systemic thinking and digital ecosystems. The research methodology used was Action Research was used in two years fieldwork with four phases (Table 3).

Table 3. Correspondence for Systemic Maturity Model

Phases and Activities	Practice
Phase 1	
A1.1: Analysis of the project, team set up, strategy for executing the project	P1
A1.2: Literature review and project documentation	P2
A1.3: Semi-structured interviews and application of Café Mundial methodology	P2
A1.4: Definition of purposes and vision and team training	P1
Phase 2	
A2.1: Initial decisions	P1
A2.2: Literature research	P2
A2.3: Deepening literature review of four theoretical themes.	P2
A2.4: Dissemination of basic concepts of theoretical themes.	P1
A2.5: Identification of domain and scope.	P1
A2.6: Interaction with the communities.	P1, P2
A2.7: Strategy for the development of the Reference Model version 1.0.	P3
A2.8: Development of the Reference Model version 1.0.	P4
Phase 3	
A3.1: Definition of the situation of interest.	P1
A3.2: Learning with behavior patterns and building of systemic map.	P2
A3.3: Learning with systemic maps.	P3
A3.4: Learning with mental models.	P2
A3.5: Build and simulation of scenarios.	P2
A3.6: Learning with computational model.	P2
A3.7: Plan of systemic development.	P1, P2
Phase 4	
A4.1: Development of the Reference Model, v2.0.	P3, P4
A4.2: Development of the Reference Model, v3.0.	P4
A4.3: Strategy for developing reference model, v4.0, a systemic version.	P3
A4.4: Design of the reference model, v4.0.	P4
A4.5: Developing the reference model, v4.0.	P5
A4.6: Validation of the reference model, v4.0.	P6

3.3   KAcq Method

KAcq Method is a term we created to mean the knowledge acquisition method for customizing Capability/Maturity Software Process Models [14]. KAcq Method was developed using a systematic approach. It considers a PAM as "best practices" knowledge repositories. Hence by focusing on the extraction and modeling of the knowledge it uses Knowledge Engineering. The method is structured in five phases: Knowledge Identification, Knowledge Specification, Knowledge Refinement, Knowledge Usage and Knowledge Evolution. Each phase is composed of a set of activities. The two last phases are outside the scope of MFMOD [Table 4]. MFMOD was used as reference for many activities in the first three phases.

Table 4. Correspondence for KAcq Method

Phase and Activities	Practice
Phase 1: Knowledge Identification	
A1.1: Familiarize with domain	P1
A1.2: Identify information sources	P2
A1.3: Define scope and goals	P3
A1.4: Formalize the working group	NC
Phase 2: Knowledge Specification	
A2.1: Develop the design/architecture of the model	P4
A2.2: Analyze and integrate existing related models	P2, P3, P4
A2.3: Develop a draft model - process dimension	P5
A2.4: Develop a draft model - capability dimension	P5
Phase 3: Knowledge Refinement	
A3.1: Evaluate draft model	P6
A3.2: Consolidate draft model	P7
A3.3: Ballot on the consolidated model	P6
A3.4: Approve the model	P7
A3.5: Publish	P7
Phase 4: Knowledge Usage	
A4.1: Support model usage	NC
A4.2: Validate model in use	NC
Phase 5: Knowledge Evolution	
A5.1: Change request management	NC
A5.2: Confirmation, revision or withdrawal	NC

3.4   SaaS Reference Model

SaaS Reference Model is a term we created to mean the Capability and Maturity Model for Software Process Improvement for Collaborative Software-as-a-Service [15]. This Model is a repository of best practices to Services Development Processes (SaaS) and Collaboration. Based on software engineering and management principles of the process, it is organized into capability and maturity levels, designed to improve processes. This Model offers a chance to adapt the quality demands from providers, offering more positive arguments in its hiring and supporting the collaboration among providers. Its development used the first three phases KAcq Method [Table 5]. The main activities are defined as specific goals.

Table 5. Correspondence for SaaS Reference Model

Activities	Practice
A.1: Preparation	P1
A.2: Identify processes of collaboration among SaaS providers	P2
A.3: Identify processes related with software services development	P2
A.4: Create a ISO/IEC 15504 conformance PRM	P3, P4, P5
A.5: Define base practices (collaboration and software system development)	P5
A.6: Define capability and maturity levels	P5
A.7: Evaluate Maturity and Capability Model	P6
A.8: Consolidate	P7

3.5   Analyses and Design Decisions

As three out of four experiences (CERTICS Model, Systemic Maturity Model and KAcq Method) explicitly used MFMOD and provided a correspondence between its activities and MFMOD's practices, we can conclude that MFMOD was useful. As the development of SaaS Reference Model uses KAcq Method as reference and the usefulness of KAcq Method was recognized, we could create the correspondence between its activities and MFMOD's practices and we can conclude that MFMOD was also useful. Following these conclusions, a design decision is to understand better how it was used and evolve MFMOD in order to improve it usefulness.

In order to support another analysis of MFMOD, a graphical representation of the usage of its practices in these four experiences for deriving activities with cycles, as described in Tables 2, 3, 4 and 5, was produced [Fig. 2]. The objective of this analysis was to identify possible model development characteristics related with patterns of activities and cycles.

Analyzing Figure 2, we noticed that there are a significant number of activities and cycles related to MFMOD Practice 1 (Strategic decisions) for CERTICS Model (four activities in three cycles) and Systemic Maturity Model (eight activities in seven cycles). For KAcq Method and SaaS Reference Model there is only one activity.

Analyzing the development of CERTICS Model and Systemic Maturity Model, we noticed that in both cases the development of a PAM was without a precise decision on to what concept and domain. In both cases, the definition of the concept and domain was part of the problem. KAcq Method does not provide activities for this decision because it assumes that this decision was taken before. For SaaS Reference Model, the decision was taken before its development. Therefore, although MFMOD works for all these four cases, an improvement opportunity is to review the Practice 1 to better support a case like CERTICS Model or Systemic Maturity Model.

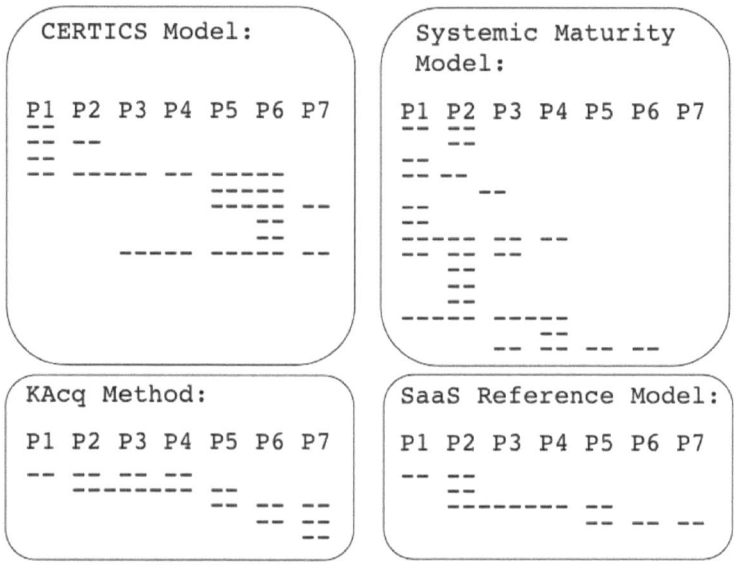

Fig. 2. Correspondence of practices with activities and cycles

In another analysis of Figure 2, we noticed that there are a significant number of activities and cycles related with MFMOD final three Practices (P5: Draft development; P6: Draft validation; and P7: Consolidation) for CERTICS Model (eight activities in four cycles) and KAcq Method (seven activities in three cycles). For Systemic Maturity Model there are only two activities and for SaaS Reference Model there are only four activities and one cycle. Analyzing the objective of the development of CERTICS Model and KAcq Method, we noticed that in both cases the objective was to produce a model to be used in practice by organizations in the market. The KAcq Method considered the actual utilization of the model as part of the method. Systemic Maturity Model and SaaS Reference Model were research project. For Systemic Maturity Model the design of the model was enough for the research goals. For SaaS Reference Model the development and the conceptual validation of the model were enough for the research goal. Therefore, although MFMOD works for all these four cases, an improvement opportunity is to include guidance in the current practices for these two types of objectives.

As ISO/IEC 15504 defines the capability dimension for a PAM, MFMOD focused on the other dimension (process or process area) as part of model design and development.

ISO/IEC 15504 also defines rules for creating an OMM from one or more PAMs. ISO/IEC 15504 has been revised as ISO/IEC 33000 Series in which there are requirements for defining Measurement Framework keeping Capability Levels as an example. CERTICS did not define yet a Measurement Framework. Systemic Maturity Model indicates maturity levels with a to be defined measurement framework based on system thinking. A design decision is to include in the practices and as one or more techniques elements to guide both dimension of a PAM and the construction of an OMM.

For KAcq Method there were activities outside of the scope of current version of MFMOD. They are Knowledge Usage and Knowledge Evolution. They are important to complete an engineering cycle. A design decision is to include, in MFMOD, practices to cover model usage and model evolution.

MFMOD is a Method Framework not a method. KAcq Method is a method. One important question is whether MFMOD should become a method or not. A design decision is to keep MFMOD as a Method Framework because still valid that no single PAM engineering method is sufficiently general and tailorable to meet the needs of all endeavors.

4   Towards a Method Framework MFMOD Version 1.1

The next version of MFMOD has been developed based on the results from four directions. The first one is described in the previous section. The second one is from updating the Systematic Literature Review (SLR) performed [5] for articles published after April 2009. The third one is from deeper revision of Firesmith's Method Framework Components [7]. The fourth one is to consider the changes from revision of ISO/IEC 15504 towards the ISO/IEC 33000 Series, specially the possibility to define a Process Quality Characteristic other than Process Capability [17].

A preliminary result from the new SLR already indicates relevant references. Stallinger and Neumann [18], for example, propose an add-on Process Reference Model for Enhancing ISO/IEC 12207 with Product Management and System-Level Reuse where systems are developed and evolved as products. A preliminary result from revisiting Firesmith's Method Framework Components indicates that the Customization rules might be evolved to a metamodel. The metamodel will define practices and how activities can be generated from these practices in order to produce processes to engineering Process Assessment Models.

References

1. Chrissis, M.B., Konrad, M., Shrum, S.: CMMI: Guidelines for Process Integration and Product Improvement, 2nd edn. Addison-Wesley (2007)
2. The Enterprise SPICE Project Team, Enterprise SPICE (ISO/IEC 15504) An Integrated Model for Enterprise-wide Improvement, Technical Report – Issue 1 (September 2010)
3. Automotive SIG, Automotive SPICE® Process Assessment Model (2010), http://www.automotivespice.com/ (last access in June 21, 2014)
4. The Int. Org. for Standardization and the Int. Electrotechnical Commission, ISO/IEC 15504 - Information Technology - Process Assessment, published as seven parts in different years: 15504-1:2004, 15504-2:2003, 15504-3:2003, 15504-4:2004, 15504-5:2006, 15504-6:2008 and 15504-7:2008

5. von Wangenheim, C.G., Hauck, J.C.R., Salviano, C.F., von Wangenheim, A.: Systematic Literature Review of Software Process Capability/Maturity Models. In: Proc. 10th SPICE International Conference, Pisa, Italy, May 18-20, pp. 1–9 (2010)
6. Salviano, C.F.: A Multi-Model Process Improvement Methodology Driven by Capability Profiles. In: The 33rd Annual IEEE Int. Computer Software and Applications Conference, COMPSAC, July 20-24, pp. 636–637 (2009)
7. Firesmith, D.G., Capell, P., Hammons, C.B., Latimer, D., Merendino, T.: The Method Framework for Engineering System Architectures. CRC Press (2008)
8. Salviano, C. F., Zoucas, A. C., Silva, J. V. L., Alves, A. M., Wangenheim, C. G., and Thiry, M.: A Method Framework for Engineering Process Capability Models. In EuroSPI 2009, The 16th European Systems and Software Process Improvement and Innovation, Industry Proc., University of Alcala, Spain, pp. 6.25–6.36, September 2-4 (2009), http://eurospi.net
9. Salviano, C.F., Martinez, M.R.M., Zoucas, A.C., Thiry, M.: Practices and Techniques for Engineering Process Capability Models. CLEI Electronic Journal 13, 1–12 (2010)
10. Salviano, C.F., Alves, A.M., Stefanuto, G.N., Maintinguer, S.T., Mattos, C.V., Zeitoum, C., Reuss, G.: Developing a Process Assessment Model for Technological and Business Competencies on Software Development. In: IEEE QUATIC: Eighth Int. Conf. on the Quality of Info. and Comm. Technology, Lisbon, Portugal, pp. 125–130 (2012)
11. Salviano, C.F., Alves, A.M., Stefanuto, G.N., Maintinguer, S.T., Mattos, C.V., Zeitoum, C., Reuss, G.: CERTICS - An ISO/IEC 15504 Conformance Model for Software Technological Development and Innovation. In: Proc. 14th SPICE International Conference, Vilnius, Lithuania (November 2014)
12. Alves, A.M., Pessoa, M., Salviano, C.F.: Towards a Systemic Maturity Model for Public Software Ecosystems. In: O'Connor, R.V., Rout, T., McCaffery, F., Dorling, A. (eds.) SPICE 2011. CCIS, vol. 155, pp. 145–156. Springer, Heidelberg (2011)
13. Alves, A.M.: Proposal of a Measurement Framework for Quality of Brazilian Public Software (Original in Portuguese: Proposta de uma estrutura de medição para qualidade do SPB - Software Público Brasileiro), PhD Thesis at Escola Politécnica da Universidade de São Paulo, São Paulo, SP, Brazil (2013)
14. Hauck, J.C.R.: A Knowledge Acquisition Method for customizing Capability/Maturity Software Process Models (Original in Portuguese: Um Método de Aquisição de Conhecimento para customização de Modelos de Capacidade/Maturidade de Processos de Software), PhD Thesis at Programa de Pós-Graduação em Engenharia e Gestão do Conhecimento da Universidade Federal de Santa Catarina, Florianópolis, Brazil (2011)
15. Cancian, M.H.: A Capability and Maturity Model for Software Process Improvement for Collaborative Software-as-a-Service (Original in Portuguese: Um Modelo de Capacidade e Maturidade para Melhoria de Processo de Software para SaaS Colaborativo), PhD Thesis at Departamento de Automação e Sistemas da Universidade Federal de Santa Catarina, Florianópolis, SC, Brazil (2013)
16. Basili, V.R., Caldiera, G., Dieter Rombach, H.: The Goal Question Metric Approach, NASA GSFC Software Engineering Laboratory (1994)
17. Varkoi, T.: Safety as a Process Quality Characteristic. In: Woronowicz, T., Rout, T., O'Connor, R.V., Dorling, A. (eds.) SPICE 2013. CCIS, vol. 349, pp. 1–12. Springer, Heidelberg (2013)
18. Stallinger, F., Neumann, R.: From Software to Software System Products: An Add-on Process Reference Model for Enhancing ISO/IEC 12207 with Product Management and System-Level Reuse. In: EUROMICRO-SEAA, pp. 307–314 (2012)

Towards Methodological Support for the Engineering of Process Reference Models for Product Software

Fritz Stallinger[1] and Reinhold Plösch[2]

[1] Software Competence Center Hagenberg, Softwarepark 21,
4232 Hagenberg, Austria
fritz.stallinger@scch.at
[2] Johannes Kepler University, Altenbergerstraße 69, 4020 Linz, Austria
reinhold.ploesch@jku.at

Abstract. Reference models available for software process improvement are often not satisfactorily suitable for application in the improvement of product-oriented software engineering. The resulting need to develop more suitable models for the engineering of software products by integrating, customizing, specializing or enhancing existing models is additionally enforced by the wide spectrum of models available, but focused on specific improvement areas or engineering paradigms, and the need of companies and industry sectors for compliance with more than one model. The goal of the research underlying this paper is thus to support the development of process reference models for the context of product-oriented software engineering by distilling methodological support for the derivation of respective model development methods. The aim of the present paper is to present the goals, identified related work and state-of-the-art, and the envisioned approach of this ongoing research to the software process improvement community.

Keywords: software product, product-oriented software development, process improvement, process reference model, reference model development.

1   Introduction, Goals, and Overview

Traditional reference models and underlying software life cycle models available for *Software Process Improvement* (SPI) (e.g. [1], [2]) are typically not satisfactorily suitable for application to the improvement of product-oriented software engineering. Reasons identified by Staples et al. [3] for e.g. not adopting CMMI include: too small organization size, too costly assessment and improvement services, and lack of time for process improvement. Additionally, according Rautiainen et al. [4] these approaches to SPI focus rather on the software process for customer projects in large organizations, while product-oriented organizations – in particular smaller ones – require a view to software engineering and management – and consequently SPI – that combines business and development considerations based on a clear product focus. Moreover, Brinkkemper et al. [5] argue that in capability based approaches improvement increments are "often too large and general, instead of local and situational". The goal of general applicability

A. Mitasiunas et al. (Eds.): SPICE 2014, CCIS 477, pp. 24–35, 2014.

to any type of software development and the often implicitly assumed project contexts of these models further imply a lack of consideration of product-specific engineering and reuse paradigms and a lack of integration with management and in particular product management activities [6].

On the other hand, the reference models emerged so far for product-oriented software engineering are rather focused on specific improvement areas or engineering paradigms like product management, requirements engineering, product line engineering, and less providing an integrated view on software product engineering.

The resulting needs to develop reference models for further focus areas as well as more complete and integrated reference models, to integrate such models with existing traditional models and standards, to customize such models to specific domains within the software product domain, or to specialize them for specific engineering paradigms, etc. requires methodological support for the development of these models beyond generic methods for from-scratch development (cf. e.g. [7]), customization (cf. e.g. [8]) or harmonization (cf. e.g. [9]).

The overall goal of the present research endeavor is thus to provide methodological support for systematically developing *Process Reference Models* (PRMs) in the domain of engineering software products or software-intensive products. The models produced by application of the envisioned methodology are typically intended to support the migration to or the improvement of product-oriented engineering of such systems. The goal is to provide support and guidance for the derivation of concrete model development methods, based on the goals and requirements of a given model development endeavor. More detailed, the objectives of the research are:

- to analyze a series of PRM developments from the software product engineering domain in order to distill the overall goals of these model developments, the pursued engineering strategies, used methods, applied validation approaches, etc.;
- to assess the methods and method elements identified in the analyzed model developments with respect to their generic applicability and include them in a pool of method elements;
- to establish an architecture and meta-model describing and putting into relation the methodology elements necessary for PRM development in the target domain;
- to distill guidelines to methodologically support the combination and orchestration of the methodology elements based on the goals and requirements of a respective model development endeavor;
- to at least partially validate the proposed methodology for PRM development.

The proposed work builds on spare existing works (cf. respective assessments of the state-of-the-art in [10], [8] or [11]) with respect to systematic methods and methodological support for developing generic processes for reference model development, methods for customizing reference models to specific domains, or harmonizing multiple reference models.

The rest of the document is structured as follows: section 2 sketches the overall research areas involved in the work and major related work representing the state-of-the-art; section 3 provides an overview on the envisioned approach and research methods; section 4 summarizes and concludes the paper and sums up the scientific as well as industrial relevance of the work.

2   State-of-the-Art: Research Areas and Related Work

The major research areas involved in the work and the most important related works representing the state-of-the-art are sketched in the following sub-sections.

2.1   Involved Research Areas

Involved research areas comprise *'assessment-based software process improvement'* as the overall research area dealing with the conceptual frameworks underlying the work as well as the application of its results, in particular setting the scene and determining the requirements for PRMs; *'reference models for product-oriented software engineering'* dealing with the scope, characteristics, challenges, and best practices of the targeted application domain; and *'Process Reference Model Engineering'* as the emerging discipline of how to systematically develop, maintain, and enhance PRMs.

Assessment-Based Software Process Improvement. Starting from the late nineteen-eighties with the proposal of a model for the organizational improvement of software engineering (cf. [12, 13]), SPI evolved as a key means to increase the quality of software and the efficiency and performance of the software producing organization.

Up to date a significant number of such models has emerged (cf. e.g. [14] or [15] for respective overviews). In Wangenheim et al. [15] a total of 52 models is identified and analyzed. The authors conclude that there exists a trend towards specialization of these models for specific domains and that most of the identified models are concentrated around either the CMM/CMMI framework [1, 16] or the ISO/IEC 15504 standard [17] as the two most relevant sources for model development.

Software Process Assessment (SPA) is related to SPI as the means to identify the actual state of processes and major process related problems, and to set priorities for process improvement. According to [18] process assessment is "a disciplined evaluation of an organization's software processes against a model compatible with the reference model" while process improvement is defined as the "action taken to change an organization's processes so that they meet the organization's business needs and achieve its business goals more effectively".

From the point of view of involved models, ISO/IEC 15504 (SPICE) distinguishes between PRMs and *Process Assessment Models* (PAMs). While a PRM defines a set of processes in terms of their purpose and outcomes, a compatible PAM extends the PRM's process definitions through the identification of a set of indicators of process performance and process capability [19, 20].

Reference Models for Product-Oriented Software Engineering. PRMs for product-oriented software engineering are expected to capture and organize best practices for engineering software products, addressing the particular characteristics and challenges of the respective software product business. In the context of SPI, such models are also expected to guide and support the transition from project- and/or customer order-driven development towards product development.

The term "productization" has been coined in [21] for that transition and defined as "the process of transforming from customer specific software development to a standard software product". According to [22], productization means "standardization of the elements in the offering", and "includes several technological elements from the very early stages of designing a product (i.e., managing requirements, selection of technological platforms, design of product architecture etc.) to the commercial elements of selling and distributing the product (i.e., delivery channels, positioning of the product and the any, and after sales activities)".

As stated by Rautiainen et al. [4], approaches to SPI as CMM and SPICE focus on the software process for customer projects in large organizations, while in particular "small product-oriented companies require a more holistic and practical view to software engineering management that combines business and development considerations and has a clear product focus".

On the other hand, although with distinct foci, a series of PRM or PRM-like models has been proposed to overcome these gaps, e.g.:

- the "Reference Framework for Software Product Management" by Van de Weerd et al. [23], accompanied by a "Productization Process" [24] describing the typical stages of transformation from customer-specific software development to a standard software product;
- the "Market-driven Requirements Engineering Process Model" by Gorschek et al. [25], aiming at organizations faced with the challenges of operating in an environment with a huge number of requirements and where a product does not have a, but any number, of customers;
- a series of process models (e.g. [26]) and best practice collections (e.g. [27]) focusing on the peculiarities of applying a product line engineering approach for software product development;
- the recently published international standard ISO/IEC 26550:2013 on "Software and systems engineering -- Reference model for product line engineering and management" [28].

The latent need for extending reference models for product-oriented software engineering beyond the mere process dimension is indicated by the proposal of the BAPO model [29]. The model proposes a four-dimensional evaluation framework for software product family engineering, covering the dimensions business, architecture, organization, and process.

Process Reference Model Engineering. The discipline of how to systematically engineer process reference – and in a wider sense process capability and maturity – models has recently gained attention as an emerging topic in literature (cf. [10, 30]).

Despite the variety of models being developed and customized Wangenheim et al. [10] assert a lack of methodological support and identify two major issues to be overcome in the still maturing discipline: 1) relating model elements systematically to quality and performance goals; and 2) supporting model validation methodologically.

Suggestions for methods for the development of such models in the recent years include (cf. section 2.2 for short descriptions):

- the proposal of a framework for the development of maturity assessment models in different application domains, based on a six-step development sequence by De Bruin et al. [31]

- the proposal of a procedure for designing maturity models that aim to match a set of defined requirements, considering design science guidelines, by Becker et al. [32];
- the analysis of the fundamentals of process maturity models, in particular the main development phases from a design science research perspective by Mettler [33];
- the proposal of a method for the development of so-called "focus area maturity models", i.e. models that are especially suited to the incremental improvement of functional domains like development or testing, by van Steenbergen et al. [34];
- the method proposal of Wangenheim et al. [8, 10] based on ISO/IEEE standard development processes and integration of knowledge engineering techniques;
- the proposal of a generic framework for the development of process capability/ maturity models by Salviano et al. [7] based on their previous experiences in developing diverse models with a 7-step process.

According [30] "most published models are based on practices and success factors from projects that showed good results in an organization or industry, but which lack a sound theoretical basis and methodology". Similarly, [8] with reference to [35] states that literature detailing how such models are developed, evolved, and adapted is extremely rare.

2.2   Related Work and State-of-the-Art

Related work in the field of method provision for process capability and maturity model development comprises the following works, aside from few exceptions due to thematic reasons, presented in chronological order:

De Bruin et al. [31] propose a generic, i.e. application domain independent, phase-oriented, six-step framework for the development of maturity assessment models. The method is exemplified by two maturity model developments from the domains of business process management and knowledge management. The generic phases proposed comprise: scope; design; populate; test; deploy; and maintain. The framework also identifies and characterizes the decisions involved in the scope and design phases.

Driven by the context of IT management and the ever-growing number of maturity models for this domain, Becker et al. [32] propose a generic procedure model for the design of maturity models that aims to match a set of defined requirements concerning the development of such models. The procedure model is based on a comparison of a selection of a few well-documented maturity models to these requirements. The procedure is applied to the development of an IT performance measurement model.

Mettler [33] analyses the fundamentals of process maturity models in information systems and the typical phases of maturity model development and application by taking a design science research perspective. The work is based on the phases proposed by [31] and assumes that development and application of maturity models are inherently connected. Consequently a phase model for both, development and application of such models is proposed and the relevant decision parameters for each phase in respect to rigor and relevance of the maturity model are discussed.

Salviano et al. [7] propose a generic framework for the development of process capability models that is based on their previous experiences in experimenting different processes to develop diverse models. The framework is composed of seven sequential practices, customization rules applied to these practices, examples of utilization and examples of techniques. The framework is reported to be initially validated. The seven sequential practices comprise: initial decisions; sources analysis; strategy for development; model design; draft model development; draft model validation; and model consolidation.

Larsson et al. [36] report a case study-based synthesis of five reference models in the area of software product integration and comparison with activities performed in seven product development projects. The authors conclude that none of the descriptions of best practices available in the different reference models covers the problem situations for the investigated product developments and that these reference models need to be merged into one set of practices. The applied procedure for combining the reference models is only shortly sketched and relying on the experience of the authors. It essentially consists of the following steps: acquire knowledge regarding the reference models; produce a summary of practices and a comparison between the models; combine the extracted information from all investigated reference models into a set of practices; investigate all reference models based on these set of practices, considering both explicit and implicit instances of the practices.

Van Steenbergen et al. [34] propose a generic method for the development of so-called "focus area maturity models", models that are especially suited to the incremental improvement of functional domains. The authors use a design science research process. The development method itself is based on a literature review on maturity model development and experience in practically applying the concept to two example models. The resulting development method is comprised of four groups of method steps (method steps provided in brackets): 1) Scoping (Identify & scope domain); 2) Design model (Determine focus areas; Determine capabilities; Determine dependencies; Position capabilities in matrix); 3) Instrument development (Develop assessment instrument; Define improvement actions); 4) Implementation & exploitation (Implement maturity model; Improve matrix iteratively; Communicate results).

Wangenheim et al. [8, 10] propose a method for the customization of process capability/maturity models to specific domains/sectors or development methodologies that is based on ISO/IEEE standard development processes and the integration of knowledge engineering techniques and experiences about how such models are currently developed. The proposed method is structured into five phases: 1) Knowledge Identification (familiarization with the target domain and characterization of the target customization context); 2) Knowledge Specification (development of a first version of the customized model); 3) Knowledge Refinement (validation of the draft model, balloting, refinement, and community approval); 4) Knowledge Usage (model usage, results collection and analysis); 5) Knowledge Evolution (continuous evolution of the model). Additionally, basic techniques, including pointers to literature, applicable in each of the five phases are identified.

Pardo et al. [9] present an ontology for harmonization projects of multiple standards and models targeted at organizations that are seeking to resolve their manifold needs through application of multiple models. The ontology is intended to provide the main concepts and a consistent terminology for supporting and leading the implementation of improvement projects where multiple models have to be harmonized. It is complemented by a guide to support the determination of the harmonization goals, a process for driving multi-model harmonization, and a set of methods and techniques. Based on preceding research [37], the authors also note that beside the terminological differences existing between models, the inconsistencies and terminological conflicts also appear in the techniques, methods and related concepts established to support harmonization of multiple models. The process for driving the harmonization is presented in more detail in [11], together with two case studies of applying the framework.

3   Approach and Methods

To achieve the goals of providing methodological support for the development of PRMs in the software product engineering domain and of distilling and systematizing insights and experience from related PRM developments the following approach is pursued.

Step 1 - Analysis of PRM Development Cases. A series of successful PRM developments from the software/system product engineering domain in which the authors have been personally involved will be analyzed post-mortem. The candidate model developments for analysis comprise:

- The OOSPICE PRM for Component-based Software Engineering [38, 39]
- The GDES-Reuse PRM for Reuse in Industrial Engineering [40]
- The Hephaistos/INSPiRE PRM for Software Product Management [6, 41]
- The SPiRE PRM for Reuse & Product-Orientation in Systems Engineering [42–44]

These cases will be analyzed with respect to the goals of model development, the specific application domain, involved source models, key stakeholders of the target model, pursued model engineering and model creation strategies, linkage with and/or positioning against established standards, key challenges of model development, used model engineering methods and techniques, applied validation approaches, etc.

The focus of this analysis will be on the goals of the model developments, the decision parameters in place and actual decisions taken, and how they influenced the path of model development and choice of methods and techniques.

Step 2 - Development of Methodology Architecture. In this step, the architecture of the methodology for the development of PRMs in the software product engineering domain together with meta-models for relevant methodology elements will be defined and preliminarily validated.

The main purpose of this artifact is to identify and put into relation the methodology elements generally necessary for PRM development in the target domain.

Major candidate architecture elements include: PRM development process, methods, work products, instantiation guidelines, and concepts and terms used in the methodology.

As an interim validation step, the emerging methodology architecture will be validated against parts of the results of the study under step 1 with respect to "coverage" of the concepts and method elements identified there.

Step 3 - Population of the Methodology. In this step, the methodology defined in step 2 will be populated with methodology elements identified in the analysis of model developments in step 1. For that purpose these elements have to be assessed with respect to their generic applicability and adapted accordingly.

For the development of the core PRM engineering process and the guidelines for process/methodology instantiation a design science-based approach [45, 46] will be pursued. The instantiation guidelines will have to link with and orchestrate the generic methodology elements according to the specific goals and requirements of a respective model development endeavor.

The methodology, in particular its pool of methods and techniques and its instantiation guidelines are foreseen to be "living artifacts", i.e. they should be enhanced based on the needs, experience, and feedback of future reference model developments.

Guidelines for methodology enhancement thus represent a further element of the methodology architecture to be developed in step 2.

Step 4 - Validation of the Methodology. The objective of this final step is to validate the proposed PRM development methodology for the software product domain at least initially and partially.

Pulm [47] discusses the scientific evaluation of methods in the context of systems theory. He points to the key question, whether a methodology has been evaluated through a case study or whether concrete developed methods have been abstracted for scientific representation. He concludes that concrete methods can be evaluated in one specific case, while abstractly represented methods that are generally applicable always require adaption and individual action so that they can only be evaluated with restrictions.

In the present case, the main strategy for methodology development is abstraction from reference model development cases, so that the second alternative applies, implying only restricted possibilities for evaluation.

For the present case, the following validation activities are foreseen:

- comparison against similar (generally less focused and less granular) reference model development method proposals,
- reflection of the proposed methodology against its originating method development cases,
- demonstration of the methodology through application to a further reference model development endeavor,
- presentation to and evaluation of the methodology by a panel of experts in the field of PRM development.

The results of each validation step will be incorporated into a revision of the methodology under development.

4   Summary, Conclusions, and Relevance

The paper presented the motivation, the state-of-the-art in the main involved research areas and in related work, and the approach regarding work-in-progress on providing methodological support for deriving methods for the development of PRMs in the software product engineering domain.

The methodology is intended to be applicable to a variety of model development scenarios. Overall, the focus of the proposed work is less on deriving in all its details one single new method for PRM development that fits all potential requirements of the targeted domain, but more on providing methodological support and guidance for the combination and orchestration of the potential method elements in order to fulfill given PRM development goals.

From a knowledge management perspective the work intends to capture, distill and systematize insights and experience from PRM development endeavors in the software product domain and systematize and prepare them for reuse under similar conditions.

The proposed work contributes to overcoming the problem with respect to a lack of systematic understanding and methodological support of how PRMs – and in a broader sense – process maturity/capability models – are developed. The relevance of this problem has been pointed out recently by a number of authors. Garcia-Mireles et al. [30] e.g. conclude that relevant literature available on which methods have been proposed to develop maturity models is spare and that the topic is recently appearing in research. Similarly, Wangenheim et al. [10] state that despite the variety of models being developed, the work seems to lack methodological support. With respect to model customization methods, Hauck et al. [8] assess that most of the customization initiatives do not adopt a systematic approach for the customization of generic standards and models and "that research on how to perform such customizations in a systematic way is sparse". With respect to the harmonization of multiple models in company contexts Pardo et al. [11] also state the lack of any other systematic solution that address harmonization in a way as to satisfy the needs of the companies.

The systematic development and provision of process reference models addressing the specific needs of companies migrating towards the development, maintenance and enhancement of a product or even multiple products within a product portfolio is regarded essential for industry. Surveys (e.g. [22]) covering software product companies highlight that the biggest challenges in growth of such companies are not technical but management and marketing related and that the most important improvement areas refer to the degree of productization and competence level of personnel. The same study also assesses that the majority of the companies is still rather immature with respect to the degree of productization and that raising the degree of productization is one of the most important issues for software product companies. According [22] the latter is especially challenging, as companies have to find a balance between long-term productization aims and short-term financial needs that are often addressed by customizing and customer projects.

Acknowledgements. This work is partly supported within the project *SPiRE (Lightweight Software Product and pRocess Evolution)* as part of the COMET-Programme of the Austrian Research Promotion Agency (FFG).

References

1. CMMI Product Team: CMMI for Development, Version 1.3 (CMMI-DEV, V1.3), http://resources.sei.cmu.edu/asset_files/TechnicalReport/2010_005_001_15287.pdf
2. International Standards Organisation: ISO/IEC 12207:2008 - Systems and software engineering — Software life cycle processes (2008)
3. Staples, M., Niazi, M., Jeffery, R., Abrahams, A., Byatt, P., Murphy, R.: An exploratory study of why organizations do not adopt CMMI. Journal of Systems and Software 80, 883–895 (2007)
4. Rautiainen, K., Lassenius, C., Sulonen, R.: 4CC: A framework for managing software product development. EMJ - Engineering Management Journal 14, 27–32 (2002)
5. Brinkkemper, S., van de Weerd, I., Saeki, M., Versendaal, J.: Process Improvement in Requirements Management: A Method Engineering Approach. In: Rolland, C. (ed.) REFSQ 2008. LNCS, vol. 5025, pp. 6–22. Springer, Heidelberg (2008)
6. Stallinger, F., Neumann, R.: Extending ISO/IEC 12207 with Software Product Management: A Process Reference Model Proposal. In: Mas, A., Mesquida, A., Rout, T., O'Connor, R.V., Dorling, A. (eds.) SPICE 2012. CCIS, vol. 290, pp. 93–106. Springer, Heidelberg (2012)
7. Salviano, C.F., Zoucas, A., Silva, J.V.L., Alves, A.M., von Wangenheim, C.G., Thir, M.: A Method Framework for Engineering Process Capability Models. In: EuroSPI 2009, The 16th EuroSPI Conference, European Systems and Software Process Improvement and Innovation, Industry Proceedings, pp. 6.25 – 6.36 (2009)
8. Hauck, J.C.R., von Wangenheim, C.G., Mc Caffery, F., Buglione, L.: Proposing an ISO/IEC 15504-2 Compliant Method for Process Capability/Maturity Models Customization. In: Caivano, D., Oivo, M., Baldassarre, M.T., Visaggio, G. (eds.) PROFES 2011. LNCS, vol. 6759, pp. 44–58. Springer, Heidelberg (2011)
9. Pardo, C., Pino, F.J., García, F., Piattini, M., Baldassarre, M.T.: An ontology for the harmonization of multiple standards and models. Computer Standards & Interfaces 34, 48–59 (2012)
10. von Wangenheim, C.G., Hauck, J., Zoucas, A., Salviano, C.F., McCaffery, F., Shull, F.: Creating Software Process Capability/Maturity Models. IEEE Software 27, 92–94 (2010)
11. Pardo, C., Pino, F.J., Garcia, F., Baldassarre, M.T., Piattini, M.: From chaos to the systematic harmonization of multiple reference models: A harmonization framework applied in two case studies. Journal of Systems and Software 86, 125–143 (2013)
12. Radice, R.A., Harding, J.T., Munnis, P.E., Phillips, R.W.: A programming process study. IBM Syst. J. 24, 91–101 (1985)
13. Humphrey, W.S.: Characterizing the software process: a maturity framework. IEEE Software 5, 73–79 (1988)
14. Sheard, S.A.: Evolution of the frameworks quagmire. Computer 34, 96–98 (2001)
15. von Wangenheim, C.G., Hauck, J.C.R., Salviano, C.F., von Wangenheim, A.: Systematic Literature Review of Software Process Capability/Maturity Models. In: Rout, T., Lami, G., Fabbrini, F. (eds.) Process Improvement and Capability Determination in Software, Systems Engineering and Service Management. Proceedings of: 10th International SPICE Conference 2010, Pisa, Italy, May 18-20, pp. 1–9. Edizioni ETS, Pisa (2010)
16. Paulk, M.C., Curtis, B., Chrissis, M.B., Weber, C.V.: Capability Maturity Model for Software, Version 1.1, http://resources.sei.cmu.edu/asset_files/TechnicalReport/1993_005_001_16211.pdf

17. International Standards Organisation: ISO/IEC 15504-1:2004 - Information technology - process assessment - part 1: concepts and vocabulary (2004)
18. International Standards Organisation: ISO/IEC TR 15504-9:1998 - Information technology — Software process assessment — Part 9: Vocabulary (1998)
19. International Standards Organisation: ISO/IEC TR 15504-1:1998 - Information technology — Software process assessment — Part 1: Concepts and introductory guide (1998)
20. International Standards Organisation: ISO/IEC TR 15504-5:1998 - Information technology — Software process assessment — Part 5: An assessment model and indicator guidance (1998)
21. Artz, P., van de Weerd, I., Brinkkemper, S.: Productization: The process of transforming from customer-specific software development to product software development, http://www.cs.uu.nl/research/techreps/repo/CS-2010/2010-003.pdf
22. Hietala, J., Kontio, J., Jokinen, J.-P., Pyysiainen, J.: Challenges of software product companies: results of a national survey in finland. In: Proceedings - 10th International Symposium on Software Metrics, METRICS 2004, pp. 232–243 (2004)
23. van de Weerd, I., Brinkkemper, S., Nieuwenhuis, R., Versendaal, J., Bijlsma, L.: Towards a Reference Framework for Software Product Management. In: Glinz, M., Lutz, R. (eds.) 14th IEEE International Requirements Engineering Conference, RE 2006, pp. 319–322. IEEE Computer Society, Los Alamitos (2006)
24. Artz, P., van de Weerd, I., Brinkkemper, S., Fieggen, J.: Productization: Transforming from developing customer-specific software to product software. In: Tyrväinen, P., Jansen, S., Cusumano, M.A. (eds.) ICSOB 2010. LNBIP, vol. 51, pp. 90–102. Springer, Heidelberg (2010)
25. Gorschek, T., Gomes, A., Pettersson, A., Torkar, R.: Introduction of a process maturity model for market-driven product management and requirements engineering. J. Softw. Evol. and Proc. 24, 83–113 (2012)
26. van der Linden, F., Schmid, K., Rommes, E.: Software product lines in action. The best industrial practice in product line engineering. Springer, Berlin (2007)
27. Software Engineering Institute, Carnegie Mellon University: A Framework for Software Product Line Practice, Version 5.0, http://www.sei.cmu.edu/productlines/frame_report/index.html
28. International Standards Organisation: ISO/IEC 26550:2013 - Software and systems engineering – Reference model for product line engineering and management (2013)
29. van der Linden, F., Bosch, J., Kamsties, E., Känsälä, K., Obbink, H.: Software Product Family Evaluation. In: Nord, R.L. (ed.) SPLC 2004. LNCS, vol. 3154, pp. 110–129. Springer, Heidelberg (2004)
30. García-Mireles, G.A., Ángeles Moraga, M., García, F.: Development of maturity models: a systematic literature review. In: Baldassarre, T., Genero, M., Mendes, E., Piattini, M. (eds.) Proceedings of 16th International Conference on Evaluation & Assessment in Software Engineering, EASE 2012, pp. 279–283. IEEE, Piscataway (2012)
31. de Bruin, T., Rosemann, M., Freeze, R., Kulkarni, U.: Understanding the main phases of developing a maturity assessment model. In: Campbell, B., Underwood, J., Bunker, D. (eds.) Australasian Conference on Information Systems (ACIS) (2005)
32. Becker, J., Knackstedt, R., Pöppelbuß, J.: Developing maturity models for IT management - A procedure model and its application. Busin. Info. Sys. Eng. 51, 249–260 (2009)
33. Mettler, T.: A Design Science Research Perspective on Maturity Models in Information Systems, https://www.alexandria.unisg.ch/Publikationen/214531
34. van Steenbergen, M., Bos, R., Brinkkemper, S., van de Weerd, I., Bekkers, W.: The Design of Focus Area Maturity Models. In: Winter, R., Zhao, J.L., Aier, S. (eds.) DESRIST 2010. LNCS, vol. 6105, pp. 317–332. Springer, Heidelberg (2010)

35. Matook, S., Indulska, M.: Improving the quality of process reference models: A quality function deployment-based approach. Decision Support Systems 47, 60–71 (2009)
36. Larsson, S., Myllyperkiö, P., Ekdahl, F., Crnkovic, I.: Software product integration: A case study-based synthesis of reference models. Information and Software Technology 51, 1066–1080 (2009)
37. Pardo, C., Pino, F.J., García, F., Piattini Velthius, M., Baldassarre, M.T.: Trends in harmonization of multiple reference models. In: Maciaszek, L.A., Loucopoulos, P. (eds.) ENASE 2010. CCIS, vol. 230, pp. 61–73. Springer, Heidelberg (2011)
38. Stallinger, F., Dorling, A., Rout, T., Henderson-Sellers, B., Lefever, B.: Software process improvement for component-based software engineering: an introduction to the OOSPICE project. In: Fernandez, M., Crnkovic, I. (eds.) Proceedings of 28th Euromicro Conference, Dortmund, Germany, September 4-6, pp. 318–323. IEEE Computer Society, Los Alamitos (2002)
39. Henderson-Sellers, B., Stallinger, F., Lefever, B.: Bridging the gap from process modelling to process assessment: the OOSPICE process specification for component-based software engineering. In: Fernandez, M., Crnkovic, I. (eds.) Proceedings of 28th Euromicro Conference, Dortmund, Germany, September 4-6, pp. 324–331. IEEE Computer Society, Los Alamitos (2002)
40. Stallinger, F., Plösch, R., Pomberger, G., Vollmar, J.: Integrating ISO/IEC 15504 conformant process assessment and organizational reuse enhancement. J. Softw. Maint. Evol.: Res. Pract. 22, 307–324 (2010)
41. Stallinger, F., Neumann, R., Schossleitner, R., Zeilinger, R.: Linking software life cycle activities with product strategy and economics: Extending ISO/IEC 12207 with product management best practices. In: O'Connor, R.V., Rout, T., McCaffery, F., Dorling, A. (eds.) SPICE 2011. CCIS, vol. 155, pp. 157–168. Springer, Heidelberg (2011)
42. Stallinger, F., Neumann, R., Vollmar, J., Plösch, R.: Towards a Process Reference Model for the Industrial Solutions Business: Integrating Reuse and Product-orientation in the Context of Systems Engineering. In: Rout, T., Lami, G., Fabbrini, F. (eds.) Process Improvement and Capability Determination in Software, Systems Engineering and Service Management. Proceedings of: 10th International SPICE Conference 2010, Pisa, Italy, May 18-20, pp. 129–139. Edizioni ETS, Pisa (2010)
43. Stallinger, F., Neumann, R., Vollmar, J., Plösch, R.: Reuse and product-orientation as key elements for systems engineering: Aligning a reference model for the industrial solutions business with ISO/IEC 15288. In: Raffo, D.M., Pfahl, D., Zhang, L. (eds.) ICSSP 2011. Proceedings of the 2011 International Conference on Software and Systems Process, Waikiki, Honolulu, HI, USA, May 21-22, pp. 120–128. Association for Computing Machinery, New York (2011)
44. Stallinger, F., Neumann, R.: Enhancing ISO/IEC 15288 with Reuse and Product-orientation: Key Outcomes of an Add-on Process Reference Model Proposal. In: EuroSPI2 2012. European Systems, Software & Service Process Improvement & Innovation, Industrial Proceedings, 19th EuroSP 2012 Conference, June 25-27, pp. 8.1–8.11. DELTA, Hørsholm (2012)
45. March, S.T., Smith, G.F.: Design and natural science research on information technology. Decision Support Systems 15, 251–266 (1995)
46. Peffers, K., Tuunanen, T., Rothenberger, M.A., Chatterjee, S.: A Design Science Research Methodology for Information Systems Research. Journal of Management Information Systems 24, 45–77 (2007)
47. Pulm, U.: Eine systemtheoretische Betrachtung der Produktentwicklung. Dissertation, Technische Universität München, Fakultät für Maschinenwesen (2004)

Towards a Process Assessment Model
for Management System Standards

Stéphane Cortina, Nicolas Mayer, Alain Renault, and Béatrix Barafort

Public Research Centre Henri Tudor, Luxembourg
{stephane.cortina,nicolas.mayer,alain.renault,
beatrix.barafort}@tudor.lu

Abstract. Certification to management system standards is more and more attractive for organisations, and many companies are today certified according to several of them (e.g., ISO 9001, ISO 14001, ISO/IEC 27001, etc.). However, in this case, it is a remaining challenge to optimise the system in place by mutualising as much as possible the different processes required by the various management systems, and thus improving the integrated overall system. In order to fill this gap, this paper presents how a process assessment model for management system standards has been built. It is based on the High Level Structure proposed by ISO, which defines a set of common requirements for management system standards. This process assessment model will provide the core content and could be the basis of all the future process assessment models that will be developed to assess domain-specific management systems.

Keywords: Process assessment, process assessment model, management system standard, management systems, integrated management system.

1   Introduction

Every year, ISO (International Organization for Standardization) performs a survey [1] of certifications to Management System Standards (MSS). The 2012 results reveal that ISO 9001 (which gives the requirements for quality management systems) has generated more than 1.1 million of certificates in 184 countries since 1993. This survey also indicates an increase between 9 and 20% of the certificates related to emerging MSS such as ISO 14001 (Requirements for environmental management systems), ISO/IEC 27001 (Requirements for information security management systems), or ISO 22000 (Requirements for food safety management systems).

Regarding this growing interest about management systems and the penetration in the market of associated certifications, ISO has published in 2012 (and revised in 2014), as part of its Directives, an annex entitled "High-level structure, identical core text, common terms and core definitions" for MSS [2]. This High Level Structure (HLS) aims at ensuring consistency among future and revised MSS, and aims at making their integrated use easier. Indeed, many companies need to implement several management systems covering complementary domains (information security, service management, quality, etc...). The challenge is then to reduce the workload by sharing processes across the different management systems.

A. Mitasiunas et al. (Eds.): SPICE 2014, CCIS 477, pp. 36–47, 2014.

Implementing and assessing the capability of the processes composing such integrated management systems are both emerging challenges. In this paper, our focus is on the process assessment activity and the purpose of this paper is to present how we have built a process assessment model for MSS (compliant with the requirement of the ISO/IEC 33000 series of standards for process assessment [3], [4], [5], [12]). This process assessment model will provide the core content and could be the basis of all the future process assessment models that will be developed to assess domain-specific management systems. The purpose of such a model is also to be used as a tool for assessing the capability of the processes that are common to any management system.

Section 2 presents the background of our research project and states its objectives. Section 3 describes our research method and the different steps followed to build the core content of a process assessment model for MSS. Then, in Section 4, the resulting core content is presented. Section 5 analyses our approach and its results by discussing the different strengths and weaknesses of the model and its building process. Finally, Section 6 concludes about the current state of the process assessment model for MSS and presents our future work.

2   Problem Statement

On the one hand, management systems are implemented by companies under the form of a management system dedicated to a specific domain, or more and more often under the form of an integrated management system targeting several domains (such as business continuity, information security, and/or service management). This kind of integrated management system results in different processes that are common to and shared between several domains. It is indeed relevant to have for example only one management review process shared across these different domains. This enables taking optimal decisions during management review meetings based on the needs, the requirements and the priorities of the different management systems. Since 2012 and the first publication of the HLS, there is a robust description of the processes that are common to all management systems. First of all, the HLS is used to revise the existing MSS at the ISO level. All of the MSS shall now be compliant with the HLS structure. Furthermore, the HLS can be used by companies to establish their integrated management system. The HLS provides the description of what processes can easily be shared among the domain-specific MSS.

On the other hand, there is a growing community of consultants using process assessment methods to support the implementation, improvement, and integration of management systems. The ISO/IEC 33000 series is a well-established series of standards for describing processes and assessing process capabilities. It also introduces its own terminology such as *"process assessment model"*, *"process reference model"*, *"purpose"* or *"outcome"* that is not further developed in this paper. However, the reader can refer to ISO/IEC 33001 [3] for terms and definitions and more generally to the whole ISO/IEC 33000 series for an exhaustive explanation about the approach. A key element of the approach, explained in ISO/IEC 33002 [4], is that an assessment shall be performed based on compliant process assessment models, as defined in ISO/IEC 33004 [6].

Consequently, there is an emerging need for a process assessment model describing the common processes of MSS as described in the HLS, and meeting the requirements of ISO/IEC 33004 [5]. Such a process assessment model will be used to perform standardized assessments of the capability of processes now required for composing any integrated management system. The objective of this paper is to present a process assessment model for common processes of MSS, and the main focus of the paper is on how to build it according to a structured and reliable approach.

3   Method

This section describes how the authors have developed a process reference and then a process assessment model for MSS compliant with the HLS. The first step was the selection of a set of key criteria that were taken into account during the development process. These criteria are detailed in 3.1. Then, as explained in 3.2, the authors applied the transformation process described in [6] to the requirements contained in the HLS in order to build the process assessment model for MSS.

3.1   Key Criteria

The following criteria have been used by the authors, all along the transformation process, to guide design choices. These criteria have been chosen on the basis of the experience of the authors in order to guarantee that the resulting process assessment model will be efficient whatever the domain assessed.

Assessability

The main objective of a process assessment model is to be used to perform process assessments. For that each process has been described in a way that facilitates its future assessment. Particularly, the process model has been designed so that:

- each process has one single purpose
- the process outcomes are necessary and sufficient to achieve the process purpose
- each process outcome is defined as a measurable objective
- the base practices reflect the process purpose and outcomes

Interoperability

The expected process assessment model needs to support interoperability between management systems. For that the produced model describes processes and work products in a way that fosters the exchanges between several management systems.

Integration

The expected process assessment model needs to facilitate the integration of multiple management systems. For that the produced process assessment model only describes the common/generic part of any management system. Thus it focuses on the core content of an integrated management system covering several domains.

Completeness

The expected process assessment model needs to address each requirement contained in the HLS. For that the traceability between the HLS and the process base practices (contained in the produced process assessment model) has been assured.

Adoption

The produced process assessment model needs to describe the common processes of MSS in a way that encourages the adoption of these processes. For that the proposed processes have been designed in a way that reflects the processes that are usually implemented in most companies. Moreover, the proposed process descriptions were worded using terms, base practices and work products that can be easily understood and that are as close as possible to those used in MSS.

Applicability

The proposed process assessment model needs to fit in with all companies, regardless of their type, size, or nature. It needs to be usable for various purposes such as: the rating of an individual process, the determination of the organizational maturity, the preparation for audit, or benchmarking. For that the produced process model has been designed in a way that ensures its compliance with all the requirements of ISO/IEC 33004 [5].

3.2   The Transformation Process

The transformation process described in [6] has been used by the authors of this paper to design and build a process assessment model for MSS compliant with the requirements of ISO/IEC 33004. Based on goal-driven requirements engineering techniques [7], this transformation process has already been used successfully to build process models in various domains [8], [9], [10].

Using this transformation process, the collection of requirements contained in the HLS are first transformed into requirements trees, then into goal trees, and finally into a process reference model and a process assessment model, as illustrated in Figure 1.

The transformation process consists in 9 steps described in details in [6] and summarized below:

Step 1 – Identify Elementary Requirements in a Collection of Requirements

This step consists in identifying all of the requirements under the form of a collection of elementary requirements. In our case, the 'shall statements' (revealing requirements) contained in the proposed text of the HLS [2] were easily identified and split into elementary requirements. The final list was composed of more than one hundred elementary requirements made up of a subject, a verb and a complement, without coordination, conjunctions, or enumeration.

Step 2 – Organize, and Structure the Requirements

Then, the elementary requirements were organized and structured. For that, a 'mind map' helped to have a graphical view of the elementary requirements having the same object (or component). The requirements were then gathered around the objects they were relating to in order to build a requirements tree.

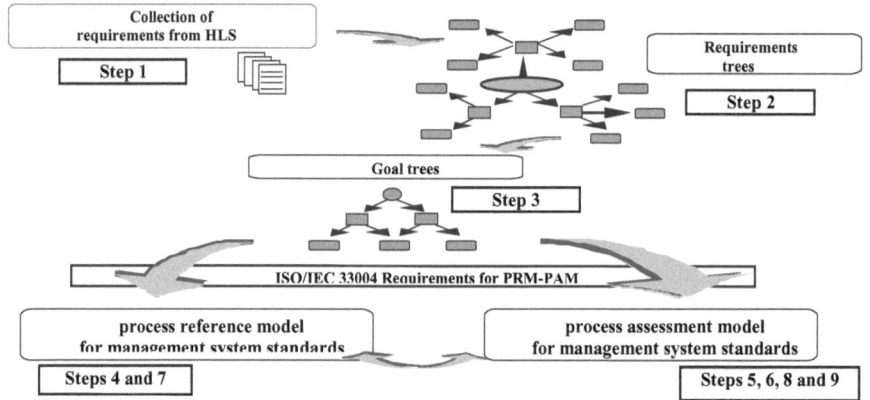

Fig. 1. Transformation process activities

Step 3 – Identify Common Purposes Upon those Requirements and Organize Them

An internal task force composed of experts in process assessment and/or domain-specific management system (service management, quality management, information security management, and electronic records management) was then set up. The task force identified common purposes for the groups of requirements and organised them accordingly, taking the original meaning of the text proposed in the HLS into account. A goal tree was then built for each process (an example can be seen in Figure 2). On these goal trees, each low-level objective is linked to an elementary requirement of the HLS (and all requirements are linked to a low-level objective of a goal-tree). Thus, thanks to these goal trees, the task force carefully grouped inter-related activities, keeping in mind the key criteria (see Section 3.1), and particularly that the main objective was to create easily assessable processes. This semantic work enabled to outline the structure of the process reference model and particularly to identify its processes.

Step 4 – Identify and Factorize Outcomes from the Common Purposes and Attach them to the Related Goals

The common purposes identified during step 3 of the transformation process can be considered as the observable results of something (i.e. the production of an artefact, or a significant change of state, or the meeting of specified constraints). These observable results are named 'outcomes' and are attached to the related purposes. Depending on the size of the goal tree, and in order to have from 3 to 7 outcomes per process, (as recommended by the ISO/IEC TR 24774 [11]) it was sometimes necessary to factorize and merge some of these outcomes.

Step 5 – Group Activities Together Under a Practice and Attach it to the Related Outcomes

The original input of the transformation process (the requirements from the HLS) contains information describing activities that should be conducted for implementing the processes. According to the number and level of detail of these activities, they were grouped as practices. Each practice represents a functional activity of the process. When implemented, a practice contributes to the achievement of at least one outcome of the performed process. During this step, we linked these activities or practices to the related outcomes and we kept traceability between each practice and the initial set of elementary requirements. Indeed, it is possible that several elementary requirements are related to (or hidden behind) only one practice of a process. The goal trees enable to keep that in mind for further activities, in particular, when questionnaires are being developed for supporting process assessment.

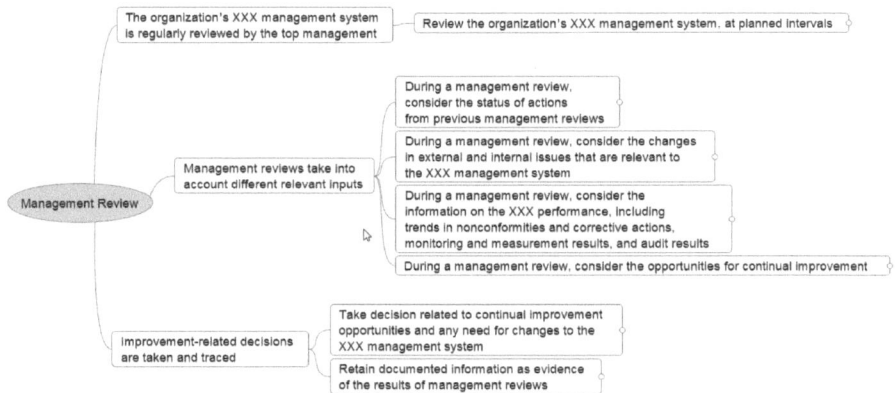

Fig. 2. Goal tree for the "Management Review" process

Step 6 – Allocate Each Practice to a Specific Capability Level

During this step and for each process, we reviewed the practices and their linked outcomes in order to be sure that they contribute to the process performance attribute (capability level 1) of their associated process. New processes were added to gather HLS activities that were normally reflecting capability levels higher than 1. Thus, we ensured that our process descriptions are such that no aspects of the measurement framework beyond level 1 are contained or implied and thus, that the created process reference and process assessment models comply with ISO/IEC 33004 [5].

Step 7 – Phrase Outcomes and Process Purpose

In order to create a process reference model that follows the guidelines of ISO/IEC TR 24774 [11], each outcome has been phrased as a declarative sentence using verbs at the present tense. Then, the purpose has been phrased to state a high-level goal for performing the process and provide measurable and tangible benefits to the stakeholders through the expected outcomes (process assessment concern). We also checked that the set of outcomes is necessary and sufficient to achieve the purpose of the process.

Step 8 – Phrase the Base Practices Attached to Outcomes

Once the purpose and outcomes of a process have been phrased, the process reference model was considered stable enough to phrase the base practices. Base practices were phrased as actions, starting with a verb at the infinitive, according to the guidance provided by ISO/IEC TR 24774 [11]. During steps 8 and 9, we paid a particular attention to choose a wording that suits and that is commonly used in organizations in order to ensure a good adoption of the models.

Step 9 – Determine Work Products among the Inputs and Outputs of the Practices

A work product is an artefact associated with the execution of a process. During the steps 1 and 5, many work products have been identified and listed as inputs or outputs. During this step, these work products were included as parts of indicators in order to finalize the process assessment model.

4   Results

The transformation process described in Section 3 resulted in the creation of the core content of a process capability assessment model for MSS. This model is composed of 10 processes, as listed in Figure 3. These processes, common to all management systems, are described in generic terms (as shown in Figure 4) and require to be contextualized before being used in an assessment.

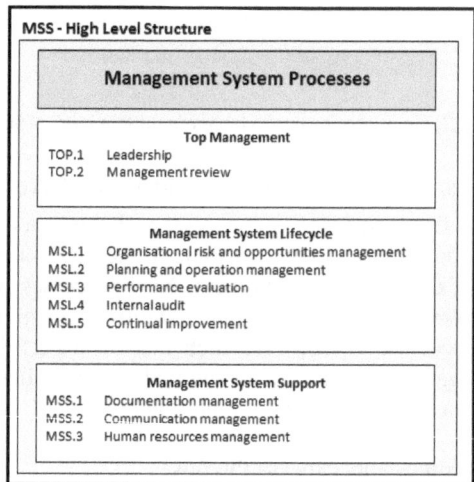

Fig. 3. Processes in the process assessment model for MSS

This list of processes and their associated descriptions have been compared with the results of one of our research project conducted at the same period in Labgroup (a digitization and archiving service provider in Luxembourg). This research project aimed at integrating requirements from various MSS such as ISO/IEC 27001 [13], ISO 31000 [15], and ISO 9001 [16] into a single integrated management system.

This experimentation permitted to consolidate and validate, through a bottom-up approach, the design choices made by the task force during the transformation process. It also helped to validate that the produced process assessment model has the required characteristics of assessability, interoperability, integration, completeness, adoption and applicability.

Process ID	TOP.2
Process Name	Management review
Process Context	This process, usually performed by the top management, consists in deciding the future improvements. This could be done only after having reviewed the management system and the policies and after having taken into account the actions from previous management reviews as well as the outputs from the "Performance evaluation", "Internal audit", and "Continual improvement" processes.
Process Purpose	The purpose of the Management review process is to decide the implementation of future improvements and changes that will enhance the XXX performance and the effectiveness of the XXX management.
Process Outcomes	As a result of successful implementation of the Management review process: 1. the organization's XXX management system is regularly reviewed by the top management; 2. management reviews include consideration of relevant and various inputs; 3. improvement-related decisions are taken and recorded.
Base Practices	**TOP.2.BP1: Review the organization's XXX management system at planned intervals** [Outcome 1] Organize reviews of the organization's XXX management system by the top management, at planned intervals, to ensure its continuing suitability, adequacy and effectiveness. *Annex SL - §5.1:* Top management shall demonstrate leadership and commitment with respect to the XXX management system by ensuring that the XXX management system achieves its intended outcome(s) *Annex SL - §9.3:* Top management shall review the organization's XXX management system, at planned intervals, to ensure its continuing suitability, adequacy and effectiveness

Fig. 4. Extract of the "Management review" process description

5   Discussion

The discussions presented in this section took place during the third step of the transformation process and all occurred within the internal task force. Most of them (5.1 to 5.4) relate to the composition of the list of processes to be included in the process assessment model. The last two ones (5.5 to 5.6) relate to process assessment aspects.

5.1   Human Resource Management and Resource Management

The HLS contains some requirements related to human resources and some others related to other resources (financial, material, etc.) needed by the management system. But should these two aspects be included into one single process? Most of the companies have persons exclusively in charge of the management of human resources. Thus, it was decided to build a dedicated "Human resources management" process. Such a dedicated process contributes to a better assessability of this process and a better adoption of the process model. The requirements related to the other resources needed by the management system were included into the "Planning and operation management" process. These resources are required whatever the domain(s) covered by the management system. Thus, the "Planning and operation management" process permits to reinforce the interoperability between and integration of multiple management systems.

5.2   Documentation Management

The HLS contains two types of requirements dedicated to documentation. The HLS is first defining generic rules for managing documentation across the assessed organization. These requirements have been grouped into a "Documentation management" process. Such a dedicated "Documentation process" is applicable whatever the domain covered by the management system and even in case of an integrated management system. This also contributes to enhance the interoperability between, and the integration of, multiple management systems. The second type of requirements relates to the creation of documents specifically related to a process (as for example the record of the results of management reviews). In that case, each of these requirements specifying the content of these documents has been directly included into the related specific process (such as "Management review" in our example), enhancing the assessability of these specific processes.

5.3   Leadership vs Management Review

When analysing the requirements linked to the activities performed by Top Management (such as the leadership-related activities or the management review activities), the question of grouping all these requirements under the umbrella of one unique process emerged. The task force finally decided to split the requirements into two different processes: "Leadership" and "Management review". This choice has been done to ensure a better and easier assessability of these two processes. Indeed, on the one side the requirements from clause 5.1 of the HLS describe leadership-related activities (such as defining policy, assigning roles and responsibilities) that take place at the beginning of the implementation of a management system. On the other side the requirements related to the management review (such as those contained in clause 9.3) describe activities that usually take place at a different period of time (i.e. prior the improvement of the management system). Moreover, while the activities of the "Leadership" process are usually well performed and organized (as the beginning of something new), the management review activities can have less priority and thus be performed with lower assurance level. From an assessment standpoint, it is thus important to be able to make the difference between the capability levels of those two processes. Consequently, even if these two kinds of activities are performed by the top management, they should be seen as two different processes.

5.4   Communication Management

To address the requirements from the HLS related to the management of the communication, the task force decided to create a dedicated "Communication management" process. Indeed, the internal and external communication activities are in most cases performed by a dedicated role, whatever the size of the company.

Having a dedicated process better reflects the situation in place in the field. Thus, this contributes to a better adoption and applicability of the process assessment model. Moreover, the "Communication management" process defines communication and awareness practices that are applicable whatever the domain covered by the management system and even in case of an integrated management system. It permits to enhance the interoperability and the integration aspects of the core content of a process assessment model for MSS.

5.5   Non-auditable Requirements

When analyzing the requirements from the HLS, we admitted that all of the elementary requirements were not equally defined or detailed. Indeed, some of these requirements were generic and not auditable as such. However, to ensure a strict traceability between the HLS and the produced process assessment model, the task force decided to include these non-auditable requirements into existing processes. For example, clause 4.4 stated that:

"The organization shall establish, implement, maintain and continually improve an XXX management system, including the processes needed and their interactions, in accordance with the requirements of this International Standard."

This generic requirement could be seen as a high-level requirement that covers all the elementary requirements described in the HLS. The task force first took the decision to split this requirement into four elementary requirements:

- *"The organization shall **establish** an XXX management system, including the processes needed and their interactions, in accordance with the requirements of this International Standard."*
- *"The organization shall **implement** an XXX management system, including the processes needed and their interactions, in accordance with the requirements of this International Standard."*
- *"The organization shall **maintain** an XXX management system, including the processes needed and their interactions, in accordance with the requirements of this International Standard."*
- *"The organization shall **continually improve** an XXX management system, including the processes needed and their interactions, in accordance with the requirements of this International Standard."*

Then, it was decided to associate the first three requirements to the "Planning and operation management" process whereas the fourth one was linked to the "Continual improvement" process.

5.6   Process Completeness

At the end of the transformation process, we reviewed the complete process model to check the completeness of each process. Indeed, the fact that they are based on a set of elementary requirements coming from the HLS does not guarantee that the processes are complete, or in other words that the process outcomes are sufficient to achieve the process purpose. For example, in the HLS [2] the requirements related to risk and opportunity management does not include aspects such as the risk assessment, the selection of the risk treatment strategy, or the monitoring of the residual risk. All these aspects are missing but should be present in order to have a well-formed and complete risk management process. Thus, we decided to enrich our process model by adding the needed but missing outcomes and practices to each incomplete process. For filling the gaps of the HLS at the risk management level, we used the ISO 31000 standard [15], which provides requirements for risk management that are applicable to any domain. By doing so, we ensure a better assessability of each process and a better adoption of the created process models.

6   Conclusion

This paper describes the construction of the core content of a process assessment model for MSS. The resulting process model is covering the processes that are common to all MSS and thus reflecting an international consensus as defined by ISO standards. This paper also explains how the produced process model could support consistency and interoperability between domain-specific MSS.

With that core content made available, only the content specific to a particular domain still needs to be described when one wants to build a process assessment model to assess a management system for a specific domain. For this reason, the proposed process assessment model will permit to avoid the construction of new process assessment models from scratch. Experts from CRP Henri Tudor are currently using this core content to design a process assessment model for information security management system (based on [13]), as well as one for business continuity management system (based on [14]).

Another future work will consist in helping the digitization and archiving services providers in Luxembourg to comply with the technical regulation requirements described in [17]. For that, we will combine the core content of a process assessment model for MSS with requirements from international standards (ISO/IEC 27001:2005, ISO/IEC 27002:2005 and ISO/IEC 30301:2011) and national regulations [18]. This will lead to the design of an integrated management system for information lifecycle management.

Finally, in order to ensure that it reflects an international consensus, the process models described in this paper has been proposed as New Work Item at the ISO level. If accepted, the new Technical Specification can contribute to enhance the adoption of our research results, i.e. the core content of a process assessment model for MSS.

References

[1] ISO Survey (2012),
     http://www.iso.org/iso/home/standards/certification/
     iso-survey.htm
[2] ISO/IEC Directives, Part1, Annex SL (2014)

[3] ISO/IEC 33001: Information technology – Process assessment – Concepts and terminology (2014)

[4] ISO/IEC 33002: Information technology – Process assessment – Requirements for performing process assessment (2014)

[5] ISO/IEC 33004: Information technology – Process assessment – Requirements for process reference, process assessment and maturity models (2014)

[6] Barafort, B., Renault, A., Picard, M., Cortina, S.: A Transformation Process for Building PRMs and PAMs based on a Collection of Requirements – Example with ISO/IEC 20000. In: 8th international SPICE 2008 Conference, Nuremberg (2008)

[7] Rifaut, A.: Goal-driven requirements engineering for supporting the ISO 15504 assessment process. In: Richardson, I., Abrahamsson, P., Messnarz, R. (eds.) EuroSPI 2005. LNCS, vol. 3792, pp. 151–162. Springer, Heidelberg (2005)

[8] Cortina, S., Picard, M., Valdes, O., Renault, A.: A Challenging Process Models Development: The ITIL v3 Lifecycle Processes. In: Proceedings of the 10th International SPICE Conference on Process Assessment and Improvement, Pisa (2010)

[9] Public Research Center Henri Tudor, ITSM Process Assessment Supporting ITIL. Amersfoort: Van Haren Publishing (2009)

[10] Togneri MacMahon, S., Mc Caffery, F., Keenan, F.: Transforming Requirements of IEC 80001-1 into an ISO/IEC 15504-2 compliant Process Reference Model and Process Assessment Model. In: Proceedings of the 20th EuroSPI[2] Conference. Dundalk (2013)

[11] ISO, ISO/IEC TR 24774: Software and systems engineering – Life cycle management – Guidelines for process description (2010)

[12] ISO/IEC 33020: Information technology – Process assessment – Process measurement framework for assessment of process capability (2014)

[13] ISO/IEC 27001: Information technology – Security techniques – Information security management systems – Requirements (2013)

[14] ISO 22301: Societal security – Business continuity management systems – Requirements (2012)

[15] ISO 31000: Risk management – Principles and guidelines (2009)

[16] ISO 9001: Quality management systems – Requirements (2008)

[17] Technical regulation requirements and measures for certifying Digitisation or Archiving Service Providers (PSDC) – Version 1.3 (2013)

[18] Circular CSSF 12/544: Optimisation of the supervision exercised on the "support PFS" by a risk-based approach (2012)

CERTICS - An ISO/IEC 15504 Conformance Model for Software Technological Development and Innovation

Clenio F. Salviano[1], Angela M. Alves[1], Giancarlo N. Stefanuto[2], Sonia T. Maintinguer[2], Carolina V. Mattos[2] and Camila Zeitoum[2]

[1] Centro de Tecnologia da Informação Renato Archer - CTI
Rodovia D. Pedro I, km 143.6, CEP 13069-90, Campinas, SP, Brazil
{clenio.salviano,angela.maria}@cti.gov.br
[2] Fundação de Apoio à Capacitação em Tecnologia da Informação – Facti
Rodovia D. Pedro I, km 143.6, CEP 13069-901, Campinas, SP, Brazil
{gianstefanuto,soniamaint,camila.zeitoum,
carol.mattos}@gmail.com

Abstract. The Brazilian Government established a public policy instrument to identify and stimulate software production resulting from technology development and innovation carried out in Brazil. In order to accomplish this effort, CERTICS software process assessment methodology was created and established in Brazil. Its construction has been based on the reality of local software development organizations, in effort to achieve consensus within the community of interest, and guided by methodological references including the ISO/IEC 15504 (SPICE) Standard. CERTICS Methodology includes an Assessment Reference Model and an Assessment Method. This article presents the CERTICS Assessment Reference Model and statements on how it is compliant with ISO/IEC 15504 Requirements for Process Reference Models, Process Assessment Models and Organizational Maturity Models.

Keywords: ISO/IEC 15504, SPICE, Process Reference Model, Process Assessment Model, Organizational Maturity Model.

1   Introduction

ISO/IEC 15504 series of standards, also known as SPICE (Software Process Improvement and Capability dEtermination) established requirements, a measurement framework, guidelines and examples of models and methods for process assessment [1] [2] [3]. Using ISO/IEC 15504, different models and methods can be developed to address specific objectives and domains. ISO/IEC 15504-2 "addresses the assessment of process and the application of process assessment for improvement and capability determination" [1]. ISO/IEC 15504-7 "addresses the expression of the results of assessment of processes in terms of the overall maturity of an organizational unit, and the application of the results of assessment of organizational maturity for process improvement and capability determination" [2].

A. Mitasiunas et al. (Eds.): SPICE 2014, CCIS 477, pp. 48–59, 2014.

The CERTICS Assessment Methodology for Software (CERTICS Methodology) is a methodology to assess software process in order to determine a specific criterion, named in this article as the Fundamental Concept: whether a given software is resulting from technological development and technological innovation carried out in Brazil. CERTICS is a name. A design decision for CERTICS Methodology was to use ISO/IEC 15504 Standard as a reference for two major methodological components: CERTICS Assessment Reference Model (CERTICS Model) and CERTICS Assessment Method (CERTICS Method). CERTICS Methodology also includes an Operational Structure for its operation, monitoring and continuous improvement. In order to improve the communication with the community of interest, some specific terms are used in CERTICS with correspondence to ISO/IEC 15504 terms. The CERTICS Model, for example, corresponds to ISO/IEC 15504's Process Reference Model (PRM), Process Assessment Model (PAM) and Organizational Maturity Model (OMM).

A special attention was given to the requirement to identify and take actions to achieve consensus within the community of interest of the model. The Brazilian Federal Government demands the CERTICS Methodology as a public policy instrument to identify and stimulate software resulting from technology development and innovation in Brazil.

The objective of this article is to present the current version 1.1 of CERTICS Model and the extent of its compliancy with ISO/IEC 15504-2 and ISO/IEC 15504-7 Standards. The CERTICS Methodology and its two major components, the CERTICS Model and the CERTICS Method, are documented in Portuguese language in three technical reports [4] [5] [6]. The CERTICS Model is complemented with another technical report about its conformity to ISO/IEC 15504 requirements [7]. This article includes overviews and English translations from selected original materials.

In the first semester of 2011, the Brazilian Ministry of Science, Technology and Innovation (in Portuguese *Ministério da Ciência, Tecnologia e Inovação* – MCTI) demanded a project for the Information Technological Center Renato Archer (in Portuguese *Centro de Tecnologia da Informação Renato Archer* – CTI Renato Archer) to provide a methodology to characterize software with respect to the Fundamental Concept. At that time, CTI Renato Archer was establishing the Poli.TIC Laboratory to develop instruments for public policies in Information and Communication Technologies (ICT). Poli.TIC emerged as a combination from previous work in Software Process Improvement and from public policy analyses in ICT in general, specially in software.

In order to characterize software with respect to the Fundamental Concept, it is necessary and sufficient to examine the processes performed to develop and commercialize the software and their relation with technological development and technological innovation carried out in Brazil. Therefore the process assessment technology was appropriate and ISO/IEC 15504 was the appropriate reference. The organizational unit is the "part of an organization responsible for all aspects of a particular product or product set" – in this case, a particular software.

2   The Development of CERTICS Methodology

CERTICS Methodology and its Operational Structure had been developed since July 2011 following five phases: Design, Version 1.0 development, Delivery, Version 1.1 development and Operation Setup. The first two phases and their results are also described in another work [8].

The first phase (Design) was carried out from July to December 2011. The objectives were to understand the demand in its technical, political and strategic dimensions, explore scenarios for local software industry, identify and interview relevant stakeholders, and review theoretical and practical references in order to design the solution. A multi-disciplinary team with eight specialists was defined. About 20 exploratory interviews with representatives from companies, governmental entities purchasing software, policy makers and funding agencies were held. A study of scenarios with 50 experts was conducted to deepen the understanding of the trajectory of the software activities in Brazil and analyze the contribution of a certification mechanism for its development. In parallel, surveys of secondary sources were conducted, both intending to characterize the software production as well as its applications to the theories related to innovation, management innovation and economy. During this phase, it could be confirmed, based on these inputs, the view that the assessment should be based on the process undertaken for the software. The concept of technological and correlated competencies was defined to guide the development of the Fundamental Concept.

The second phase (Version 1.0 development) was carried out from October 2011 to May 2012, overlapped with the first phase. The objective was to perform cycles of development and experiences in order to produce the first version of the methodology. Preliminary versions of this methodology with more detailed levels of abstraction were exercised for software from 15 software companies, and the results oriented new and more detailed versions. An expert panel with 60 participants, among entrepreneurs, academics, consultants, policy makers and representatives from government, acquisition departments, agencies and others entities was conducted to present and review one of these versions. The results of this Panel guided a new version with improvements in the methodology. This version was presented in different sections to more than 30 stakeholders from software organizations associations and other entities, where more elements of improvement were identified and implemented. The methodology was named CERTICS Methodology and its consolidated version was published as version 1.0 in May 2012. A CERTICS web site was launched at www.certics.cti.gov.br to disclose the methodology. CERTICS Assessment Reference Model was defined with 24 outcomes organized into five competence areas.

The third phase (Delivery) was performed from June to December 2012. At this stage the requirements and characteristics of an operational structure have been identified for operation CERTICS, including an organizational arrangement, a business model to estimate and address the potential demand and the design of a software platform to support assessments. From August to December 2012 a formal public review and two public hearings were performed to collect comments and improvement proposals from any person or group. In this period there were 4,686 visits to the CERTICS site and the page was viewed 18,922 times. In this public review, 333 comments and proposals were received: 122 from individual participants and 91 from institutions. In addition, a survey was carried out with 49 micro and small software companies, from all regions of Brazil, to verify if CERTICS was suitable for micro and small software companies. The result was positive with some suggestions for improvements.

The fourth phase (Version 1.1 development) was performed from January to July 2013. The objective was to analyze the results from public review and the survey, and to produce a new version of the methodology. The results were positive to the CERTICS Methodology. The general structure was validated. CERTICS Assessment Reference Model was reviewed. The 24 outcomes were reviewed and reduced to 16 outcomes. They were organized into four competence areas, instead of five. CERTICS Assessment Method was then, redesigned. An operational structure, identified in the previous phase, was designed and a software platform was developed to support a CERTICS assessment. The CERTICS Methodology version 1.1 and its components CERTICS Model and CERTICS Method were published in June 2013, in Portuguese language in three technical reports [4] [5] [6]. In June 2013, MCTI launched the CERTICS Methodology and the characteristics of its operational structure in a public event in CTI Renato Archer.

The fifth phase (Operation Setup) started in August 2014 and it is planned to be completed in December 2015 when the operation is going to be in full capacity. The operational structure designed in the previous phases began to operate gradually. CERTICS went into operation on September 19, 2013. Approximately eleven months later, on August 27, 2014, 191 professionals have been trained in the methodology, 10 organizations have been authorized to perform the preparation and visit phases of the assessment method, 121 software have been registered in the software platform to exercise the methodology, 12 assessments are under the way and 8 assessments had been completed.

3   CERTICS Assessment Reference Model

CERTICS Assessment Reference Model (CERTICS Model) is structured with four conceptual hierarchical layers. Figure 1 illustrates the layered structure of the reference model and its use for the assessment method. This figure presents the logic and top-down structure, which is driven by the fundamental concept that guided the development of the model. The information processing that guides the use of this framework in conducting an assessment following the method is, by its turn, based on evidence and bottom-up engineered.

The first layer is the fundamental concept: software resulting from development and technological innovation carried in Brazil. From this fundamental concept, the context in which it was formulated and the reality of software industry in Brazil, operational concepts were defined to guide the construction of the next layers. These operational concepts can be summarized in promoting sustainable national development by the creation and improvement of technological and correlated competencies, contributing, thus, to the creation of knowledge-based businesses, the increase of technological autonomy and innovative capacity of Brazilian software industry.

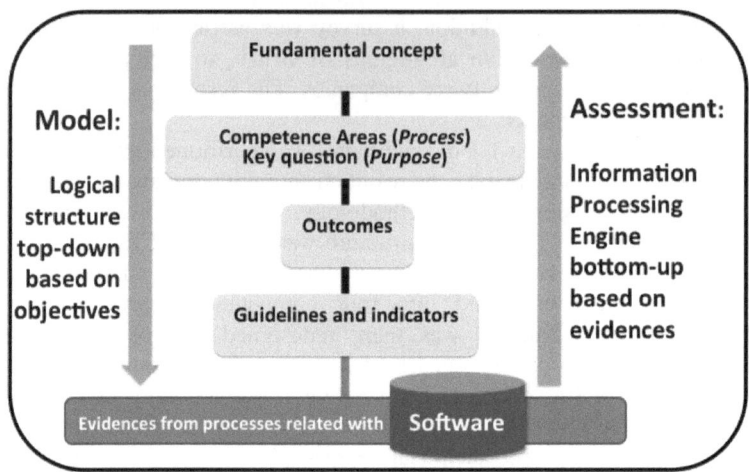

Fig. 1. Structure with four layers

The second layer emerged from these operational concepts based on technological and correlated competencies concepts and organized as competencies areas. A competencies area corresponds to an ISO/IEC 15504's process. The fundamental concept is then, unfolded into four competence areas named as Technological Development (DES), Technological Management (TEC), Business Management (GNE) and Continuous Improvement (MEC). Each Competence Area involves, with different emphases, aspects of both technological and correlated competencies. Each Competence Area is characterized by a key question, followed by a brief description and a set of Outcomes. Each Competence Area is achieved if their outcomes are achieved.

The third layer is comprised of Outcomes, detailing each competence area. There are sixteen outcomes: six for DES, four for TEC, three for GNE and three for MEC. Each outcome is characterized in the model by a definition, preceded by an ID and a label and followed by a brief description. The fourth layer consists of guidelines and indicators for each outcome. Each set of guidelines and indicators guides the assessment of an outcome in order to verify if it is achieved.

Table 1 presents the descriptions of the four competence areas. These descriptions address layers 2 and 3.

The fourth layer consists of guidelines and indicators for each outcome. As well as indicators for each outcome, there are a set of practices and examples of types of evidences [5, p. 25-26]. Thus, for the outcome "TEC.1. Use Results from Technological R&D: Software development uses results from Technological Research and Development", for example, there are practices related with the presence of "information about results from R&D projects and their incorporation in the software" and "documentation about technological competencies generated with the results from R&D projects". Types of evidences for this outcome are, for example, "report for R&D projects", "software design document with indication of the usage of R&D results", and "registries on the diffusion of R&D results".

Table 1. Descriptions of CERTICS Competence Areas

Technological Development (DES)	Technology Management (TEC)
Key question: "Is the software the result of technological development in Brazil?"	**Key question:** "Does the software remain autonomous and technologically competitive?"
Outcomes: DES.1. Competence in Architecture: The Organizational Unit has competencies over the relevant elements of the software architecture and its implementation; DES.2. Competence in Requirements: Organizational Unit has competencies over the relevant requirements related to software technology; DES.3. Compatibilities of Phases and Disciplines to the Software: The development phases and disciplines are compatible with the generated software; DES.4. Identified Roles and Personnel: The roles and people who worked in the software are identified, they are compatible with development and technological expertise generated in the Organizational Unit; DES.5. Documented Relevant Technical Data: The technical data relevant to software technology are documented and of easy reach; and DES.6. Competence in Support and Evolution of Software: The Organizational Unit is competent to perform support and related software development activities.	**Outcomes:** TEC.1. Use Results from Technological R&D: Software development uses results from Technological Research and Development; TEC.2. Appropriation of Relevant Technologies: The relevant technologies used in software are appropriated by the Organizational Unit; TEC.3. Introduction of Technological Innovations: Actions to introduce technological innovations in the software are stimulated and handled at the Organizational Unit; and TEC.4. Decision-making Capacity: Organizational Unit has decision-making capacity on the relevant technologies in the software.

Business Management (GNE)	Continuous Improvement (MEC)
key question: "The software leverages knowledge-based business and is driven by these business?"	**key question:** Is the software resultant of continuous improvement actions originated in the management of people, processes and knowledge to support and enhance their development and technological innovation?"
Outcomes: GNE.1. Monitoring Market Shares: Monitoring of aspects related to potential market and related software functionalities are performed; GNE.2. Anticipate and Meet Customers' Needs: Anticipation and meeting of customers needs related with the software are performed; and GNE.3. Software Related Business Evolution: Actions to guide the evolution of software-related business are taken.	**Outcomes:** MEC.1. Hiring, Training and Encourage Qualified Professionals: Qualified professionals are hired, trained and encouraged to perform software-related activities; MEC.2. Software related Knowledge diffusion: The information from technological and business activities related to the software is diffused; and MEC.3. Process Improvements: Improvements in processes of technological and business activities related to software are performed.

4   Statements of Conformity with ISO/IEC 15504 Requirements

There are three types of conformity models to the requirements of ISO/IEC 15504: PRM, PAM and OMM. Accordance to the requirements of ISO/IEC 15504 may be verified by self-declaration (first party), a second party, or a third party. A Technical Report presents conformity statements of CERTICS Model with ISO/IEC 15504-2 and ISO/IEC 15504-7 requirements [7]. The CERTICS Team (in this case first party) elaborated and verified these statements. This Section presents excerpts and overviews from that Technical Report.

We identified two approaches to document such statements: a complete list of each requirement with a declaration on how and where it is addressed, as, for example, in Enterprise SPICE model [9], and a list with a selection of some requirements, as, for example, in Automotive SPICE Process Assessment Model [10]. We used the complete list approach.

The conformity statements are described in a set of tables with three columns: a sequential identification starting from S01, an ISO/IEC 15504 requirement and a conformity statement. A conformity statement starts with a reference to the CERTICS Model document [5] and section where the requirement is addressed. Then, a conformity statement concludes with a comment on how the requirement is addressed. Table 2 presents the statements of conformity to the requirements for a PRM.

Table 2. Statements of conformity to the requirements for a PRM

Id	Requirements in ISO/IEC 15504-2	Statement of CERTICS Model Conformity
S01	6.2.3.1 A PRM shall contain:	The following statements attend this requirement.
S02	a) a declaration of the domain of the PRM;	The declaration of the domain is in CERTICS Model Section 2.2: Fundamental Concept. The domain includes software technological development and innovation.
S03	b) a description, meeting the requirements of clause 6.2.4 of this International Standard, of the processes within the scope of the PRM;	The description is in CERTICS Model Section 3: Competence Areas. There are descriptions of four Competence Areas, identified as DES, TEC, GNE and MEC within the scope of CERTICS Model. A Competence Area corresponds to a process, as explained in Statement S12.
S04	c) a description of the relationship between the PRM and its intended context of use;	The description is in CERTICS Model Section 2.2: Fundamental Concept. The intended context of use is to assess software process for the Fundamental Concept. CERTICS Model is intended for use in multiple organizational contexts and to meet a full range of different business needs, application domains, and sizes. It is flexible with regard to the type of software.

Table 2. *(Continued)*

Id	Requirements in ISO/IEC 15504-2	Statement of CERTICS Model Conformity
S05	d) a description of the relationship between the processes defined within the PRM;	The description is in CERTICS Model Section 3.4: Continuous Improvement (MEC) Competence Area. There is one relevant relationship. It is between MEC and the other three competence areas.
S06	6.2.3.2 The PRM shall document the community of interest of the model and the actions taken to achieve consensus within that community of interest:	There are at least two related communities of interest: the Brazilian Federal Government and the relevant software stakeholders. CERTICS Methodology is a public policy instrument supported by federal law. From the federal government perspective, MCTI is responsible to implement CERTICS. Therefore, the federal government, represented by MCTI, is a community of interest. In order to be accepted, the other community of interest includes buyers, governmental agencies, specialists, software organizations, software organization associations, and others.
S07	a) the relevant community of interest shall be characterized or specified;	The characterization is indicated in CERTICS Model Sections 1: Introduction and 2. Objectives. An overview is described in the previous Statement S07.
S08	b) the extent of achievement of consensus shall be documented;	The actions taken to achieve consensus within the Brazilian Federal Government as a community of interest are related to a continuous relationship, as well as a demanding and joint public presentations and publications. The extent of consensus achieved is evidenced by the publication of legal instruments indicating CERTICS Methodology as the implementation of the related federal law. The actions taken to achieve consensus and the extent of consensus achieved within the relevant software stakeholders, as well as the other community of interest, are described in Section 2 of this article.
S09	c) if no actions are taken to achieve consensus, a statement to this effect shall be documented;	Not applicable because actions were taken to achieve consensus as described in the previous Statement S08.
S10	6.2.3.3 The processes defined (...) shall have unique (...) descriptions and identification.	The descriptions and identification are in CERTICS Model Section 3: Competence Areas.

Table 2. *(Continued)*

Id	Requirements in ISO/IEC 15504-2	Statement of CERTICS Model Conformity
S11	NOTE Any elements contained in a PRM that are not included in this clause are to be considered informative.	All elements that are not included in this clause are considered informative.
S12	6.2.4 Process descriptions: The fundamental elements of a PRM are the descriptions of the processes (...). The process descriptions (...) incorporate a statement of the purpose of the process which describes at a high level the overall objectives of performing the process, together with the set of outcomes which demonstrate successful achievement of the process purpose. These process descriptions shall meet the following requirements:	The descriptions are in CERTICS Model Section 3: Competence Areas. The fundamental elements of CERTICS Model are the descriptions of four Competence Areas, identified as DES, TEC, GNE and MEC. A Competence Area corresponds to a process. Each Competence Area is defined by a key question and outcomes. A key question represents the purpose written as a question. The key question for TEC, for example, which is "Does the software remain autonomous and technologically competitive?" correspondents to the purpose "to maintain the software autonomous and technologically competitive". Therefore each Competence Area is a process to achieve its purpose.
S13	a) a process shall be described in terms of its purpose and outcomes;	The descriptions are in CERTICS Model Section 3: Competence Areas. Each Competence Area (process) is described in terms of key question (purpose) and outcomes.
S14	b) in any process description the set of process outcomes shall be necessary and sufficient to achieve the purpose of the process;	They are necessary and sufficient to achieve the purpose of the process. Technical reviews were performed to adjust and validate the outcomes as necessary and sufficient to answer the key question (achieve the purpose) of the competence area (process).
S15	c) process descriptions shall be such that no aspects (...) beyond level 1 are contained or implied.	No aspect beyond level 1 are contained or implied. Technical reviews were performed to adjust and validate the "level 1" competence area (process) descriptions.
S16	An outcome statement describes one of the following: Production of an artefact; A significant change of state; Meeting of specified constraints (...).	All outcome statements follow this description. Technical reviews were performed to adjust and validate the sixteen outcomes.

Similar tables were produced with conformity statements to the requirements for PAM and OMM. Basically, in order to be a PAM, CERTICS Model already includes:

a) a set of indicators for each outcome that explicitly addresses the purpose and outcomes, as described in subsections "Guidelines" and "Examples of Types of Evidences" for each outcome in CERTICS Model Section 3 - Competence Areas; and

b) the capability level 1 selected from the ISO/IEC 15504 Measurement Framework, as indicated in CERTICS Methodology Section 4 – Rating Rules.

Basically, in order to be an OMM, CERTICS Model already defines the maturity level 1 with the four competence areas as the Basic Process Set with no additional elements, as indicated in CERTICS Methodology Section 4 – Rating Rules.

5   Conclusion

From an analysis of the conformity statements of CERTICS Model with the ISO/IEC 15504-2 requirements for PRM and PAM, we conclude that CERTICS Model can be considered both as PRM and PAM. From an analysis of the conformity statements of CERTICS Model to ISO/IEC 15504-7 requirements for OMM, we also conclude that CERTICS Model can be considered as an OMM. The documentation of CERTICS Model, however, should be improved in order to facilitate the understanding of how these requirements are addressed.

Thus, there are some remarks on how CERTICS Model uses ISO/IEC 15504 requirements and possible further research work:

a) In the current revision of ISO/IEC 15504 Standard, it has been renumbered as ISO/IEC 33000 Series. In this revision the new concept of Process Quality has been introduced as "an ability to satisfy stated and implied stakeholder needs when used in a specific context" [11]. Measurement aspects, named as process quality characteristics, define process quality. Process capability, defined in current ISO/IEC 15504, and safety [11] are examples of process quality characteristic. Technological and correlated competencies, as defined and used in CERTICS Model, can be considered as another example of process quality characteristic. After the final publication of the relevant standards of ISO/IEC 33000 Series there are at least two further research work to be performed: an investigation on competence as a process quality characteristic and the development of maturity levels 2 and beyond using competence. This second issue is discussed in the next remark.

b) Although the fundamental and operational concepts together with the competence areas were defined as a reference both for improvement and for assessment, this current version of CERTICS Model is written with an assessment perspective. In order to provide a more systematic reference for improvement one of the further research work stated in the previous remark should be performed: the development of maturity levels 2 and beyond. This development can be made using the current process capability or using competence as a candidate process quality characteristic.

c) CERTICS Model is defined as an OMM with only maturity level 1. The main reason was due to its assessment focus. However, a feedback from some assessments pointed out that it has been useful to drive a documentation of current practices and results of technological development and innovation. This finding is consistent with the reasons for defining maturity level 1, given that the most popular maturity model starts from level 2: maturity level 1 as defined in ISO/IEC 15504-7 guides the awareness of current practices and assures good practices on basic processes, before levels 2 and on.

d) The requirement of "document the community of interest of the model and the actions to achieve consensus within that community of interest" is the only requirement that directly addresses the process to develop models. The other requirements are more related with the models themselves. In addition, this requirement was considered very important for CERTICS Model. Therefore, special care was taken to address this requirement since the very beginning of the development.

e) From the previous remark, the process used to develop a model should be considered an important issue. Similar to the process view on software there should be a process view on process models. Since 2006, a research group is working on processes to develop ISO/IEC 15504-based models. From an analysis of processes used to develop different models, this work generated a Method Framework for Engineering Process Assessment Models (MFMOD) [12]. MFMOD has been used to CERTICS Models, as described in more details in another work [8].

f) CERTICS Model uses the terms Competence Area and Key Question instead of the ISO/IEC 15504's terms process and purpose. These two terms were chosen to facilitate the understanding of the model by the community of interest. As demonstrated in a previous section, they are correspondent to the ISO/IEC 15504 terms.

g) During CERTICS development, a literature search was performed to identify other related reference models. Among these references, for example, the Enterprise SPICE model [9] and the Innovation Capability Maturity Model [13] provided some ideas for CERTICS. Recently, an Innovation, Knowledge and Technology Transfer Capability Maturity Model was identified [14]. An analysis between CERTICS and this model shall be performed.

CERTICS offers a Reference Model in an innovative domain: technological development and technological innovation carried out in Brazil. The usage of ISO/IEC 15504 was essential to CERTICS Methodology in achieving its objectives.

Acknowledgments. The authors thank the financial support from projects MCTI/01200.001832/2011 - CTENIC and FINEP 0113009300 - *Implementação da CERTICS*, the work and efforts from all CERTICS team, and the anonymous referees for their comments and suggestions to improve this article.

References

1. The International Organization for Standardization and the International Electrotechnical Commission (ISO/IEC): ISO/IEC 15504-2 - Information technology - Process assessment - Part 2: Performing an assessment (2003)
2. ISO/IEC: ISO/IEC 15504-7 - Information technology - Process assessment - Part 7: Assessment of organizational maturity (2008)
3. Rout, T.P., El Emam, K., Fusani, M., Goldenson, D., Jung, H.-W.: SPICE in retrospect: Developing a standard for process assessment. J. Syst. Software (2007)
4. Equipe CERTICS: Metodologia de Avaliação da CERTICS para Software - Documento de Definição - Versão 1.1. Relatório Técnico CTI Renato Archer – TRT0012113 (2013) (in Portuguese), http://www.certics.cti.gov.br
5. Equipe CERTICS: Modelo de Referência para Avaliação da CERTICS - Documento de Detalhamento - Versão 1.1. Relatório Técnico CTI Renato Archer – TRT0084113 (2013) (in Portuguese), http://www.certics.cti.gov.br
6. Equipe CERTICS, Método de Avaliação da CERTICS - Documento de Detalhamento - Versão 1.1, Relatório Técnico CTI Renato Archer – TRT0083113 (2013)
7. Equipe CERTICS, CERTICS Assessment Reference Model Conformity to ISO/IEC 15504, Technical Report CTI Renato Archer TRT0129114 (2014)
8. Salviano, C.F., Alves, A.M., Stefanuto, G.N., Maintinguer, S.T., Mattos, C.V., Zeitoum, C., Reuss, G.: Developing a Process Assessment Model for Technological and Business Competencies on Software Development. In: Proc. of Eighth IEEE QUATIC Conference, Lisbon, September 3-6, pp. 125–130 (2012)
9. Project Team: Enterprise SPICE (ISO/IEC 15504) An Integrated Model for Enterprise-wide Improvement. Technical Report – Issue 1 (September 2010)
10. Automotive SIG, Automotive SPICE® Process Assessment Model (2010), http://www.automotivespice.com/ (last access in June 21, 2014)
11. Varkoi, T.: Safety as a Process Quality Characteristic. In: Proc. of the 13th SPICE International Conference, Bremen, Germany, June 4-6, pp. 1–12 (2013)
12. Salviano, C.F., Zoucas, A.C., Silva, J.V.L., Alves, A.M., Wangenheim, C.G., Thiry, M.: A Method Framework for Engineering Process Capability Models, In: EuroSPI, The 16th European Systems and Software Proc. Imp. and Innovation (2009)
13. Essmann, H., Preez, N.: An Innovation Capability Maturity Model – Development and initial application. World Academy of Science, Engineering and Technology 53, 435–446 (2009)
14. BONITA Project Team, innoSPICE An Innovation, Knowledge and Technology Transfer Capability Maturity Model, Technical report (January 2012), http://innospice.ning.com/ (last accessed in July 9, 2014)

Development of the Project Management SPICE (PMSPICE) Framework

Antoni-Lluís Mesquida[1], Antònia Mas[1], Marion Lepmets[2],
and Alain Renault[3]

[1] University of the Balearic Islands, Department of Mathematics
and Computer Science, Cra. de Valldemossa, km 7.5,
Palma de Mallorca, Spain
{antoni.mesquida,antonia.mas}@uib.es
[2] Regulated Software research Centre, Dundalk Institute of Technology,
Dundalk, Ireland
marion.lepmets@dkit.ie
[3] Public Research Centre Henri Tudor, 29 J.F.Kennedy ave.,
Luxembourg, Luxembourg
alain.renault@tudor.lu

Abstract. This paper proposes the development of a project management process assessment framework (PMSPICE). The paper describes three stages for the construction of the proposed PMSPICE process models. PMSPICE will include a process reference model (PRM), a process assessment model (PAM) and an organizational maturity model (OMM). The PMSPICE PRM is based on the project management processes defined in the ISO 21500 standard. The PMSPICE PAM will be used to perform ISO/IEC 15504 conformant assessments of the project management process capability in accordance with the requirements of ISO/IEC 15504-2. The processes also support compliance with OMM established in ISO/IEC TR 15504-7.

Keywords: Project management, process improvement, ISO/IEC 15504 (SPICE), ISO 21500, Process Reference Model (PRM).

1 Introduction

The process approach considers that all activities and tasks performed in an organization are part of a process and details the interactions among all processes. The maturity of an organization is associated with its capability to define, implement and maintain continuous improvement of all the processes it uses to perform the work. There are large benefits obtained in a process-oriented organization. Processes are well known and therefore can be controlled, analysed and improved. All employees work by applying the same guidelines. The management of processes also facilitates obtaining work results and improves the efficiency of the organizational activities and the performance of their employees.

A. Mitasiunas et al. (Eds.): SPICE 2014, CCIS 477, pp. 60–71, 2014.
© Springer International Publishing Switzerland 2014

A process-oriented organization may consider different process frameworks. On the one hand, it must take into account the processes in its business area related to the activity performed. On the other hand, it must also consider the processes related to the management of the company.

A project is the set of activities to be performed to achieve a certain goal within the limits imposed by previously established budget, quality requirements and duration. Project management is a dynamic process of leading, coordinating, planning and controlling a diverse and complex set of processes and people in the pursuit if achieving project objectives [1]. Organizing work in projects allows knowing the value of the indicators established for each process and, from experience, refines the estimates used during planning. This way deadlines and budgets for the products and services requested by customers can be set, resulting in an increase of their confidence and satisfaction.

We have observed that interest in project management has become increasingly apparent in recent years. One of the indicators that can corroborate this statement is related to the number of professionals that have been certified by one of the certification schemes or models most recognized and adopted: Project Management Professional (PMP)®, PRINCE2 and Certified ScrumMaster® (CSM). If practitioners have shown interest in this field and aim to acquire and demonstrate their experience and knowledge, it is because professionals with this profile are highly requested.

The interest of companies in implementing project management best practices has also continued to grow. Managing projects efficiently provides greater control of the work done in the company at all levels and allows the organization to be in competitive position in an increasingly globalized market. Moreover, the emergence of the ISO 21500 standard has attracted much interest from the business sector, on the one hand, to implement project management processes, and on the other hand, for the recognition that this standard could report back to the organization.

This paper outlines the development of a project management process assessment and improvement framework, called Project Management SPICE (PMSPICE). The experience we have gained over the years working with different frameworks and standards has made us recognize the importance of having the new PMSPICE Framework and has been the main factor and the origin of the work presented in this article.

The paper is structured as follows. Section 2 describes the motivation for the development of the PMSPICE Framework. Section 3 presents the previous works related to this new research. Section 4 details the planned stages for the development of PMSPICE. Section 5 finally summarizes the results obtained and opens discussion about future work.

2 The Need for the Project Management SPICE Framework

In order to define, implement and maintain continuous improvement in the processes related to project management, organizations need to establish a set of project management processes as a reference framework. Certainly the ISO/IEC 12207:2008 [2] standard includes a group of 7 processes, named *Project Processes*, intended to establish and evolve project plans, to assess actual achievement and progress against the plans and to control the execution of the project through to fulfilment, at any time in the life cycle. However, these 7 processes are not sufficient to cover all aspects of project management that are necessary for an organization since they are specific to the context of software development.

The recent standard ISO 21500:2012 [3] provides generic guidance and a high-level description of the project management concepts and processes that are important for and have impact on the achievement of projects. It describes 39 processes for project management, which are similarly structured to the PMBOK Guide [4], to be used during a project as a whole, for individual phases or both. The project management processes may be viewed from two different perspectives: either as the management of the project in a more timely manner, described as *process groups* (Initiating, Planning, Implementing, Controlling and Closing), or presenting the processes as *subject groups*. There are ten different subject groups: Integration, Stakeholder, Scope, Resource, Time, Cost, Risk, Quality, Procurement and Communication. Each process is shown in the process group and subject group in which most of the activity takes place.

The ISO 21500 standard does not follow the formal approach of other ISO standards that describe standard processes using a Process Reference Models (PRMs). According to the ISO/IEC 15504-2:2003 [5] standard, a PRM defines a set of processes characterized by statements of process purpose and process outcomes. The description of the processes in ISO 21500 is brief and the list of outcomes is not provided. Specific activities and tasks are also not described. This is the primary reason for developing a new PRM specific for project management.

In addition, an organization may be interested in knowing the different capability levels of its project management processes. The measurement framework of ISO/IEC 15504-2, which defines the requirements for performing a process assessment as a basis for use in process improvement and capability determination, can be used to assess the capability of the processes of the new project management PRM. Thus, we also propose the development of a Process Assessment Model (PAM) for the project management. A PAM expands the PRM process definitions by including two sets of process assessment indicators: process performance and process capability indicators. The proposed PAM will offer a structured definition of the project management processes specifically meant to allow process assessment. It will enable to compare the project management processes in an organization to the standard processes of ISO 21500 and to determine their capability level.

Finally, an organization may also be interested in knowing in which order it should implement and/or improve the various project management processes. To that end it an Organizational Maturity Model (OMM) could be used, which is aligned with the framework for determining the organizational maturity of ISO/IEC TR 15504-7:2008 [6]. Therefore, we also aim to develop a project management organizational maturity model.

The new PMSPICE Framework will thus define a PRM, a PAM and an OMM for project management. The PMSPICE PRM is based on the project management processes described in ISO 21500. The PMSPICE PAM will be used to perform ISO/IEC 15504 conformant assessments of the project management process capability in accordance with the requirements of ISO/IEC 15504-2. The project management processes also support the OMM conformant structure established in ISO/IEC TR 15504-7.

3   Related Work

In this section, we summarize the research that the authors have conducted in the past decade to support the development of the proposed PMSPICE Framework. Our work in the quality area began in the early 2000s. We focused on the assessment and improvement of software life cycle processes using the ISO/IEC 12207 and ISO/IEC 15504 standards. The work related to the ISO/IEC 15504 standard [7-10] has allowed us to observe its evolution, from the time ISO/IEC 15504-2 was published in 2003 [5] until the appearance of specific PAMs for different PRMs related to different disciplines or knowledge fields that have been emerging. After working on the assessment and improvement of software and system life cycle processes, we decided to delve into the application of the exemplar OMM defined in ISO/IEC TR 15504-7 [6].

In 2008, we started a new research line related to IT service management process quality. The objective of our research was to analyse which of the processes and best practices of IT service management were related, in whole or in part, to any of the software life cycle processes. The main result was the development of a framework to facilitate the integration of IT management standards in mature organizations [11-12]. During this research, we worked with ISO/IEC 20000-4:2010 [13] as a PRM and ISO/IEC TS 15504-8 as a PAM.

In 2010, our research was redirected to project management. This was mainly due to a greater industry demand to implement and improve the project management processes in the companies with which we were collaborating. Moreover, we had a deeper knowledge of the subject that had been acquired through a decade of teaching project management courses both in undergraduate and postgraduate programmes. For example, we analysed the project management practices of CMMI-DEV [14], ISO/IEC 15504 [5], PMBOK [4] and project management literature in 2007 [15], which clearly indicated the need for a more comprehensive set of project management practices to be established than were currently defined in the process models of CMMI-DEV and ISO/IEC 15504.

The interest of the SPICE community in developing different PRMs and PAMs specific to certain areas has recently increased, resulting in the appearance of new process models. This is the case with MDevSPICE®, a software process assessment model which is being developed to meet the specific safety-critical and regulatory requirements of the medical device domain [16, 17]. Other frameworks have also been developed for regulated domains, such as the aerospace (SPICE4SPACE), automotive (ASPICE) and nuclear (NuclearSPICE). Another example is TIPA® for ITIL®, a framework that uses the principles of ISO/IEC 15504 standard for IT service management process assessment [18]. Other proposals address the development of specific process models for areas, such as information security management [19] or software product management [20]. Moreover, there are PAMs already published as standards such as ISO/IEC 15504-5:2012 [21] for software life cycle processes, ISO/IEC 15504-6:2013 [22] for system life cycle processes or ISO/IEC TS 15504-8:2012 [23] for IT service management processes. With the replacement of ISO/IEC 15504 by the ISO/IEC 33001-99 series of standards, these parts related to the definition of PRMs and PAMs are currently being revised.

4   The Development of the PMSPICE Framework

The Project Management SPICE (PMSPICE) Framework is the result of a construction process divided into three sequential stages, which are detailed in next three subsections. The first stage has recently been completed. The second stage will be initiated very soon and the last stage will start once the results of the other two have been analysed and validated. As a result of these three stages the PMSPICE Framework will be composed of:

- PMSPICE Process Reference Model (PRM). It expands the descriptions of the project management processes in ISO 21500 to be aligned to the ISO/IEC TR 24774:2010 [24] standard for process description and be compliant with ISO/IEC 15504-2.
- PMSPICE Process Assessment Model (PAM). It will expand upon the PMSPICE PRM by including a set of assessment indicators compliant with ISO/IEC 15504-2.
- PMSPICE Organizational Maturity Model (OMM). It will follow the guidelines provided by ISO/IEC 15504-7 to perform assessments of project management organizational maturity.

4.1   Stage 1: Building the PMSPICE Process Reference Model

The first step in the development of the PMSPICE Process Reference Model (PRM) was the definition of the process map. In our case, we focused on the project management processes contained in the ISO 21500 standard. Having agreed on the processes (39) and the structure of the PRM (5 process groups and 10 subject groups), work then commenced on the development of the contents of the processes. We carefully analysed the information provided by the ISO 21500 standard for each process. This standard defines a process in terms of the purpose it serves, the relationships among the processes, the interactions within the processes, and the primary inputs and outputs associated with each process.

In order to follow a methodological approach, we followed the guidelines of ISO/IEC TR 24774:2010 [24] standard for the description of the processes in the new PRM. This technical report identifies descriptive elements and rules for the formulation of processes. It characterizes the following elements of process description: the title, the purpose, the outcomes, the activities and specific tasks to achieve an activity and other information items.

From the ISO 21500 process descriptions, and in line with the requirements of ISO/IEC 15504-2, each process in the PRM was assigned an ID and a name, i.e. a descriptive title. The process purpose, which describes the goal of performing the process, was also derived from the ISO 21500 process description. Figure 1 shows the standards and the components they define that were used for the design of the PMSPICE PRM.

Based on the ISO 21500 process purposes, the next step in our work was to identify the process outcomes. The outcomes express the observable results expected from the successful performance of the process. They are necessary and sufficient measurable results that demonstrate the successful achievement of the process purpose. According to ISO/IEC 15504-2 an outcome statement describes: the production of an artefact, a significant change of state or the compliance to specified constraints, e.g. requirements, goals, etc.

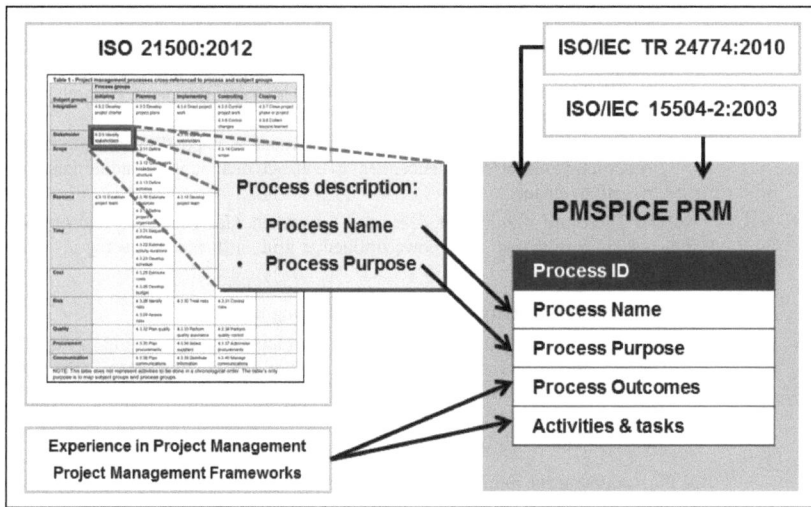

Fig. 1. Procedure followed for the construction of the PMSPICE Process Reference Model

Finally, in order to complete the description of the processes in the PMSPICE PRM, the activities and tasks for each process were added. The activities are a list of actions that may be used to achieve the process outcomes. Each activity may be further elaborated as a grouping of related lower level actions. The tasks are specific actions that may be performed to conduct an activity. Multiple related tasks are often grouped within an activity.

The process descriptions in the PMSPICE PRM are summarized in a table containing the above-mentioned information. Table 1 shows the example of the description of the *STK.2 Manage stakeholders* process defined in the PRM.

Table 1. The Manage stakeholders Process described in the PMSPICE PRM

Process ID	STK.2
Process Name	Manage stakeholders
Process Purpose	The purpose of *Manage stakeholders* is to ensure appropriate attention is given to stakeholders.
Process Outcomes	As a result of the successful implementation of this process:
	1. The impact stakeholders have on the project is analysed.
	2. Stakeholders' expectations are understood.
	3. Stakeholders' concerns are addressed.
	4. Stakeholders' issues are resolved or escalated in accordance with the organization to a higher authority.

Table 1. *(Continued)*

Process ID	STK.2
Activities and tasks	**1. Stakeholder analysis**. This activity consists of the following tasks: • Identify stakeholders' relevant information, such as their interests, knowledge, expectations and influence levels. Create the stakeholder register. • Analyse the potential impact or support each stakeholder could generate, and classify them so as to define an approach strategy. The engagement level of the stakeholders can be classified as follows: Unaware, Resistant, Neutral, Supportive and Leading. • Assess how key stakeholders are likely to react or respond in various situations, in order to plan how to influence them to enhance their support and mitigate potential negative impacts. NOTE: There are multiple models used for stakeholder's analysis and classification such as: power/interest grid, power/influence grid, influence/impact grid or salience model. **2. Meetings**. This activity consists of the following tasks: • Conduct project meetings designed to develop an understanding of major project stakeholders, and to exchange and analyse information about roles, interests, knowledge, and the overall position of each stakeholder. • Hold meetings with experts and the project team to define the required engagement levels of all stakeholders. **3. Plan stakeholder management**. This activity consists of the following tasks: • Identify the management strategies required to effectively engage stakeholders. • Create the stakeholder management plan. In addition to the data gathered in the stakeholder register, the stakeholder management plan can include: scope and impact of change to stakeholders, interrelationships and overlaps between stakeholders, communication requirements, information to be distributed, time frame and frequency for the distribution of information and the method for updating the stakeholder management plan. **4. Manage stakeholder engagement**. This activity consists of the following tasks: • Apply interpersonal skills to manage stakeholder's expectations: building trust, resolving conflict, active listening and overcoming resistance to change. • Apply management skills to coordinate and harmonize the group toward accomplishing the objectives, influencing people to support the project and modifying organizational behaviour to accept the project outcomes. **5. Control stakeholder engagement**. This activity consists of the following tasks: • Compare the current engagement level of all stakeholders to the planned engagement levels required for successful project completion. • Use status review meetings to exchange and analyse information about stakeholder engagement. • Obtain expert judgment to ensure comprehensive identification and listing of new stakeholders and reassessment of current stakeholders. **6. Update documents**. This activity consists of the following tasks: • Update project documents such as project schedule and stakeholder register. • Update organizational process assets such as stakeholder notifications, project reports, project presentations, project records, feedback from stakeholders and lessons learned documentation.

ISO/IEC 15504-2 requires that descriptions of the processes included in a PRM satisfy the following requirements:

- A process shall be described in terms of its purpose and outcomes.
- In any description the set of process outcomes shall be necessary and sufficient to achieve the purpose of the process.
- Process descriptions shall be such that no measurement aspects are contained or implied.

Since process purposes and outcomes were derived directly from ISO 21500, the first requirement was satisfied. The second and third requirements were also met during the construction of the PMSPICE PRM, as can be observed in the process example in Table 1.

4.2   Stage 2: Designing the PMSPICE Process Assessment Model

A PRM and the capability dimension defined in ISO/IEC 15504-2 cannot be used alone as the basis for conducting reliable and consistent assessments of process capability. The descriptions of process purposes and outcomes in a PRM, and the process attribute definitions in ISO/IEC 15504-2, need to be supported with a comprehensive set of indicators of process performance and process capability that are used for performing an assessment [21].

The work in the second stage will consist of the development of a Process Assessment Model (PAM) that expands upon the developed PMSPICE PRM by including a defined set of assessment indicators with lower-level details on each particular process that will be necessary to perform an accurate and detailed assessment. Assessment indicators comprise of process capability indicators, which apply to capability levels 1 to 5, and process performance indicators, which apply exclusively to capability level 1.

Process capability indicators provide an indication of the extent of achievement of the attribute in the instantiated process. These indicators are: Generic Practice (GP), Generic Resource (GR), and Generic Inputs/Outputs (GIO). The new PMSPICE PAM will adopt the GPs, GRs and GIOs which are defined in other PAMs such as ISO/IEC 15504-5 [21] and ISO/IEC 15504-8 [23].

Process performance indicators relate to individual processes defined in the process dimension of the process assessment model and are chosen to explicitly address the achievement of the defined process purpose. Process performance indicators included in a PAM are:

- The activities that are recommended for the achievement of process outcomes, which are called Base Practices (BP), and
- Its inputs and outputs, also named Work Products (WP) that are either used or produced (or both) when performing the process.

The base practices for each process in the PAM will be defined from the list of activities and tasks of the process description in the PRM. Base practices will be described with a sequence number identifying them within the process, a name starting with a verb, a description with more details as a sentence also starting with a verb and a reference between brackets indicating to which outcome(s) the base practice relates to.

Regarding the WPs, the list of primary inputs and primary outputs from ISO 21500 process descriptions will be taken as a basis and further work will be done in order to define the structure and contents of each item. The inputs and outputs in the PMSPICE PAM will be described with an identification number, a name, a reference number for the outcome they contribute to and a reference number for the base practice during which they are used or produced.

Figure 2 shows the elements for each process in the PMSPICE PAM and their relationships with the PRM and other international ISO standards.

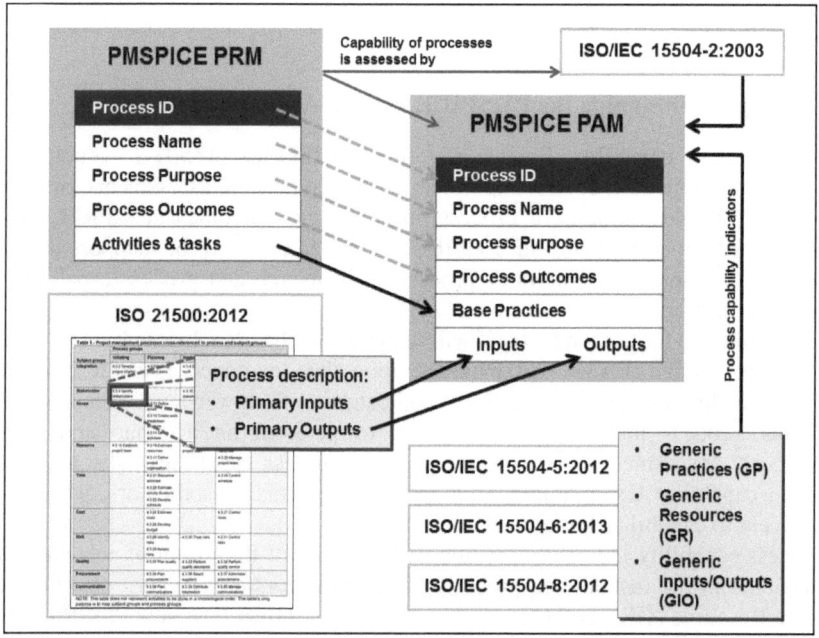

Fig. 2. Design of the PMSPICE Process Assessment Model

4.3   Stage 3: Designing the PMSPICE Organizational Maturity Model

As defined in ISO/IEC 15504-7, organizational maturity is an expression of the extent to which an organization has explicitly and consistently performed, managed and established processes within a defined scope with predictable performance and demonstrated the ability to change and adapt the performance of the processes fundamental to achieving the organization's business goals (current or projected). An Organizational Maturity Model (OMM) is based upon one or more specified PAM(s), and addresses the domains and contexts for use of the PRM(s) from which the PAM(s) are derived.

The work in the third stage will consist of defining the content of an OMM for Project Management, based upon PMSPICE PRM and PMSPICE PAM. This new

OMM will specify a continuous subset of maturity levels for the assessment of project management organizational maturity.

Organizational maturity is defined by ISO/IEC TR 15504-7 [6] on a six point ordinal scale that enables maturity to be assessed from the bottom of the scale, Level 0 Organization - the Immature Organization, through to the top end of the scale, Level 5 Organization - the Innovating Organization. The scale for organizational maturity retains the semantic intent of the process capability levels that are defined in ISO/IEC 15504-2. ISO/IEC TR 15504-7 contains guidance on implementing the requirements for constructing an OMM, on performing assessments of organizational maturity, and on the application of organizational maturity ratings for process improvement and capability determination. It also defines the conditions under which organizational maturity are valid.

From the PMSPICE PAM, a set of elements will constitute the basic process set for the model. The basic process set will include: a minimum set of elements that define Level 1 Organization Maturity for all assessments based on the model, additional elements that are required for assessments in particular domains or scope of application, and additional elements that are optional depending on the particular circumstances of the organization.

Figure 3 shows the relationships between the PMSPICE OMM, PAM and PRM.

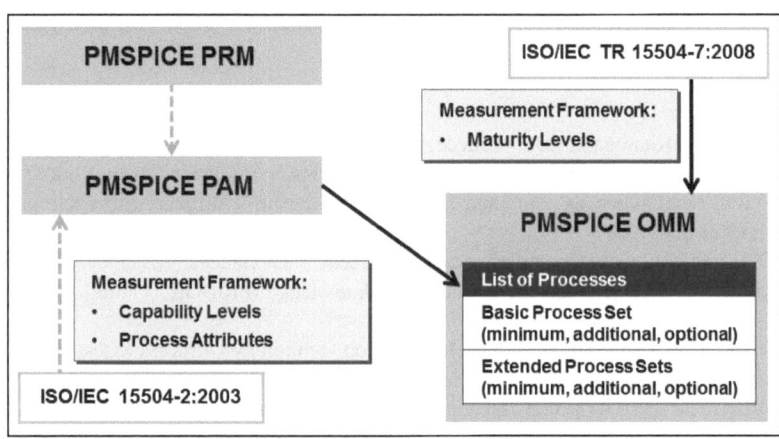

Fig. 3. Design of the PMSPICE Organizational Maturity Model

5   Conclusions and Future Work

This paper presents a Project Management Process Reference Model (PMSPICE PRM) developed from the project management processes contained in the ISO 21500 standard, in accordance to ISO/IEC TR 24774 for the description of the processes and in line with the requirements of ISO/IEC 15504-2. The experience of the authors in project management derived from teaching, applying best practices to our own research projects and also supporting software development companies in the application of project management best practices has been very useful when building this first version of the model.

This result is just the first step in the development of PMSPICE, a proposal of a complete framework composed by a PRM, a PAM and an OMM. As the second stage we propose to develop a PAM that expands upon the developed PMSPICE PRM by including a defined set of assessment indicators. Finally, we plan to complete the framework by designing a Project Management Maturity Model.

We are aware that this contribution represents only the starting point of a large-scale work. We aim to secure international support of both institutions and experts in the fields of project management and process maturity to jointly refine and collaboratively improve the work we have done building the PMSPICE PRM. This external support will be crucial to carry out the construction of the PMSPICE PAM and PMSPICE OMM. We believe that the PAM can only be of high quality when it is a result of the collaborative efforts mentioned. For this reason our goal was to present this first version in the most appropriate forum to gather experts who can help us make this initiative possible. The PMSPICE Framework would not be complete without the development of accompanying process assessment method for the PMSPICE PAM and OMM, which will be described in the future.

Acknowledgments. This work has been partially supported by the Spanish Ministry of Science and Technology with ERDF funds under grants TIN2013-46928-C3-2-R and TIN2010-20057-C03-03.

References

1. Pinto, J.K., Kharbanda, O.P.: Successful Project Managers - Leading Your Team to Success. Van Nostrand Reinhold, International Thomson Publishing, New York (1995)
2. ISO/IEC 12207:2008 Systems and software engineering - Software life cycle processes. ISO, Geneva (2008)
3. ISO 21500:2012 Guidance on project management. ISO, Geneva (2012)
4. A guide to the project management body of knowledge (PMBOK® Guide) - fifth edition. Project Management Institute (2013)
5. ISO/IEC 15504-2:2003/Cor 1:2004 Information technology - Process assessment - Part 2: Performing an assessment. ISO, Geneva (2004)
6. ISO/IEC TR 15504-7:2008 Information technology - Process assessment - Part 7: Assessment of organizational maturity. ISO, Geneva (2008)
7. Mas, A., Amengual, E.: A Method for the Implementation of a Quality Management System in Software SMEs. In: 12th International Conference on Software Quality Management, pp. 61–74. The British Computer Society (2004)
8. Mas, A., Amengual, E., Mesquida, A.L.: Application of ISO/IEC 15504 in Very Small Enterprises. In: Riel, A., O'Connor, R., Tichkiewitch, S., Messnarz, R. (eds.) EuroSPI 2010. CCIS, vol. 99, pp. 290–301. Springer, Heidelberg (2010)
9. Mas, A., Fluxà, B., Amengual, E.: Lessons learned from an ISO/IEC 15504 SPI programme in a company. Journal of Software Maintenance and Evolution - Research and Practice 24(5), 493–500 (2012)
10. Mas, A., Mesquida, A.: A successful case of Software Process Improvement programmes implementation. In: Colomo-Palacios, R., Calvo-Manzano, J.A., De Amescua, A., San Feliu, T. (eds.) Agile Estimation and Innovative Approaches to Software Process Improvement, pp. 243–257. IGI Global (2014)

11. Mesquida, A.L., Mas, A., Amengual, E., Calvo-Manzano, J.A.: IT Service Management Process Improvement based on ISO/IEC 15504: A systematic review. Information and Software Technology 54(3), 239–247 (2012)
12. Lepmets, M., Mesquida, A., Cater-Steel, A., Mas, A., Ras, E.: The Evaluation of the IT Service Quality Measurement Framework in Industry. Global Journal of Flexible Systems Management 15(1), 39–57 (2014)
13. ISO/IEC TR 20000-4:2010 Information technology - Service management - Part 4: Process reference model. ISO, Geneva (2010)
14. CMMI® for Development, Version 1.3. Software Engineering Institute (2010)
15. Lepmets, M.: Evaluation of Basic Project Management Activities - Study in Software Industry, Tampere University of Technology, Pori. Doctoral dissertation (2007)
16. Casey, V., McCaffery, F.: Development of the Medi SPICE PRM. In: Mas, A., Mesquida, A., Rout, T., O'Connor, R.V., Dorling, A. (eds.) SPICE 2012. CCIS, vol. 290, pp. 265–268. Springer, Heidelberg (2012)
17. Lepmets, M., Clarke, P., McCaffery, F., Finnegan, A., Dorling, A.: Development of a Process Assessment Model for Medical Device Software Development. In: EuroSPI 2014 Industrial Proceedings (2014)
18. Barafort, B., Betry, V., Cortina, S., Picard, M., St-Jean, M., Renault, A., Valdés, O.: ITSM Process Assessment Supporting ITIL Van Haren Publishing, Zaltbommel (2009)
19. Mangin, O., Barafort, B., Heymans, P., Dubois, E.: Designing a Process Reference Model for Information Security Management Systems. In: Mas, A., Mesquida, A., Rout, T., O'Connor, R.V., Dorling, A. (eds.) SPICE 2012. CCIS, vol. 290, pp. 129–140. Springer, Heidelberg (2012)
20. Stallinger, F., Neumann, R.: Extending ISO/IEC 12207 with Software Product Management: A Process Reference Model Proposal. In: Mas, A., Mesquida, A., Rout, T., O'Connor, R.V., Dorling, A. (eds.) SPICE 2012. CCIS, vol. 290, pp. 93–106. Springer, Heidelberg (2012)
21. ISO/IEC 15504-5:2012 Information technology - Process assessment - Part 5: An exemplar software life cycle process assessment model. ISO, Geneva (2012)
22. ISO/IEC 15504-6:2013 Information technology - Process assessment - Part 6: An exemplar system life cycle process assessment model. ISO, Geneva (2013)
23. ISO/IEC TS 15504-8:2012 Information technology - Process assessment - Part 8: An exemplar process assessment model for IT service management. ISO, Geneva (2012)
24. ISO/IEC TR 24774:2010 Systems and software engineering - Life cycle management - Guidelines for process description. ISO, Geneva (2010)

The Development and Validation of a Traceability Assessment Model

Gilbert Regan, Fergal McCaffery, Kevin McDaid, and Derek Flood

Dundalk Institute of Technology, Dundalk, Ireland
{gilbert.regan,fergal,mccaffery,kevin.mcdaid,
derek.flood}@dkit.ie

Abstract. Regulation normally requires critical systems to be certified before entering service. This involves submission of a safety case - a reasoned argument and supporting evidence that stringent requirements have been met and that the system is acceptably safe. A good safety case encompasses an effective risk mitigation process which is highly dependent on requirements traceability. However despite its many benefits and regulatory requirements, most existing software systems lack explicit traceability links between artefacts. Reasons for the lack of traceability include cost, complexity and lack of guidance on how to implement traceability. To assist medical device organisations in addressing the lack of guidance on how to implement effective traceability, this paper aims to present the development and validation of a traceability process assessment model and the actions to be taken as a result of the validation. The process assessment model will allow organisations to identify strengths and weaknesses in their existing traceability process and pinpoint areas for improvement.

Keywords: Traceability, requirements traceability, process assessment, safety critical software.

1 Introduction

Manufacturers of safety critical software must ensure their software meets stringent guidelines and is safe to use as intended. Guidelines such as DO-178B (aerospace) [1], EN50128 (railway) [2] and IEC 62304 (medical devices) [3] represents industry consensus opinion on the best way to ensure safe software, e.g. IEC 62304 provides a framework of life cycle processes with activities and tasks necessary for the safe design and maintenance of medical device software. Traceability is an important tool in ensuring that a rigorous software development process has been established and that software is safe, hence these guidelines provide specific guidance for the creation and maintenance of traceability e.g. IEC 62304 states that the manufacturer shall create an audit trail whereby each: a) Change request, b) relevant Problem report, and c) approval of the Change request can be traced.

However despite its many benefits and regulatory requirements, most existing software systems lack explicit traceability links between artefacts [4]. Numerous reasons have been identified for reluctance in implementing traceability including cost

A. Mitasiunas et al. (Eds.): SPICE 2014, CCIS 477, pp. 72–83, 2014.

and complexity. Other reasons include the task of building a requirements trace matrix (RTM) is time consuming, arduous and error prone [5], there are few metrics for measuring the return on investment for traceability, stakeholders within an company have differing perceptions as to the benefits of traceability [6], the need for documentation can cause resentment among developers who may fear that traces could be used to monitor their work [7], difficulties with trace tools including selecting between available tools, and difficulties configuring a general purpose tool or developing a custom tool [8]. Finally almost no guidance is available for practitioners to help them establish effective traceability in their projects and as a result, practitioners are ill-informed as to how best to accomplish this task [9, 10].

To assist medical device organisations in addressing the lack of guidance on how to implement effective traceability, this paper presents the development and validation of a traceability process assessment model (PAM). To be effective, organisations need to know how well their current traceability process helps them achieve their goals. Additionally an assessment of a process will lead to an increased understanding of the actual performance and management of activities, and the potential for improvement.

2   Related Work

A literature review was conducted to determine what other traceability assessment models were available in the general, safety critical or medical device domains. This review returned only one model on traceability compliance/ capability assessment called Med-Trace [9]. Med-trace is a lightweight traceability assessment method, completed in 8 stages, whose goal is to assist medical device organisations to improve their software development traceability process. The authors completed assessments on two medical device companies and were able to identify areas for improvement in each company's traceability process.

There are a number of process assessment models which provide common frameworks for assessing software process capability. These models include ISO/IEC 15504 SPICE [11], Automotive SPICE [12], SPICE 4 SPACE [13], and the Capability Maturity Model CMMI [14] among others. These frameworks assess processes such as software design process, software construction process, software testing process etc. However the frameworks do not include a dedicated traceability assessment process. The frameworks do include traceability assessment but it is spread out across a lot of processes and sometimes difficult to interpret e.g. base practice 4 of the software construction process (Eng. 6) in SPICE states;

"Verify software units. Verify that each software unit satisfies its design requirements by executing the specified unit verification procedures and document the results". Explicit traceability is not required in the above statement but it may be implied. It is open to interpretation.

3   Methodology

It was decided to base the traceability assessment model on the ISO/IEC 15504 (SPICE) assessment model for two reasons;

1. ISO/IEC 15504 is used extensively in other safety critical industries such as the automotive industry (Automotive SPICE), space industry (SPICE 4 SPACE) and the medical device industry (Medi SPICE).
2. ISO/IEC 15504 is derived from ISO/IEC 12207 [15] and since IEC 62304:2006 (Software lifecycle processes for medical device software) is also derived from ISO/IEC 12207 it was determined that there was good synergy between IEC 62304:2006 and ISO/IEC 15504.

The PRM was developed using the requirements from traceability (taken from the medical device standards and guidelines), and ISO/IEC 15504-2 section 6.2 which sets out the requirements for a Process Reference Model. Additionally it was felt necessary to assess the best practices for implementing traceability. These best practices (23 in total) were the result of an extensive literature review [16].

While ISO/IEC 15504-2 details the minimum requirements that a PRM and a PAM should meet, it provides no guidance on how to develop the models i.e. it does not tell you how to transform requirements into a PRM or PAM. To address this issue, this study based the development of the PAM on the Tudor IT Service Management Process Assessment (TIPA) transformation process. The TIPA transformation process complies with the requirements for PRMs and PAMs as expressed in ISO/IEC 15504-2. The TIPA transformation process contains the following steps [17];

1) Identify elementary requirements in a collection of requirements
2) Organise and structure the requirements
3) Identify common purposes upon those requirements and organize them towards domain goals
4) Identify and factorize outcomes from the common purposes and attach them to the related goals
5) Group activities together under a practice and attach it to related outcomes
6) Allocate each practice to a specific capability level
7) Phrase outcomes and process purpose
8) Phrase the Base Practices attached to Outcomes
9) Determine Work Products among the inputs and outputs of the practices

4   Traceability PAM

The traceability PAM, illustrated in Figure 1, consists of 4 traceability processes which are Change Management (CM) traceability, Risk Management (RM) traceability, Software Development Lifecycle traceability, and Best Practice traceability. Each of the processes contains: (i) Title; (ii) Purpose, which contains the unique functional objectives of the process when performed in a particular environment; (iii) Outcomes, which are a list of expected positive results of the process performance; (iv) Base practices, whose performance provides an indication of the extent of achievement of the process purpose and process outcomes; and (v) Work Products (WPs) are either used or produced (or both), when performing the process.

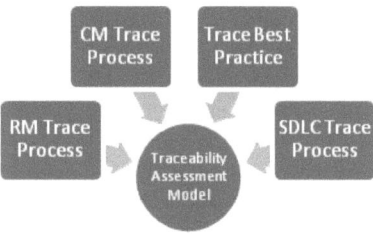

Fig. 1. Traceability PAM

The CM Traceability Process: Five requirements for traceability, extracted from IEC 62304 and depicted in Figure 2, have been grouped to form a change management traceability process. The double head arrows represent bi-directional traceability, even though 'bidirectional' is not a requirement of IEC 62304 but is included because it is considered good engineering practice.

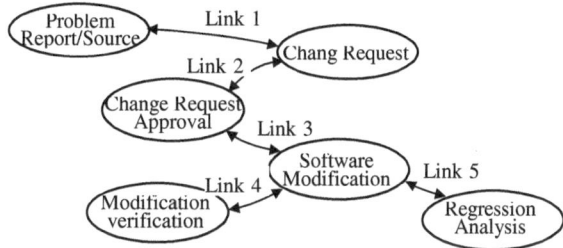

Fig. 2. Change Management Traceability Requirements

From these above requirements a common purpose (to ensure that traceability is adequately addressed throughout all stages of the Change management/Problem reso- lution process) was developed. A list of expected results (Outcomes) generated from performing the process was established, and five base practices which provide a definition of the tasks and activities needed to accomplish the process purpose and fulfil the process outcomes were identified as follows;

Base Practice 1: Establish bidirectional traceability between each change request and relevant problem report (Link1).

Base Practice 2: Establish bidirectional traceability from each change request to approval of the change request (Link 2).

Base Practice 3: Establish bidirectional traceability from each approval of change request to software modifications (Link 3).

Base Practice 4: Establish bidirectional traceability from each software modification to verification of the modification (Link 4).

Base Practice 5: Establish bidirectional traceability from each software modification to regression analysis (Link 5).

Additionally the PAM contains a set of assessment questions whose objective is to determine if the base practices are being implemented and how successful the organisation is at achieving the process purpose.

The RM Traceability Process: The purpose of this process is to ensure that traceability is adequately addressed throughout all stages of the risk management process by assessing the following application of bi-directional traceability: between analysis of risk to the identification of hazards; between hazardous situation and software item; between software item and specific software cause; between each hazard to estimation of risk of each hazard; between each risk estimation to evaluation of acceptability of the risk; between hazards and identification and implementation of risk control measures; between implementation and verification of risk control measures; and between residual risk to assessment of acceptability of those risks.

The SDLC Traceability Process: The purpose of the SDLC Traceability Process is to ensure that traceability is adequately addressed throughout all stages of the SDLC process by assessing the following application of bi-directional traceability: between software requirements and system requirements; between software requirement and software architectural and software detailed design; between software detailed design and source code; between software requirements and source code; and between each phase of the SDLC and test for that phase.

Traceability Best Practice Process: The purpose of the Traceability Best Practices process is to ensure that traceability best practices are established when implementing traceability through the SDLC and the supporting processes of risk management and change management. This is achieved by assessing if a company policy and a standard operating procedure for traceability have been developed, the resources required for successful traceability implementation are made available, and the appropriate techniques for successful implementation are deployed.

5   Validation of the PAM

An initial validation of the traceability PAM has been conducted by expert review. Experts were chosen based on the following criteria; their expertise in a) ISO/IEC 15504, b) medical device standards and c) requirements traceability and d) medical device software development:

Expert 1 is a provisional ISO/IEC 15504 assessor and is a member of the ISO/IEC JTC 1 SC7 WG10 standardisation subcommittee working on the ISO/IEC 15504 standard. **Expert 2** has thirteen years industrial experience in software development and is a member of the ISO/IEC JTC 1 SC7 WG10 standardisation subcommittee working on the ISO/IEC 15504 standard. **Expert 3** has worked in the field of systems engineering for forty five years and worked as senior staff engineer on medical device software for a large multinational. He is an INCOSE certified ESEP and an ACM distinguished engineer. **Expert 4** has forty five years in software engineering. He has eighteen years in medical device software including developing processes that included traceability and has seventeen years in international standards activities for software engineering, medical device software and medical IT networks.

Each reviewer was asked to fill in a questionnaire which focused on the PAMs 'fit for purpose'. A number of minor comments (mainly about terminology) and major comments were returned. The major comments are listed below.

a) Why would anyone want to assess traceability in isolation to all the other process activities?

b) Change management and Problem resolution might be considered by some to be separate processes.

c) Outcome 2 (Traceability is provided from each change request or problem report to analysis/evaluation of the change request/ problem report) and Outcome 4 (Traceability is provided from each denial of change request/problem report to reason for denial) of Change Management traceability process are not outcomes for traceability

d) Outcome 2 of Risk Management traceability process (Traceability is provided from each hazard to estimation of risk of each hazard) does not look like an outcome for traceability but for risk estimation.

e) Outcome 3 of Risk Management (Traceability is provided from each risk estimation to evaluation of the acceptability of the risk) does not look like a traceability related outcome. This should belong to risk acceptance criteria instead.

f) Outcome 6 of Risk Management traceability process (Traceability is provided from any residual risk(s) to the assessment of the acceptability of those risks). I don't see this as a traceability related requirement. Each residual risk has to have the justification attached to it, which comes from the risk evaluation.

g) In the SDLC traceability process, some of the outcomes are duplicating the contents of 80002-3 PRM.

h) Outcome 2 (Bi-directional traceability is established between system requirements and software requirements, including system architectural design) of the SDLC process is a requirement of architectural design and of software requirements analysis process. Not sure it should be duplicated from there.

i) Outcomes 4, 5 and 6 of the SDLC process (Bi-directional traceability is established between software requirements, software architectural design, software detailed design and source code, and between software requirements and source code, and between each phase of the SDLC and Test Specification for that phase) could be deleted and replace by 1 outcome such as "Ensure consistency of software requirements throughout software development lifecycle".

j) Traceability best practices process: Not sure how you can call a process a best practice? Is it not more like Planning? I would integrate both planning the traceability and implementing the plan within the other three processes.

k) Outcome 1 of the Traceability best practice process should be "Establish a plan for establishing traceability in the organisation/project" and not "a company policy on traceability and procedures for its implementation are established".

l) Some of these process outcomes in the Traceability best practices process are already required in 62304;2006 section 5.1.1

m) In Traceability best practices process: Why does this process table not have a link back to source documents (as in the other processes)

n) In Traceability best practices process, Improvement would appear to be outside the scope of Outcome 1(a company policy on traceability and procedures for its implementation are established). Therefore BP2 (Establish traceability improvement communication method) is not clearly defined.

o) Most products are upgrades or enhancements to previous products. As such, the issue of traceability, releases and upgrades become very important. It seems to me that your best practices consider only the greenfield case, which is the exception rather than the rule. How does one trace when building an upgrade to an existing product? Start from scratch? Just do the delta? Etc.

p) Often, a product is to be released in multiple countries, with product variations for different regions. I don't see any discussion of best practices under those circumstances. In a broader context, your assessments seem to ignore the existence of product lines

q) My personal opinion is that the entire hazard mitigation process is flawed (the standard approach, not just yours). If you look closely at your risk mitigation process you will see that it is a "stovepipe", e.g. a look at a single requirement and risk pair, or related requirements associated with a single risk. The world is moving away from this view. Very often risks are associated with combinations of hazards, or a chain of flaws rather than a single (requirement, hazard, mitigation) tuple. Furthermore, in systems engineering, we look at the entire environment, rather than a narrow stovepipe view of the tuple (e.g. fukishima).

r) Who does something is almost as important as what is being done e.g. if the QA checks on tracing are done by someone reporting to the project manager, I would invariably expect deterioration in the quality of the work done.

s) Your process best practices suffer from the same inadequacy as just about all such processes, a lack of detail and implementation guidelines. It is one thing to say "Ensure consistency between system architectural design and software requirements" and quite another to do it. What if there are impedance mismatches between the architecture and software tooling?

t) The Change management process does not identify traceability of problem reports to change requests. The change management traceability process seems to consider problem reports and change requests as the same thing. This is not correct. I don't believe that 62304 requires that the origin of a change request be specified unless the change request is the result of a problem report.

u) IEC 62304 also requires that risk control measures implemented in software be included in the software requirements. So traceability from risk control measures in software to software requirements should be included.

v) It is not clear why the 14971 traceability needs to be bidirectional.

w) For the SDLC traceability process: In outcome 3, all system requirements may not be implemented in software, so there can only be traceability between the software requirements and the system requirement, not traceability between the system requirements (or at least not all of them) and the software requirements. 62304 does not require bidirectional traceability, only traceability from software to system.

x) For the SDLC traceability process: Outcomes 4 and 5 are not required by 62304. I think outcome 4 should be stated more clearly as traceability between requirements and architecture, traceability architecture and detail design, and traceability between detailed design and code. The way it is currently stated makes it sound like everything must trace to everything.

y) For the SDLC traceability process: Outcome 6 indicates that there should be a test specification for each phase of the SDLC. Phase is not a term used in 62304, but assuming that phase = 62304 software development activity then there would not be testing at each phase since tests require code to have been developed. 62304 does require that verification tasks for each development activity be planned and that acceptance criteria be identified, but it does not require a verification specification for each development activity.

To assist with their analysis, the comments were then categorised as shown in Table 2. The '✓' indicates comments on which the authors agree to amend the model. The 'x' indicates comments that will not cause the model to be amended. Categories are:

- Structure - Comments related to the structure of the PAM
- Terminology – Comments related to terminology used
- Outcomes - Comments related to outcomes in the PAM
- Duplication - Comments relating to duplication of traceability requirements from standards
- Scope - Comments relating to scope of PAM
- General – Comments that are general in nature

Table 1. Categorisation of reviewer comments

Category	Review Comments																								
	a	b	c	d	e	f	g	h	i	j	k	l	m	n	o	p	q	r	s	t	u	v	w	x	y
Structure		✓						✓				✓							✓						
Terminology										✓				X							X				
Outcome			X	X	X	X			X												✓		✓	✓	X
Duplication								X	X			X													
Scope															✓	✓	X								
General	X																X	X							

6 Discussion

The review comments are discussed under their categorisations.

Structure: Two experts made similar comments (b and t) that change management and problem resolution are different processes and that the change management process does not identify traceability of problem reports to change requests. On reflection, this is considered to be correct, therefore the change management process is to be amended to include traceability of problem reports to change requests.

Comment 'j' considers the title of the Traceability best practice process to be incorrect and that it would be better to integrate planning the traceability and implementing the plan within the other three processes. As the purpose of this process is to assess if known best practices are established and applied when implementing traceability, the process name will be amended to Traceability best practice management. However the integration of the best practices with the other three processes is not considered, as the best practices are generic across the other three processes and would mean a lot of repetition.

The traceability best practices process does not have a link back to source documents, as with the other processes (comment 'm'). The source documents are academic publications and, on reflection, it is agreed that amending the process to include references to these documents in an appendix would improve the process.

Terminology: Comment k is considered to be an improvement and so Outcome 1 of the Traceability best practice process will be changed from "a company policy on traceability and procedures for its implementation are established" to "Establish a plan for establishing traceability in the organisation/project".

Comment 'n' asserts that 'improvement' (in base practice 2) would appear to be outside the scope of Outcome 1(a company policy on traceability and procedures for its implementation are established) in Traceability best practice process. However, it is thought that communication of improvement should be part of company policy and so will remain a base practice for outcome 1.

Expert 4 remarks that ISO 14971 does not require bidirectional traceability through risk management (comment 'v'). While this is correct, 'bidirectional' traceability is considered good practice and so a note will be added to the risk management traceability process indicating that it is good practice, even though it is not a requirement of IEC 62304 or ISO 14971.

Outcome: Comment 'c' remarks that Outcomes 2 and 4 (Traceability is provided from each change request or problem report to analysis/evaluation of the change request/ problem report, and Traceability is provided from each denial of change request/problem report to reason for denial) of change management traceability process are not outcomes for traceability. As IEC 62304 states that the manufacturer shall create an audit trail whereby each Change request, relevant Problem report and approval of the Change request can be traced [Class A, B, C], it is the interpretation of this study that outcomes 2 and 4 are outcomes for traceability and considered good practice.

Comments 'd' 'e' and 'f' consider outcomes 2,3 and 6 (Traceability is provided from each hazard to estimation of risk of each hazard, Traceability is provided from each risk estimation to an evaluation of the acceptability of the risk, and Traceability is provided from any residual risk(s) to the assessment of the acceptability of those risks) of the risk management process to be outcomes for risk estimation, risk acceptance criteria and risk evaluation, and not outcomes for traceability. This study considers this not to be the case as ISO 14971 states that the risk management file shall provide traceability for each identified hazard to the risk analysis(which includes estimation of risk), risk evaluation (evaluation of the acceptability of the risk), the assessment of the acceptability of any residual risk(s).

Comment 'i' states that outcomes 4,5 and 6 (Bi-directional traceability is established between software requirements, software architectural design, software detailed design and source code, and between software requirements and source code, and between each phase of the SDLC and Test Specification for that phase) of the SDLC traceability process could be replaced by one outcome i.e. "Ensure consistency of software requirements throughout software development lifecycle". This point was considered during development of the SDLC traceability process, but for reasons of clarity it was felt better to have three separate outcomes. Comment 'x' asserts that outcome 4 and 5 are not required by IEC 62304, which is true, however they are required by the FDA's GPSV. As outcome 5 is only required where requirements cannot be addressed in the software design (e.g. nonfunctional requirements), outcome 5 will be removed and a note added to the process to address this issue.

In addition to the above, for outcome 3 of the SDLC traceability process, all system requirements may not be implemented in the software (comment 'w'). This point is accepted, therefore the process will be amended to include only system requirements that are included in the software.

Expert 4 maintains that IEC 62304 requires that risk control measures implemented in software be included in the software requirements (comment 'u'). This study considers this comment to be correct and as a result traceability from risk control measures in software to software requirements should be included. The risk management traceability process will be amended to reflect this.

Finally, comment 'y' states that IEC 62304 does not require a verification specification for each development activity but does require that verification tasks for each development activity be planned and that acceptance criteria be identified. However GPSV requires that traceability is established from unit tests to detailed design and to source code, and from integration tests to high level design.

Duplication: This category consists of comments on outcomes that relate to the outcomes being duplicated from other models and processes. For example comment 'g' states that some of the outcomes in the SDLC traceability process are duplicating the contents of 80002-3 PRM (yet to be officially published) or is a requirement of architectural design and of software requirements analysis process. Part of the rationale behind the traceability PAM is to include all requirements for traceability in one model. IEC 80002-3 PRM, in addition to any individual medical device standard or guideline, does not include all the requirements for traceability through the SDLC and supporting processes of risk management and change management.

Comment 'l' states that some of the outcomes in the traceability best practice process are already required in IEC 62304:2006 Section 5.5.1. However it is determined that this does not seem to be the case as section 5.1.1 contains detail about what the software development plan shall address and does not contain any of the outcomes in the traceability best practice process.

Scope: This category contains comments which relate to the scope of the PAM. Comments 'o' and 'p' make the point that the traceability best practice model does not consider best practice for traceability across product lines, that the model just considers the greenfield case. On reflection it is agreed that product lines do need to be considered in the traceability best practice process and the process needs to be amended to reflect this.

Expert 4 feels that the whole hazard mitigation process is flawed (comment q). While there may be some truth in this, ISO 14971 is the current standard for the application of risk management to medical devices and therefore is the standard that will be adhered to.

General: This category contains general comments on the traceability PAM. Comments 'r' and 's' relate to the fact that the PAM does not contain any details as to 'who does what ' and 'how is it done'. While these comments are true, it is not the place of a PAM to detail the 'who' and 'how', but to assess 'what' traceability is implemented. The development of a traceability implementation roadmap will answer the 'how' question and is considered future work for this study.

The final comment (comment 'a') questions the need for a traceability assessment model. It is the view of this study that traceability of hazards to implementation and verification of mitigations is important in producing safety critical software, and that tracing user requirements to software requirements and to test of those software requirements is important in product validation. Additionally numerous publications have highlighted the fact that most software systems don't employ explicit traceability between artefacts (despite the fact the existing assessment models such as ISO/IEC 15504 and CMMI assess for traceability) and that one reason for this is a lack of guidance on how to implement traceability. The traceability PAM will assert focus on traceability to identify strengths and weaknesses in existing traceability processes and set the foundation for improvement. Additionally the traceability assessment model, developed in this study will assess for traceability implementation best practices.

7   Conclusion

To assist medical device organisations improve their traceability, a traceability assessment model has been developed. This model, which consists of four processes, is based on the ISO/IEC 15504 structure and used the TIPA transformation process for development. By assessing for all traceability requirements from the medical device standards and guidelines and by assessing for traceability implementation best practices, this traceability assessment model will assist medical device organisations understand their actual traceability performance and management of activities, and the potential for improvement.

Four experts (two ISO/IEC 15504 experts, one medical device standards expert and one medical device industry expert) reviewed the model and returned twenty five review comments. Nine of the twenty five review comments were accepted for change as it was felt they would improve the model. Most of the changes are to the structure and outcome categories, with two coming from the terminology category. Based on the review feedback and resulting amendments, the model is now ready for pilot assessment within two medical device organisations.

References

1. RTCA, DO-178B Software Considerations in Airborne Systems and Equipment Certification, ed. Washington, DC (1992)
2. CENELEC, Railway applications – Communications, signalling and processing systems – Software for railway control and protection systems ed. (2001)
3. ANSI/AAMI/IEC, 62304:2006 Medical device software—Software life cycle processes, ed. Arlington, VA: AAMI (2006)
4. Lucia, A.D., et al.: Information Retrieval Methods for Automated Traceability Recovery. In: Cleland-Huang, J., et al. (eds.) Software and Systems Traceability, pp. 88–111. Springer, Heidelberg (2012)
5. Cleland-Huang, J.: Just Enough Requirements Traceability. Presented at the Proceedings of the 30th Annual International Computer Software and Applications Conference, vol. 01 (2006)
6. Kannenberg, A., Saiedian, D.H.: Why Software Requirements Traceability Remains a Challenge. CrossTalk The Journal of Defense Software Engineering, p. 5 (2009)
7. Jarke, M.: Requirements tracing. Commun. ACM 41, 32–36 (1998)
8. Regan, G., et al.: The Barriers to Traceability and their Potential Solutions: Towards a Reference Framework. Presented at the 38th Euromicro Conference on Software Engineering and Advanced Applications, Cesme, Turkey (2012)
9. McCaffery, F., Casey, V.: Med-Trace: Traceability Assessment Method for Medical Device Software Development. Presented at the EuroSPI Denmark (2011)
10. Mader, P., et al.: Motivation Matters in the Traceability Trenches. Presented at the Proceedings of the 2009 17th IEEE International Requirements Engineering Conference, RE (2009)
11. ISO/IEC, 15504-5: An exemplar Process Assessment Model, ed. Switzerland: ISO (2006)
12. Sig, A.: Automotive SPICE® Process Assessment Model, ed (2010)
13. ECCS, Space Product Assurance- Software process assessment and improvement – Part 2: Assessor instrument, ed. Netherlands: ESA Requirements and Standards Division (2010)
14. S. E. Institute, CMMI® for Development, Version 1.3, in Improving processes for developing better products and services, ed. (2010)
15. ISO/IEC, 12207: Systems and software engineering — Software life cycle processes, ed. Geneva, Switzerland: ISO (2008)
16. Regan, G., et al.: Implementation of traceability best practices within the medical device domain. Presented at the EuroSPI 2013, Dundalk, Ireland (2013)
17. Barafort, B., et al.: A transformation process for building PRMs and PAMs based on a collection of requirements – Example with ISO/IEC 20000. Presented at the SPICE, Nuremberg, Germany (2008)

Test Process Models: Systematic Literature Review

Cecilia Garcia[1], Abraham Dávila[2], and Marcelo Pessoa[3]

[1]Posgraduate School, Pontificia Universidad Católica del Perú, Lima, Perú
garcia.cecilia@pucp.pe
[2]Engineering Department, Pontificia Universidad Católica del Perú, Lima, Perú
abraham.davila@pucp.edu.pe
[3]Polytechnic School, University of Sao Paulo, Sao Paulo, Brasil
mpessoa@usp.br

Abstract. Software products quality is strongly influenced by the quality of the process that generated them; particularly, the testing process contributes to product quality and represents a significant effort in software development projects. In this context, this study aim to find which test process models has been defined, adapted or extended in software industry from 1990 to the current date. For this purpose, a systematic literature review has been performed according to relevant guidelines. This study has identified 23 test process models, many of them adapted or extended from TMMi and TPI, which have different architectures and the new ISO/IEC 29119 with an architectural approach aligned to other ISO/IEC software process models.

Keywords: Test Process Model, Systematic Literature Review, Maturity Model, TMMi, TPI.

1 Introduction

Systems play an important role in our lives, both economically and socially, therefore there is pressure for the software engineering discipline to focus on quality issues [43]. As stated by Humphrey [5], software products quality is significantly influenced by the quality of the processes that generates them. Process improvement has become increasingly important over the years, with many organizations trying to reduce their production cost by improving the efficiency of their development processes [48]. This understanding is marked by a progression of software process models, such as ISO/IEC 12207 [27], RUP [31], CMMI [32], MoProSoft [41] o MPS.Br [3], among others. However, despite software process models have been broadly studied over the past four decades, [9], [8], only limited attention is given to testing issues, which have not been adequately addressed in the detail required by industry and academy [14], [30], [34].

As a consequence, a number of approaches has been specifically developed for that purpose, such as TMMi [30], TPI [34], and the standard ISO/IEC 29119-2 [19] among others. These models contribute to disciplined software testing practice; moreover, its adoption adds value to those buying and selling software engineering goods and services [11].

A. Mitasiunas et al. (Eds.): SPICE 2014, CCIS 477, pp. 84–93, 2014.

There are various benefits from the research of software process models [11]. From the industry perspective, quality assurance tasks accounts for the 50% to 60% of the total effort of software development [4], [42], from which software testing are the most used in industry [7]; organizations were experienced the negative outcomes of faulty systems and have become aware of aware of the increasing need to improve their test process. From an academic perspective, Bertolino [7], in her study "Software Testing Research: Achievements, Challenges, Dreams" refers that the establishment of an adequate test process has been considered among the main topics in the specialized software testing forums. Hence, there are various benefits from the research of software process models [11].

For this study it was chosen to undertake a systematic literature review (SLR), which is a secondary study that uses a well-defined methodology to identify, analyze and interpret all available evidence related to a specific research question in a way that is unbiased and (to a degree) repeatable [1], [2]. As part of our work we found a SLR by Wangenheim et al [9] focused on software process models. These authors identified 52 software process capability/maturity models marked in 29 domains, however only 5 models close to software testing domain. The models identified were [9]: Test Maturity Model (TMM), Test Improvement Model (TIM), SAMM Modern software assurance and five-level model of software assurance model, MB-V2M2 Metrics Based Verification and Validation Maturity Model and CB-VVCM Criticality-Based V&V Capability Model; most of them adapted from CMM and TMM.

This study is motivated by the problem mentioned by some authors [12], [14], [26] to select an adequate software testing process model, in contrast with the various process models or best practices that already exists. The goal of this research is to identify such models that has been defined, adapted or expanded, as well as to trends regarding the development of those models. The remainder of this paper is structured as follows: section 2, presents the methodology of the systematic literature review; section 3, the identified models and findings; and finally, in section 4 it is presented the final discussion and future work.

2   Bibliographic Review Approach

The approach of this study is a systematic literature review. This section describes the method used and its application.

2.1   Method Used in the Systematic Literature Review

The research method used in this study is a systematic literature review based on the guidelines and lessons learned proposed by Berenson [13] y Kitchenham [2], [6]. Fig. 1 show the review process performed.

The research question is which test process models are developed or expanded or adapted? In order to frame the research question and define the search string, it was used the PICOC (Population, Intervention, Comparison, Outcome, Context) criteria applied to software engineering [2]. The strategy consisted in perform trial searches using various combinations of search terms derived from the research question, and also checking trial research against lists of already know primary studies, such as TMMi, TPI and ISO/IEC 29119-2. As a result, the more effective search terms were considered, avoiding a very large and unrelated first search result list. Table 1 shown such keywords aligned to the PICOC criteria for this. Table 2 present the search strings used on the selected data sources.

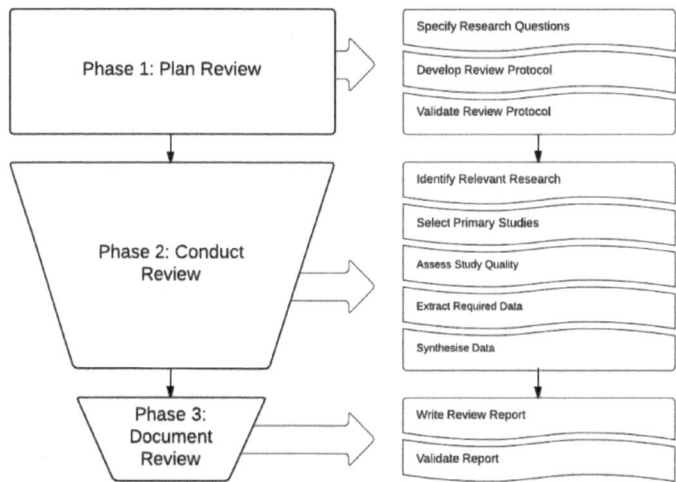

Fig. 1. The Systematic Literature Review Process proposed by Berenson [13]

Table 1. Keywords used based on PICOC criteria

Population	test*
Intervention	maturiry model, process improvement, improvement model, maturity standard
Comparison	Comparison models have not been considered for this study
Outcome	The outcomes are not limited to any particular result
Context	Software Engineering

2.2   Review Protocol

A review protocol was defined and adjusted later to reduce the possibility of researcher bias. First, the exclusion and inclusion criteria were tested in a random set of 5 articles, the independent results were similar, hence the remaining number of articles was analyzed by one of the researchers, considering the article Title and Abstract only and identifying them by Included, Excluded and Uncertain. Uncertain articles were verified by peer review to determine their exclusion or inclusion. The exclusion and inclusion criteria considered were:

- Inclusion criteria: Selected articles included any research type (experiment, case study, comparisons, systematic reviews and mappings, etc.) and any test process structure: maturity or non-maturity models, assessment models and standards. Although the primary articles that answers the research question of this study were only the ones describing a model per se, other research types were considered mainly because these contributed to add to the conclusions of this report, especially in the cases were the information available of the model definition was difficult to obtain. It was also included the reference list from all primary papers, as another source of evidence, in addition to the selected scientific databases (see Table 3).

- Exclusion criteria: The search scope in the selected scientific databases was limited to the following publication types: Journals, Conferences, Transactions, Magazines or Standards. There were excluded Newsletters, Books or Doctoral and Master Thesis

Table 2. Search Strings

Data Source	Search String
IEEE Xplore	("Document Title":test* AND ("Document Title": "maturity model" OR "Document Title": "process improvement" OR Document Title": "improvement model" OR "Document Title": "standard" OR "Document Title": "maturity") AND ("Publication Title": software OR "Publication Title":test*))
ACM Digital Library	itle:test* AND (Title:"process improvement" OR Title:"maturity model" OR Title:"improvement model" OR Title: maturiry OR Title:standard) AND (PublicationTitle:*test OR PublicationTitle:software) AND (PublishedAs:journal OR PublishedAs: proceeding OR PublishedAs:transaction OR PublishedAs:magazine)
Science Direct	title(test*) AND (title(maturity) OR title("maturity model") OR title("process improvement") OR title("improvement model") OR title(standard))[Journals(Computer
ISI Web Of Science	Title: (test*) AND Title: (("maturity level" OR "process improvement" OR "improvement model" OR maturity OR standard))

In a second stage, a more in depth analysis was conducted over the included arti-cles, reading other sections of these articles, such as conclusions or, in some cases all sections.

As a result, 12 articles were selected as primary studies aligned to the research question. Additionally 4 test process model comparison articles were selected [14], [46], [37], [38] which allowed contrasting the data extracted.

Table 3. Data Sources of the Systematic Review

Data Source	Name of Database and Publication Type	Date of search	Years covered by search
Digital Libraries	IEEE Xplore, Conferences Publications, Journals & magazines and Standards, that contains terms "software" or "test*"	June, 2014	1990-2014
	ACM Digital Library; journal , proceeding, transaction or magazine	June, 2014	1990-2014
	Science Direct, Journals in Computer Sciences	June, 2014	1990-2014
	ISI Web Of Science, refined by Science technology and Compturer Science	June, 2014	1990-2014
Other Sources	References from articles presented in Table 3, that includes Books, master or doctorate dissertation thesis or Private company's tailored test process models.	June, 2014	1988-2014

Despite it was not considered in a pre-defined protocol, in a later iteration it was decided to include other source of evidence in addition to the selected data sources. The reason was that various test process models, existence of which was known pre-viously, were not published in scientific databases, but they do add an academic or industry value, therefore the authors considered important to include them in this study. Therefore, a new search was conducted in the reference list from all 12 relevant primary studies identified in previous stage, resulting in new 11 relevant articles [18], [20], [47], [14], [22], [24], [28], [31], [43], [33], [40].

3   Analysis of the Results

As a result of the systematic review described in section 2, we identified 23 test process models, which are presented in Table 4. Each model is characterized by its do-main or the context in which it was defined, a reference to the data source where the model is described, the model source or sources on which it is based and a sequential identification (from m01 to m23). Among the main findings we have:

- About the adoption degree of each model. The mainstream models are TMMi (m17) and TPI (m20). They have been used very often as a base to describe or extend other test models: m02, m07, m11, m15, m17, m20, m21, m23. Both TMMi and TPI were published in mid-90s. Other models that were published around the same year, such as TOM (m18), MMAST (m08), TAP (m12), TCMM (m13), STEP (m10) y CTP (m04) have had a very low adoption rate and in some cases they are not used anymore, as it is observed by the low number of research undertaken about adoption experiences since its appearance.
- About the models architecture. TPI (m20) and TMMi (m17) are maturity models and ISO/IEC-29119 (m05) in conjunction with future ISO/IEC 33063 [10] is a capability model. TMMi is based on CMMI [32] and it is structured by process areas, generic and specific goals, and generic and specific practices. TPI uses a test maturity matrix based on key areas, checkpoints, 4 maturity levels and clusters [33], [34]. ISO/IEC 29119 architecture is defined in terms of Process Reference Models (PRMs) and Process Assessment Models (PAMs).
- About the domains. There are 13 general purpose process models and 9 process models applied to specific contexts, like test automation, embedded systems or small organizations, which indicates exists a trend to the specialization of models to specific domains.
- About the source models used. Many models have been developed using as a reference one or more source models as shown in Table 4. It was found that the models TPI and TMM have been used more often as a basis to define other models. We can observe in Fig. 2 that 17% of model is based on TMM and 19% based on TPI, followed by a 12% of practical experience models.
- About the trend analysis for the publications. 7 model were defined around the year 1996, as shown Table 4, among them TPI and TMMi became mainstream models. However, several models that were adapted or extended based on these were not published until 10 year later: m23, m21, m19, m17, m14, m11, m09, m05, m02 y m01, as it is shown in Fig. 3.
- About the minimum information available of the models. TOM (m18), MMAST (m08), TAP (m12) and TCMM (m13) are process models found in the references list from in Swinkels work [14]. However, there is no information available of these models in the scientific databases, and a minimal piece of information was

found outside scientific databases. Therefore it was not possible to do an in-depth analysis of these models and, in the case of TOM (m18), the publication year remain unknown.

Table 4. Software Testing Process Models

ID	Test Process Model Name	Reference	Model Source	Domain	Publication
m01	TIF, A test improvement framework for embedded software testing	[15]	NA	Embedded Systems	2007
m02	ATG-TPI, A test process improvement model for automated test generation	[16], [36]	TPI	Test Automation	2012
m03	BS 7925-2, the software component testing standard	[17]	None	General	1998
m04	CTP, Critical Testing Process	[18]	Practical Experience	General	2003
m05	ISO/IEC 29119 - 2	[19]	ISO	General	2013
m06	ISTQB Expert Level Syllabus - Improving the Testing Process	[20][47]	None	General	
m07	MB-V2M2, A metrics based verification and validation maturity model	[21]	TMM	General	2002
m08	MMAST, A Maturity Model for Automated Software Testing	[14]	None	Medical	1994
m09	MPT.BR A Brazilian Maturity Model for Testing	[23]	ISO/IEC 29119 - 2, TMMi	small organizations	2012
m10	STEP, Systematic Test and Evaluation Process	[24]	None	General	1988
m11	TAIM, A Test Automation Improvement Model	[25]	TPI, TMMi, TIM	Test Automation	2014
m12	TAP, The Testing Assessment Programe	[14]	NA	General	1995
m13	TCMM, Testing Capability Maturity Model	[14]	NA	General	1996
m14	TEST SPICE	[22][28]	ISO/IEC 15504-5	Test Process Assessment	2012
m15	TIM, A test improvement model	[29]	Practical Experience	General	1997
m16	TMM, Testing Maturity Model	[30], [44],[45]	CMM, ISO	General	1996
m17	TMMi, Testing Maturity Model Improved	[31], [42]	CMM, TMM	General	2005
m18	TOM, Test Organization Model	[14]	None	NA	NA
m19	TPI NEXT, Business Driven Test Process Improvement	[33]	TPI	General	2009
m20	TPI, Test Process Improvement	[34]	Practical Experience	General	1999
m21	TPI-Emb, A Test Process Improvement Model for Embedded Software Developments	[35]	TPI	Embbeded Systems	2009
m22	MTPF, Minimal Test Practice Framework	[39]	NA	small organizations	2005
m23	TPI-Automotive	[40]	TPI	Automotive	2004

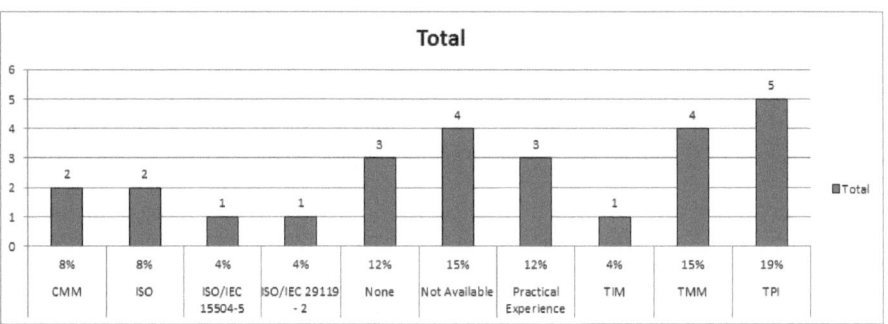

Fig. 2. Source Models used

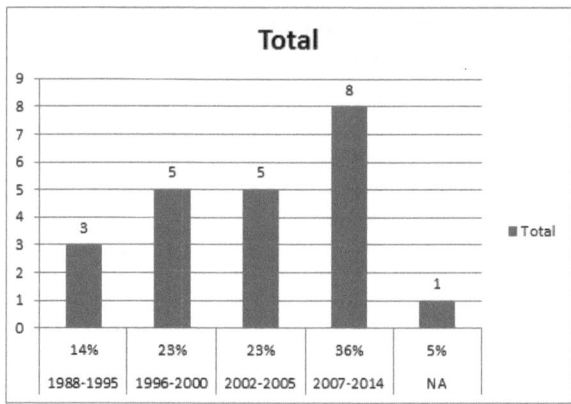

Fig. 3. Trend of Publications

4   Conclusions and Future Work

By this systematic literature review, it was identified that TMMi and TPI are the test process models with more presence and influence in the software industry since mid 90s. Both TPI and TMMi have a maturity approach; TMMi is based on CMMI [32], while TPI uses an evolution axis approach that generates a matrix that is used as an assessment base. ISO/IEC 29119 was published in 2013 with a different architectural approach from TMMi and TPI. This new model is aligned to other ISO/IEC stand-ards, for that reason ISO/IEC 29119 part 2 is a process reference model and ISO/IEC DIS 33063 is an example of a process assessment model for software testing.

This systematic literature review attempted to have a wide coverage of test process models, both in time and number of articles analyzed. Initial searches for primary studies were undertaken using digital libraries. Since this was not sufficient for the systematic review, other sources of evidence were searched manually, such as refer-ence lists from relevant primary studies.

This study will be used as a basis for further analysis (test process models charac-terization) of the selected test process models presented in Table 3 and the identifica-tion of experience if use of the models in particular contexts, for example, the case of small organizations that tests software (organizations or specialized business units under a test factory business model). Likewise, it will aim to gather lessons learned in the application of this models and determined best practices.

Acknowledgements. This work is framed within ProCal-ProSer Project under con-tract 210-FINCYT-IA-2013 and supported, in part, by Engineering Department of Pontificia Universidad Católica del Perú.

References

1. Petersen, K., Feldt, R., Mujtaba, S., Mattsson, M.: Systematic Mapping Studies in Software Engineering. In: 12th International Conference on Evaluation and Assessment in Software Engineering, vol. 17, pp. 68–77 (2008)
2. Kitchenham, B.A., Charters, S.: Guidelines for Performing Systematic Literature Reviews in Software Engineering. Technical Report EBSE-2007-01 (2007)
3. Softex: MPS.BR - Melhoria de Processo do Software Brasileiro Guia Geral MPS de Software (2012)
4. Kollanus, S., Koskinen, J.: Survey of Software Inspection Research. The Open Software Engineering Journal 3, 15–34 (2009)
5. Humphrey, W.S.: Managing the Software Process. Addison-Wesley Professional (1989)
6. Kitchenham, B.A., Budgen, D., Brereton, P.: Using mapping studies as the basis for further research–a participant-observer case study. Information and Software Technology 53(6), 638–651 (2011)
7. Bertolino, A.: Software Testing Research: Achievements, Challenges, Dreams. In: Future of Software Engineering, pp. 85–103. IEEE Computer Society (2007)
8. Paulk, M.C.: Surviving the Quagmire of Process Models, Integrated Models, and Standards. In: Annual Quality Congress Proceedings, Toronto, Ontario, Canada, pp. 429–438. Carnegie Mellon University, Pittsburgh (2004)
9. Wangenheim, C.G., Hauck, J.C.R., Salviano, C.F., Wangenheim, A.: Systematic Literature Review of Software Process Capability/Maturity Models. In: Proceedings of International Conference on Software Process Improvement and Capability Determination (SPICE), Pisa, Italy (2010)
10. Software Testing Standard., http://www.softwaretestingstandard.org/
11. Moore, J.W.: An integrated collection of software engineering standards. IEEE Software 16(6), 51–57 (1999)
12. Toroi, T., Raninen, A., Vaatainen, L.: Identifying Process Improvement Targets in Test Processes: A Case Study. In: 29th IEEE International Conference on Software Maintenance (ICSM), pp. 11–19 (2013)
13. Brereton, P., Kitchenham, B.A., Budgen, D., Turner, M., Khalil, M.: Lessons from Applying the Systematic Literature Review Process within the Software Engineering Domain. The Journal of Systems and Software 80(4), 571–583 (2007)
14. Swinkels, R.: A Comparison of TMM and other Test Process Improvement Models. Technical Report Frits Philips Institute, Technische Universiteit, Eidhoven, Netherlands (2000)
15. Kim, E., Jang, Y.: A test improvement model for embedded software testing. In: Proceedings of the 11th IASTED International Conference on Software Engineering and Applications, pp. 79–84. ACTA Press (2007)
16. Heiskanen, H., Maunumaa, M., Katara, M.: A Test Process Improvement Model for Automated Test Generation. In: Dieste, O., Jedlitschka, A., Juristo, N. (eds.) PROFES 2012. LNCS, vol. 7343, pp. 17–31. Springer, Heidelberg (2012)
17. Reid, S.C.: BS 7925-2: The Software Component Testing Standard. In: Proceedings of First Asia-Pacific Conference on Quality Software, pp. 139–148. IEEE (2000)
18. Black, R.: Critical Testing Processes: Plan, Prepare, Perform, Perfect. Addison-Wesley Professional (2004)
19. ISO/IEC: ISO/IEC/IEEE 29119-2:2013 Software and systems engineering – Software testing – Part 2: Test processes. Geneva (2013)

20. Veenendaal, E., Evans, I., Black, R.: Foundations of Software Testing: ISTQB Certification. Course Technology Cengage Learning (2008)
21. Jacobs, J.C., Trienekens, J.J.M.: Towards a Metrics Based Verification and Val-idation Maturity Model. In: Proceedings of 10th International Workshop on Software Technology and Engineering Practice, STEP 2002, pp. 123–128. IEEE (2002)
22. Steiner, M., Blaschke, M., Philipp, M., Schweigert, T.: Make Test Process As-sessment Similar to Software Process Assessment—the Test SPICE Approach. Journal of Software Maintenance and Evolution Research and Practice
23. Furtado, A.P.C.C., Gomes, M.A.W., Andrade, E.C., de Farias, I.H.: MPT. BR: A Brazilian Maturity Model for Testing. In: 12th International Conference on Quality Software (QSIC), pp. 220–229. IEEE (2012)
24. Hetzel, W.C., Hetzel, B.: The Complete Guide to Software Testing. QED Information Sciences, Wellesley (1988)
25. Eldh, S., Andersson, K., Ermedahl, A., Wiklund, K.: Towards a Test Automation Im-provement Model (TAIM). In: 2014 IEEE Seventh International Conference on Software Testing, Verification and Validation Workshops (ICSTW), pp. 337–342. IEEE (2014)
26. Jacobs, J., van Moll, J., Stokes, T.: The Process of Test Process Improvement. XOOTIC Magazine 8(2), 23–29 (2000)
27. ISO/IEC ISO/IEC 12207:2008 Systems and software engineering — Software life cycle processes, Geneva (2008)
28. Steiner, M., Blaschke, M., Philipp, M., Schweigert, T.: Make test process assessment similar to software process assessment—the Test SPICE approach. Journal of Software: Evo-lution and Process 24(5), 471–480 (2012)
29. Ericson, T., Subotic, A., Ursing, S.: TIM - A Test Improvement Model. Software Testing, Verification and Reliability 7(4), 229–246 (1997)
30. Burnstein, I., Suwanassart, T., Carlson, R.: Developing a testing maturity model for soft-ware test process evaluation and improvement. In: Proceeding of International Test Conference, pp. 581–589. IEEE (1996)
31. IBM, Rational Unified Process, IBM Rational Method Composer, Version 7.1.1
32. SEI: CMMI for Development, Version 1.3, CMU/SEI-2010-TR-033 (November 2010)
33. SOGETI: TPI Next – Business Driven Test Process Improvement. UTN Publishers (2009)
34. Koomen, T., Pol, M.: Test Process Improvement: A practical step-by-step guide to struc-tured testing. Addison-Wesley Longman Publishing Co., Inc. (1999)
35. Jung, E.: A test process improvement model for embedded software developments. In. 9th International Conference on Quality Software, QSIC 2009, pp. 432–437. IEEE (2009)
36. Heiskanen, H., Maunumaa, M., Katara, M.: Test Process Improvement for Au-tomated Test Generation. Tampere: Tampere University of Technology, Department of Software Systems (2010)
37. Kulkarni, S.: Test Process Maturity Models–Yesterday, Today and Tomorrow. In: Proceedings of the 6th Annual International Software Testing Conference, Delhi, India (2006)
38. Zhang, L.: The software test improvement model in practice (2005)
39. Karlström, D., Runeson, P., Norden, S.: A minimal test practice framework for emerging software organizations. Software Testing, Verification and Reliability 15(3), 145–166 (2005)
40. SOGETI: TPI Automotive. Tech. Rep. version 1.01 (2004), http://www.tpiautomotive.de/produkte.html (visited June 2014)
41. Oktaba, H., Alquicira C., Su A.: Modelo de Procesos para la Industria de Softwa-re, Mo-ProSoft. Versión 1.3 (2005)

42. Veenendaal, E.: Test Maturity Model Integration (TMMi). Version1.0. TMMi Foundation (2008), `http://www.tmmifoundation.org/html/tmmiorg.html` (last access June 2014)
43. ISTQB. Improving the Testing Process - ISTQB® International Software Testing Qualification Board, `http://www.istqb.org`
44. Suwanassart, B.T., Carlson, C.R.: Developing a testing maturity model (part 1). CrossTalk, Journal of Defense Software Engineering 9(8), 21–24 (1996)
45. Burstein, I., Suwannasart, T., Carlson, C.R.: Developing a testing maturity model, part II. Crosstalk The Journal of Defense Software Engineering (1996)
46. Gelperin, D., Hetzel, B.: The growth of software testing. Communications of the ACM 31(6), 687–695 (1988)
47. ISTQB. International Software Testing Qualification Board, `http://istqb.org/`
48. Reid, S.: The Personal Test Maturity Matrix. In: CAST 2006: Influencing the Practice, Indianapolis, June 5-7, vol. 133 (2006)

Government Process Capability Model: An Exploratory Case Study

Ebru Gökalp and Onur Demirörs

Informatics Institute, Middle East Technical University
Ankara, Turkey
{egokalp,demirors}@metu.edu.tr

Abstract. The customization of software process capability/maturity models to specific domains/sectors or development methodologies represents one of the most critical challenges of the process improvement domain. As a result of the literature review, it is observed that there is a lack of a guideline for how to improve process quality in governmental institutions. Therefore, in this study, development of a government process capability model based on ISO/IEC 15504 is aimed in order to ensure that processes are consistently applied, managed, and controlled across a governmental institution. Towards this goal, a government business process classification framework consisting of management of government resources and support processes and government specific processes is constructed. As a government specific process; public investment management process is defined and assessed as a case study to explore the applicability of this framework. Initial findings of the study indicate the usefulness and adequacy of the proposed approach.

1 Introduction

Improving quality in public sector is sometimes problematic because of the specific characteristics of its environment. These characteristics are defined in [1,2] as the necessity of being firmly based in law of decisions, culture, multiple stakeholders for many processes. While Information Technologies (IT) have the potential to improve the quality of governmental services, existing processes should be improved beforehand [3]. Automation practices in governmental institutions have not provided the expected efficiency improvements in Turkey, since the automation of processes are carried out with existing process defects [4]. As pointed out in [5;6], Enterprise Architecture (EA) in the public sector has to be transformed from being IT-centric to business-centric. However only a few papers deal with the necessary changes in business processes in the government domain [7]. Public organizations are not profit-oriented and experience unconditional demand while their processes are frequently unstructured, and depend on employee judgment. Thus, low productivity and process performance, high defect rates, employee and citizen dissatisfaction and high costs arise.

There are various well-accepted generic Software Process Capability/Maturity Models (SPCMMs), such as ISO/IEC TS 15504 [8], CMMI-DEV (Capability Maturity Model Integration for Development) model [9]. These models are used as an

A. Mitasiunas et al. (Eds.): SPICE 2014, CCIS 477, pp. 94–105, 2014.

evaluative and comparative basis for process improvement and/or assessment, assuming that higher process capability or organizational maturity is associated with better performance. As a result of observed benefits of these models, many process capability models are generated based on ISO/IEC 15504 [8], i.e: Spice4Space [10] AutomotiveSPICE [11], Medi SPICE [12], Enterprise SPICE [13], etc.

We intend to utilize the same approach for the government domain by developing the Government Process Capability Model (GPCM) based on ISO/IEC15504 standard. The aim of GPCM is providing the base for improving the processes of governmental organizations. It pursues a structured and standardized approach by assessing relevant processes in order to perform quality improvement initiatives in a consistent, repeatable manner, assessed by adequate metrics with guidance on what to do to increase quality in government institutions.

The model is intended to fulfill the following four high-level requirements:

- Enable each public agency to evaluate its processes in detail.
- Enable each public agency to identify current state of its process capability.
- Enable each public agency to compare itself against other agencies evaluated with the same model.
- Suggest feasible improvement roadmaps that public agencies can follow to improve their levels of process capability.

Towards this goal, a government business process classification framework consisting of management of government resources and support processes as well as government specific processes is constructed. In addition, public investment management process, which is a government specific process, is defined and assessed as an exploratory case study to check the usefulness and adequacy of the proposed approach. The remainder of the paper includes a brief literature review related to existing quality improvement models for the government domain, description of the proposed GPCM approach, explanation of the exploratory case study performed and finally the findings obtained from the case study.

2   Literature Review

Quality improvement models developed for public sector, including the Total Quality Management approach, enterprise architecture models, and e-government maturity models, are investigated in this section.

2.1   Total Quality Management in Public Sector

Total quality management (TQM) consists of organization-wide efforts to install and make permanent a climate in which an organization continuously improves its ability to deliver high-quality products and services to customers. Important aspects of TQM include customer-driven quality, training, leadership, preventing defects and continuous improvement. TQM highlights defining quality, making quality measurable and standardization. ISO 9000 [14] was published as an international standard in 1988. Some of the Turkish public sector institutions began to implement TQM practices in the second half of 1990s. It should be stated that such practices are being adopted at individual, organizational and departmental levels, rather than having a systemic character and being organized by the central government, as has been the case in some other developed countries [15]. TQM practices in public institutions is a controversial issue in the literature [16,17,18]. It is asserted in [17] that TQM should be modified based on the characteristics of public sector. Because of its specific characteristics, number of governmental institutions among OECD countries having ISO 9000 certification is limited [19].

Common Assessment Framework. [20] is the common European quality management instrument for the public sector. It is developed based on EFQM and TQM to assess and measure public management qualities. The evaluation criteria are: results orientation, leadership, strategy & planning, people, partnerships & resources, processes, and results. These criteria are further broken down into 28 sub-criteria, where a self-assessor gives points for each of them. According to a survey carried out in [21], the most difficult criteria to evaluate are performance results and processes.

2.2   Maturity Models in Public Sector

Governments have started transformation and modernizations after TQM initiatives. Enterprise Architecture (EA) and e-government initiatives have arisen [22].

Public EA describes organizational structures, information and technology infrastructure. It includes relationships among layers of business, application, information, technology, and security.

Enterprise Architecture Maturity Models (EAMM) is developed to improve performance and efficiency of EA. Thus, increasing information sharing, and reducing incorrect and unnecessary information are provided. Level of the EA is determined as a result of evaluation of Critical Success Attributes. EAMM developed for public domain can be listed as EAMMF [23], E2AMM [24], ACMM [25], EAAF [26].

E-Government is the use of information and communication technologies (ICTs) to improve the activities of public sector organizations. It provides government services as electronically secure, seamless and fast to be delivered to citizens through a common point. Benefits of e-government are as follows; reducing paperwork, loss of time, and increasing individual participation, and hence developing a democratic culture; reducing intensive communication between agencies.

E-government Maturity Models provide IT-based assessment to transition to e-government applications by evaluating technological, organizational, functional adequacy. Increasing maturity level which is observed as a result of assessment provides more sophisticated e-government structure. They focus on e-services, web-based communication, and interoperability. Examples of e-government maturity models can be listed as United Nation's Model [27], Gartner's Model [28], Siau and Yong's Model [29], MAGENTA [30], Deloitte&Touché's Model [31], Layne&Lee's Model [32], Andersen&Henriksen's Model [33], Hiller's Model [34], Moon's Model [35].

Literature review points out that, there are studies for improving quality in public domain, however, although they provide benefits from different aspects, they don't aim to improve process quality directly to guarantee the consistency of services with each other through the use of standard processes where the capability level can be assessed and improved with guidance. The aim of developing GPCM is to address this aspect.

3   Government Process Capability Model

GPCM offers a common point-of-reference with different levels that describe behaviors, practices, and processes that regularly produce desired outcomes. It becomes a roadmap that shows the next steps to take when creating solid, sophisticated, repeatable process management capabilities and can direct organizations that lack process discipline on how to become highly organized and efficient. In order to define the scope of GPCM, we first develop the Government Business Classification Framework (GBCF) as shown in Figure 1, which is based on the Business Reference Model of Federal Enterprise Architecture [36] including the business functions of government and American Productivity and Quality Centre (APQC) Process Classification Framework [37]. GBCF consists of Governmental Business Services and Management of Government Resources and Support Processes. The Governmental Business Services describes the mission and purpose of the government in terms of the services it provides both to and on behalf of the citizen. They include the delivery of citizen-focused, public, and collective goods and/or benefits as a service and/or obligation of government to the benefit and protection of the nation's general population. It is classified into 10 classes. Government specific processes are performed to deliver these services. For instance; civil domain under citizen services includes birth, death and marriage registration processes.

Management of Government Resources and Support Processes incorporating common processes across the governmental agencies refer to the support activities that enable the government to operate efficiently. There are 6 main classes for management of government resources processes as shown in Figure 1.

Structure of the GPCM is Made Up of Two Dimensions

- The process dimension consists of processes derived from the Government Business Process Classification Framework. This dimension is characterized by process purpose statements which are the essential measurable objectives of a process; process outcomes, base practices, and work products which are constructed based on the standard of ISO/IEC TS 15504 [8].
- The process capability dimension, which is characterized by a series of process attributes, is applicable to any process, which represents measurable characteristics necessary to manage a process and improve its capability to perform. It is adapted from ISO/IEC TS 15504 [8].

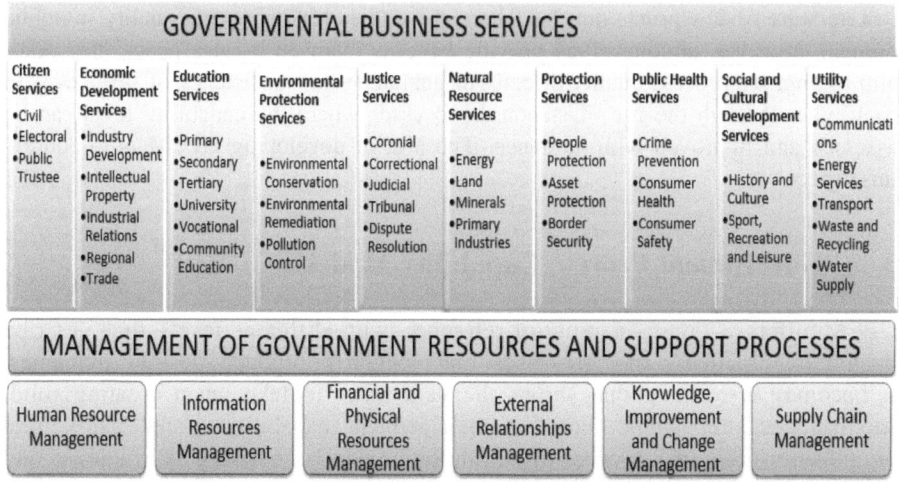

Fig. 1. Government Business Process Classification Framework

4   Case Study

An exploratory case study is performed for a governmental-specific process in order to evaluate the adequacy of the proposed approach. Public Investment Management Process of Ministry of Development in Turkey is selected for the case study. This process is selected because of its importance for the development of the country. National financial resources should be used properly to enrich people's lives and improve organizational performance. Evaluating and improving investment management capabilities provides significant benefits for the government. Thus, authorities in the Ministry of Development need to discover the weaknesses of the process to improve the process performance.

4.1   Process Definition

Public Investment Management Process is defined *(ad-hoc)* by one of the authors together with the process owners. In particular, the process is defined in a prescriptive procedural manner. So, the first task to be undertaken is to define the process based on the standard of ISO/IEC TS 15504- part 2 whose process elements are as follows:

- The title is a descriptive heading for a process;
- The purpose describes the goal of performing the process;
- The outcomes express the observable results expected from the successful performance of the process;
- The base practices are a list of actions that may be used to achieve the outcomes;
- The work products are separately identifiable bodies of information produced and stored for human use during a system or software life cycle.
- Defining a governmental-specific process includes the following steps:

- Defining the scope by selecting the business segment and its corresponding engagement from the available categories in the GBCF. In our case, the Public Investment Management Process is performed within the Industry Development Domain under the Economic Development Services in the GBCF, as given in Figure 1.
- Investigating documents related to Policies & Business Rules of the Turkish Government. (Decree law concerning the organization as well as duties, and process-specific documents containing the corresponding business-rules are examined in order to define the process.)
- Interviewing the stakeholders.
- Reviewing worldwide best practices related to the process in hand.
- Taking similar processes from international standards as a reference.
- The definition is formally reviewed and approved by the management with executive responsibility within the organizational unit and by one of the authors who has both professional and academic experience in using ISO/IEC 15504. Accordingly, the defined Public Investment Management Process is given in Table 1. Once approved, the process definition became our Government Process Reference Model (albeit including only one process). At this point it is necessary to build a Process Assessment Model (PAM).

4.2   Process Assessment

Audit procedures related to details of activities such as planning, briefing of the participants, data collection and validation and reporting are based on ISO/IEC 15504 [8] where Process Capability is classified into six levels; Level 0: Incomplete; Level 1: Performed; Level 2: Managed; Level 3: Established; Level 4: Predictable; Level 5: Optimizing.

The measure of capability is based upon a set of process attributes (PA). Process capability indicators are the means of achieving the capabilities addressed by the considered process attributes. Evidence of process capability indicators supports the judgment of the degree of achievement for the process attribute.

Process Attribute of Level 1 is Process performance attribute which is a measure of the extent to which the process purpose is achieved. Process definition as given in Table 1 are used for Level 1 assessment. For the assessments of levels 2 to 5, we use exactly the same 'generic practices indicators', 'generic resources indicators' and 'generic work products indicators' as the exemplar PAM provided by the ISO/IEC 15504-part 5.

Table 1. Process Definition of Public Investment Management

Process Title	Public Investments Management
Process Purpose	The Purpose of the Public Investment Management Process is to provide public investment politics that are consistent with priorities identified in development plans and programs; to create, monitor and review the public investment program; and also to coordinate, analyze, investigate and support the public investments projects.

Table 1. *(Continued)*

Process Title	Public Investments Management	
Process Outcomes	1) Investment politics are identified and evaluated in light of 5 years-development plan and middle-term financial plan which are interpreted at sector or sub-sector levels to determine priorities. 2) Pre-feasibility study is performed to identify relevant alternatives before undertaking a full-fledged feasibility study to improve agencies projects effectiveness. 3) Public investment policies and guideline are determined. 4) Budget allocation for each public agency in the strategic level is performed. 5) Public investment projects are submitted by the public agencies with basic project information, including project objective, expected results and estimated budget (Feasibility analysis). 6) Submitted projects are evaluated. 7) Accepted public investment projects are monitored and reported. 8) Funding review is performed for the accepted public investment projects and revisions are done if necessary.	
Base Practices	BP1: Create and manage public investment politics, policies and plans. [Outcomes: 1] BP2: Evaluate pre-feasibility study: [Outcomes: 1;2] BP3. Develop public investment policies and guideline. [Outcomes: 1;3] BP4: Allocate budget to public agencies as high-level planning. [Outcomes:1;4] BP 5: Submit public investment projects. [outcomes 1;2;3;4;5] BP 6: Evaluate public investment projects.[Outcome 3;6] BP 7: Evaluate submitted as aggregated or bulk project [Outcome 6] BP 8: Announce accepted projects. [Outcome 6] BP 9: Monitor accepted public investment projects [Outcome 7] BP 10: Track projects progress against plans [Outcomes: 5;7] BP 11: Adjust projects[Outcome: 8] BP 12: Perform project close-out review[Outcomes: 5;6;7]	
Work Products		
Inputs	**Outputs**	
5-years Development Plan [Outcome:1]		
Middle-Term Financial Plan [Outcome:1]		
Public Investment Policies and strategies [Outcome:5]	Public Investment Policies and strategies [Outcome:3]	
Public Investment Project Preparing Guideline [Outcome:5]	Public Investment Project Preparing Guideline [Outcome:3]	
Investment Allocation Ceiling by Agencies [Outcome: 6]	Investment Allocation Ceiling by Agencies [Outcome: 4]	
Project proposals[Outcome:6]	Project proposals [Outcome:5]	
Feasibility report [Outcome:6]	Feasibility report [Outcome:5]	
Project financial plan[Outcome:6]	Project financial plan[Outcome:5]	
Project schedule[Outcome:6]	Project schedule[Outcome:5]	
	Public Investment Program [Outcome:6]	
	Book of Public Investments Breakdown by Province [Outcome:6]	
	Progress status record[Outcome:7]	
Project status report[Outcome:8]		
	Review Records[Outcome:7]	
Project Performance Data [Outcome: 7]		
Tracking system [Outcome:7]		
Additional-allocation request[Outcome:8]		

Process Assessment is performed by the participants in the organization responsible for the quality assurance and by the authors, one of whom is a competent assessor formally certified by INT-ACS (International ISO/IEC 15504 Assessors Schema). Accordingly, the assessment team follows the 'ISO/IEC 15504-part 3: Guidance on Performing an Assessment' as the documented procedural approach for conducting the assessment. Details of the assessment activities such as planning, briefing of the participants, data collection and validation, and reporting are put together into an assessment plan document and an assessment report.

The result of this assessment in the case study is that the capability level of the investment management process performed in the Ministry of Development in Turkey is Level 2 with the following rationale based on collected and validated evidence. More details of the assessment is given in the technical report [38].

Table 2. Public Investment Management Assessment Result

Level	Attribute	Evidences	Assessment Value	Result
Level 1	Process Performance	The process clearly achieved its purpose by maintaining steady public investment management selection and monitoring.	Fully Achieved	
Level 2	Performance Management	The performance is planned and managed but quality assurance objectives and performance quality criteria are not defined.	Largely Achieved	
	Work Product Management	Work products are defined but their quality criteria are not identified. Additionally, change control is not established, and real time data for revised project is not gathered.	Partially Achieved	
Level 3	Process Definition and Tailoring	The standard process is defined in governmental documents but the sequence and interaction of standard process with other process, plus infrastructure and work environment needs of the process are not defined. Definition of metrics/methods/ criteria monitoring effectiveness and suitability of the process is missing.	Partially Achieved	LEVEL 2
	Process Deployment	The deployment rules are known by the personnel. Required human, information, infrastructure resources are available but there is no conformance/test to verify the defined process satisfies the requirements. Additionally, data required to understand the behavior, suitability and effectiveness of the defined process are not identified/collected.	Partially Achieved	

5   Analysis of the Results

In order to improve the capability level of the public investment management process to Level 3, assessment values of the process attributes should be as follows; Performance and Work Product Management attributes: Fully Achieved, Process Definition and deployment attributes: Largely or Fully Achieved.

5.1   Guideline for Improvement Capability of the Process

The road map to improve the capability level of investment management processes is derived from the assessment evidences in the technical report [38]. The aim is to turn negative evidences into positive evidences of process capability indicators supporting the judgment of the degree of achievement of the process attribute. For example; for performance management attribute; first indicator is to identify the objectives for the performance of the process. However, the quality assurance objectives of the process are not defined for the performed process. Thus, necessity of defining quality assurance objectives and other issues are indicated in the guideline as follows:

- Quality assurance objectives of the process should be defined.
- Metrics/methods/criteria should be defined for monitoring effectiveness and suitability of the process.
- Performance quality criteria should be defined and performance of the employees should be monitored.
- Quality criteria of the work products should be identified.
- Quality criteria for reviewing and approving the content of the work products should be defined.
- For HR Qualification, personnel qualifications should be identified, Required exam scores and bachelor degree are not sufficient.
- Standardization for evaluation project should be applied. Criteria and their weights should be determined.
- Monitoring and reporting processes should be performed with real-time data.
- Data required understanding the behavior; suitability and effectiveness of the defined process should be identified/ collected and used for improvement.
- Internal audit and management review should be conducted.
- Training for deploying the process should be performed.
- Change Control of the projects should be established.
- Project revisions should be controlled systematically.
- Revision status of the projects should be available.
- Real-time data for revised project details should be available.
- Revised project details should be available to everyone.
- Resolving issues arising from work product reviews should be tracked systematically.
- The sequence and interaction of standard process with other process should be defined.
- The infrastructure and work environment needs of the process should be defined.

5.2   Comparing the Result with ITIM

ITIM (Information Technology Investment Management) [39] which is developed for improving capability of IT investment projects management process is an accepted federal management framework for IT investment decision making in USA Government. It is an independent specific capability model developed for public investment management. It is used to check whether our proposed approach and findings are consistent with such an accepted domain specific framework.

Public Investment Management Process performed in Ministry of Development is assessed with ITIM by the authors and process owners. Since critical maturation steps required to move to the next stage is described properly in the ITIM, the assessment is performed easily. The capability level is assessed as Level 2 and improving to level 3 is described as follows in the ITIM;

- Criteria should be created and maintained.
- The analysis associated with examining the merits of each investment should be performed.
- Performance reviews should be conducted.
- Evaluation with classifying projects should be standardized.

As a result; our findings with the developed model are consistent with the ITIM; our proposed approach covers improvement list of ITIM, additionally, it provides more detailed guidance on what improvement activities to implement.

5.3   Interviews with the Stakeholders

In order to check usefulness and adequacy of the proposed approach, interviews are conducted with stakeholders. Open-ended structured questionnaire below is utilized.

- Are measuring process capability and obtaining guideline for improvement useful?
- Do you think that applying these suggestions will improve the process performance?
- Is there any information you want to add in process definition?
- Is there any missing item in guideline for improvement list?

Interviews are conducted with 5 process owners, 4 of them have more than 5 years' work experiences. One of them has 2 years' work experiences as public investment project manager. The findings in the conducted interviews support our proposed approach. All of answers for the first two questions are positive. They think that generated guideline is useful, and applying this suggestion will improve the process performance of the public investment management process, and they also confirm the process definition. While answering the last question, they point out some possible improvement areas such as interoperability with other government agencies. However, this is out of our scope and is primarily related to e-government initiatives.

6   Conclusion

Initial findings of the case study indicate the usefulness and adequacy of the proposed approach of using process assessment in the government domain. Lessons learned from this case study as follows:

- Governmental process can be defined using requirements in ISO/IEC 15504.
- ISO/IEC 15504-5 is of great help in identifying indicators for levels 2 to 5.
- The exemplar documented process in ISO/IEC 15504-3 can be used by a competent assessor to perform a conformance assessment.

- In the software engineering field, processes tend to be more 'creative' and frequently tailored for specific contracts/assignments. This makes it harder to assure a systematic performance. However, governmental processes tend to be more repetitive and stable. This difference is a positive variance to depict the usability of the model in public domain.

In parallel with ISO/IEC 15504, our approach aims to provide a variety of benefits for government organizations including the following: cost savings; more involved employees; improved and predictable quality as well as productivity; generating a consistency of process capture and use. Future studies include creating a methodology incorporating guidelines for government specific process definition based on experiences of this exploratory case study, and validating the GPCM by performing different case studies in various government agencies. The findings from the exploratory case study will be shown to be equally applicable in the wider public sector context.

References

1. Teicher, J., Hughes, O., Dow, N.: E-government: a new route to public sector quality. Managing Service Quality 12(6), 384–393 (2002)
2. Hutton, G.: Business process re-engineering a public sector view. In: Armistead, C., Rowland, P. (eds.) Managing Business Processes BPR and Beyond. John Wiley and Sons, Chichester (1996)
3. Indihar Stemberger, M., Jaklic, J.: Towards E-government by business process change—A methodology for public sector. Int. J. of Information Management 27(4), 221–232 (2007)
4. Acar, M., Kumaş, E.: Türkiye'ninDönüşümSürecindeAnahtarBirMekanizmaOlarak E-Devlet, E-DönüşümVeEntegrasyonStandartları (2008)
5. Isomäki, H., Liimatainen, K.: Challenges of government enterprise architecture work – stakeholders' views. In: Wimmer, M.A., Scholl, H.J., Ferro, E. (eds.) EGOV 2008. LNCS, vol. 5184, pp. 364–374. Springer, Heidelberg (2008)
6. Hjort-Madsen, K., Gotze, J.: Enterprise Architecture in Government – Towards a multi-level framework for managing IT in government. In: Proceedings of European Conference on e-Government, Dublin, Ireland, pp. 365–374 (2004)
7. Bradford Rigdon, W.: Information Management Directions: The Integration Challenge.
8. In: Architecture and Standards, ch. 17 (1989)
9. ISO/IEC 15504: composed of seven parts (15504-1 to 15504-7) Parts: Under the general title Information technology — Process assessment (2008)
10. Software Engineering Institute (SEI): CMMI Product Team, CMMI® for Development, Version 1.3, Improving processes for developing better products and services (2010)
11. Cass, A., et al.: SPICE for SPACE trials, risk analysis, and process improvement. Software Process: Improvement and Practice 9(1), 13–21 (2004)
12. Automotive, S.: Automotive SPICE - Process Assessment Model (2007), http://www.itq.ch/pdf/AutomotiveSPICE_PAM_v23.pdf
13. McCaffery, F., Dorling, A.: Medi SPICE Development, Software Process Maintenance and Evolution. Improvement and Practice Journal 22(4), 255–268 (2010)
14. Ibrahim, L.: Improving Process Capability Across Your Enterprise. In: 4th World Congress on Software Quality (4WCSQ), Bethesda/USA (2008)
15. ISO 9001, Quality management systems – Requirements (2008)
16. Deming, E.: Out of the Crisis. MIT Center for Advanced Engineering Study (1994)

17. Üstüner, Y., Coşkun, S.: Quality management in the Turkish public sector: a survey. Public Administration and Development 24(2), 157–171 (2004)
18. Swiss, J.: Adopting TQM to government. Public Administration Review 52(4), 352–356 (1992)
19. Rago, W.: Adopting Total Quality Management (TQM) to government: another point of view. Public Administration Review 54(1), 61–64 (1994)
20. Saner, R.: Quality assurance for public administration: a consensus building vehicle. Public Organization Review 2(4), 407–414 (2002)
21. EIPA: The Common Assessment Framework (CAF) Improving An Organization Through Self-Assessment, European Institute of Public Administration (2013)
22. Cappelli, L., Guglielmetti, R., Mattia, G., Merli, R., Renzi, M.F.: Peer evaluation to develop benchmarking in the public sector. Benchmarking: An International Journal 18(4), 490–509 (2011)
23. Pollitt, C., Bouckaert, G.: Public Management Reform. Oxford University Press (2004)
24. Saha, P.: A Methodology for Government Transformation with Enterprise Architecture. In: Advances in Government Enterprise Architecture, pp. 1–29 (2009)
25. IFEAD: Extended Enterprise Architecture Maturity Model (E2AMM) v2.0 (2004)
26. TOGAF Architecture Capability Maturity Model, in TOGAF Version 9 (2009)
27. NASCIO.: NASCIO Enterprise Architecture Maturity Model, Version 1.3 (2003), http://www.nascio.org/publications/documents/nascio-eamm.pdf
28. United Nations and American Society for Public Administration Global Survey of E-government (2001), http://www.unpan.org/egovernment2.asp
29. Baum, C., Di Maio, A.: Gartner's Four Phases of E-Government Model, Gartner Group, Research Note (2000), http://aln.hha.dk/IFI/Hdi/2001/ITstrat/Download/Gartner_eGovernment.pdf
30. Siau, K., Long, Y.: A stage model for e-government implementation. Paper Presented at the 15th Information Resource Management Association International Conference (IRMA 2004), New Orleans, LA, May 23-26, pp. 886–887 (2004)
31. Saha, P.: A Methodology for Government Transformation with Enterprise Architecture. In: Advances in Government Enterprise Architecture, pp. 1–29 (2009)
32. Deloitte, Touche: The citizen as customer. CMA Management 74(10) (2001)
33. Layne, K., Lee, J.: Developing fully functional e-government: a four stage model. Government Information Quarterly 18(2), 122–136 (2001)
34. Andersen, K.V., Henriksen, H.Z.: E-Government maturity models: Extension of the Layne and Lee model. Government information quarterly 23(2), 236–248 (2006)
35. Hiller, J., Bélanger, F.: Privacy Strategies for Electronic Government. Pricewaterhouse Coopers Endowment for the Business of Government, E-Government Series (2001)
36. Moon, M.J.: The evolution of e-government among municipalities: rhetoric or reality? Public Administration Review 62(4), 424–433 (2002)
37. Council, C. I. O., Federal Enterprise Architecture Consolidated Reference Model Document. Version 2.3 (2007)
38. American Productivity & Quality Center (APQC)., Process Classification Framework, APQC, Washington, DC (2012), http://www.apqc.org/free/framework.htm
39. Gokalp, E.: Technical Report of Public Investment Management Process Assessment (2014), http://smrg.ii.metu.edu.tr/smrgp/index.php?option=com_jresearch&view=publication&task=show&id=718&Itemid=54
40. GAO. Information Technology Investment Management (2004), http://www.gao.gov/new.items/d04394g.pdf

Tool for Usage of Multiple Process Assessment Models

Stasys Peldzius and Saulius Ragaisis

Vilnius University, Universiteto Str. 3, LT-01513 Vilnius, Lithuania
{Stasys.Peldzius,Saulius.Ragaisis}@mif.vu.lt

Abstract. CMMI and ISO/IEC 15504 are two main models for software process assessment and improvement. Both models have staged and continuous representations but these are different. It is desirable for organizations to have assessments according to more than one model but every assessment is expensive both financially and time-wise. Furthermore, a new assessment is required when a new model's version is released. Transitional Process Assessment Model (TPAM) is proposed as tool supporting these opportunities. It enables assessment results according to one Process Assessment Model (PAM) to be transformed to other PAMs. The requirements and the main principles of TPAM construction have been presented in [1, 2]. This paper details the methodology for inclusion of a new model into TPAM and presents application of this methodology for CMMI-DEV V1.3 and ISO/IEC 15504-5:2012 inclusion. It has been concluded that TPAM is a suitable tool for usage of multiple PAMs.

Keywords: CMMI, ISO/IEC 15504, models mapping, transitional process assessment model.

1 Introduction

Investigations in software process capability provided a deep insight into software activities and introduced various software process assessment models which helped assess and improve both software process capability and maturity of organization producing software or software-based systems. The evolution of software process assessment models has stabilized two main models widely known as CMM and SPICE with their current revisions: CMMI-DEV V1.3 and ISO/IEC 15504-5:2012. These 2 models are prevalent and the most important worldwide [3].

Organizations want to get the advantages of different process assessment models that stimulate their harmonization and investigation of process improvement in multimodel environments [4, 5, and 6]. Companies that work both with European and US customers often need to have assessments based on CMMI and SPICE at the same time because an assessment according to one of the SPICE models is required most often by European customers, whereas exclusively CMMI is required in USA. This is particularly the case with companies that specialize in aerospace, automotive or defense industries [7].

A. Mitasiunas et al. (Eds.): SPICE 2014, CCIS 477, pp. 106–117, 2014.

We propose the Transitional Process Assessment Model (TPAM) [1, 2] as a tool helping organizations to tackle problems related to multiple software process assessment models. This paper describes the methodology for inclusion of a new model into TPAM. As an example of the application of this methodology the inclusion of CMMI-DEV V1.3 and ISO/IEC 15504-5:2012 into TPAM is presented. Resulting TPAM enables transformations of the assessment results into all PAMs included. This is demonstrated by transforming the assessment results according CMMI-DEV Engineering process areas into ISO/IEC 15504-5:2006 and 2012 versions.

2   Background and Related Works

Software process modeling examines two aspects: the activities of software product development or services provision; and the soundness of how well these activities' are performed, i.e. ability to meet the defined schedule, cost, scope, and quality goals. A software process model defines the standard process that provides the basis for assessment and improvement of organization's processes. It should ensure the usage of the same concepts, relevance with the best software engineering practices and compatibility with internationally accepted standards. All software process models summarize the best practices of software development and services worldwide. But although the source is almost the same, the resulting models are different.

An analysis of the conceptual relationships between two main software process assessment models CMM and SPICE is performed during their evolution [8]. Taxonomy and approaches for comparison of software process improvement models is analyzed in [1, 7, and 9].

Fundamental ideas for CMMI and ISO/IEC 15504 mapping have been proposed in [10]. Mappings of the CMMI-DEV V1.2 and ISO/IEC 15504:5-2005 models are presented in [11]. They show how CMMI maturity levels can be expressed by ISO/IEC 15504 Processes capability profiles and vice versa. Mappings show what is common in the models and how they differ. These mappings have been employed as the basis for TPAM development using the new versions of the source models. An approach for the control of model evolution and compliance maintenance is proposed in [12].

Studies [13, 14, 15, 16, and 17] examine ways to harmonize different models so that each of them would not require separate implementation and conclude that these models often have much in common and once these common elements are found, the only thing left to be done is to implement the differences that exist between the models. Companies often need to have ITIL, COBIT, CMMI, ISO 27001 and other models because it is a requirement imposed by customers or internal business rules.

TPAM is intended to facilitate companies in assessing their process capability based on different PAMs. Using TPAM transformations, the company having assessment result according one source PAM or TPAM can obtain approximate assessment results according to all other included PAMs. The requirements and the main principles of TPAM construction have been introduced in [1]. The further development of TPAM and supporting software tool is discussed in [2]. This paper details the methodology for inclusion of a new model into TPAM, provides examples of the application of this methodology and representative transformations performed by TPAM obtained.

3   Approach for PAM Inclusion

The usefulness of TPAM directly depends on how many PAMs are included into TPAM. The first decision should be taken was the selection of the module to be included first, i.e. the initial basis of TPAM. After thorough investigation of potential candidates ISO/IEC 15504-5:2006 has been chosen. The decision is based on the following considerations:

- ISO/IEC 15504 is de-jure international standard.
- ISO/IEC 15504-5:2006 is the first exemplar PAM conformant with ISO/IEC 15504-2.
- It uses process definitions from ISO/IEC 12207:1995/Amd.1:2002; Amd.2:2004 that serve as processes source for industry widespread PAMs also: Automotive SPICE and SPiCE for Space (S4S).
- The usefulness of several versions of the same model included into TPAM could be proved having both versions of ISO/IEC 15504-5 (2006 and 2012) and the historical order of the inclusion is preferable.

Currently, TPAM contains the following source models: ISO/IEC 15504-5:2006, CMMI-DEV V1.3, and ISO/IEC 15504-5:2012 (Software Implementation Processes Group).

It has been decided do not include the older CMMI-DEV V1.2 because its inclusion is not very important from both theoretical and practical points of view: the changes between CMMI versions V1.2 and V1.3 are not essential, except refusal of capability levels 4-5 that also does not affect the design of TPAM and validation of its transformations; according information provided by Software Engineering Institute the last 10 organizations have had appraisals according CMMI-DEV V1.2 in 2012 so these assessments' results will not be relevant for transformation now.

The sections of this chapter are organized the following way: first, the elaborated methodology for inclusion of a new PAM into TPAM is presented; then inclusion of CMMI-DEV V1.3 and ISO/IEC 15504-5:2012 and the transformations obtained are analyzed.

3.1   Methodology for PAM Inclusion

The inclusion of a new model into TPAM is accomplished in 4 steps.

Step 1. Check compatibility of a new model and TPAM.
Compatibility check consists of two subchecks: 1) application domains of PAM to be included and TPAM should overlap and 2) it should be possible to align the concepts of PAM with TPAM ontology [1]. Current TPAM is constructed for software development capability assessment. So, the application domain of PAM should cover software development at least partially. For example, Enterprise SPICE is appropriate to assess the capability of the company operating any business. Therefore, it is suitable but when including into TPAM Enterprise SPICE processes should be approached only from the perspective of software development. Compliance with ISO/IEC 15504-2 requirements for PAMs is sufficient but not necessary condition to pass the second subcheck. For example, CMMI-DEV does not satisfy all ISO/IEC 15504-2 requirements but its concepts could be aligned with TPAM ontology as shown in next section.

Step 2. *Select PAM processes to be included into TPAM.*
Usually all processes of the new model are included into TPAM but it is not a requirement. Any set of PAM processes could be selected for inclusion. This corresponds to ISO/IEC 15504-2 requirement 6.3.2.1 for PAM construction from Process Reference Model (PRM): PAM shall relate to at least one process from the specified PRM.

It may be sufficient for the moment to obtain a capability profile for some group or any other set of PAM processes. In such case only these processes are included into TPAM at once. This was done for ISO/IEC 15504-5:2012: only processes of Software Implementation Processes Group are included yet.

It should be noted that the order of processes inclusion is irrelevant, i.e. the order does not affect the resulting TPAM. If PAM to be included has staged representation, it could be preferable to include the processes according their assignment to maturity levels starting from the lowest one. Such approach has been chosen for CMMI-DEV inclusion. Just having process areas of second maturity level included into TPAM, the process capability profiles of ISO/IEC 15504-5 for enterprises having CMMI-DEV second maturity level could be obtained through TPAM transformations.

Step 3. *Determine overlap of each PAM practice with TPAM practices.*
The practices of the selected PAM processes are included one by one. Since TPAM and PAM to be included deal with software development or PAM is approached from the perspective of software development, it could be expected that most of PAM practices are covered by pre-existing TPAM practices. But each model could have specific areas that are not presented in other models. The Full Coverage rule should always be fulfilled: each TPAM practice should be covered fully by one or more practices of included models. Therefore, 4 variants of overlapping could occur:

1. Unique PAM practice (not overlapping with existing TPAM practices) should be simply added into TPAM.
2. If PAM practice is essentially the same as single TPAM practice, no changes are needed.
3. If PAM practice is a part of TPAM practice, this TPAM practice should be split because of the Full Coverage rule.
4. In case of partial overlapping both PAM and TPAM practices should be split.

These 4 variants and their application together have been discussed thoroughly in [1]. The search for the related practices and determination of the overlapping is a complex task and it requires good knowledge of both models.

It should be noted that description of the practice itself could not be sufficient for the correct mapping and a broader context (e.g. the context of related outcome) should be taken into account. For example, the description of CMMI-DEV practice *SP 2.2 Manage Interfaces* is not enough for correct determination of the application area of the practice. In general such practice could be employed in Product Integration as well as in Technical Solution context. In the last case it would be related with practices of ISO/IEC 15504 *ENG.5 Software design process*. Because the practice belongs to CMMI Product Integration Process Area and ISO/IEC 15504-5 does not define explicitly practices ensuring interface compatibility, this practice and all other practices of the same CMMI specific goal have been added into TPAM as new ones.

Additional difficulties are caused by alternative terms used in models, for example: CMMI-DEV uses the term 'component design' while ISO/IEC 15504 names it as 'software design'. It is important to understand what activities the practice defines in the actual process of a company and what work products it should produce. The search of related practices could be narrowed as a rule by linking the processes. For example, practices of CMMI-DEV Engineering process areas are likely related with practices of TPAM processes that originated from ISO/IEC 15504 Engineering Process Group.

When relationship between PAM practice and TPAM practices (pre-existing, split, and/or new ones) is one-to-many it is very important to indicate for each TPAM practice correct percentage value showing the extent of PAM practice covered. When PAM practice simply becomes a new TPAM practice, it is evident that coverage is 100%.The opposite coverage is always 100% because of the Full Coverage rule.

Splitting of TPAM practices does not affect the outcomes of the named process the practices belong. But adding of a new practice into TPAM as a rule requires outcome(s) of the process to be updated because the achievement of current outcomes is ensured without this new practice. This leads to extending of the context of TPAM process. The source for outcome(s) update is the relevant outcome of PAM to be included. In case of CMMI, the specific goal supported by practice is used as a source for update. If all practices of that specific goal are included into TPAM as new ones, the specific goal simply becomes a new outcome of TPAM named process.

When creating a new TPAM practice first of all attempt to assign it to existing TPAM process should be made. But if application domain of PAM or its set of processes to be included is wider than current application domain of TPAM, a new TPAM named process needs to be created.

Step 4. Adjust generic practices.
The model compatible with TPAM must have the equivalents of process attributes and generic practices. For PAMs fully compliant with ISO/IEC 15504 requirements (i.e. having the process attributes as defined in ISO/IEC 15504-2 and the generic practices as defined in ISO/IEC 15504-5) this step is to be omitted because PAM capability dimension will already be consistent with TPAM capability dimension, since ISO/IEC 15504-5 has been taken as initial TPAM.

If PAM to be included has different capability dimension, the equivalents of generic practices should be included into TPAM. This is accomplished according the same rules as inclusion of the base/specific practices described in step 3.

Step 4 is required if transformation of the assessment results higher than capability level 1 is necessary. In case of CMMI, generic practices need to be included into TPAM.

3.2   CMMI-DEV V1.3 Inclusion

As it has been already mentioned, the initial TPAM has been made directly from ISO/IEC 15504-5:2006. Then CMMI-DEV V1.3 was included into TPAM applying the methodology defined in the previous section.

CMMI-DEV is compatible with the TPAM: its application domain covers software development (i.e. evidently overlaps with TPAM application domain); the mapping of CMMI concepts with TPAM ontology is presented in Table 1.

Table 1. Mapping of CMMI and TPAM concepts

TPAM	CMMI
Organizational Process	Process
Named Process	Process Area
Purpose	Purpose Statement
Outcome	Specific Goal
Practice	Specific Practice
Generic Property	Generic Goal
Generic Practice	Generic Practice
Capability Level	Capability Level

All CMMI-DEV process areas have been included into TPAM because possibility to transform complete assessment results according CMMI-DEV are important for the organizations. But this section discusses only the inclusion of the Engineering process areas into TPAM as it is enough for the representative example.

Third step is the inclusion of specific practices. Let's start from *Requirements Development (RD)* process area, its first specific goal *SG1 Develop Customer Requirements*, and the first practice *SP 1.1 Elicit Needs*. It should be checked whether TPAM practices (for the moment the same as base practices of ISO/IEC 15504-5:2006) include a requirement to elicit stakeholder needs, expectations, constraints, and interfaces for all phases of the product lifecycle. TPAM practices do not state explicitly that needs should be obtained. But there is a related TPAM practice *ENG.1.BP1 Obtain customer requirements and requests* because stakeholder expectations and constraints as a rule are obtained as requests. Therefore, this TPAM practice has been divided into two practices: *ENG.1.BP1_1 Obtain customer expectations, constraints, and other requests* and *ENG.1.BP1_2 Obtain customer requirements*; and both of them cover 50% of the original practice ENG.1.BP1 of ISO/IEC 15504-5:2006.

It has been expertly evaluated that the new practice ENG.1.BP1_1 covers 30% of the practice *SP 1.1 Elicit Needs*, because stakeholder expectations and constrains essentially is a subset of all needs. Since no more relationships have been found in TPAM, a new practice *RD_SP1.1 Elicit Needs* has been introduced into TPAM, and it covers 70% of the original practice *SP 1.1 Elicit Needs* of CMMI-DEV. Also, TPAM named process ENG.1 is supplemented with the following new outcome: *Needs are elicited*. Table 2 summarizes the results of specific practice RD SP 1.1 inclusion into TPAM.

The following naming convention has been applied for the practices of TPAM:

- The identifier of TPAM practice starts with process abbreviation (e.g. ENG.1, RD).
- If TPAM practice is fully consistent with the practice of source model, it gets the practice number of source model (e.g. ENG.1.BP1 until splitting, RD_SP 1.1).
- When splitting TPAM practice, the sequential number of the part of original practice is added.

Table 2. Results of RD SP 1.1 inclusion into TPAM

CMMI practice	%	TPAM practices
SP 1.1 Elicit Needs Elicit stakeholder needs, expectations, constraints, and interfaces for all phases of the product lifecycle.	70	**RD_SP 1.1 Elicit Needs** Elicit stakeholder needs and interfaces for all phases of the product lifecycle.
	30	**ENG.1.BP1_1 Obtain customer expectations, constraints, and other requests** Obtain customer expectations, constraints, and other requests through direct and continuous solicitation of customer and user input.

In such a way, all other specific practices are included into TPAM. It should be noted that because of different aspects explicitly emphasized in CMMI-DEV and ISO/IEC 15504-5:2006 the inclusion of CMMI-DEV into TPAM has affected essentially definitions of some TPAM practices. As an example of such practice ENG.5.BP1 could be taken. Table 3 shows the five TPAM practices obtained from the original ENG.5.BP1 during the inclusion of all CMMI-DEV Engineering process areas: Requirements Development (RD), Product Integration (PI), Technical Solution (TS), Validation (VAL), and Verification (VER).

Table 3. TPAM practices covering original ENG.5.BP1 after CMMI-DEV inclusion

TPAM practices	%	ISO/IEC 15504 practice
ENG.5.BP1_1 Transform the software requirements into a software architecture design	30	ENG.5.BP1 Describe software architecture
ENG.5.BP1_2 Describe software architecture	10	
ENG.5.BP1_3 Select Solutions	20	
TS_SP 2.1_1 Develop preliminary design	30	
TS_SP 2.4 Perform Make, Buy, or Reuse Analyses	10	

The last step was the inclusion of CMMI generic practices. It has been performed in accordance with [18], where it is proved that the capability dimensions of ISO/IEC 15504 and CMMI are compatible. The 1st CMMI and ISO/IEC 15504 capability levels are fully compatible as both require base/specific practices to be performed. Each generic practice of the 2nd CMMI capability level partially covers one or more generic practices of 2nd ISO/IEC 15504 capability level. The 3rd capability level of CMMI and ISO/IEC 15504 has 2 and 11 generic practices correspondingly, but the requirements of generic goals and process attributes level are basically compatible.

Using this approach, all CMMI-DEV process areas have been included into TPAM. Summarizing the results it could be stated that the most complicated and time consuming task is finding the relationships between CMMI-DEV and TPAM practices. The major part of CMMI-DEV has been fully covered by TPAM, but a large part of TPAM practices have been split to fulfill the Full Coverage rule. Only a few practices of CMMI-DEV (e. g. *Perform Peer Reviews, Monitor Data Management, Evaluate Alternatives*) have no related TPAM practices and have been added as new ones.

CMMI-DEV - ISO/IEC 15504-5:2006 Transformations

When CMMI-DEV is included, TPAM provides possibility to transform a capability profile according CMMI-DEV to other source models covered by TPAM. Let's take a CMMI-DEV capability profile with all Engineering process areas having capability level 1 and assume that all their specific practices are fully (100%) performed. As the company owning this capability profile develops exclusively software, the transformation does not cover system related processes of ISO/IEC 15504-5:2006. The capability profile of ISO/IEC 15504-5:2006 obtained by TPAM transformation is presented in Figure 1, where "CL" means Capability level, "N"- Not achieved, "P" - Partially achieved, "L" - Largely achieved, "F" - Fully achieved. It may be noted that the scope of CMMI Engineering process areas is much broader than ISO/IEC 15504 Engineering process group. The main reason why the most of ISO/IEC 15504-5:2006 Engineering processes do not achieve capability level 1 is that CMMI process area Requirements Management (REQM) is assigned to Project Management and therefore it is not included in this representative transformation.

ISO/IEC 15504-5:2006 Processes	Base practices											PA 1.1				CL
	1	2	3	4	5	6	7	8	9	10	11	N	P	L	F	
ENG.1 Requirements elicitation	100	100		100												0
ENG.4 Software requirements analysis	100	100	100	100	100											1
ENG.5 Software design	100	50	100													0
ENG.6 Software construction	100	100														0
ENG.7 Software integration	100	100	100	100	100	100										1
ENG.8 Software testing	100	100														1
ENG.11 Software installation	100	100	100	100	100	100										1
OPE.2 Customer support		100														0
SUP.2 Verification	100	10	100	100												1
SUP.3 Validation	100	100	100	100	100											1
SUP.7 Documentation						10										0
SPL.2 Product release	100	100	100	100	100	100	100	100	100	100	100					1
MAN.5 Risk management			30													0
RIN.4 Infrastructure	20	20	20	20	20	20										0
REU.2 Reuse program management		10			40											0

Fig. 1. ISO/IEC 15504-5:2006 capability profile obtained from CMMI-DEV Engineering process areas

For the opposite transformation let's take ISO/IEC 15504-5:2006 capability profile with all Engineering group processes (except system processes) having capability level 1 and assume that all their base practices are fully (100%) performed. The resulting CMMI-DEV capability profile obtained by TPAM transformation is presented in Figure 2, where "CL" means Capability level, "NI"- Not Implemented, "PI" - Partially Implemented, "LI" - Largely Implemented, "FI" - Fully Implemented, and "SG" – specific goal. CMMI Engineering process areas Validation (VAL) and Verification (VER) are not addressed (and not presented in Figure 2) because the corresponding processes of ISO/IEC 15504-5:2006 are assigned to Support process group that has not been included into original capability profile.

CMMI-DEV V1.3 Process Areas	Specific practices														SG1	SG2	SG3	CL
	1.1	1.2	1.3	1.4	1.5	2.1	2.2	2.3	2.4	3.1	3.2	3.3	3.4	3.5				
Product Integration (PI)	100	40	100			0	0			0	100	100	40		LI	NI	LI	0
Requirements Development (RD)	30	80				100	100	100		10	0	30	20	0	LI	FI	NI	0
Technical Solution (TS)	100	80				95	0	80	90	100	0				FI	LI	PI	0
Requirements Management (REQM)	100	100	100	37	70										LI			1

Fig. 2. CMMI-DEV capability profile obtained from ISO/IEC 15504-5:2006 Engineering processes

3.3   ISO/IEC 15504-5:2012 Inclusion

For practical application of TPAM it is very important to have the current version of ISO/IEC 15504-5 included. This will facilitate the companies to migrate from 2006 version to 2012 model version.

Table 4 shows the relationships between these versions. ISO/IEC 15504-5:2012 uses the Process Reference Model (PRM) defined in ISO/IEC 12207:2008. The grouping of the processes has been changed essentially. For example, new PRM does not contain the Engineering (ENG) process group; it has been split into two new groups: Technical Processes (ENG) and Software Implementation Processes (DEV).

Table 4. Comparison of ISO/IEC 15504-5 versions

ISO/IEC 15504-5:2006		ISO/IEC 15504-5:2012	
Life Cycle	Process Group	Process Group	Life Cycle
Primary	Acquisition	Agreement	System
	Supply		
	Engineering	Software Implementation	Software
	Operation	Technical	System
Organizational	Management	Project	System
	Process Improvement	Organizational Project-Enabling	System
	Resource and Infrastructure		
	Reuse	Software Reuse	Software
Supporting	Support	Software Support	Software

Also, two new types of processes – subprocesses and lower-level processes – were added to the revised SPICE model. Unfortunately, the standard does not define explicitly these concepts and does not reveal their differences. But it is clear that subprocesses and lower-level processes detail some process. It should be noted that hierarchy of subprocesses is possible. For example, the subprocess AGR.2C is detailed by two subprocesses AGR.2D and AGR.2E defined in Annex D of ISO/IEC 15504-5:2012.

ISO/IEC 15504-2 defines the measurement framework only for capability of processes. Meanwhile, ISO/IEC 15504-5:2012 does not provide any explanation how capability of subprocesses and lower-level processes should be assessed.

Because subprocesses and lower-level processes meet ISO/IEC 15504-2 requirements for process definition, their capability assessment is exactly the same as defined for processes. When defining the scope of assessment the appropriate level of detail should be taken. For example, the company specializing in software development should assess all lower-level processes of ENG.4 process when assessment of the company developing systems could be limited to ENG.4 process level. Therefore, the processes of all levels should be included into TPAM.

Currently Software Implementation Processes (DEV) of ISO/IEC 15504-5:2012 have been included into TPAM. It should be noted that the new model version places a greater emphasis on software implementation. For example, the ISO/IEC 15504-5:2006 process *ENG.5 Software design* splits into two processes: *DEV.2 Software architectural design* and *DEV.3 Software detailed design*. Consequently, the same happens with the base practices.

ISO/IEC 15504-5:2006 has been designed for both: companies that engage in system development and companies that develop exclusively software. According to ISO/IEC 15504-7, the company developing exclusively software does not have to assess processes ENG.2, ENG.3, ENG.9, and ENG.10. Following the same rule, it can be stated that the company developing exclusively software should assess ISO/IEC 15504-5:2012 process *ENG.1 Stakeholder requirements definition* approaching it only from the perspective of software development.

Inclusion of Software Implementation Processes (DEV) of ISO/IEC 15504-5:2012 shows that while structural changes of versions are essential, the contents do not substantially changed by.

CMMI-DEV - ISO/IEC 15504-5:2012 Transformations

To verify the inclusion of ISO/IEC 15504-5:2012 and transformation abilities, let's take ISO/IEC 15504-5:2012 capability profile with all Software Implementation Processes having capability level 1 and assume that all their base practices are fully (100%) performed as in the previous examples. The resulting CMMI-DEV capability profile obtained by TPAM transformation is presented in Figure 3 (notation is exactly the same as used in Figure 2). CMMI Engineering process areas Validation (VAL) and Verification (VER) are not addressed because the corresponding processes of ISO/IEC 15504 remain assigned to Support process group. It should be noted that the resulting CMMI-DEV capability profile is exactly the same for both transformations from ISO/IEC 15504-5:2006 and ISO/IEC 15504-5:2012 and the ratings of the specific goals are also very similar.

CMMI-DEV V1.3 Process Areas	Specific practices														SG1	SG2	SG3	CL
	1.1	1.2	1.3	1.4	1.5	2.1	2.2	2.3	2.4	3.1	3.2	3.3	3.4	3.5				
Product Integration (PI)	100	40	100			0	0			0	100	100	0		LI	NI	PI	0
Requirements Development (RD)	0	10				100	100	100		10	0	30	0	0	NI	FI	NI	0
Technical Solution (TS)	100	80				100	0	80	90	90	0				FI	LI	PI	0
Requirements Management (REQM)	90	0	0	100	70										LI			1

Fig. 3. CMMI-DEV capability profile obtained from ISO/IEC 15504-5:2012 Software implementation processes

4   Conclusions and Future Work

The methodology for inclusion of a new model into TPAM has been elaborated and successfully applied for inclusion of CMMI-DEV V1.3 and ISO/IEC 15504-5:2012. The transformation of assessment results between three PAMs already integrated into TPAM have been performed. The following major conclusions can be drawn from the work performed:

- ISO/IEC 15504 compatible models as well as CMMI like models (e.g. TMMI) could be included into TPAM.
- Although structural changes of ISO/IEC 15504-5:2006 and ISO/IEC 15504-5:2012 are essential, there are no substantial changes in the contents thereof.
- TPAM provides possibility to convert assessment results between the models integrated.
- TPAM is a suitable tool for usage of multiple PAMs.

The following future work is planned:

- Finishing inclusion of ISO/IEC 15504-5:2012;
- Inclusion of Automotive SPICE and Enterprise SPICE;
- An extensive verification and validation of TPAM transforming agile methodology DSDM Atern assessment results according to TPAM and comparing them with assessment results directly according to CMMI-DEV [19].

References

1. Peldzius, S., Ragaisis, S.: Framework for Usage of Multiple Software Process Models. In: Mas, A., Mesquida, A., Rout, T., O'Connor, R.V., Dorling, A. (eds.) SPICE 2012. CCIS, vol. 290, pp. 210–221. Springer, Heidelberg (2012)
2. Peldzius, S., Ragaisis, S.: Usage of Multiple Process Assessment Models. In: Woronowicz, T., Rout, T., O'Connor, R.V., Dorling, A. (eds.) SPICE 2013. CCIS, vol. 349, pp. 223–234. Springer, Heidelberg (2013)
3. Pino, F., Garcia, F., Piattini, M.: Software Process Improvement in Small and Medium Software Enterprises: A Systematic Review. Software Quality Journal 16(2) (2008)
4. Ferreira, A., Machado, R.: Software Process Improvement in Multimodel Environments. In: Fourth International Conference on Software Engineering Advances, pp. 512–517 (2009)
5. Khoshgoftar, M., Osman, O.: Comparison of maturity models. In: 2nd IEEE International Conference on Computer Science and Information Technology, pp. 297–301 (2009)
6. Garcia, I., Pacheco, C., Coronel, N.: Learn from Practice: Defining an Alternative Model for Software Engineering Education in Mexican Universities for Reducing the Breach between Industry and Academia. In: Proceedings of the International Conference on Applied Computer Science, Malta, pp. 120–124 (2010)
7. Bella, F., Hörmann, K., Vanamali, B.: From CMMI to SPICE – Experiences on How to Survive a SPICE Assessment Having Already Implemented CMMI. In: Jedlitschka, A., Salo, O. (eds.) PROFES 2008. LNCS, vol. 5089, pp. 133–142. Springer, Heidelberg (2008)

8. Rout, T.: CMMI conformance to ISO/IEC 15504. In: 5th International SPICE Conference on Process Assessment and Improvement, pp. 27–29 (2005)
9. Halvorsen, C.P., Conradi, R.: A Taxonomy to Compare SPI Frameworks. In: Ambriola, V. (ed.) EWSPT 2001. LNCS, vol. 2077, pp. 217–235. Springer, Heidelberg (2001)
10. Rout, T.P., Tuffley, A., Cahill, B.: CMMI Evaluation: Capability Maturity Model Integration Mapping to ISO/IEC 15504 2:1998., Griffith University, Brisbane (2001)
11. Peldzius, S., Ragaisis, S.: Investigation Correspondence between CMMI-DEV and ISO/IEC 15504. International Journal of Education and Information Technologies 5(4), 361–368 (2011)
12. Soto, M., Münch, J.: Using Model Comparison to Maintain Model-to-Standard Compliance. In: CVSM 2008 Proceedings of the 2008 International Workshop on Comparison and Versioning of Software Models, pp. 35–40 (2008)
13. Pardo, C., Pino, F., García, F., Romero, F.R., Piattini, M., Baldassarre, M.T.: HProcess-TOOL: A Support Tool in the Harmonization of MultipReference Models, pp. 370–382 (2011)
14. Pardo, C., Pino, F.J., Garcia, F., Baldassarre, M.T., Piattini, M.: From chaos to the systematic harmonization of multiple reference models: A harmonization framework applied in two case studies. Journal of Systems and Software 86(1), 125–143 (2013)
15. Pardo, C., Pino, F.J., García, F., Piattini, M., Baldassarre, M.T.: An ontology for the harmonization of multiple standards and models. Computer Standards & Interfaces 34(1), 48–59 (2012)
16. Pardo, C., Pino, F.J., García, F., Piattini, M., Baldassarre, M.T.: A process for driving the harmonization of models. In: Proceedings of the 11th International Conference on Product Focused Software - PROFES 2010, pp. 51–54 (2010)
17. Pricope, S., Lichter, H., Rosenkranz, C.G.: Efficient Adoption and Assessment of Multiple Reference Models. In: 5th IFIP TC2 Central and Eastern European Conference on Software Engineering Techniques, pp. 25–26 (2011)
18. Rout, T.P., Tuffley, A.: Harmonizing ISO/IEC 15504 AND CMMI. Software Process Improvement and Practice 12, 361–371 (2007)
19. Peldzius, S., Ragaisis, S., Valaitis, V.: Seeking Process Maturity with DSDM Atern. Computational Science and Techniques (2), 193–204 (2013)

Software Process Lines: A Systematic Literature Review

Daniel Dias de Carvalho, Larissa Fernandes Chagas,
Adailton Magalhães Lima, and Carla Alessandra Lima Reis

Graduate Program in Computer Science, Federal University of Pará
Belém, Brazil
{danieldias,larissafc,adailton,clima}@ufpa.br

Abstract. Software Process Line (SPrL) has been claimed as a suitable paradigm for tailoring and reuse of software processes. However, despite its increasing importance, there is still a lack of research that systematically characterizes and analyzes the state of the art of SPrL approaches, in particular focusing on how such a paradigm has been used to improve software processes. This paper presents the method followed to perform a systematic literature review on SPrL in order to investigate the state of the art of this area, as well as the results of this review focusing especially on how variability is represented. We found 40 primary studies about this topic published from 1996 to 2013. Our results indicate that the software engineering community has increasingly invested effort in this area. However, it is still considered an immature area with many open issues such as the lack of the modeling of well-known process standards and models using SPrL concepts and the lack of empirical evaluations.

Keywords: Software Process Lines, Software Process Variability, Variability Management, Feature Model, Systematic Literature Review.

1 Introduction

The ultimate goal of improving software quality is the main motivation for software process definition, based on the premise that the process by which a software is developed strongly influences the quality of that software [44], [40]. However, process definition is a complex activity, requiring experience and knowledge of a variety of disciplines of software engineering [12], [17]. Additionally, defining software processes from scratch for each new project creates high risks and requires a significant amount of effort and time [46].

For this purpose, the Software Process Line (SPrL) paradigm has been proposed. SPrL is a set of similar processes within a particular domain or for a particular purpose, having common characteristics and built based upon common and reusable process assets [47]. By adopting the SPrL paradigm, an organization takes a proactive initiative for reuse, actively preparing its software processes for a number of anticipated needs beforehand, whereas classic process tailoring typically modifies a process individually for a specific project [13].

A. Mitasiunas et al. (Eds.): SPICE 2014, CCIS 477, pp. 118–130, 2014.
© Springer International Publishing Switzerland 2014

In this paper we present a Systematic Literature Review (SLR) that aims to characterize existing approaches on SPrL. The rest of this paper is structured as follows: Section 2 describes the SLR method followed. Section 3 presents the data extraction and the results of the SLR. Section 4 presents related work. Section 5 discusses some threats to validity. Finally, Section 6 presents the conclusion and plans for future work.

2   Research Method

Systematic Literature Review (SLR) is a type of secondary study that uses a well-defined method to identify, analyze, evaluate and interpret all available evidence (i.e., primary studies) related to a particular research question in a way that is unbiased and (to a degree) repeatable [2]. The outcomes of a SLR are far more convincing than a more informal approach to elaborate a research background [1].

The SLR process we performed was driven by process guidelines specified in [2] and [5] and is composed of the following phases: (i) planning the SLR, (ii) conducting the SLR and (iii) reporting the SLR. The writing and publication of this paper partially fulfills the reporting phase. The first author of this paper was the main responsible for performing the SLR, with some help from the other authors when needed.

2.1   Planning the SLR

The planning phase consists of the following steps: (i) identification of the need for a SLR; (ii) specifying the research questions; and (iii) developing the protocol.

Need for a Systematic Literature Review: Regarding the aforementioned benefits of conducting a SLR and the lack of this kind of study focused specifically on SPrL, the authors of this paper judged that it would be important to conduct a SLR study to investigate this research area and to develop well-founded future work.

Research Questions: Specifying the research questions is the most critical part of a SLR and it drives the study as a whole [2]. The research questions of this SLR are presented in Table 1.

Table 1. Research questions

Id.	Research Question
Q1	Which are the main contributions of the proposed approaches?
Q2	How to represent variability?
Q2.1	Which variability types are provided?
Q2.2	Which dependency types are provided?
Q2.3	Which types of software process elements are targets of variability?
Q3	Which process modeling languages are being used?
Q4	Which process quality models and standards are being used?
Q5	Which software engineering paradigms have been applied in conjunction with SPrL?
Q6	Which software process line concepts are being used?
Q7	Are there tools to support the approaches?
Q8	How the proposed approaches are being validated?

SLR Protocol: The SLR protocol documents the method that was used to conduct the systematic review, in a way to reduce the researcher bias and increase repeatability.

Search Strategy: In order to maximize the number of papers retrieved, the search strings, one for each digital library, were built considering both singular and plural forms (e.g., "process line" and "process lines") and possible synonyms (e.g., "process line", "process family" and "variant rich process") of the main terms. Unnecessary plural terms that had no impact on results were omitted. A required condition was that all papers inside the control group had to be retrieved by this search string.

Inclusion Criteria: The list of inclusion criteria is presented in Table 2.

Table 2. Inclusion Criteria

Id.	Inclusion Criteria
IC-01	The paper addresses variability, similarity or flexibility in process models.
IC-02	The paper addresses product lines.
IC-03	The paper addresses process reuse or process tailoring.
IC-04	The paper addresses process lines.

Exclusion Criteria: If a paper was classified in at least one of the exclusion criteria, then it was rejected. The list of exclusion criteria is shown in Table 3.

Table 3. Exclusion Criteria

Id.	Exclusion Criteria
EC-01	The publication refers to a proceeding, technical report, tutorial, minitrack or any kind of non-scientific work.
EC-02	The paper is not related to the area of Software Engineering (or even to the area of Computer Science).
EC-03	The paper addresses reuse only in software.
EC-04	The paper addresses variability/similarity only in software or other entity.
EC-05	The paper employs variability/similarity only in the sense of generic comparison, structural similarity matching, process mining, statistical process control, process deviation, or process unpredictability.
EC-06	The paper uses "feature" term only in the sense of functionality.
EC-07	The paper addresses software process, but not considering variability modelling.
EC-08	The paper was not found without cost.
EC-09	The paper was not found.
EC-10	The paper addresses software process reuse, but not using SPrL concepts.
EC-11	The paper is not written in English.
EC-12	The paper addresses only product line.
EC-13	The paper represents a systematic literature review.

2.2   Conducting the SLR

In this phase, the process specified in the protocol was carried out. The main steps were: (i) identification of research; (ii) selection of primary studies; (iii) data extraction; and (iv) data analysis.

Identification of Research: In this step, three digital libraries (Scopus, IEEE Xplore and Engineering Village) were queried in February 2014. Table 4 shows the search strings. The search strings retrieved, respectively, 1376, 778 and 1195 papers.

Table 4. Search Strings and Additional Settings

Scopus' Search String: TITLE-ABS-KEY(("process line" OR "process lines" OR "process family" OR "process families" OR "variant rich process" OR "variant-rich process") OR (("business process" OR "business processes" OR "software process" OR "software processes" OR "process model" OR "process models") AND (variability OR variabilities OR variation OR variations OR variant OR variants OR commonality OR commonalities OR similarity OR similarities OR "feature model" OR "feature models" OR "feature modeling" OR "feature-based"))) AND (PUBYEAR > 1995) AND (PUBYEAR < 2014) AND (LIMIT-TO(SUBJAREA, "COMP"))   **Additional Settings:** "Advanced search" mode selected.
IEEE Xplore's Search String: ("process line" OR "process lines" OR "process family" OR "process families" OR "variant rich process" OR "variant-rich process") OR (("business process" OR "business processes" OR "software process" OR "software processes" OR "process model" OR "process models") AND (variability OR variabilities OR variation OR variations OR variant OR variants OR commonality OR commonalities OR similarity OR similarities OR "feature model" OR "feature models" OR "feature modeling" OR "feature-based"))   **Additional Settings:** "Advanced search" and "command search" modes selected. Option "metadata only" checked as true. "Publication year" in mode "range" from 1996 to 2013. "Content Type" with values "Conference Publications", "Journals & Magazines" and "Early Access Articles" selected.
Engineering Village's Search String: ((((("process line" OR "process lines" OR "process family" OR "process families" OR "variant rich process" OR "variant-rich process") OR (("business process" OR "business processes" OR "software process" OR "software processes" OR "process model" OR "process models") AND (variability OR variabilities OR variation OR variations OR variant OR variants OR commonality OR commonalities OR similarity OR similarities OR "feature model" OR "feature models" OR "feature modeling" OR "feature-based"))) WN KY) AND (723* WN CL) AND ({ca} OR {ja} OR {ip}) WN DT))   **Additional Settings:** "Expert search" mode selected. "Limit to" ranging from 1996 to 2013.

Selection of Primary Studies: In the first filter, only the title, abstract and keywords of the papers were read. When papers apparently addressed only process variability, product line or process reuse, rather than reject them in the first filter, we applied the inclusion criteria IC-01, IC-02 and IC-03, respectively. After this step, 1133 papers were classified as duplicated, 1753 were rejected and 463 were accepted.

In the second filter, a more detailed analysis was done upon the 463 papers that were accepted in the first filter, since a complete reading was performed. After the second filter, 423 papers were rejected and 40 were accepted.

3   Data Extraction and Results

In this step, the information from the accepted papers was extracted in order to answer the research questions of the SLR.

Primary Studies and Publishing Vehicles

As Figure 1a shows, the 40 primary studies were published in a range of 18 years (from 1996 to 2013. There is evidence that the interest in the area is increasing, since between 1996 and 2003 only 2 (5%) of the papers had been published; and 26 (65%) of them were published over the last 4 years (between 2010 and 2013).

Despite the small number of papers, there is evidence that researches in the area are maturing, considering that until 2005, there were no papers published in journals. The papers were published among 28 different publishing vehicles; and, in 21 (75%) of them, only 1 paper was published. Figure 1b shows the types of publishing vehicles.

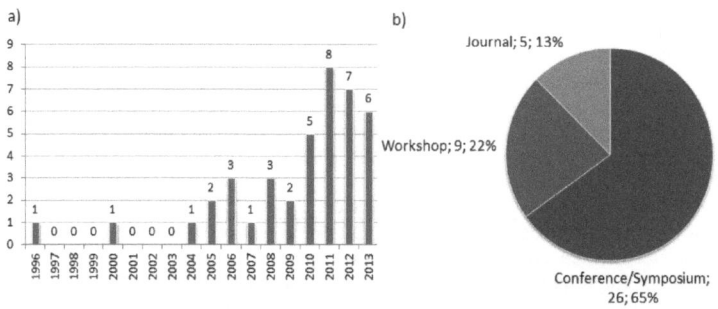

Fig. 1. Papers by Year and Type of Publishing Vehicles

Main Contributions (Q1)

"Method" definition is the most common contribution (Figure 2a). As stated by [40], the SPrL engineering process is composed by two phases: (i) domain engineering and (ii) application engineering. Considering only the 28 papers that proposed methods for SPrL engineering, Figure 2b shows the methods phases covered. It may indicate that more effort is being conducted in researches on how to create reusable processes than on how to tailor processes from SPrL.

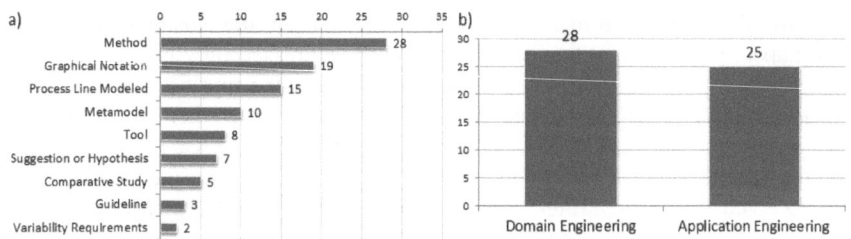

Fig. 2. Main Contributions and Coverage of the SPrL Engineering Methods

Variability Types (Q2.1)

As stated by [43], the notation expressiveness for specifying variability is one of the most relevant factors for successful SPrL adoption. Thus, the purpose of this question is to investigate how variability can be expressed in the proposed approaches for SPrL. Initially, we considered the most used variability types in SPrL, as investigated by [3]: "alternative/variation point", "optional" and "mandatory". However, other values emerged during the conduct of the review: "invariant" and "crosscutting". Figure 3a shows the variability types found.

Dependency Types (Q2.2)
Dependency is an important mechanism to support the decisions on variabilities and to ensure the consistency of the generated processes. The two types considered were "requirement" (e.g., if A is included, then B must also be included) and "exclusion/mutual-exclusion" (e.g., if A is included, then B must not be included). Figure 3b shows the dependency types found and the number of related studies.

Software Process Elements (Q2.3)
We realized that it is a difficult task to establish a closed set of types (e.g., considering elements defined in SPEM as a basis) due to the variety of synonyms and conflicting meanings for process elements. Thus, the authors' original terminology was kept. Figure 4a shows the types of process elements found and the number of related studies using it.

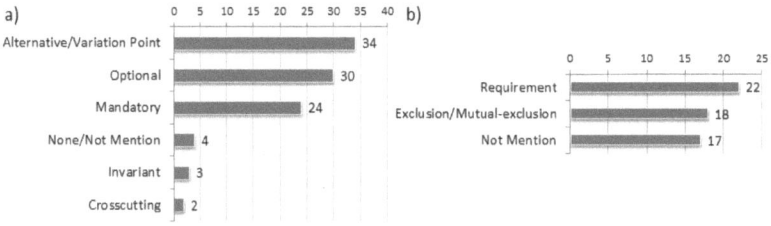

Fig. 3. Variability and Dependency Types

Modeling Languages (Q3)
A total of 29 different languages were found and Figure 4b shows the most common ones. Six languages were found in 2 papers and 4 languages were found in 1 paper. In 5 primary studies (13%), the authors claimed that its approaches were independent of language. Only 7 primary studies (18%) did not mention any language. Thus, the majority of the primary studies (33, representing 82%) have mentioned at least one language. This result may show the importance of representing process elements and variabilities in the context of SPrL.

Process Quality Models and Standards (Q4)
Whether an organization desires to certify or evaluate its software development process, such a process must be rigorously defined as established by the most popular models and standards (e.g., CMMI-DEV, MR-MPS-SW, ISO/IEC 12207) and SPrL is a suitable approach for this purpose [17], [26], [30].

This SLR has identified 19 unique quality models, standards, process frameworks and process life cycles modeled considering SPrL concepts. The most common were: V-Modell XT, found in 4 primary studies (10%); and Scrum, found in 3 primary studies (8%). However, 12 of the 19 (63%) were modeled only in a single primary study. In addition, 21 primary studies (53%) did not mention any of them.

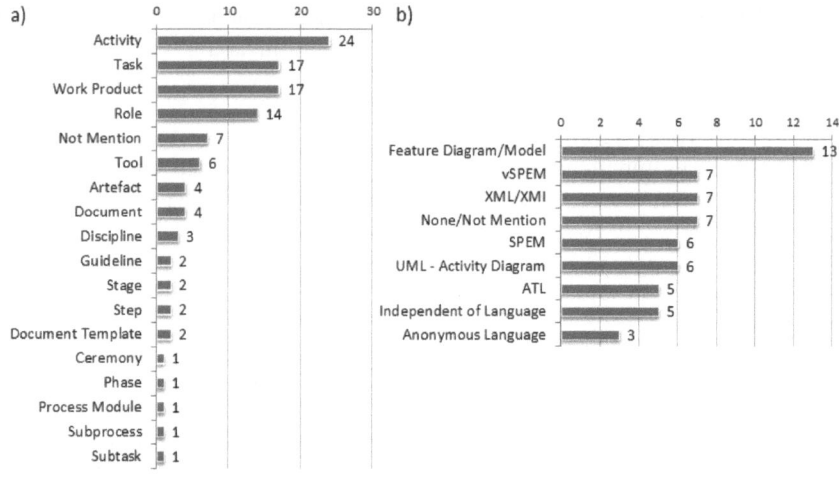

Fig. 4. Process Elements and Modeling Languages

It is also important to consider that in most cases, these standards were modeled only as an example of application, without the authors worrying about defining their scope, consistency, applicability and validation. This is an evidence of the lack of papers that apply SPrL concepts to the most widely adopted process models and standards in the software engineering community. This kind of modeling could help software organizations to take advantage of the benefits of SPrL.

Software Engineering Paradigms (Q5)

There are several concepts and paradigms in software engineering that can complement and benefit the SPrL paradigm [26], [32]. The most frequently paradigm applied in combination with SPrL was "Model-Driven Engineering (MDE)", which was found in 9 primary studies (23%). Such a paradigm is related to transformations between models in order to automate some steps of the SPrL engineering.

"Rationale Management" was the second most common paradigm, found in 4 primary studies (10%). It can be explained because SPrL is based on variability representation and decisions must be made in order to include or not some elements and which is the most suitable alternative from a variety of possible ones. Thus, some authors apply rationale management to systematically resolve variabilities trade-offs.

"Aspect-Oriented Engineering" was found in 3 primary studies (8%) and it was the third most common paradigm used in conjunction with SPrL. Some authors used such a paradigm in order to represent crosscutting variabilities.

In addition, "Service-Oriented Architecture (SOA)", "Experience Factory", "Business Process Management" and "Situational Method Engineering (SME)" were found each one in 2 papers; and "Global Software Development (GSD)" and "Agent-Oriented Engineering" were found in 1 paper each one.

SPrL Concepts Used (Q6)

"Process Line" is the most common concept used, found in 29 (73%) of the primary studies; followed by "Product Line" and "Feature Modeling", both found in 16 primary studies each one (40%); "Process Family", was found in 15 primary studies (38%); and "Process Line Architecture", was found in 12 primary studies (30%). In addition, "Variability Management" 6; "Variant Rich Process" 4; "Product Family" 3; "System Family" 2; "Domain Modeling" 1.

The terms "Process Line" and "Process Family" were used together in 10 papers (25%), and in 67% of the time that the former was used, the latter was also used. At a first glance, it may seem strange the use of terms such as "Product Line", "Product Family" and "System Family". This can be explained by the fact that some authors claim to use these concepts applied to processes.

Our conclusion is that there is no standardized nomenclature and semantic of concepts, which may hinder the understanding and comparison. This may be a sign of lack of maturity of the area.

Supporting Tools (Q7)
Figure 5a shows the number of approaches with and without supporting tools.

Validation Methods (Q8)
The following empirical strategies defined by [6] were considered: "Survey", "Case Study" and "Experiment". In addition, nonscientific strategies were also considered, such as: "Expert Review", "Comparison", "Example", and "Experience Report". Figure 5b shows the validation methods used.

We found that 18 papers (45%) have used only "Example"; 1 paper (3%) has used only "Comparison"; and 6 papers (15%) have used only "Experience Report". Many authors claimed to have performed case study in order to validate their proposed approaches. However, we realized that none of them actually used this methodology, as they did not follow a rigorous process (e.g., as defined by [6]).

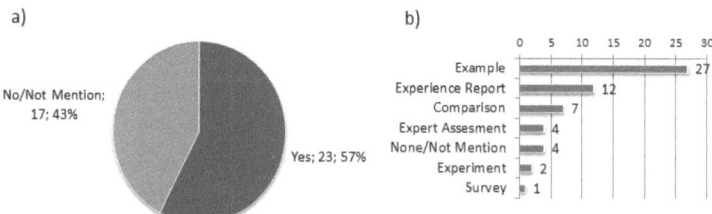

Fig. 5. Supporting Tools and Validation Methods

4   Related Work

Table 5 presents related work. In the first related work [3] (line 1), the authors conducted a SLR aiming to identify requirements of notations and mechanisms for software process tailoring. Although considering software process, the scope is wider, as SPrL is just one of the process tailoring approaches addressed by the authors.

In the second related work [4] (line 2), it was performed a SLR on business process lines with special attention to dynamic variability, like changes that need to be carried out at run-time. Despite of the similarity with our work, their work focused only on business processes[1].

Table 5. Comparison of related SLRs

SLR	Period	Digital Libraries	# of retrieved	# of accepted
[Martínez-Ruiz et al. 2012]	1991-2009	Science Direct, Wiley InterScience, Springer-Link, IEEE Xplore, ACM Digital Library	1172	32
[Rocha and Fantinato 2013]	2003-2012	Scopus, ISI Web of Science, IEEE Xplore, ACM Digital Library, SpringerLink, ScienceDirect, Engineering Village.	3649	63
This	1996-2013	Scopus, IEEE Xplore, Engineering Village.	3349	40

5   Threats to Validity

In order to analyze threats to validity related to this SLR, key concerns are addressed separately as follows:

Discovering the highest number of primary studies: for this purpose, the search strings were reviewed by the second author. In addition, they contain synonym and both singular and plural forms of the main terms. However, the number of digital libraries used (i.e., only three) may be considered low compared with related work (that used five [3] and seven [4]). Other risk was the lack of access to some papers that are paid or not found. Finally, only papers written in English were read. Therefore, this SLR may have ignored some potentially relevant primary studies.

Avoiding early rejection of potentially relevant primary studies: in order to avoid it, in the first filter of the selection process, papers were accepted even though SPrL concepts were not evident at a first glance. In addition, in case of doubt the papers were accepted too. However, the lack of clarity and inconsistencies found in some papers together with schedule constraints (preventing consulting other authors) may have led to the rejection of some potentially important primary study.

Avoiding misclassification of primary studies: data extraction was a difficult task, as there were many conflicting and overlapping concepts, in addition to missing or even erroneous information in the primary studies. As a measure to mitigate the risk of erroneous classification, the other authors were consulted in case of doubt; however it was not always possible. For all these factors, some misclassification may be occurred and it is not guaranteed that the outcome of the extraction made by other researches would be identical to those presented in this paper.

Increasing transparency and repeatability: it is improved by documenting and disseminating the research questions, search strings, inclusion and exclusion criteria, digital libraries used, process undertaken and all accepted primary studies in the references. But, full transparency is not possible as some information cannot be presented here for the sake of space.

---

[1] E.g. processes related to purchasing, manufacturing, advertising and sales.

6   Conclusion and Next Steps

This paper presented the process followed to perform a SLR aiming to get an overview of existing researches on software process lines.

The results show an increasing interesting in SPrL research. They also suggest the immaturity of the area, since there is no a well-defined taxonomy and the quality assessment of the proposed approaches needs improvement in terms of empirical validation. Another weakness is the low number of works that performed comparative studies to highlight advantages and disadvantages between their approaches and related work. However, this area has been showing signs of an increase in maturity as the numbers of published papers are increasing and SPrL has been applied in practice.

Taking into account the fact that this SLR has accepted only 40 papers and related work [4] has accepted 63 (57% more), it may also indicate a lower level of maturity of software process lines in relation to business processes lines.

A research trend we identified was the increasing number of experience report in industry and academy showing evidences that the SPrL paradigm is feasible and beneficial to be applied in real context. But, we suggest the use of a more rigorous method like case study for this purpose.

A future work is the modeling of widely adopted process models and standards. The authors of this paper have already modeled a SPrL for CMMI-DEV in conjunction with Scrum [7]. Our next goal is to investigate the effectiveness of SPrL paradigm for this purpose through an empirical study, since it is a promising area.

References

1. Budgen, D., Brereton, P.: Performing Systematic Literature Reviews in Software Engineering. In: 28th International Conference on Software Engineering (ICSE), pp. 1051–1052. ACM, New York (2006)
2. Kitchenham, B.: Guidelines for performing systematic literature reviews in software engineering. EBSE Technical Report EBSE-2007-01, Keele University (2007)
3. Martínez-Ruiz, T., Münch, J., García, F., Piattini, M.: Requirements and constructors for tailoring software processes: a systematic literature review. Software Quality Journal 20(1), 229–260 (2012)
4. Rocha, R., Fantinato, M.: The use of software product lines for business process management: A systematic literature review. Information and Software Technology 55(8), 1355–1373 (2013)
5. Souza, G.: Ambientes de Engenharia de Software Orientados a Corporação. PhD thesis, Federal University of Rio de Janeiro, 2008 (2008)
6. Wholin, C., Runeson, P., Höst, M., Ohlsson, M., Regnell, B., Wesslén, A.: Experimentation in Software Engineering (2012)
7. Carvalho, D., Chagas, L., Reis, C.: Definition of Software Process Lines for Integration of Scrum and CMMI. In: XL Latin American Computing Conference (CLEI) (2014)

Appendix (Primary Studies of the SLR)

8. Adam, S., Doerr, J.: The role of service abstraction and service variability and its impact on requirements engineering for service-oriented systems. In: 32nd Annual IEEE International Computer Software and Applications (COMPSAC), pp. 631–634. IEEE, Turkux (2008)

9. Alegría, J., Bastarrica, M.: Building software process lines with CASPER. In: International Conference on Software and System Process (ICSSP), pp. 170–179. IEEE, Zurich (2012)

10. Alegría, J., Bastarrica, M., Quispe, A., Ochoa, S.: An MDE approach to software process tailoring. In: International Conference on Software and Systems Process, pp. 43–52. ACM, New York (2011)

11. Aleixo, F., Freire, M., Alencar, D., Campos, E., Kulesza, U.: A comparative study of compositional and annotative modelling approaches for software process lines. In: Brazilian Symposium on Software Engineering, pp. 51–60 (2012)

12. Aleixo, F., Freire, M., Santos, W., Kulesza, U.: A model-driven approach to managing and customizing software process variabilities. In: 12th International Conference on Enterprise Information Systems (ICEIS), pp. 92–100 (2010)

13. Armbrust, O., Katahira, M., Miyamoto, Y., Münch, J., Nakao, H., Ocampo, A.: Scoping software process models - initial concepts and experience from defining space standards. In: Wang, Q., Pfahl, D., Raffo, D.M. (eds.) ICSP 2008. LNCS, vol. 5007, pp. 160–172. Springer, Heidelberg (2008)

14. Armbrust, O., Katahira, M., Miyamoto, Y., Münch, J., Nakao, H., Ocampo, A.: Scoping software process lines. Software Process: Improvement and Practice - Examining Process Design and Change 14(3), 181–197 (2009)

15. Azanza, M., Sosa, J., Trujillo, S., Díaz, O.: Towards a process-line for MDPLE. In: 2nd International Workshop on Model-Driven Product Line Engineering, pp. 3–12 (2010)

16. Barreto, A., Murta, L., Rocha, A.: Software process definition: a reuse-based approach. Journal of Universal Computer Science 17(13), 1765–1799 (2011)

17. Barreto, A., Nunes, E., Rocha, A., Murta, L.: Supporting the definition of software processes at consulting organizations via software process lines. In: Seventh International Conference on the Quality of Information and Communications Technology, pp. 15–24. IEEE (2010)

18. Biffl, S., Winkler, D., Höhn, R., Wetzel, H.: Software process improvement in Europe: potential of the new V-Modell XT and research issues. Software Process: Improvement and Practice 3(11) (2006)

19. Laporte, C.Y., Alexandre, S., O'Connor, R.: Software Engineering Lifecycle Standard for Very Small Enterprises. In: O'Connor, R.V., et al. (eds.) EuroSPI 2008. CCIS, vol. 16, pp. 129–141. Springer, Heidelberg (2008)

20. Castro, J., Pimentel, J., Lucena, M., Santos, E., Dermeval, D.: F-STREAM: A flexible process for deriving architectures from requirements models. In: Salinesi, C., Pastor, O. (eds.) CAiSE Workshops 2011. LNBIP, vol. 83, pp. 342–353. Springer, Heidelberg (2011)

21. Costache, D., Kalus, G., Kuhrmann, M.: Design and validation of feature-based process model tailoring - A sample implementation of PDE. In: 19th ACM SIGSOFT symposium and the 13th European conference on Foundations of software engineering (ESEC/FSE), pp. 464–467. ACM, New York (2011)

22. Durán, A., Benavides, D., Bermejo, J.: Applying system families concepts to requirements engineering process definition. In: van der Linden, F.J. (ed.) PFE 2003. LNCS, vol. 3014, pp. 140–151. Springer, Heidelberg (2004)

23. Gallina, B., Sljivo, I., Jaradat, O.: Towards a safety-oriented process line for enabling reuse in safety critical systems development and certification. In: 35th Annual IEEE Software Engineering Workshop (SEW), pp. 148–157. IEEE, Heraklion (2012)

24. Golpayegani, F., Azadbakht, K., Ramsin, R.: Towards process lines for agent-oriented requirements engineering. In: IEEE International Conference on Computer as a Tool (Euro-Con), pp. 550–557. IEEE, Zagreb (2013)

25. Gomaa, H., Kerschberg, L., Farrukh, G.: Domain modeling of software process models. In: Proc. Sixth IEEE International Conference on Engineering of Complex Computer Systems (ICECCS), pp. 50–60. IEEE (2000)

26. Hurtado, J., Bastarrica, M., Ochoa, S., Simmonds, J.: MDE software process lines in small companies. Journal of Systems and Software 86(5), 1153–1171 (2013)

27. Jafarinezhad, O., Ramsin, R.: Development of situational requirements engineering processes: A process factory approach. In: IEEE 36th Annual Computer Software and Applications Conference (COMPSAC), pp. 279–288. IEEE, Washington (2012)

28. Jaufman, O., Münch, J.: Acquisition of a project-specific process. In: Bomarius, F., Komi-Sirviö, S. (eds.) PROFES 2005. LNCS, vol. 3547, pp. 328–342. Springer, Heidelberg (2005)

29. Kiebusch, S., Franczyk, B., Speck, A.: Process-Family-Points. In: Wang, Q., Pfahl, D., Raffo, D.M., Wernick, P. (eds.) SPW 2006 and ProSim 2006. LNCS, vol. 3966, pp. 314–321. Springer, Heidelberg (2006)

30. Martínez-Ruiz, T., García, F., Piattini, M., Münch, J.: Modelling software process variability: an empirical study. IET Software 5(2), 172–187 (2011a)

31. Martínez-Ruiz, T., García, F., Piattini, M.: Managing process diversity by applying rationale management in variant rich processes. In: Caivano, D., Oivo, M., Baldassarre, M.T., Visaggio, G. (eds.) PROFES 2011. LNCS, vol. 6759, pp. 128–142. Springer, Heidelberg (2011)

32. Martínez-Ruiz, T., García, F., Piattini, M., Münch, J.: Applying AOSE concepts to model crosscutting variability in variant-rich processes. In: 37th EUROMICRO Conference on Software Engineering and Advanced Applications (SEAA), pp. 334–338. IEEE Computer Society, Washington (2011c)

33. Martínez-Ruiz, T., García, F., Piattini, M.: Towards a SPEM v2.0 extension to define process lines variability mechanisms. In: International Conference on Software Engineering, Re-search, Management And Applications (SERA), pp. 115–130. Springer, Heidelberg (2008)

34. Martínez-Ruiz, T., García, F., Piattini, M., Lucas-Consuegra, F.: Process variability management in global software development: A case study. In: International Conference on Software and System Proces (ICSSP), pp. 46–55. ACM, New York (2013)

35. Martínez-Ruiz, T., Ruiz, F., Piattini, M.: Towards understanding software process variability from contextual evidence of change. In: International Workshop on Variability Support in Information Systems (VarIS), pp. 417–431. Springer, Heidelberg (2013)

36. Magdaleno, A., Araujo, R., Werner, C.: COMPOOTIM: An approach to software processes composition and optimization. In: Congresso Ibero-Americano em Engenharia de Software (CIbSE), pp. 1–14 (2012)

37. Moser, T., Biffl, S., Winkler, D.: Process-driven feature modeling for variability management of project environment configurations. In: 11th International Conference on Product Focused Software Development and Process Improvement (PROFES), pp. 47–50 (2010)

38. Nunes, V., Werner, C., Santoro, F.: Context-based process line. In: International Conference on Enterprise Information Systems (ICEIS), pp. 277–282 (2009)

39. Rausch, A., Kuhrmann, M.: A proposal for principles and values from the perspective of the german standard it-development process V-modell XT. In: International Conference on Software and Systems Process (ICSSP), pp. 230–233. ACM (2011)

40. Rombach, H.D.: Integrated software process and product lines. In: Li, M., Boehm, B., Osterweil, L.J. (eds.) SPW 2005. LNCS, vol. 3840, pp. 83–90. Springer, Heidelberg (2006)

41. Rouillé, E., Combemale, B., Barais, O., Touzet, D., Jézéquel, J.: Leveraging CVL to manage variability in software process lines. In: 19th Asia-Pacific Software Engineering Confer-ence (APSEC), pp. 148–157. IEEE Computer Society (2012)

42. Rouillé, E., Combemale, B., Barais, O., Touzet, D., Jézéquel, J.: Improving Reusability in Software Process Lines. In: 39th EUROMICRO Conference on Software Engineering and Advanced Applications (SEAA), pp. 90–93. IEEE Computer Society (2013)

43. Simmonds, J., Bastarrica, M., Silvestre, L., Quispe, A.: Variability in software process models: Requirements for adoption in industrial settings. In: 4th International Workshop on Product Line Approaches in Software Engineering (PLEASE), pp. 33–36 (2013)

44. Sutton, S., Osterweil, L.: Product families and process families. In: 10th International Soft-ware Process Workshop (ISPW), pp. 109–111. IEEE Computer Society (1996)

45. Ternité, T.: Process lines: a product line approach designed for process model develop-ment. In: 35th Euromicro Conference on Software Engineering and Advanced Applica-tions (SEAA), pp. 173–180. IEEE Computer Society, Washington (2009)

46. Washizaki, H.: Building software process line architectures from bottom up. In: Münch, J., Vierimaa, M. (eds.) PROFES 2006. LNCS, vol. 4034, pp. 415–421. Springer, Heidelberg (2006)

47. Washizaki, H.: Deriving project-specific processes from process line architecture with commonality and variability. In: IEEE International Conference on Industrial Informatics (INDIN), pp. 1301–1306. IEEE Computer Society (2006)

Assessment-Based Innovation System Customization for Software Product Line Organizations

Fritz Stallinger[1], Robert Neumann[2], and Robert Schossleitner[3]

[1] Software Competence Center Hagenberg, Softwarepark 21, 4232 Hagenberg, Austria
fritz.stallinger@scch.at
[2] Softwareforen Leipzig GmbH, Hainstraße 16, 04109 Leipzig, Germany
neumann@softwareforen.de
[3] STIWA Automation GmbH, Salzburger Straße 52, 4800 Attnang-Puchheim, Austria
robert.schossleitner@stiwa.com

Abstract. Innovation is regarded a key element for an organization's business success. The models and methods available for innovation management mainly concentrate on the product and service businesses in consumer or business-to-business markets. Software Product Line Engineering (SPLE) allows delivering customized software at reduced costs and development time while simultaneously enhancing quality. To reach that, SPLE employs proactive planning and engineering which require prescribing product features, variants, etc. Innovating and flexibly adapting a product line is thus highly challenging. We present a holistic approach for systematically evaluating and adapting an innovation system for SPLE organizations based on the organization's business characteristics and discuss how the process dimension is embedded into this approach and related to the concept of process assessment and improvement.

Keywords: software business characteristics, product line engineering, innovation management system, innovation process, evaluation, customization.

1 Introduction, Goals, Research Context, and Approach

Innovation is considered a key element for an organization's business success and gaining and maintaining competitive advantage. However, as organizations are constantly challenged by competition, just spawning new ideas does not guarantee success. Therefore, the systematic management of innovations from idea creation to market introduction has been subject to research for a long time, mainly driven by the product and service businesses in consumer or business-to-business markets.

On the other hand, *Software Product Line Engineering* (SPLE) employs systematic variability management and proactive planning and engineering which to a significant extent require prescribing the features of the products in the *Software Product Line* (SPL), the allowed variants, etc. in order to deliver a widely predefined spectrum of software products at reduced costs and development times and enhanced quality. Potential innovations to a SPL may thus be impeded if they require changes to the pre-planned models and structures of the SPL and overall innovations may be prevented.

A. Mitasiunas et al. (Eds.): SPICE 2014, CCIS 477, pp. 131–143, 2014.
© Springer International Publishing Switzerland 2014

As SPLE approaches generally lack a systematic approach for innovation management, SPLE organizations often do not fully exploit their innovation potential.

We therefore present a business characteristics-driven approach for systematically customizing an innovation management system for software businesses applying SPLE, consisting of a conceptual framework and a method for supporting SPLE organizations in developing a customized innovation management system that allows them to exploit their business-specific innovation benefits, increase competitiveness, reduce innovation risks, and embed innovation in the organization's culture.

The work is based on the results of work with an industry partner in order to foster the establishment of systematic innovation management within the *industrial solutions business* (ISB), based on the assumption that *system family approaches* are a key enabler for enhancing productivity and quality in the ISB. Innovations in the ISB are mostly driven by customer requests within a specific project and typically need a systematic, fast and accurate feasibility study for which resources and know-how are often not available within a project. Further problems arise from a lack of willingness to change and take risks, a lack of top management support or a too strong focus on technical innovation. Establishing systematic innovation management was thus considered a promising contribution to the goal of systematically improving the ISB.

To get an overview of state-of-the-art concepts, models and methods in innovation and innovation management a literature review has been performed [1-15]. As an understanding of SPL-based businesses and their characteristics were assumed to be the foundation for further investigations, a comparison of the SPL-based business with other business types has been performed. The identification and evaluation of appropriate comparison criteria was supported by researching literature from related domains [16-19] and by discussions with domain experts. Based on this, the different topics that need to be addressed by innovation management and the challenges and requirements posed on these topics by SPLE characteristics have been identified. A high-level description of the resulting conceptual framework for representing generic innovation system requirements for SPLE has been presented as a short paper at SEAA 2013 [20]. The present paper extends this work with more details, background, and related work, and adds the presentation of a method for applying the framework to improve an organization's specific innovation system.

The remainder of the paper is structured as follows: Section 2 provides background and related work on SPLE and innovation management; Section 3 provides details on the performed literature research on innovation system design and innovation process models, and identifies key innovation challenges for SPLE; Section 4 summarizes the conceptual framework developed for innovation system customization; Section 5 outlines the method for application of the framework; Section 6 summarizes and concludes the paper and discusses directions for further work.

2   Background and Related Work

Innovation is typically not restricted to new ideas and invention, but encompasses the exploitation of an idea and its successful introduction in a market as important aspects. Innovation management is the systematic planning, implementation, and controlling of innovations. An overview on the various approaches to define innovation and innovation management is provided by Hauschildt [6].

2.1   Innovation and Innovation Management

Innovations are typically distinguished by their subject, their degree of novelty, or their initiating driver. The subject can be a product or service, a process, a technology, the business model, the organization, etc. Along the novelty dimension, typically radical and incremental innovations are distinguished [1] [6] with radical innovations causing a major change in the corresponding subject, while incremental innovations only introduce small improvements. The initiating driver can stem from either technology or market [5] [6]. When new technologies are available (e.g. RFID), new ideas will spawn on how to make use of these technologies (e.g. RFID-tags in logistics). Such innovations are in a way pushed into the market by these new opportunities ("*technology push*"). On the other hand, innovations are initiated to fulfill customer needs, so in a way they are pulled by the market ("*market/demand pull*"). Importantly, different types of innovation need different handling.

Hauschildt points out, that innovations disturb the well-established routines in an organization and have the inherent potential for conflicts [6]. Therefore, an organization has to determine rules on how to handle such conflicts so that neither routine nor innovation dominates. Typical elements of innovation management are identified by Davila et al. [1] and comprise amongst others *innovation strategy*, *organizational structure*, and *innovation process*. Due to different business characteristics, e.g. with respect to targeted markets, offered products and services, applied engineering approaches, or position in the value chain, each organization has to develop or at least customize its own innovation management system.

2.2   Software Product Lines

A SPL is defined as a set of software or software-intensive systems that share a common, managed set of features that satisfy the specific needs of a particular market and are developed from a common set of core assets in a prescribed way [21]. The benefits of SPLE include the delivery of customized products at reduced costs and development times and enhanced quality, and the ability to master the increasing complexity of software products. According to Matys [22] the group of products of a SPL may share different kinds of relationships, e.g. products may provide similar functionality and share common features, complement each other, or target the same market. The core of SPLE is that products are generated based on the planned, systematic reuse of components, methods, tools, and other resources [23].

Typically SPLE is divided into order-independent *domain engineering* and order-specific *application engineering*. Domain engineering defines and realizes the commonalties and variability of the SPL, whereas application engineering builds the software products by reusing domain artifacts provided by domain engineering and exploiting the SPL's variability [24] [25]. In the recently released standard ISO/IEC 26550 this distinction is reflected by two lifecycles, the domain engineering lifecycle and the application engineering lifecycle [26].

2.3   Innovation vs. Product Management, Lifecycle Processes, and SPLE

Own research [27] [28], carried out to identify software product management best practices for product-oriented software development from selected software product line and product management frameworks, showed that only few of these frameworks explicitly foresee innovation and innovation management practices. Innovation in these contexts addresses the extension of the product portfolio with new or enhanced products that satisfy customer needs or various strategies (e.g. innovation leader, product imitation) and suggests sources for idea generation (e.g. Pohl et al. [24]).

This research also highlighted that product innovation – in terms of extending the product portfolio – is not in the scope of software engineering lifecycle process models like ISO/IEC 12207 [29]. Although various processes handle change requests provided by stakeholders, systematically managing and utilizing these sources and generating, evaluating, and realizing ideas for new or enhanced products, etc. is not addressed.

Key outcomes for a potential *Product Innovation Process,* which aims at extending a product portfolio with new or enhanced products, are identified in [28] and comprise:

- the development and establishment of a strategy for product innovation,
- the systematic search for new ideas according to this innovation strategy,
- the systematic evaluation and selection for implementation of ideas for new products or product enhancements, and
- the identification and continuous assessment of technologies for their immediate benefit and potential future applicability.

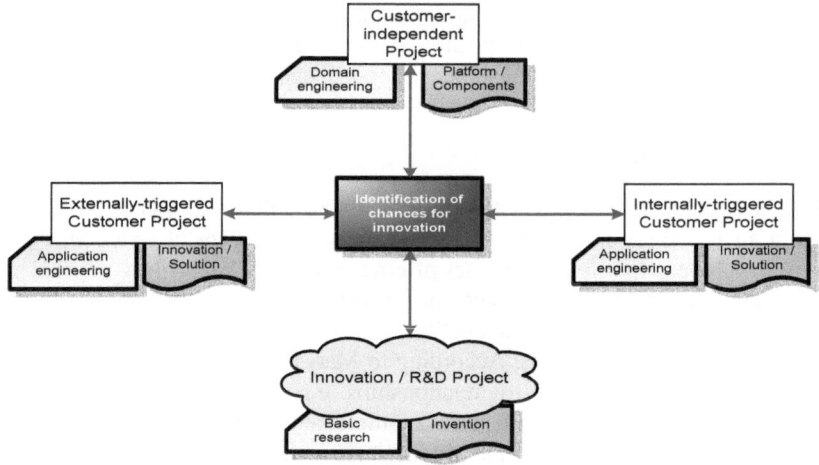

Fig. 1. Project scenarios with different kinds of innovation

In an SPLE environment, potential innovations may be hindered or not even considered if they require changes to the pre-defined and established models and structures of the SPL, since changes to the SPL's variability model may imply high effort for the existing and planned products [30]. Thus innovations may be prevented and the SPL may encounter a lock-in effect [30] which puts at risk the SPL's long-term competitiveness and ability to adapt to changing business factors and parameters.

With respect to software organizations applying SPLE, Böckle [30] provides a series of innovation management measures aimed at preventing this lock-in effect, but without detailing how to select appropriate measures for a particular organization's situation.

In SPLE, the customer-specific product development is typically assumed to take place within the *application engineering* part of the overall engineering process. As a consequence, innovation management in SPLE contexts has to address the specific challenge that innovation will happen within and outside such customer-specific projects, and that there is by nature a tension between customer-specific and reusable innovations. The SPLE innovation and innovation management process thus need to cover multiple project scenarios (cf. Fig. 1) and potentially multiple instantiations of those. Scenarios include customer projects which employ internally, i.e. from within the organization, or externally triggered innovations, customer-independent projects to develop an innovation for marketability, and research and development projects.

Chances for innovation can potentially spawn from and be further handled in any of these scenarios and the life cycle of an innovation can run through multiple such project scenarios, which requires additional processes to manage, control, coordinate, and synchronize innovations across projects and products or solutions.

The key characteristics of the innovation and innovation management process for SPLE contexts identified during development of the approach are:

- *"Identification of chances for innovation"* is a central and ongoing activity that is closely linked with all other processes. It also links the different project scenarios where different kinds of innovation take place (cf. Fig. 1).
- *"Strategy development"* drives and at the same time is driven by *"Identification of chances for innovation"* and is an ongoing activity.
- A distinction between *"problem"* and *"idea"* has to be made. A specific problem requires *"Idea generation"* to find solutions to the problem.
- A recurring activity for *"Rating & Selection"* of problems and ideas is necessary and may be triggered regularly or on occasion. It has to be performed within and beyond the boundaries of projects, organizational units and disciplines.
- Activities like development, test, or market launch of traditional product-oriented innovation process models are widely covered through other processes and typically already well-established in SPLE contexts.

3   Innovation System Design Challenges in SPLE

Innovation management literature provides a plethora of innovation models [1], processes [2], success factors [1] [3] [4] and techniques and tools that an organization may apply. Depending on the innovation subject, degree of novelty, and initiating driver, there are many different types of innovation that require different handling and need to be considered in designing an innovation management system. Davies and Hobday [18] [19] particularly focus on the specifics of project-based organizations in the domain of complex products and systems (COPS). A key element of their work is how the nature of COPS affects innovation and how projects can drive innovation.

The innovation process is a central element of innovation management and there exist a lot of innovation process models in literature. A summary has been compiled by

Verworn and Herstatt [15]. Many of these models are based on a stage-and-review concept. Such sequential models are not very flexible, time consuming, and often too much focused on technology. Consequently, more recent models, e.g. the model of *Hughes et al.* [15], explicitly comprise parallel and iterative execution of activities.

Nevertheless, none of the reviewed innovation process models explicitly addresses SPL-based businesses, but particular features appropriate for this business type can be identified. The models of *Ebert et al.* and *Pleschak et al.* [15] for instance, cover idea generation in detail, while other models require an existing idea to start the innovation process. *Ebert et al.* identify the sources of problems that trigger innovations, including market development, competitive situation, customer requests, technological advance, or social, public, and environmental developments. Both models explicitly mention strategy as a necessary input for idea generation and evaluation. The model of *Ulrich et al.* [15] emphasizes a multi-disciplinary approach by integrating different business functions (marketing, design, finance, etc.) into each stage of the innovation process.

Based on an analysis of the identified project scenarios (cf. Fig. 1) and discussions with project management and innovation experts the following key innovation challenges have to be addressed for SPLE contexts (extended from [20]):

- *Innovations happen within and outside customer-specific projects*: The goals and constraints in both innovation contexts differ greatly and require a different handling of innovations. The innovation strategy has to make statements on the role and importance of innovation in each context. For customer-specific projects, quick and accurate feasibility and risk evaluation and flexible development have to be ensured. The innovation process has to integrate the two contexts and the organizational structure must support innovations in both contexts.
- *There is a tension between customer-specific and reusable innovations*: Innovation management has to find a balance between these contradicting goals. On the one hand, providing customized solutions is essential, on the other hand, cost saving pressure demands for reusable solutions. Innovation strategy has to define objectives and where to focus innovation efforts. The innovation process has to support the innovation strategy for example by defining appropriate evaluation criteria or allowing different paths an innovation can take.
- *Coordination of innovation across multiple organizational units and product sub-systems*: In the development of a customer-specific product many different organizational units are involved. Innovation strategy must define the role of innovations and specific objectives for these units as well as for the different elements in the product structure. The extensive range of innovation possibilities requires clear statements regarding objectives and focus of innovation efforts. Organizational units need to be integrated into a multi-disciplinary process.
- *Integration of customers, suppliers, and partners as well as multiple disciplines and competencies*: Developing and delivering customized products often involves broad and dynamic networks of suppliers and partners, and also of the individual customer. In specific engineering contexts, systems often integrate multiple disciplines and require extensive knowledge. These sources of innovation need to be considered in the innovation strategy and integrated by the innovation process.

4   Innovation System Customization Concept

The conceptual framework for innovation system customization, as outlined in [20], prescribes generic innovation management system requirements for SPLE across two dimensions (cf. Fig. 2): firstly, *innovation management elements*, like innovation strategy or innovation process, that have to be considered in defining an innovation system; secondly, *software business characteristics*, that differentiate businesses or organizations. The requirements are then defined at the intersection of a specific *software business characteristic* with an *innovation management element*.

The approach provides a structured representation of the requirements that are posed on innovation management in SPLE contexts. Each of the identified *software business characteristics* is analyzed regarding its potential values and its impact on specific *innovation management elements*.

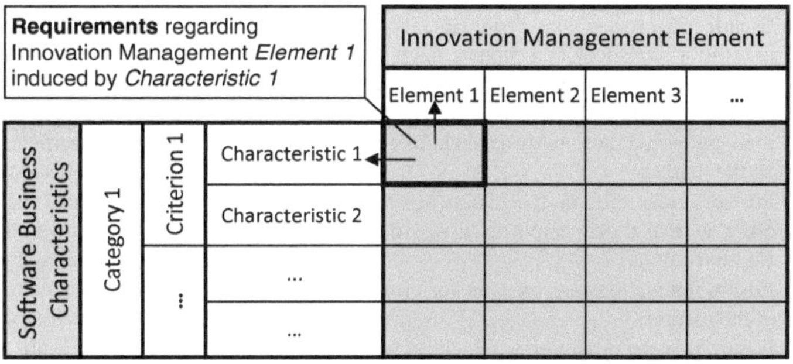

Fig. 2. Framework for innovation system customization (adapted from [20])

According to Davila et al. [1] the following elements have to be considered in order to develop an innovation management system: *Innovation Strategy, Organizational Structure, Innovation Process, Innovation Culture, Innovation Measurement, Incentives and Rewards,* and *Learning*. They are described in more detail in [20].

The criteria that are suitable to differentiate and characterize software businesses and organizations can be ordered into the following categories (extended from [20]):

- The *'Customers and Market'* category that characterizes an organization's customers and approached markets and comprises criteria such as anonymity of customers or markets, strength and duration of customer-relationships, the degree to which customers are involved with or are able to control product developments, the structure and competiveness of markets, or buying decisions of customers.
- The *'Products and Services'* category that characterizes an organization's products and services according e.g. to their typical life-span and life cycle costs, the degree of customization, product complexity, or competitive advantage.
- The *'Engineering and Production'* category that characterizes the process of developing and generating the products and services. These criteria comprise e.g. typical volumes or batches produced, the repeatability of the process, the type of order fulfillment, the distribution of effort between order-independent and order-specific engineering, or the number and kind of involved engineering disciplines.

- The *'Organization'* category that characterizes the role of the organization towards its customers, i.e. where in the value chain the organization positions itself, core competencies of the organization, structure of supplier and partner networks, etc.

For each criterion a set of typical characteristics or values the criterion could have for a specific organization is foreseen in the framework. These criteria and their characteristics stem from an initial criteria set for business characterization in the ISB, which was further enhanced to cover SPLE contexts. Overall, the identified software business characteristics suggest that innovation management concepts, which are well-established in other business types, should not be applied in SPLE contexts without careful analysis and appropriate adaptation.

Table 1. Requirements for business criterion *'anonymity of customers or market'* vs. innovation management element *'Innovation Process'*

	Anonymous markets	Individual customers
Innovation Process	• Establish a process that systematically gathers ideas in a repository and funnels them through different stages into marketable innovations • Establish systematic risk evaluations and ensure innovations are thoroughly tested before roll out on the market • Provide clear criteria for evaluating ideas in order to make transparent go/no-go decisions for innovations • Ensure innovations are relevant for broad parts of the market • Ensure that the possibilities the current product line offers for innovations are systematically and constantly analyzed and exploited	• Establish a process that ensures quick evaluation of customer requests and respective innovation risks • Ensure innovations initiated by or realized for a specific customer are not forgotten but collected and evaluated for reusability for other customers or integration into the product line • Focus on maintaining a flexible product line that can be adapted to changing customer needs • Ensure customers are integrated into the innovation process or innovation activities as early as possible

We exemplarily illustrate the generic requirements provided by the framework by showing which requirements for the innovation management element *Innovation Process* can be derived for each of the characteristics of the criterion *'anonymity of customers or market'* in order to demonstrate the power of the approach in identifying innovation system requirements tailored to the specific needs of an organization.

For the selected criterion two basic characteristics can be differentiated. The organization may target an *anonymous market* with its products, which is typical for high volume consumer products with no direct contact to customers. On the other hand, an organization may provide its products to *individual customers*, typically accompanied with direct contact, strong customer relationships, and the need to fulfill customer requests. The requirements that can be derived for these two characteristics are shown in Table 1 (excerpted from [20]).

The identification of the framework's requirements is based on the knowledge and information gathered during the preceding analysis of innovation and innovation management literature and incorporation of the results of the analysis of the different SPLE-related project scenarios (cf. Fig. 1) and the specific challenges they pose.

5   Innovation System Evaluation and Adaptation Method

As sketched in Fig. 2, the identification of an organization's business characteristics allows identifying the requirements shaping the innovation management system. The result is a set of requirements for each of the innovation management elements that are linked with and induced by a specific business characteristic. This way, an organization can on the one hand gather the relevant requirements the innovation management system has to fulfill. On the other hand, gaps in currently implemented innovation management systems can be identified and improvements derived.

The purpose of the innovation system evaluation and adaptation method is thus to tailor the provided generic innovation system according to the organization's specific business characteristics and to assess the state of fulfillment of the requirements associated with and adapted for these characteristics. This provides the foundation for the subsequent identification of areas in need for taking appropriate measures and the derivation of respective improvement measures. The method steps are:

Step 1 - Tailoring of Criteria and Characteristics. The provided generic innovation system with all its software business criteria and characteristics is tailored to the specific organization. For each criterion there are multiple characteristics defined and those that most apply to the organization have to be selected.

Step 2 - Consolidation and Refinement of Requirements. The generic requirements linked to the selected business characteristics are consolidated and refined according to the specifics of the organization. The requirements associated with each business characteristic should be discussed among the stakeholders and their validity for the organization confirmed. If for a specific criterion multiple characteristics apply, the stakeholders typically have to deal with some contradicting requirements. If such requirements are valid, it has to be clearly stated for which contexts of the organization they apply. Additionally, it should be identified whether the organization has any specific requirements regarding innovation not covered by the provided innovation system. As a result, the tailored innovation system contains only the requirements that will shape the organization-specific innovation system. This step also fosters a common understanding between the stakeholders.

Step 3 - Requirements Fulfillment Assessment. An evaluation of the fulfillment of the consolidated and refined requirements is performed. We recommend using an NPLF-scale, i.e. is N(ot), P(artially), L(argely), or F(ully) fulfilled, with percentages of fulfillment as in ISO/IEC 15504 [31]. For this step it may be appropriate to perform multiple sessions, each focusing on specific innovation management elements like innovation strategy or innovation process, which supports use of existing evaluation results, e.g. from process assessment or strategy evaluation.

Step 4 - Identification of Need for Action. For each requirement its importance for the organization's business and innovation success is estimated. Indicators typically include the contribution of fulfilling a requirement to achieving the business goals or its strategic fit. A simple scale of low, medium, and high importance is considered sufficient. Based on this assessment, the need for action can be identified by combining the identified requirement fulfillment and its importance. As a result, each requirement can be put into a simple portfolio of requirements fulfillment vs. requirements importance.

Step 5 - Identification of Improvement Measures. For those requirements that were identified to require urgent action measures are elaborated and defined which implement the requirement. Since such a measure in itself is an innovation and may imply more or less changes within the organization, all affected stakeholders should be incorporated into planning and performing the measure.

Step 6 - Re-Evaluation. A re-evaluation should be performed regularly. The initial tailoring step can be reduced to checking if the selected business characteristics still apply or the organization has changed significantly. The consolidation and refinement of requirements in the second step is only necessary if business characteristics have changed or new stakeholders are involved and typically can be performed quickly. The evaluation of requirements fulfillment and the subsequent steps should then be performed with great care, but may focus only on those requirements, which are new or previously were the trigger of an improvement measure.

The outlined approach allows organizations to make more informed, transparent, and documented innovation management decisions. Moreover, foreseeable changes to business characteristics may be evaluated early for changes to the innovation system.

6   Summary, Conclusions, Future Work

The paper presented research on innovation management in SPL-based businesses, based on the assumption that these businesses are substantially different from others and therefore classical innovation concepts and methods need adaptation.

The presented innovation system customization framework and method are based on the identification of relevant software business characteristics and the generic, in-advance identification of the requirements these characteristics pose on specific innovation management elements. These generic requirements are envisioned to serve as major input into the discussion related to innovation system design, based on and tailored through an assessment of an organization's specific business characteristics.

The sets of requirements identified show significant, important, and valid differences for each of the innovation management elements. The current state of the requirements is considered sufficient to demonstrate the capabilities of the approach. The requirements are consistent within each and across all innovation management elements. Potential dependencies between requirements induced by dependencies between characteristics of different business criteria are currently not modeled within the framework and require consolidation within the application of the framework.

The developed innovation system customization approach can thus serve as a sound basis for understanding the specific innovation challenges and deriving a sound basis of requirements for implementation or improvement of an organization's specific innovation system. The separation of the resulting requirements into innovation management elements, should further allow integration with existing approaches to process improvement, e.g. by interpreting the requirements identified for *'innovation process'* as a kind of *process outcomes*. On the other hand, process improvement can be seen as one specific kind of innovation (cf. also section 2.1 on innovation subjects). Establishing this mutual link to process assessment and improvement (e.g. SPICE type process assessment [31]) is a candidate path for future work.

The collection of innovation system requirements for SPLE linked to software business characteristics is intended to be a living framework that is continuously updated with and evaluated against the results of its application. The incorporation of feedback from application into the framework is an essential pillar of the approach and envisioned to satisfactorily stabilize the framework as part of future work.

The approach builds on work in the field of system family-oriented systems engineering and has been partly applied in contexts targeting the improvement of product management and engineering in SPLE contexts, but is not yet fully validated. Due to this initial focus on SPLE, aspects of service innovation as an important innovation subject are currently only marginally addressed.

In the course of future work, part of the requirements definitions need to be sharpened and refined to make their SPLE-focus more explicit where appropriate. On the other hand, explicit application of SPLE is not a fundamental prerequisite for applying the conceptual framework to other businesses. In particular, organizations that develop multiple software products without explicitly applying SPLE could also use the framework and benefit from it by improving their innovation systems. In this context, it is of particular interest to analyze the extent to which peculiarities of SPLE are reflected in the currently defined characteristics and requirements.

Acknowledgements. The work presented builds on work carried out in the project *"Systematic Improvement of the Solutions Business" (SISB)* with *Siemens AG*. The work on product management and the customization framework for innovation was supported within the COMET-Programme of the Austrian Research Promotion Agency (FFG) within the projects *INSPiRE (INtegrated and Sustainable PRoduct Engineering)* and *SPiRE (Lightweight Software Product and pRocess Evolution).*

References

1. Davila, T., Epstein, M.J., Shelton, R.: Making Innovation Work: How to Manage It, Measure It, and Profit from It. Wharton School Publishing (2006)
2. Cooper, R.G., Kleinschmidt, E.J.: Stage-Gate process for new product success. Innovation Management U3 (2001), http://stage-gate.eu/articles/stage-gate.pdf (accessed: June 2013)
3. Cooper, R.G.: The invisible success factors in product innovation. Journal of Product Innovation Management 16(2), 115–133 (1999)
4. Jiménez-Zarco, A.I., Pilar Martínez-Ruiz, M., Llamas-Alonso, R.: The Impact of Success Factors on New Services Performance. In: Proceedings to the International Federation of Scholarly Associations of Management (IFSAM) and the Association of University Professors of Management (VHB) VIIIth World Congress in Berlin (2006)

5. Perl, E.: Grundlagen des Innovations- und Technologiemanagements (in German). In: Strebel, H. (ed.) Innovations- und Technologiemanagement (in German), Vienna, Austria. UTB, vol. 2455, pp. 15–48. WUV Universitätsverlag (2003)

6. Hauschildt, J., Salomo, S.: Innovationsmanagement. 4/E, Verlag Franz Vahlen (2007)

7. Vahs, D., Burmester, R.: Innovationsmanagement, Stuttgart, Germany (2002)

8. Schröder, H.H.: Paradigmen für das Management von Innovationen - eine kritische Analyse. In: Strebel, H. (ed.) Innovation und Umwelt, Graz/Vienna, pp. 23–76 (2002)

9. Cooper, R.G.: Winning at New Products: Pathways to Profitable Innovation. Microsoft Whitepaper (December 2005)

10. Cooper, R.G., Edgett, S.J., Kleinschmidt, E.J.: Optimizing the Stage-Gate Process: What Best Practice Companies Are Doing – Part 1. Research Technology Management 45(5) (2002)

11. Armbruster, H., Kirner, E., Lay, G.: Patterns of Organisational Change in European Industry. Fraunhofer ISI (2006)

12. Specht, G., Beckmann, G., Amelingmayer, J.: F&E-Management, Stuttgart (2002)

13. Osterwalder, A.: The Business Model Ontology: A Proposition in a Design Science Approach, Dissertation, University of Lausanne (2004)

14. Hofbauer, G.: Erfolgsfaktoren bei der Einführung von Innovationen, Heft Nr. 3. aus der Reihe Arbeitsberichte – Working Papers (2004),
http://opus4.kobv.de/opus4-haw/files/18/ABWP_03.pdf
(accessed: June 2013)

15. Verworn, B., Herstatt, C.: Modell des Innovationsprozesses. Arbeitspapier (6) (September 2000),
http://www.tu-harburg.de/tim/downloads/arbeitspapiere/Arbeitspapier_6.pdf (accessed: June 2013)

16. Schaible, J., Hönig, A.: High-Tech Marketing in der Praxis. Verlag Vahlen (1996)

17. Backhaus, K., Voeth, M.: Industriegütermarketing, 8. Auflage, Vahlen (2007)

18. Davies, A., Hobday, M.: The Business of Projects: Managing Innovation in Complex Products and Systems. Cambridge University Press (2005)

19. Hobday, M.: Product Complexity, Innovation and Industrial Organisation. Research Policy 26, 689–710 (1998)

20. Stallinger, F., Neumann, R.: A Framework for Innovation System Customization for Product Line-based Software Businesses. In: 39th Euromicro Conference on Software Engineering and Advanced Applications (SEAA 2013), Santander, Spain, September 4-6, pp. 94–97. IEEE CS (2013)

21. Northrop, L.: Software Product Line Essentials, Software Engineering Institute, Carnegie Mellon University, Pittsburg, PA (2008),
http://www.sei.cmu.edu/library/assets/spl-essentials.pdf
(accessed: June 2013)

22. Matys, E.: Praxishandbuch Produktmanagement: Grundlagen und Instrumente (in German), 3rd edn. Campus Verlag (2005)

23. Sneed, H.M., Hasitschka, M., Teichmann, M.-T.: Software-Produktmanagement (in German). Dpunkt Verlag Heidelberg (2005)

24. Pohl, K., Böckle, G., van der Linden, F.: Software Product Line Engineering – Foundations, Principles, and Techniques. Springer, Berlin (2005)

25. van der Linden, F.J., Schmid, K., Rommes, E.: Software Product Lines in Action: The Best Industrial Practice in Product Line Engineering. Springer, New York (2007)

26. ISO/IEC 26550:2013. Software and systems engineering — Reference model for product line engineering and management. International Standards Organization (2013)

27. Stallinger, F., Neumann, R., Schossleitner, R., Zeilinger, R.: Linking Software Life Cycle Activities with Product Strategy and Economics: Extending ISO/IEC 12207 with Product Management Best Practices. In: O'Connor, R.V., Rout, T., McCaffery, F., Dorling, A. (eds.) SPICE 2011. CCIS, vol. 155, pp. 157–168. Springer, Heidelberg (2011)

28. Stallinger, F., Neumann, R.: Extending ISO/IEC 12207 with Software Product Management: A Process Reference Model Proposal. In: Mas, A., Mesquida, A., Rout, T., O'Connor, R.V., Dorling, A. (eds.) SPICE 2012. CCIS, vol. 290, pp. 93–106. Springer, Heidelberg (2012)

29. ISO/IEC 12207:2008. Systems and software engineering — Software life cycle processes. International Standards Organization (2008)

30. Böckle, G.: Innovation Management for Product Line Engineering Organizations. In: Obbink, H., Pohl, K. (eds.) SPLC 2005. LNCS, vol. 3714, pp. 124–134. Springer, Heidelberg (2005)

31. ISO/IEC 15504-2. Information Technology – Process Assessment. International Standards Organization (2003)

A Lightweight Assessment Method for Medical Device Software Processes

Fergal McCaffery, Paul Clarke, and Marion Lepmets

Regulated Software Research Centre, Dundalk Institute of Technology, Dundalk, Ireland
{Fergal.Mccaffery,Paul.Clarke,Marion.Lepmets}@dkit.ie

Abstract. This paper outlines the MDevSPICE-Adept process assessment method. MDevSPICE-Adept is a lightweight process assessment method that has been created for the MDevSPICE software process assessment model which is currently being developed for the medical device industry. MDevSPICE is a fully validated release of a medical device software process assessment model (formerly known as Medi SPICE), which was developed by the authors. While the MDevSPICE process assessment model is detailed and comprehensive, there is industry demand for a lightweight medical device software process assessment method. To address this requirement the MDevSPICE-Adept method has been developed. Details on how this has taken place and the procedures for implementing an MDevSPICE-Adept process assessment are presented. Information is also provided regarding how an MDevSPICE process assessment was undertaken in an Irish based medical device company. A summary of the issues identified from this process assessment and the actions taken to facilitate process improvement is also presented. Finally, plans for future work are discussed.

Keywords: Medical Device Software, Software Process Improvement, Lightweight Process Assessment Method, Medical Device Software Process Assessment, MDevSPICE.

1   Introduction

Due to the potential threat that medical devices pose to patients, clinicians and third parties their development is highly regulated. In recent years there has been a significant increase in the role and importance that software plays in the healthcare industry [1]. The outcome of this has been the substantial increase in the functionality, complexity and size of software components in medical devices [2]. This development has been recognized by the European Union (EU) in their latest amendment to the Medical Devices Directive (MDD) (2007/47/EC) [3]. As a result, standalone software may now be classified as an active medical device in its own right in the EU. Given the importance and relevance of this measure, the European Commission released a guidance document for the qualification and classification of standalone medical device software MEDDEV 2.1/6 [4] in January 2012. In the United States (US), the Food and Drug Administration (FDA) are responsible for the

A. Mitasiunas et al. (Eds.): SPICE 2014, CCIS 477, pp. 144–156, 2014.

regulation and approval of medical devices and have published software specific guidance documents for medical device software developers, such as the *General Principles of Software Validation* [5], *Off-the-Shelf Software Use in Medical Devices* [6] and *Guidance on the Content of Premarket Submissions for Software Contained in Medical Devices* [7]. To address the increasingly important role that software now plays, the FDA recently published the *Medical Device Data Systems Final Rule* [8] and *Draft Guidance in Relation to Mobile Applications* [9].

Given the mission critical nature of medical device software compliance with the relevant regulations, international standards and guidance documents of the region where a medical device is to be marketed is obligatory [10]. In the EU, the receipt of the CE mark is essential and in the US, FDA approval is required. There are approval bodies performing similar roles in other countries including China, Canada, India, Japan, and Australia. A key international standard for achieving regulatory compliance is IEC 62304:2006 [11] and its aligned standards ISO13485:2003 [12], ISO 14971:2007 [13], EN 60601-1:2005 [14], IEC 62366:2007 [15] and IEC 60812:2006 [16]. Information is also provided in relevant technical reports IEC/TR 80002-1:2009 [17] and IEC/TR 61508:2003 [18]. Despite the provision of these international standards, technical reports, regulations and guidance documents, the information they offer is high-level and no specific methods for performing the essential activities required have been provided [19].

It is therefore not surprising, given the importance that achieving regulatory approval plays, that organizations developing medical device software have focused on achieving compliance rather than implementing efficient processes and undertaking process improvement [20]. Previously this was not a critical issue due to the limited proportion of software in medical devices and it was acceptable to take a compliance centric approach. This is no longer the case and there is now a particular requirement for highly effective and efficient software development processes to be in place. These processes need to be defined in a regulatory compliant manner and then adopted to produce the required deliverables in order to achieve approval [19]. To address this requirement, MDevSPICE (formerly known as Medi SPICE [21]), a medical device software process assessment model (PAM) is being developed and validated, which will be made available to the international medical device industry during November 2014. While the MDevSPICE PAM is a comprehensive and detailed process assessment model based on process reference model (PRM) both of which are described in Section 2, there is also industry demand for a lightweight medical device software process assessment method [22]. The MDevSPICE-Adept process assessment method has been developed to help address this requirement and this is discussed in section 3 along with the procedure for its implementation. Section 4 outlines how a MDevSPICE-Adept process assessment was undertaken and provides a summary of the process improvement plan which was collaboratively developed based on the findings report. Section 5 provides a summary and context for future work based on this research.

2   PRM and PAM of MDevSPICE

Existing software process models like the Capability Maturity Model Integration (CMMI) [23] and ISO 15504-5:2012 [24] (SPICE) describe generic software development best practices and were not developed to provide coverage of all the necessary areas required to achieve domain specific requirements such as medical device regulatory compliance [25]. To address the requirement for a medical device software development, the Regulated Software Research Centre (RSRC) at Dundalk Institute of Technology (DkIT) undertook extensive research in the area [19]. This resulted in work commencing on the development of MDevSPICE PAM (initially known as Medi SPICE), a medical device specific process assessment model, which is being developed in collaboration with the SPICE community, the international medical device standards community and the international medical device software industry. This process assessment model is in line with Automotive SPICE [26], a domain specific process assessment model for the automotive industry.

The MDevSPICE PAM is based upon the latest version of ISO/IEC 15504-5:2012 and provides coverage of the relevant medical device regulations, standards, technical reports and guidance documents, as illustrated on Fig.1. These include IEC 62304:2006 and its aligned standards (ISO 14971 [13], ISO 13485 [12], IEC TR 80002-1 [17], IEC 62366 [15], IEC 60601-1 [14], IEC 82304 [27]), the FDA guidance documents on premarket submission [7], off-the-shelf software use [6] and software validation [5]. The MDevSPICE PAM is partly founded upon the process reference model for IEC 62304 (IEC TR 80002-3:2014 [28]) as this is the standard for medical device software life cycle processes and is therefore the pivotal standard for medical device software development. It is also worth noting that the development of IEC TR 80002-3 was initiated and lead by the authors (since October 2010) in association with the International medical device standards community combining the requirements from IEC 62304:2006 and ISO/IEC 12207:2008 [29]. Both IEC 62304 and IEC TR 80002-3 describe the process requirements for different software safety classes. This feature has also been carried forward to the MDevSPICE PAM where each process outcome derived from IEC 62304 indicates the safety class for which it is required.

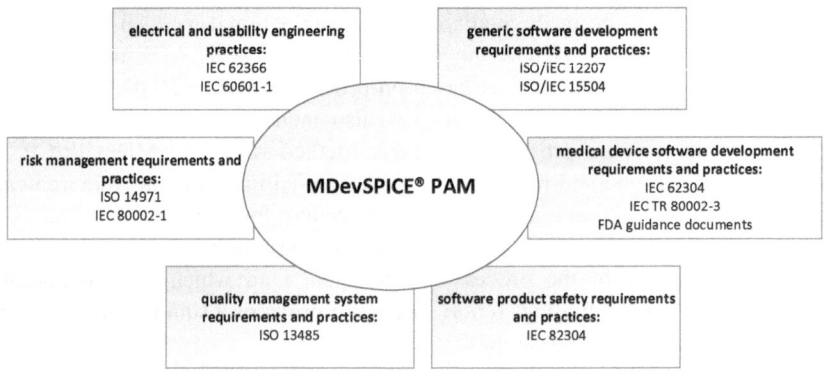

Fig. 1. Collection of requirements and practices of MDevSPICE PAM

The MDevSPICE PAM contains a Process Reference Model (PRM) which extends the requirements from IEC TR 80002-3 to include requirements from system level and supporting processes described in ISO/IEC 12207:2008. The MDevSPICE PRM consists of 24 processes which are fundamental to the development and maintenance of regulatory compliant medical device software. Each process has a clearly defined purpose and process outcomes that must be accomplished to achieve that purpose. One way to achieve these process outcomes is through implementing the base practices described in the MDevSPICE PAM. The MDevSPICE PAM extends the PRM with additional process elements of base practices and work products and the measurement framework allowing process capability ratings. Similarily to ISO/IEC 15504-5, the MDevSPICE PAM also has two-dimensional view of process capability. In one dimension, it describes a set of base practices that allow the achievement of the process outcomes and purpose defined in the PRM; this is termed the process dimension. In the other dimension, the PAM describes capabilities that relate to the process capability levels and process attributes, this is termed the capability dimension.

The MDevSPICE PAM extends the PRM with a set of work products for every process that are the inputs and outputs of the processes. In ISO/IEC 15504-5, work products are the informal evidence collected to support the process capability rating. In MDevSPICE PAM, these are both informal as well as normative, i.e. mandatory work products as required in the regulatory standards. The existence of these mandatory work products together with their required content are addressed as process outcomes during the process assessment.

The MDevSPICE PAM also includes the measurement framework, which is based on ISO/IEC 15504-2:2003 [30]. Similarly to ISO/IEC 15504-2, the MDevSPICE PAM also has six process Capability Levels, with one or more process attributes per Capability Level from Level 1 onwards.

The objective of undertaking an MDevSPICE process assessment is to determine the state of a medical device organisation's software processes and practices in relation to the regulatory requirements of the industry and to identify areas for process improvement [31]. It can also be used as part of the supplier selection process when an organisation wishes to outsource or offshore part or all of their medical device software development to a third party or remote division [32]. An MDevSPICE process assessment can also be conducted for pre-qualification purposes as it provides a preliminary readiness overview of regulatory compliance.

The MDevSPICE PRM and PAM were released in stages and each stage was extensively reviewed by interested parties from the SPICE community, representatives from international standards bodies and medical device industry experts. This collaborative approach is seen as a key element in the development of the MDevSPICE PAM to ensure coverage of both the generic software best practices and medical device software regulatory requirements [31]. The MDevSPICE PAM is a comprehensive and detailed process assessment model and its overall objective is to provide both process capability and conformity assessment ratings to support first, second or third party assessments. It is envisaged that results from these assessments may be recognized by the relevant regulatory bodies.

3   Requirements for MDevSPICE-Adept Process Assessment Method

As outlined in section two, there is a specific requirement for a detailed and comprehensive process assessment model, which is specific to the medical device domain and that MDevSPICE PAM is addressing. as with other process models i.e. CMMI and IEC 15504-5:2012. A full MDevSPICE process assessment will require considerable planning and resources to successfully undertake. While MDevSPICE process assessment is being developed with the objective of being as efficient as possible, the necessity for rigour dictates the level of planning, resources and analysis required for its successful implementation. While the need for and importance of MDevSPICE process assessment is understood [21], it was also appreciated by the RSRC that there is a specific requirement for a lightweight assessment method in the medical device software industry [33]. In particular, there was industry led demand for a lightweight assessment method based on the MDevSPICE PAM. This was communicated directly to the RSRC by numerous medical device organisations. To address this specific requirement, the MDevSPICE-Adept method was developed. This also provided an opportunity to leverage the extensive research [19] and level of detail, which developing the MDevSPICE PAM required.

A process assessment method provides a process description for conducting process assessments. The rigour of the method depends on the purpose of the process assessment. For Class 3 third-party assessment, the rigour is highest i.e. the amount of evidence collected and analysed is greatest, and assessor competence and experience highest. The more rigorous the chosen process assessment method, the more detailed are the process assessment results. On the other hand, the more rigorous the method, the more resource-demanding and time-consuming is the process assessment.

To be effective, MDevSPICE-Adept required the employment of a lightweight approach for undertaking software process assessment and improvement. This included the use of a limited number of personnel to carry out and participate in the assessment while also maximising the benefit of the time and effort of those involved. It was envisaged that MDevSPICE process assessment would eventually encompass all the MDevSPICE PAM processes. It was therefore recognized that an assessment could take place over a day or a number of days depending on how many processes were being assessed. It was also important that organizations could select the specific processes which were of most benefit for achieving their business goals. The focus of the method had to be on the evaluation of the essential base practices, key work products and the achievement of the process outcomes which were necessary for the attainment of the specific process purpose being assessed. MDevSPICE-Adept therefore needed to be process dimension centric in its focus. Finally, the objective of undertaking an MDevSPICE-Adept process assessment was not to receive formal certification, but rather to identify an organization's strengths and weaknesses and to facilitate process improvement. Having defined the criteria which had to be met, the next step was to undertake the development of MDevSPICE-Adept method.

3.1   Developing the MDevSPICE-Adept Method

The RSRC, having previously successfully developed and implemented three lightweight software process assessment methods Adept [33], Med-Adept [34] and Med-Trace [35], the objective was to leverage that experience and utilise it for the development of MDevSPICE-Adept. It was in this context that work commenced on the development of MDevSPICE-Adept. It was recognized that this process assessment method needed to cover more processes and provide more detailed analysis than those methods which had been previously developed. While this was the case, MDevSPICE-Adept was still required to be lightweight to satisfy the industry demand. The MDevSPICE-Adept method was developed through process assessment engagements in medical device industry.

The first task was to identify the initial set of processes that would be included in the MDevSPICE process assessment. The goal was to select a limited number of processes that would be most beneficial and relevant to industry with the onsite process assessment no longer than 2 days. To achieve this, industry experts were consulted on the 24 processes of the PAM from which they selected the preliminary 11 processes (most of which are from IEC 62304):

- System requirements analysis
- Software development planning
- Software requirements analysis
- Software architectural design
- Software detailed design
- Software unit implementation and verification
- Software integration and integration testing
- Software system testing
- Software risk management
- Software configuration management
- Software problem resolution

While these were the initial processes selected for inclusion in MDevSPICE-Adept, it is also possible to extend this list of processes to provide coverage of all the MDevSPICE processes. This can only be done with an extended onsite process assessment demanding more time and resources from the company that is being assessed.

The MDevSPICE PAM had been developed for each of the initial processes which were based on best practice as outlined by the latest version of ISO/IEC 15504-5 and the specific requirements of the medical device regulations, standards, technical reports and guidance documents. As a result, each process had a defined purpose and process outcomes, base practices and work products were also included for the achievement of these process outcomes and process purpose. In addition, each outcome and base practice was cross referenced to the standard they were derived from. To facilitate the process assessment, each of the initial processes were evaluated and specific questions identified based on the MDevSPICE PAM. This work was undertaken by six members of the RSRC team with extensive experience in SPI and knowledge of medical device software development. Having defined the assessment instrument, the next step was to develop the specific process for undertaking an MDevSPICE assessment.

The objective of MDevSPICE-Adept is to assist an organisation to gain an understanding of the state of their current software development processes when measured against the selected MDevSPICE PAM processes. The MDevSPICE PAM is essentially a "one stop shop" for all associated medical device software related requirements. The MDevSPICE PAM contains the requirements of all the software related medical device standards and the additional software engineering best practices from ISO/IEC 15504-5. Even though the MDevSPICE process assessment does not provide any official certification against any of the medical device standards, the output of the assessment will provide both the MDevSPICE process capability rating as well as the gaps that exist against the requirements of the medical device software standards included in the MDevSPICE PAM. This type of combinatory process assessment result allows targeted activities for both process improvement and an increased regulatory compliance to be undertaken by the assessed organization.

3.2   The Procedure for Undertaking a Lightweight MDevSPICE Process Assessment Following the MDevSPICE-Adept Method

Based on the RSRC's previous experience of developing and undertaking lightweight software process assessments [33], the seven stage procedure for undertaking an MDevSPICE Assessment following the MDevSPICE-Adept method was defined. It was decided the assessment team should normally consist of two assessors who share responsibility for conducting the assessment.

The seven stages of the procedure are as follows: As a precursor to undertaking an assessment a preliminary meeting between the lead assessor and the company takes place. This is the first stage in the procedure and during this meeting the lead assessors discusses the main drivers for the company wishing to undertake an assessment. In this context the expectations regarding what can be realistically achieved are discussed and the procedure for undertaking the assessment is outlined. If there is agreement a schedule is drawn up.

At the second stage the lead assessor has a meeting with the staff and management from the company who will be participating in the assessment where an overview of the MDevSPICE-Adept assessment method is presented and details of what their participation will involve is outlined.

On the agreed date the onsite assessment commences which is the third stage in the procedure. For each process the lead assessor conducts interviews based on the scripted MDevSPICE-Adept questions with the relevant personnel and evaluates the responses. The second assessor who also participates in the interviews prepares interview notes and may ask additional questions when clarification is required. In addition work products may also be requested and reviewed as part of this stage.   A maximum of five processes are assessed in a single day with the interviews for each process taking approximately one hour.

At the fourth stage the findings report is prepared off site based on the data gathered at stage three. Each process is reviewed in turn and relevant strengths and issues (weaknesses) are identified based on the evaluation and interview notes. Suggested actions to address these issues and to facilitate process improvement are outlined and discussed. The possibility for the use of appropriate agile and lean practices is also considered. These are then documented and included in the findings report. This is a joint effort between the assessors and may include other SPI and/or lean and agile experts if required.

The findings report is then presented to the management and staff who took part in the assessment which is the fifth stage in the procedure.

Having provided adequate time for the findings report to be read and considered by the organization, at the sixth stage the contents of the report is discussed in detail with the relevant management and staff. At this point specific objectives for process improvement are collaboratively defined based on the findings report which results in the development of a process improvement plan. Given the lightweight nature of MDevSPICE-Adept improvements that offer the greatest benefits in terms of compliance, quality and the achievement of business goals are selected for inclusion in this plan.

At the seventh stage in the procedure the organization having implemented the process improvement plan have the opportunity of having the processes reassessed. Based on this, a final detailed report is prepared which highlights what has been achieved and an updated improvement plan is also provided.

4   Conducting the Lightweight MDevSPICE Process Assessment Following the MDevSPICE-Adept Method

Having developed the MDevSPICE-Adept Assessment method and the procedure for its implementation the first assessment took place in an Irish based medical device company Irish Medical (a pseudonym). The company develops both automotive and medical device software. Each of their products contains both hardware and software and the role that software plays has considerably increase over the last number of years. They produce software for medical devices that will be marketed in the EU and the US so their products must conform to the MDD to receive the CE mark and the FDA regulations.

Having agreed that an assessment would take place (Stage 1), it was decided by the company that 10 out of the 11 processes would be assessed over a two day period (Stage 2). Software problem resolution process was omitted as an explicit process for managing problems did not exist in the Irish Medical at the time of the process assessment. The process assessment, i.e. Stage 3, was undertaken by two assessors from the RSRC. Based on the results of the process assessment, a findings report was prepared and presented in Stage 4. The focus of the report was that for each process the strengths and issues were highlighted, in addition suggested actions to facilitate process improvement were provided. Based on the findings report, the process improvement objectives and process improvement plan were collaboratively defined and developed with the company (Stage 5-6). A summary of the issues identified for each process and the actions taken to address these issues and facilitate improvement were outlined in the process improvement plan of Stage 7.

Irish Medical decided that the 10 critical processes to be assessed are the following:

- System requirements analysis
- Software development planning
- Software requirements analysis
- Software architectural design
- Software detailed design
- Software unit implementation and verification
- Software integration and integration testing
- Software system testing
- Software risk management
- Software configuration management

All of the 10 processes are described in IEC 62304 and IEC TR 80002-3 with the exception of System requirements analysis. This is an important process for Irish Medical as it develops software for embedded medical device systems and requires efficient traceability of requirements from system level to software level.

In conducting the process assessment in Irish Medical, it was possible to not just highlight strengths and weaknesses in the process implementation, but it was also possible to tailor the scope of the process assessment to suit the needs of the organisation. Fig 2 below demonstrates the coverage of the process assessment from the underlying standards perspective. In practice, additional standards can be added to full MDevSPICE assessments but for the purpose of this MDevSPICE-Adept process assessment, this coverage was deemed sufficient.

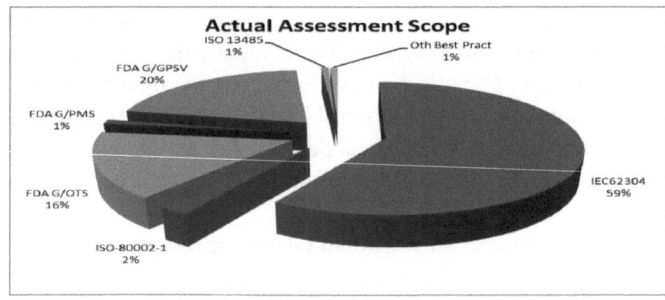

Fig. 1. Scope of Irish Medical process assessment from the underlying standards perspective

One of the primary observations from this process assessment was the extent to which the basic requirements of IEC 62304 were in fact supplemented with best practice know-how from a range of other standards, thus resulting in a more thorough evaluation of the software development process capability. It is furthermore the case that for each of the underlying sources, it is possible to also produce findings in relation to coverage of that particular standard – and not just for individual processes but for groups of processes and the process set as a whole. For example, Figure 3 demonstrates how an overall coverage of software development process requirements for safety class C software development based on IEC 62304 might appear.

At an individual process level, the participating company was provided with detailed information on the process capability rating and areas of greatest weakness. One example of such related to software configuration management, an area that the organisation is now actively addressing.

The findings report was positively received by Irish Medical as was the whole process assessment. The collaborative nature of the development of the process improvement plan provides motivation for it successful implementation. The plan is currently being implemented and when this is complete the opportunity to have the processes reassessed is available – and the company in question is positively predisposed to introducing a regular process assessment in order to better understand and improve their software processes. The process assessment also identified areas of strength in the organisation. For example, the company had very good risk management and traceability procedures in place. It is important to state that the MDevSPICE-Adept process assessment method highlights the strengths as well as the weaknesses in an organization.

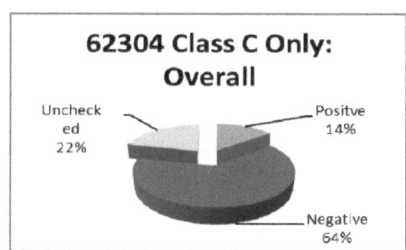

Fig. 2. Sample IEC 62304 safety class C coverage

5   Conclusion

The MDevSPICE framework consists of both the MDevSPICE PAM and the MDevSPICE-Adept process assessment method. The MDevSPICE PAM is a comprehensive and detailed domain specific process assessment model for medical device software development. It provides the basis for in-depth analysis and assessment of each process including the measurement framework for process capability determination. As a result, the findings from a Class 3 MDevSPICE process assessment can be comprehensive and detailed. On the other hand, MDevSPICE-Adept as a Class 1 lightweight assessment method has a different purpose. Its focus is high level and its role is to provide a snap shot of medical device software development processes, and to assist with regulatory compliance and process improvement in this context.

MDevSPICE-Adept is the largest and most detailed of the lightweight assessment methods developed by the RSRC. It is the result of industry demand and was developed to meet the requirement for an extensive yet lightweight medical device software assessment method. A pilot MDevSPICE-Adept assessment has recently been successfully implemented in Ireland. Feedback from the assessment was very positive. In line with our strategy for MDevSPICE-Adept method, we will develop various sets of initial processes based on the different demands of medical device software development organizations based on compliance requirements with specific standards. Given the level of demand it is also our objective to carry out additional MDevSPICE-Adept assessments both in Ireland and in collaboration with our international colleagues. We also plan to release Class 1 and Class 2 MDevSPICE process assessment methods in November 2014.

Acknowledgments. This research is supported by Enterprise Ireland and the European Regional Development Fund (ERDF) under the National Strategic Reference Framework (NSRF) 2007-2013, grant number CF/2012/2631, and in part by the Science Foundation Ireland (SFI) Stokes Lectureship Programme, grant number 07/SK/I1299, and the SFI Principal Investigator Programme, grant number 08/IN.1/I2030, and in part by Lero.

References

1. Abraham, C., Nishiharas, E., Akiyama, M.: Transforming healthcare with information technology in Japan: A review of policy, people, and progress. International Journal of Medical Informatics 80(3), 157–170 (2011)
2. Lee, I., Pappas, G., Cleaveland, R., Hatcliff, J., Krogh, B., Lee, P., Rubin, H., Sha, L.: High-Confidence Medical Device Software And Systems. Computer 39(4), 33–38 (2006)
3. European Council, Council Directive 2007/47/EC (Amendment). In: Official Journal of The European Union: Luxembourg (2007)
4. European Commission, MEDICAL DEVICES: Guidance document- Qualification and Classification of stand alone software (MEDDEV 2.1/6). Brussels, Belgium (2012)
5. US FDA Center for Devices and Radiological Health, General Principles of Software Validation; Final Guidance for Industry and FDA Staff. CDRH: Rockville (2002)
6. US FDA Center for Devices and Radiological Health, Off-The-Shelf Software Use in Medical Devices; Guidance for Industry, medical device Reviewers and Compliance. CDRH: Rockville (1999)
7. US FDA Center for Devices and Radiological Health, Guidance for the Content of Premarket Submissions for Software Contained in Medical Devices. CDRH: Rockville (2005)
8. US FDA, 21 CFR Part 880 Medical Devices; Medical Device Data Systems Final Rule. Federal Register, 2011. vol. 76(31), pp. 8637 – 8649 (2011)
9. US FDA, Draft Guidance for Industry and Food and Drug Administration Staff Mobile Medical Applications (2011)
10. Vogel, D.A.: Medical Device Software Verification, Validation and Compliance, p. 432. Artech House, Norwood (2010)

11. IEC 62304:2006, Medical device software—Software life cycle processes. IEC: Geneva, Switzerland (2006)
12. ISO 13485:2003, Medical devices — Quality management systems — Requirements for regulatory purposes. ISO: Geneva, Switzerland (2003)
13. ISO 14971:2007, Medical Devices — Application of risk management to medical devices. ISO: Geneva, Switzerland (2007)
14. BS EN 60601-1:2005Medical electrical equipment – Part 1: General requirements for basic safety and essential performance. IEC: Geneva, Switzerland (2005)
15. IEC 62366:2007, Medical devices - Application of usability engineering to medical devices. IEC: Geneva, Switzerland (2007)
16. IEC 60812:2006, Analysis technique for system reliability - Procedure for failure modes and effects analysis (FMEA). IEC: Geneva, Switzerland (2006)
17. IEC/TR 80002-1:2009, Medical device software Part 1: Guidance on the application of ISO 14971 to medical device software. BSI: London (2009)
18. IEC/TR 61508:2005, Functional safety of electrical/electronic/ programmable electronic safety related systems. BSI: London (2005)
19. Mc Caffery, F., Burton, J., Casey, V., Dorling, A.: Software Process Improvement in the Medical Device Industry. In: Laplante, P. (ed.) Encyclopedia of Software Engineering, pp. 528–540. CRC Press Francis Taylor Group, New York (2010)
20. Denger, C., Feldmann, R., Host, M., Lindholm, C., Shull, F.: A Snapshot of the State of Practice in Software Development for Medical Devices. In: First International Symposium on Empirical Software Engineering and Measurement, Madrid, Spain (2007)
21. Mc Caffery, F., Dorling, A.: Medi SPICE: An Overview. In: International Conference on Software Process Improvement and Capability Determinations (SPICE), Finland (2009)
22. Casey, V., Mc Caffery, F.: Med-Trace: Traceability Assessment Method for Medical Device Software Development. In: European Systems and Software Process Improvement and Innovation Conference. Roskilde University, Denmark (2011)
23. CMMI Product Team, Capability Maturity Model Integration for Development Version1.3. Software Engineering Institute, Pittsburg PA (2010)
24. ISO/IEC 15504-5:2012, Information technology - Process Assessment - Part 5: An Exemplar Software Life Cycle Process Assessment Model. ISO (2012)
25. Mc Caffery, F., Dorling, A.: Medi SPICE Development. Software Process Maintenance and Evolution: Improvement 22(4), 255–268 (2010)
26. Automotive SIG, Automotive SPICE Process Assessment V 2.2 (August 21, 2005)
27. IEC/CD 82304:2014, Health Software - Part 1: General Requirements for Product Safety. ISO: Geneva, Switzerland (2014)
28. IEC/TR 80002-3:2014, Medical Device Software - Part 3: Process reference model for medical device software life cycle processes (IEC 62304). ISO: Geneva, Switzerland (2014)
29. ISO/IEC 12207:2008, Systems and software engineering - Software life cycle processes. ISO: Geneva, Switzerland (2008)
30. ISO/IEC 15504-2:2003, Software engineering - Process assessment - Part 2: Performing an assessment, ISO: Geneva, Switzerland (2003)
31. Mc Caffery, F., Dorling, A., Casey, V.: Medi SPICE: An Update. In: International Conference on Software Process Improvement and Capability Determinations (SPICE), Pisa, Italy (2010)
32. Casey, V.: Virtual Software Team Project Management. Journal of the Brazilian Computer Society 16(2), 83–96 (2010)

33. Mc Caffery, F., Richardson, I., Coleman, G.: Adept – A Software Process Appraisal Method for Small to Medium-sized Irish Software Development Organisations. In: European Systems & Software Process Improvement and Innovation (EuroSPI 2006), Joensuu, Finland (2006)
34. Mc Caffery, F., Casey, V.: Med-Adept: A Lightweight Assessment Method for the Irish Medical Device Software Industry. In: European Systems & Software Process Improvement and Innovation Conference (EuroSPI), Grenoble, France (2010)
35. Casey, V., Mc Caffery, F.: A lightweight traceability assessment method for medical device software. Journal of Software Maintenance and Evolution Research and Practice (2011)

A Safety-Critical Assessment Process

Risto Nevalainen[1] and Timo Varkoi[2]

[1] Finnish Software Measurement Association – FiSMA ry, Finland
[2] Spinet Oy, Finland
risto.nevalainen@fisma.fi, timo.varkoi@spinet.fi

Abstract. Use of systems containing software is increasing rapidly in the safety-critical domain. It creates pressure to develop more rigorous process assessment methods for assessing systems and software development. The assessment process aims to ensure credibility and repeatability of assessment results. The Nuclear SPICE method consists of a process assessment model and a documented assessment process for safety-critical domain. The Nuclear SPICE method applies a classification scheme for assessment type that is a combination of assessment class and rigour in safety. This paper presents the Nuclear SPICE assessment process, analyses its strength in covering regulatory requirements, and proposes new lines for its development.

Keywords: software process, safety, process assessment.

1 Introduction

Safety, by definition, means the expectation that a system does not, under defined conditions, lead to a state in which human life, health, property, or the environment is endangered [1]. Use of systems containing software is increasing rapidly in the safety-critical domain. This, consequently, creates pressure to develop more rigorous process assessment methods for assessing systems and software development.

Safety of a system is always considered as a characteristic of a product. There is no direct causality from the development process to the safety of a product. Despite of this, characteristics of the development process certainly can affect the safety of the product. [2]

Process assessment is a means to improve the quality of a software process or to ensure that process related requirements are met. A process assessment process guides the performance of an assessment and identifies the requirements that an assessment needs to meet. The assessment process aims to ensure credibility and repeatability of assessment results.

An example of the strictest safety-criticality is the nuclear power domain. We have been developing the Nuclear SPICE assessment method to meet the requirements of the domain. The Nuclear SPICE method consists of a process assessment model (PAM) and a documented assessment process for safety-critical domain. The method follows the principles found in ISO/IEC 15504. Our work is a part of the Finnish national nuclear safety program SAFIR2014, where new approaches and verification

A. Mitasiunas et al. (Eds.): SPICE 2014, CCIS 477, pp. 157–164, 2014.

and validation methods are developed for software-intensive system safety. Nuclear SPICE assessments are performed to evaluate the capability of systems and software development process applied in systems and software engineering for nuclear industry.

This paper describes the main elements of the Nuclear SPICE assessment process. Next, in Section 2, the assessment process is explained. Section 3 discusses the importance and applicability of the assessment process in safety-critical assessments, and section 4 presents some of the development ideas for the assessment process. Section 5 summarizes the discussion.

2   Main Elements of the Nuclear SPICE Assessment Process

Process assessment can be utilized for two purposes: to determine the capability of the processes for particular requirements or to gain understanding of an organization's own processes for process improvement. In this context, our main interest is to ensure product quality by demanding that the systems and software development processes meet appropriate process capability targets.

Determination of process capability typically aims to objectively resolve the state of the processes against a given set of requirements. These requirements express the necessary attributes of the processes and are typically documented in a Process Assessment Model (PAM). Often capability determination is carried out by a party external to the assessed organization and the result can be used for supplier selection or organization's recognition. Capability determination can also be used as an input for process improvement.

Typically an assessment process has at least five phases. 1) Planning is needed to identify the scope of the assessment (which processes to assess), when and where the assessment takes place, who will participate, material required and so on. 2) Data collection may consist of interviews, revision of related documents and measurements. 3) Data validation ensures that consistent and correct data has been collected. 4) Process attribute rating means that the elements of an implemented process are analyzed and their contribution to the achievement of the goals of the process are evaluated. 5) Reporting is needed to declare and record the results of the assessment.

In the Nuclear SPICE method the assessment process begins by

- identifying the sponsor and ensuring commitment to proceed,
- defining the purpose of the assessment (why it is being carried out),
- defining the scope of the assessment (which processes are being assessed), the assessment type (supplier selection, certification, etc.), the required rigor of the process, and what constraints, if any, apply to the assessment,
- deciding on an appropriate, documented assessment process,
- defining any additional information that needs to be gathered, and
- nominating the assessment participants and the assessment team and the roles of team.

Next, an assessment plan is developed and documented, where all activities to be performed in conducting the assessment together with a detailed assessment timetable is described. Also coordination with the assessment participants is planned to ensure that both the nuclear power license holder and the supplier resources are available as needed. The Lead Assessor ensures that the assessment team understands the assessment input, process and required output. The Organizational Unit to be assessed is briefed on the performance of the assessment.

Data required for evaluating the processes within the scope of the assessment is collected in a systematic manner. The strategy and techniques for the selection, collection, analysis of data and justification of the ratings need to be identified and demonstrable, as appropriate for the chosen assessment type. Each process identified in the assessment scope is assessed on the basis of objective evidence. The objective evidence gathered for each attribute of each process assessed must be sufficient to meet the assessment purpose and scope according to the selected assessment type. Objective evidence that supports the assessors' judgment of process attribute ratings is recorded and maintained in the assessment records that provide evidence to substantiate the ratings and to verify compliance with the requirements.

Actions are taken to ensure that the data is accurate and sufficiently covers every process instance identified in the assessment scope, including seeking information from first hand, independent sources; using past assessment results; and holding feedback sessions to validate the information collected. Some data validation may occur as the data is being collected.

For each process assessed, a rating is assigned for each process attribute up to and including the highest capability level defined in the assessment scope. Process attribute ratings provide the basis for repeatability across assessments. The Nuclear SPICE method applies NPLF-rating scale to process attributes as defined in ISO/IEC 33020 [3]. Additionally, rating can be addressed e.g. to each task of a sub-process or each expected outcome of a process. More important than the rating is the information provided for process improvement by identifying the weaknesses and strengths of the current practices in an organization.

Information that is relevant to the assessment and supports understanding of the output of the assessment is compiled. During this phase, the results of the assessment are analyzed and presented in a report. The report also covers any key issues raised during the assessment such as observed areas of strength and weakness and findings of high risk. The assessment results are presented in a way that enables comparison of the results, and communication to the sponsor and affected parties. An important feature of the Nuclear SPICE method is to report compliance with the domain specific standards.

According to ISO/IEC 33002 [4], a process assessment shall be performed according to a class of assessment. Factors determining the selection of the class of assessment shall include the following:

a)   level of rigour for performing an assessment that is relevant to the assessment purpose;
b)   level of confidence required in the assessment results;
c)   repeatability of assessment results;
d)   relative costs for an assessment in relationship to the needs of the business.

In the Nuclear SPICE method we use a classification scheme for the assessment type [5]. It is a combination of assessment class and rigour in safety. The Nuclear SPICE assessment process includes methods and techniques as evidences to cover needs for rigour. Selection of the assessment type has effects on the required resources: assessor competence and effort, timetable, cost, involvement of assessees, detail of reporting etc. Main driver in selecting an appropriate class are the expectations of the assessment sponsor or, when providing qualification evidence, the requirements of the regulator.

3   Applicability of the Nuclear SPICE Assessment Process

The usefulness of process assessment depends on stakeholder goals and expectations. Legislation in nuclear domain gives much power to the national regulatory body. For historical and political reasons each country has prepared a large number of regulatory guides, which have to be satisfied to qualify any system for operational use. For example, in Finland the regulator is STUK, Radiation and Nuclear Safety Authority. STUK has recently renewed their regulatory YVL Guides for design and construction of nuclear facilities [6]. Guides have a good and clear structure, where each requirement is identified, named and defined. As a whole, approximately 10 000 requirements are set.

The most important guide for digital safety systems including software is the YVL E.7 Electrical I&C systems for nuclear power plants. It has 379 requirements, of which approx. 50 are directly related to software. When also system and hardware are considered, about 140 requirements are relevant. Some general requirements can also be counted in, and then we have about 180 requirements. This is almost half of the E.7 requirements, and it is also the maximum Nuclear SPICE assessments can cover.

The other relevant regulatory guide is Common Position 2013 [7] (later CP2013). It has been prepared in cooperation by most of the Western European countries having nuclear power. CP2013 has around 600 requirements and about as many additional best practice recommendations. About 340 requirements are related to software, hardware or system (or all of them). CP 2013 is quite detailed and has a major overlap with the relevant nuclear software standards IEC 60880 and IEC 62138. Many of the requirements are even more detailed than the standards.

Table 1. Amount of selected requirements in relevant regulatory sources [5]

Regulatory source	# of relevant requirements	...of which belong to Safety Class 2	... of which belong to Safety Class 3	... of which are directly verifiable by Nuclear SPICE[1]
YVL E.7	185	157	127	118
Common Position 2013	337	241	210	109

---

[1] Criteria is that max. 3 processes are needed to verify the requirement. Extensive requirements requiring for example whole ENG or DEV categories of Nuclear SPICE are excluded here.

Table 1 explains some classifications we applied to the E.7 and CP2013 sets. One very important is the safety class. STUK defines three safety classes: 1, 2, and 3. Software is allowed only in safety class 2 and 3. In Table 1 we use the STUK definitions for safety classes to support Nuclear SPICE development.

Most of the requirements are common for both Safety Class 2 and 3. We can also see from Table 1 that about 30 – 60 % of YVL E.7 and Common Position requirements could be in principle verified by using Nuclear SPICE. That is not the case in real life. Most requirements are targeted for the licensee organization, whereas real development happens in the technology and/or in manufacturing companies. They are only indirectly interested in regulatory requirements, as a part of the customer requirements. So, we have to classify the requirements further also by the target organization or stakeholder. The result is presented in Table 2. [5]

Table 2. Amount of selected requirements by target stakeholder [5]

Regulatory source	# of relevant requirements	...of which belong licensee only	... of which belong to supplier only	... of which can be agreed between licensee and supplier[2]
YVL E.7	185	64	37	52
Common Position 2013	337	60	64	122

We can see that if process assessment is limited to the supplier organization, only approximately 20 % of requirements can be directly verified by Nuclear SPICE [5]. This proportion is quite low and needs more attention in the future.

4   Future Development of the Nuclear SPICE Assessment Process

Nuclear SPICE can be developed to cover all general and system/hardware/software requirements in the regulatory guides and nuclear standards. For that, we need to renew process assessment as a method to verify the requirements in relevant guides and standards.

The challenge is to integrate adequate data needed to demonstrate safety of a system. Process assessment serves as a means to look through all the evidences that are characterized as process outcomes that include the system itself. The evidences need to be collected partly from the system development processes and partly from the actual product and its verified requirements. (In this context we skip the validation/qualification process, mainly because in the nuclear domain we can find other approaches that validate the system products before they are taken into use.)

---

[2] Logic is 'either or', meaning that licensee and supplier can in principle agree which organisation has the main responsibility to satisfy the requirement.

The major problems with this approach are 1) the large amount of evidence data; 2) the timeliness of the findings; and 3) the trustworthiness of the result. Overall, the effect of development process to product quality, or a specific product characteristic like safety, is inexplicit. The extended assessment context is depicted in Fig. 1.

Fig. 1. The extended assessment context

First, to meet the requirements for rigour and applicable assessment type, the assessment scope tends to increase. It is also common that organizations in this domain have well-defined processes: amount of positive evidence needed is higher than in cases when negative evidence is met. The safety regulations and standards create further needs to be covered with added evidence collection. Finally the evidence needs to be addressed to not only the process outcomes, but to other safety requirements as well.

Second, the process evidence is collected of the development process, i.e. of a process applied before the system related to safety is deployed. This puts extra pressure to strict control in change management and requirements traceability.

Third, it is extremely difficult to evaluate when there is enough evidence that we can trust the result of an assessment. Especially with safety-critical assessments the method shall be trustworthy. It is easy to think that we should collect as much evidence as possible, but at some point the assessment is no more feasible. In the nuclear domain the regulator makes the decision and information for that decision is always collected from multiple sources with several approaches, and not only isolated process or product evaluations.

As a solution we must also consider other type of process qualities than capability. In the safety critical domain process capability seems to have less importance – the assumption is that the system development organizations meet at minimum the quality management system requirements of ISO 9001. One possibility is to define process quality attributes that address safety issues more directly, as in [2].

One promising topic is the use of process assessment data and results as claims or evidences in a safety case. Then we can improve safety demonstration capabilities and make qualification and licensing process easier for the nuclear power companies.

Also regulatory bodies want to see clear and well-reasoned safety documents to support their licensing process.

Some topics in the YVL E.7 and CP2013 are currently only weakly or not at all presented in Nuclear SPICE. Examples are operational experience, safety demonstration and cybersecurity. They need to be defined as processes and made assessable by the normal SPICE approach.

New evidences are needed, too. In the current SPICE (ISO/IEC 15504-5), the evidences are base and generic practices, resources and work products [8]. To demonstrate, and hopefully also to evaluate, achievement of safety, we need to include methods and techniques as evidence. They are reasonably well documented in the IEC 61508 set of standards, and for software in the Part 3 Annexes A, B and C. Strength of the methods as evidence for safety still remains partially open, because some methods are clearly outdated. New substituting methods have been developed but also their validity as the demonstration for safety is open.

5   Summary

The Nuclear SPICE method consists of a process assessment model and a documented assessment process for safety-critical domain. This paper presents the main elements of the Nuclear SPICE assessment process and the use of the process. Further, we analysed its strength to cover some of the relevant regulatory requirements. We concluded that only a small proportion of the regulatory requirement can be covered with traditional process assessment. As a result, we propose to extend process assessment towards safety assurance by using safety cases, new evidence types, and possibly new characteristics for process quality.

Acknowledgements. This work has been partially funded by Finnish national nuclear safety program SAFIR2014. In its project CORSICA, new approaches and V&V methods have been developed for software-intensive system safety. A method called Nuclear SPICE implements an assessment approach for safety-critical domain.

References

1. ISO/IEC/IEEE 24765:2010, Systems and Software Engineering Vocabulary,
   http://pascal.computer.org/sev_display/index.action
2. Varkoi, T.: Safety as a process quality characteristic. In: Woronowicz, T., Rout, T., O'Connor, R.V., Dorling, A. (eds.) SPICE 2013. CCIS, vol. 349, pp. 1–12. Springer, Heidelberg (2013)
3. ISO/IEC 33020, Information technology – Process assessment – Process measurement framework for assessment of process capability (2014)
4. ISO/IEC 33002, Information technology – Process assessment – Requirements for performing process assessment (2014)

5. Varkoi, T., Nevalainen, R.: Compliance and Rigour in Process Assessment for Safety-Critical Domain. In: Barafort, B., O'Connor, R.V., Poth, A., Messnarz, R. (eds.) EuroSPI 2014. CCIS, vol. 425, pp. 296–308. Springer, Heidelberg (2014)
6. STUK: New YVL guides, https://ohjeisto.stuk.fi/YVL/?en=on (accessed July 14, 2014)
7. Common Position revision 2013. Licensing of safety critical software for nuclear reactors. Common position of seven European nuclear regulators and authorised technical support organisations (2013)
8. ISO/IEC 15504-5:2012, Information technology – Process assessment – Part 5: An exemplar Process Assessment Model (2012)

Towards Transparent and Efficient Process Assessments for IT Service Management

Anup Shrestha, Aileen Cater-Steel, Mark Toleman, and Terry Rout

School of Management and Enterprise,
University of Southern Queensland
Toowoomba, Australia
{Anup.Shrestha,Aileen.Cater-Steel,Mark.Toleman,
Terry.Rout}@usq.edu.au

Abstract. IT service organisations recognise the value of conducting regular process assessments for continual service improvement. However lack of transparency and substantial costs deter industry adoption. We propose that the use of the international standard for process assessment ISO/IEC 15504 offers a transparent approach to address this challenge. Moreover, efficiency can be realized by a Decision Support System (DSS) tool to automate data collection and process capability calculations. This paper details a Design Science Research project to develop a software-mediated process assessment (SMPA) approach based on ISO/IEC 15504, ISO/IEC 20000 and the IT Infrastructure Library (ITIL®). We discuss the architecture of the SMPA approach and the role of ISO/IEC 15504 in the approach. This work contributes to practice as it may help IT managers to self-assess their processes using a standard model. The SMPA approach can also support assessors who perform formal assessments.

Keywords: ITSM Process Assessment, ISO/IEC 15504, automated process assessments, IT Service Management, Process Improvement.

1   Introduction

Research has shown that IT services account for 60-90 percent of the total cost of IT ownership [1]. The discipline of IT Service Management (ITSM) uses a process approach along with service-oriented thinking to manage IT in businesses. To provide guidance to implement the ITSM model, most organisations have chosen the IT Infrastructure Library (ITIL®) framework. ITIL was initially created by the UK government in the late 1980s [2]. The ITIL framework led to the creation of the international standard for ITSM: ISO/IEC 20000 [3]. The increasing role of ITSM in facilitating business requires continual improvement of IT service processes [4]. In the current ITIL framework, Continual Service Improvement (CSI) has been proposed as an important service lifecycle phase. CSI emphasises that there should be an ongoing effort to identify opportunities for improvement in ITSM processes [5]. The CSI concept further stresses that "continual assessment" is important to identify improvement opportunities for all processes [6].

A. Mitasiunas et al. (Eds.): SPICE 2014, CCIS 477, pp. 165–176, 2014.

In performing CSI activities many organisations have adopted process assessment techniques that employ a systematic measurement of processes [6]. The measurement results are then used to determine the capability of each process and monitor improvements. Process assessment, however, needs to be differentiated from audit: while the quality standard ISO 9001, for instance, can be used to conduct audits by checking conformance [7], process assessment goes one step beyond conformance checks and provides evaluation of process capabilities on a continuous scale [8].

Organisations would normally engage consulting firms to perform process assessments and to recommend on the ITSM areas requiring improvement [4]. However, qualified and experienced ITSM consultants can be scarce and expensive, particularly for small IT service providers. It is reported that process assessments are costly and time-consuming [6, 9]. In addition, assessment outcomes are often dictated by proprietary methods and tools employed by the assessors [5]. ITSM process assessment needs to be standardized in order to have any confidence in the assessment process and outcomes. Therefore, lack of transparency and increasing costs deter regular and consistent IT service process assessments.

An alternative to reliance on expensive consultants with proprietary process assessments is for the organisation to carry out a standard process assessment itself using software tools that may be integrated with a knowledge base of ITSM best practices. Risks of internal self-assessments include lack of objectivity, poor acceptance of findings and internal politics [6]. In order to mitigate these risks, during the assessment a decision support system (DSS) tool can facilitate a standards-based approach to collect data for process assessments and analyse process capabilities to recommend process improvements. This opportunity led us to develop a novel approach for ITSM: *Software-mediated Process Assessment (SMPA)*. The SMPA approach is a standards-based process assessment approach by which organisations can self-assess their processes using a DSS tool to determine process capabilities.

To lend objectivity and consistency to the SMPA approach, its activities are aligned with the international standard for process assessment: ISO/IEC 15504 [10]. The application of the standard in ITSM is relatively new [11]. An exemplar process assessment model for ITSM has been published as a part of the international standard for process assessment [12]. This paper illustrates development of the SMPA approach using the process assessment model for ITSM.

A literature review on ITSM process assessment is presented next to articulate the research problem. Research methodology is then discussed before a detailed account of the design and development of the SMPA architecture. Finally the conclusion section discusses the role and value of the SMPA approach that is supported by the application of ISO/IEC 15504.

2   Literature Review

The literature associated with ITSM process assessment is rooted in the concept of service and quality. Existing work on IT service quality has looked to the service marketing literature and focused on adapting the SERVQUAL instrument [13] to the context of IT service. Research on IT service quality has largely focused on user satisfaction measures while there is limited research related to processes [14].

While it is a widely-agreed concept that service quality is ultimately determined by what the customer perceives, service providers should also strive to improve their processes. Organisations can conduct customer satisfaction surveys to assess the outcome of the service provision. However this is unlikely to assist service providers in improving their processes [15]. There is a need for organisations to redefine their ITSM processes to manage IT service quality [14]. Existing literature on IT service quality in terms of processes has shown a lack of research on this topic [16].

Measuring IT services is a challenging feat that requires both quantitative and qualitative metrics based on diverse service quality measures such as IT service quality, information systems quality, process quality, customer satisfaction, service value and service behaviour [14]. Few studies provide methodological guidance on an approach to determine process quality measures. A self-assessment methodology based on business excellence models and Six Sigma process improvement techniques used ITIL maturity assessments [17] for several ITIL service delivery processes. However several critical flaws in the assessment approach were reported, such as surveys with compound questions that allowed only a "yes" or "no" response [18].

Using ITIL processes and the international standard for process assessment ISO/IEC 15504, evidence of repeatable and objective improvement in IT service quality has been reported [7]. Extensive work on the combination of ITIL and ISO/IEC 15504 led to the development of a popular ITSM process assessment approach called Tudor's IT Process Assessment (TIPA) [4]. TIPA has been promoted as a commercial framework for ITSM process assessment [19].

ITSM process assessment approaches are discussed as best practice guidelines in the IT industry. Many of the solutions offered for ITSM process assessment are commercially available (for example, ITIL assessment services or Pink Elephant). These services can be considered as a black box since the rationale behind the assessment activities is not fully disclosed. Moreover, due to proprietary assessment processes, inconsistent outcomes from different assessment services hinder comparisons. Non-ITIL approaches such as CMMI for Services or eSCM for service providers have transparent models and methods but lack DSS support in order to conduct process assessments.

Based on the academic literature review and existing industry practices, the two key problems of lack of transparency and lack of efficiency in ITSM process assessments are apparent. Addressing transparency and efficiency are two major challenges of process assessments [6]. These challenges are taken into account as important problems that must be solved by the SMPA approach. The research methodology used to develop the novel SMPA approach is discussed next.

3   Research Methodology

Design science research (DSR) is the underpinning research methodology applied for the development of the SMPA approach. The DSR approach [20] has the primary goal to develop a new artefact. DSR methodology is outcome-oriented and thereby provides guidelines for development and evaluation of research artefacts that contribute to specific bodies of knowledge. The artefact, referred to as the SMPA approach in this paper, is a method for IT service process assessments using ISO/IEC 15504 and facilitated by a DSS tool.

In DSR projects, researchers are advised to use established kernel theories to inform and justify the research work [21]. Task-technology fit (TTF) theory [22] is presented as the kernel theory for the design process to advise how the task challenges of process assessment and technology requirements for a new DSS tool fit together to articulate SMPA design and development. The TTF theory from Zigurs and Buckland [22] was adopted since the DSS tool used in the SMPA approach shares similar technology dimensions as proposed in the theory, viz. communication support, process structuring and information processing.

The six DSR methodology steps [23] were followed in the research: problem identification and motivation, objectives of a solution, design and development, demonstration, evaluation, and communication. Problem identification and solution objectives have been discussed in the Literature Review section. Details of the design and development of the SMPA approach as the research artefact are discussed next.

4   Design of the SMPA Architecture

The existing challenges of lack of transparency and need for efficiency in process assessment have been discussed in the Literature Review section. The task challenges can be grouped as a typical "decision task" since process assessments are conducted to make informed decisions on improving processes. According to TTF theory, technology requirements for the challenges of a decision task must focus on "information processing" and "process structuring" dimensions of technology for enhanced performance [22].

In the context of this research, facilitation of ITSM process assessment represents process structuring. The SMPA approach must define a workflow by which the entire assessment is conducted as explicitly documented in the process assessment standard [10]. We considered the assessment workflow steps proposed in the TIPA framework that define a structure in the assessment activities: Definition, Preparation, Assessment, Analysis, Results Presentation and Closure phases [4]. Likewise, the ability to automate activities of process assessment is considered as the information processing requirement for the design of SMPA approach. The steps of assessment data collection and validation, process capability ratings and reporting of the assessment results require gathering, aggregating, evaluating and finally presenting information as listed in ISO/IEC 15504-2 [10].

After a careful analysis of the task challenges identified in the Literature Review and the technology requirements stated earlier, a fit profile between the task challenges and technology requirements was established to articulate the SMPA design architecture (shown in Table 1).

Table 1. Fit profile for design principles to develop the SMPA approach

Process Assessment (Task challenges)	Decision support system (Technology Requirements)	Design Principles
Transparency	Process Structuring	Facilitate Assessment Workflow
Efficiency	Information Processing	Automate Assessment Activities

4.1   Facilitate Assessment Workflow

Emergent from the task requirement of *transparency* and technology requirement of *process structuring*, it would be worthwhile to establish an ITSM assessment approach that uses the ISO/IEC 15504 standard as a matter of consistency and in order to establish norms for a transparent approach. The SMPA approach has been developed with this design principle.

In order to facilitate the assessment workflow, alignment with ISO/IEC 15504 is critical while developing the SMPA approach. A thorough review of the normative reference of the standard [10], the process reference model [24] and the process assessment model for ITSM [12] was conducted to develop the SMPA approach. Likewise, a top-down approach in ITSM process assessment ensured that the measurement follows a transparent workflow of assessment activities. This work was guided by the Goal-Question-Metric (GQM) approach [25]. The concept of GQM defines a process measurement model on three levels: goal (conceptual level), question (operational level) and metric (quantitative level) [25]. The GQM approach was applied to define the assessment workflow in the SMPA approach.

ISO/IEC 20000-4 defines a reference model where each process is defined in terms of its purpose and outcomes [24]. Attainment of the process purpose by meeting the outcomes defines achievement of capability level 1 (process performance) in the assessment. The goals for assessment of higher capability levels are specified in the process attributes provided in ISO/IEC 15504-8 [12].

To provide information that can drive improvement of IT service processes, the standard practices were mapped to a set of assessment questions for a sample of four ITSM processes: Service Level Management, Change Management, Configuration Management and Problem Management. A total of 46 specific questions for the four processes at PA1.1 and 127 general questions at PA2.1 to PA5.2 that applied to all processes was generated from 63 standard indicators.

Every question was measured using the scale: "Not" (N), "Partially" (P), "Largely" (L), "Fully" (F) and "Not Applicable" (NA) also referred to as the NPLF scale in ISO/IEC 15504-2 [10]. Rather than the assessment team making a subjective choice of the indicator rating, the SMPA approach objectively measures feedback from the relevant process stakeholders based on their responses to the assessment questions.

4.2   Automate Assessment Activities

Based on the task requirement of *efficiency* and technology requirement of *information processing*, automating the activities of ITSM process assessment was necessary for cost-effective process assessments. The design principle of automation in assessment activities was adopted by developing a DSS tool. The lack of efficiency in the existing approaches is based on the time and resource requirements to organise process assessments. The SMPA approach has the potential to address this challenge since the use of a DSS tool can automate several assessment activities including assessment data collection, analysis and reporting.

The DSS tool in the SMPA approach allocates assessment questions to the survey participants based on three process roles: process performers; process managers; and external process stakeholders. The three process roles are confirmed as the norm for ITSM processes [4]. The approach of asking questions directly in a web-based survey represents a faster and more efficient data collection method compared to assessment interviews while maintaining the same level of rigour in service research [26].

The DSS tool determines a final process attribute score for each process. This is done by calculating the mean value of all the responses for every process attribute. The coefficient of variation (*CoV*) of all the responses is also computed by the tool: $CoV_x = \delta x / \overline{x}$ where CoV_x is the coefficient of variation, δx is the standard deviation and $\overline{x}$ is the mean value of x responses for a particular process attribute score.

The mean and the *CoV* are simple statistical measures to understand what the critical mass of assessment respondents think about the processes being assessed. The method of process capability determination and calculation of the reliability of the survey responses is a new feature of the DSS tool that is not explicitly stated in the ISO/IEC 15504 standard.

5   Structure of the SMPA Approach

The SMPA approach that is developed during the research project has four phases. During the first phase, preparation, information about processes to assess and assessment participants is captured using the DSS tool. The first phase represents the input in the SMPA approach as it demonstrates preparation to conduct assessments. The second and third phases survey the process stakeholders according to the process assessment model and measure process capability from the survey responses. The final phase produces a report with process improvement recommendations.

The structure of the DSS tool illustrated in Figure 1 facilitates the SMPA approach.

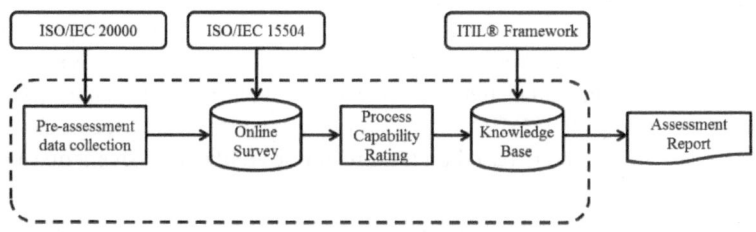

Fig. 1. Structure of the DSS tool for the SMPA approach

Phase 1 Preparation. Phase 1 represents preliminary data collection before the process assessment survey commences. The standard ISO/IEC 15504 [10] defines four key scoping dimensions to prepare before the commencement of the process assessment: (a) organisation context for assessment, (b) organisation unit to be assessed, (c) highest capability level to assess, and (d) processes to assess. Since the first three dimensions depend largely on the specific organisational context, an organisation profile form was generated to capture that information. For the fourth dimension however, the SMPA approach developed a general method to select processes to assess and improve. The processes listed in ISO/IEC 20000 [3] were considered for the initial list to choose the ITSM processes to assess. A method to select critical ITSM processes to improve has been developed and [27].

Phase 2 Survey. The process assessment model for ITSM in ISO/IEC 15504-8 [12] provides a set of base practices to fulfil the process outcomes (level 1) and a set of generic practices for process management (level 2), standardisation (level 3), quantitative measurement (level 4) and innovation (level 5). In a formal ISO/IEC 15504 assessment, these practices would be used as indicators to enable a formal evaluation of the process capabilities. In the context of the SMPA approach, the emphasis is on providing information that can drive improvement of ITSM processes. These indicators were translated into a set of assessment questions for the survey.

There are a number of best practices that are designed to assess ITSM processes, such as the process assessment model (PAM) for ITSM from ISO/IEC 15504-8 and the ITIL process maturity framework [17]. However, existing ITSM process assessment approaches used assessment indicators that were not designed to act as a direct information gathering instrument for automated data collection. Instead all assessment indicators were designed for assessors to use during assessment interviews. In contrast, we developed assessment questionnaires for direct input from process stakeholders. The questionnaires map each of the standard assessment indicators from ISO/IEC 15504-8. The questions were then allocated to the three process stakeholder groups according to the relevance of each question to each process role. Assessment questions for the survey were generated by analysing all standard indicators in the process assessment model from ISO/IEC 15504-8 so as to construct singular, fine-grained and close-ended assessment questions.

The DSS tool ensures quality data is collected for measurement. The responsibility to provide information about process capability was transferred to the process stakeholders. This shift removes the need for assessors to ask open-ended questions during assessment and avoids subjective judgments on process capability. For example, an assessor's open-ended question for the problem management process based on the base practice "RES.3.1 Identify problems" could be "Can you tell me about recording of the problems?". Instead, assessment questions in the survey are formed such as "Do you know if identified problems are properly recorded?" in a close-ended format, so that the assessment facilitator can analyse survey responses objectively and generate reports based on a concrete set of answer options. The questions progress based on the process attribute indicators at each process capability level defined by the ISO/IEC 15504-2 standard.

The survey uses a cross-sectional, self-administered web-based questionnaire, offered online. The procedure and design of the survey was chosen to be online as it is low cost, easily accessible, provides a fast response, and data collected would be available in electronic format [28]. The survey questionnaire has specific questions for each process for process attribute 1.1 (capability level 1) since this level relates to specific base practices (process dimension). The survey questionnaire has common questions for all the processes for process attributes 2.1 (level 2) to 5.2 (level 5) since these process attributes relate to generic practices (capability dimension).

Phase 3 Measurement. The assessment questions are grouped to determine process capability levels 1-5 and every question is rated using uniform answer options following the NPLF scale. This rating is a knowledge metric for ITSM process stakeholders to capture what they know about the process. Rather than the assessment team making a subjective choice of the indicator ratings based on objective evidence, the SMPA approach uses a coherent metric to collect and objectively measure feedback directly from the stakeholders.

Besides the four-point NPLF rating scale, every question also has a "Don't Know" (DnK) option and a "Don't understand the question" (DnQ) option. The DnK option suggests that the survey participant understands the question but there is a lack of communication and understanding in regard to the aspect of the process being questioned. The DnQ option is a metric to prompt the assessment facilitator to have a discussion about the question for clarity of the concepts. Every question also features a free text comment box to capture qualitative contextual data. Such textual information can be analysed by an assessor to validate responses and provide specific recommendations in the assessment report.

The ISO/IEC 15504-2 requirements were used for the calibration of process attribute ratings. Since the objective of our research project is to provide a transparent and consistent method to conduct process assessments, the final score of each process attribute is determined by calculating the arithmetic mean value of all the responses for all the questions belonging to a particular process attribute. Table 2 provides the rating scale defined by the ISO/IEC 15504-2 standard along with the mean value of the scale percentage that is used for score calculation. For example when an answer option is "Yes, most of the time", it corresponds to the "Largely" rating scale where the scale percentage is in the range 50 to 85%. Therefore, the score for that response is the average of 50 and 85 which is 67.5.

Table 2. NPLF rating scale based on the ISO/IEC 15504 standard

Answer Options	Rating score	Scale %	Mean score value (x)
No, never	N	0 - 15	7.5
Yes, but only sometimes	P	>15 - 50	32.5
Yes, most of the time	L	>50 - 85	67.5
Yes, always	F	>85 - 100	92.5

The coefficient of variation (CoV) is also computed to analyse the trustworthiness of the process attribute score based on data dispersion among the respondents. The algorithm used in the measurement of process capability is discussed next.

The process attribute scores are calculated based on the following steps:

1. Each one of the four valid answer responses (NPLF) is mapped to the rating scale and the mean value of each response (x) is determined based on Table 2.

2. For all m responses belonging to one question, the arithmetic mean of x is calculated (y). The reliability of the process attribute score increases when there is a larger value of m due to higher number of respondents representing a process.
3. y is normalised to the NPLF rating scale (f_{nplf}) defined in Table 2 (y').
4. For all n questions belonging to one process attribute, the arithmetic mean of y' is calculated (z).
5. z is normalised to the NPLF rating scale (f_{nplf}) as defined in Table 2 (z'). z' is the process attribute score for the process.

The calculation of process attribute reliability score follows five steps:

1. Each of the four valid answer responses (NPLF) is mapped to the rating scale and the mean value of a response (x) is determined based on Table 2.
2. For all p responses belonging to all questions of a process attribute, the arithmetic mean of x is calculated (μ_p). The reliability of the process attribute score increases when there is a larger value of p due to higher number of respondents representing a process.
3. For all p responses belonging to all questions of a process attribute, the standard deviation of x is calculated (σ_p). The standard deviation σ_p shows how much dispersion from the arithmetic mean μ_p exists. A low σ_p indicates that all responses are close to μ_p. A high σ_p suggests that the responses are spread over a wide range of answer options.
4. Coefficient of variation (CoV_p) is calculated from the σ_p and μ_p. CoV_p is expressed as an absolute value percentage (relative standard deviation) that can be analysed to determine trustworthiness of the process attribute score based on data dispersion of the responses. A lower CoV_p suggests low variability in the responses that boosts the degree of confidence of the process attribute score and vice versa.
5. The reliability score (CoV_p') is determined based on the percent value of CoV_p and the range of acceptable variation of responses as defined by a function (f_{hmp}). The logic of the function f_{hmp} groups the CoV_p value into one of three scores based on a scale of dispersion of responses. We considered the logic to cluster a CoV_p value of less than 30% to be a reliable score, CoV_p value of over 50% to be an unreliable score and anything in between to be a "moderate" score. Therefore, the following algorithm of the function f_{hmp} is determined.

```
If CoVp < 30%, CoVp' = "HIGH"
If CoVp between 30% and 50%, CoVp' = "MODERATE"
If CoVp > 50%, CoVp' = "POOR"
```

The final outcome is the development of an assessment process profile that includes all the process attribute scores and their reliability scores along with the rationale for the ratings [29].

The need to provide an explanation of the logic of process capability measurement is paramount, as one of the critical factors for assessors and process managers was openness and transparency of how the process capability scores are derived. Lack of transparency can be a barrier to adoption in the process assessment discipline as assessors and process managers must be able to justify the assessment and process improvement efforts by explaining the calculations on which the process capability results were based. An explanation of sound logic of the process measurement is expected to lead to increased satisfaction and trust in the SMPA approach outcome by process managers. The provision of reliability scores provides confidence in accepting the assessment results. The consistency and simplicity of the process measurement ensures that the SMPA approach is flexible and easy to change in the event of alterations to the questions, standard measurement framework and/or calculation logic. This consideration is important in view of the anticipated change of the process assessment standard ISO/IEC 15504 to the ISO/IEC 330xx series.

Phase 4 Improvement. The SMPA approach not only provides assessment process profiles but also attempts to present process improvement recommendations. After each process questionnaire was formulated, knowledge items were generated for all questions based on the ITIL® framework. After conducting an assessment, a knowledge item for each question is extracted from the knowledge base and compiled in the assessment report when the normalized mean of all responses to the question demonstrates risks (i.e. a knowledge item score of Not or Partially).

Two aspects of a knowledge item for every assessment question are combined to generate a process improvement knowledge base: observation and recommendation. The observation component of a knowledge item lists the current state of the process capability. For instance, if a process is at capability level 2, observations provide an account of the current state of what is being done to ensure this capability level is maintained. This information is transformed from the relevant question itself. Likewise the recommendation component of a knowledge item for the process is based on the best practice guidelines from the ITIL® framework to achieve higher capability levels. To illustrate the generation of a knowledge item, a scenario can be considered. If a question asked "Do you know if X is performed?" the associated knowledge item may consist of two components: Observation: "X is not performed well"; and Recommendation: "According to ITIL®, consider doing Y to perform X". Based on the assessment question, an observation is formulated stating what needs to be done. To develop the recommendation component of a knowledge item, process metrics defined in terms of critical success factors and key performance indicators in the ITIL® framework were contextualised to the question. At PA1.1 the recommendations were specific to the process in question. From PA2.1 onwards, the recommendations were developed as general guidelines that may apply to any process. However specific examples were provided where applicable.

6   Conclusion

Lack of transparency and need for efficiency were recognized as two significant problems for ITSM process assessments. To address these problems, the SMPA approach was developed to assist organisations to self-assess their processes for improvement using a standard model. The SMPA approach incorporates a DSS tool that has four main areas of functionality: pre-assessment data collection, online survey for assessment questions, calculation of process capability score and generation of process improvement recommendations in an assessment report.

The SMPA approach was designed to work in an efficient and transparent manner for continual improvement of IT services. Evaluation of the SMPA approach is being undertaken at two case study organisations in Australia by determining the usability of the DSS tool supporting the SMPA approach. The SMPA approach provides a new opportunity for automation and transparency in the way process assessments are conducted. Beyond the discipline of service management, the SMPA approach can potentially be applicable to other domains where a process assessment model is available. Using the SMPA approach, a compliant process assessment model can be used to develop survey questions. Likewise, process improvement recommendations can be generated based on industry best practice guidelines such as ITIL® in our case. With the expanding significance and reach of the ISO/IEC 15504 standard and the soon-to-be-published ISO/IEC 330xx series, the SMPA approach can be applicable for process assessments in any discipline that comprises a compliant assessment model.

The SMPA approach is not intended to replace a formal conformity assessment. However it is expected that organisations use this approach when the focus is not on the precision but on a consistent approach to measure process improvements. The SMPA approach can also be used by assessors in a formal appraisal environment as one of the evidence sources to determine process capability and maturity.

Acknowledgements. This work is supported by the Australian Research Council. We thank Mr. Paul Collins, Chief Technology Officer of Assessment Portal Pty Ltd. for his involvement and support in providing the platform to implement the DSS tool.

References

1. Galup, S.D., Dattero, R., Quan, J.J., Conger, S.: An overview of IT Service Management. Communications of the ACM 52(5), 124–127 (2009)
2. TSO, The Official Introduction to the ITIL Service Lifecycle: The Stationery Office (2011)
3. ISO/IEC, ISO/IEC 20000-1:2011 – Information Technology – Service Management – Part 1: Service Management System Requirements, ISO (2011)
4. Barafort, B., Betry, V., Cortina, S., Picard, M., St-Jean, M., Renault, A., Valdès, O.: ITSM Process Assessment Supporting ITIL. In: Chittenden, J. (ed.) Zaltbommel. Van Haren Publishing, Netherlands (2009)
5. Bernard, P.: Foundations of ITIL 2011 Edition. In: Chittenden, J. (ed.) Zaltbommel. Van Haren Publishing, Netherlands (2012)
6. Lloyd, V.: ITIL Continual Service Improvement. The Stationery Office, London (2011)
7. Barafort, B., Di Renzo, B., Merlan, O.: Benefits Resulting from the Combined Use of ISO/IEC 15504 with the Information Technology Infrastructure Library (ITIL). In: Oivo, M., Komi-Sirviö, S. (eds.) PROFES 2002. LNCS, vol. 2559, pp. 314–325. Springer, Heidelberg (2002)
8. Rout, T.P., El Emam, K., Fusani, M., Goldenson, D., Jung, H.W.: SPICE in retrospect: Developing a standard for process assessment. Journal of Systems and Software 80(9), 1483–1493 (2007)
9. Peldzius, S., Ragaisis, S.: Usage of multiple process assessment models. In: Woronowicz, T., Rout, T., O'Connor, R.V., Dorling, A. (eds.) SPICE 2013. CCIS, vol. 349, pp. 223–234. Springer, Heidelberg (2013)
10. ISO/IEC, ISO/IEC 15504-2:2004 – Information Technology – Process Assessment – Part 2: Performing an Assessment. International Organization for Standardization (2004)

11. Mesquida, A.L., Mas, A., Amengual, E., Calvo-Manzano, J.A.: IT Service Management Process Improvement based on ISO/IEC 15504: A Systematic Review. Information and Software Technology 54(3), 239–247 (2012)
12. ISO/IEC, ISO/IEC TS 15504-8:2012 - Information Technology - Process Assessment - Part 8: An Exemplar Process Assessment Model for IT Service Management, International Organization for Standardization (2012)
13. Parasuraman, A., Zeithaml, V.A., Berry, L.L.: A Conceptual Model of Service Quality and its Implications for Future Research. Journal of Marketing 49(4), 41–50 (1985)
14. Lepmets, M., Cater-Steel, A., Gacenga, F., Ras, E.: Extending the IT Service Quality Measurement Framework through a Systematic Literature Review. Journal of Service Science Research 4(1), 7–47 (2012)
15. Jia, R., Reich, B.H.: IT Service Climate—An Essential Managerial Tool to Improve Client Satisfaction with IT Service Quality. Information Systems Management 28(2) (2011)
16. Spath, D., Bauer, W., Praeg, C.-P.: IT Service Quality Management: Assumptions, Frameworks and Effects on Business Performance. In: Quality Management for IT Services-Perspectives on Business and Process Performance, pp. 1–21. IGI Global (2011)
17. MacDonald, I.: ITIL Process Assessment Framework. The Co-operative Financial Services, Manchester (2010)
18. Edgeman, R.L., Bigio, D., Ferleman, T.: Six Sigma and Business Excellence: Strategic and Tactical Examination of IT Service Level Management at the Office of the Chief Technology Officer of Washington, DC. Quality and Reliability Engineering International 21(3), 257–273 (2005)
19. Renault, A., Barafort, B.: TIPA for ITIL – From Genesis to Maturity of SPICE Applied to ITIL 2011. In: European System & Software Process Improvement and Innovation (EuroSPI2), Henri Tudor Institute, Luxembourg (2011)
20. Gregor, S., Jones, D.: The Anatomy of a Design Theory. Journal of the Association for Information Systems 8(5), 312–335 (2007)
21. Venable, J.R.: The Role of Theory and Theorising in Design Science Research. In: 1st International Conference on Design Science Research in Information Systems and Technology. CGU, CA (2006)
22. Zigurs, I., Buckland, B.K.: A Theory of Task/Technology Fit and Group Support Systems Effectiveness. MIS Quarterly 22(3), 313–334 (1998)
23. Peffers, K., Tuunanen, T., Rothenberger, M.A., Chatterjee, S.: A Design Science Research Methodology for Information Systems Research. Journal of Management Information Systems 24(3), 45–77 (2008)
24. ISO/IEC, ISO/IEC TR 20000-4:2010 – Information Technology – Service Management – Part 4: Process Reference Model. International Organization for Standardization (2010)
25. Basili, V.R., Caldiera, G., Rombach, H.D.: Goal Question Metric Paradigm. In: Encyclopedia of Software Engineering - 2 Volume Set, pp. 528–532. John Wiley & Sons, Inc., New York (1994)
26. Deutskens, E., de Ruyter, K., Wetzels, M.: An Assessment of Equivalence Between Online and Mail Surveys in Service Research. Journal of Service Research 8(4), 346–355 (2006)
27. Shrestha, A., Cater-Steel, A., Tan, W.-G., Toleman, M.: A Model to Select Processes for IT Service Management Improvement. In: 23rd Australasian Conference on Information Systems, Geelong, Victoria (2012)
28. Sheehan, K.B.: E-mail Survey Response Rates: A Review. Journal of Computer-Mediated Communication 6(2) (2001)
29. ISO/IEC, ISO/IEC TS 15504-9:2011 – Information Technology – Process Assessment – Part 9: Target Process Profiles, ISO (2011)

Systematic Literature Review on the Characteristics of Agile Project Management in the Context of Maturity Models

Larissa Fernandes Chagas, Daniel Dias de Carvalho, Adailton Magalhães Lima, and Carla Alessandra Lima Reis

Graduate Program in Computer Science, Federal University of Pará, Belém, Brazil
{larissafc,danieldias,adailton,clima}@ufpa.br

Abstract. Popularity of Agile Methods is growing up and along with this popularity is also growing the interest in adopting these methods in conjunction with maturity models, like CMMI. Dozens of reports about this topic can be found with different results. Therefore, a Systematic Literature Review was conducted with the goal of identifying characteristics of agile project management in organizations using agile methods and maturity models. We accepted 34 primary studies published from 2001 to 2013. The results show that the area still lacks details on how to perform the software development activities, what techniques can be used to meet issues not directly addressed by agile methods without losing the desired agility and what tools can be used to facilitate the combination of approaches.

Keywords: Scrum, XP, Agile Management, CMMI, Process Improvement, Maturity Model, Systematic Literature Review.

1 Introduction

Discussion on joint applicability of agile methods and maturity models is growing up. Agile Methods and maturity models practices, such as the Capability Maturity Model Integration (CMMI), are often perceived to be at odds with each other. However, each approach includes principles of good software development often overlooked but needed by the other approach [1]. The joint application of these approaches has challenges. A plausible rationale for many of the challenges faced by organizations using CMMI is likely the fact that they work with CMMI as a standard, instead of work with it as a model [1]. From the agile methods perspective, the Agile Manifesto [2] is frequently read in such a way that ignores the last line ("That is, while there is value in the items on the right, we value the items on the left more."). According to [5] there is a need for research that could lead to practical guidelines for achieving agility harmonizing traditional and agile approaches. In this context, a Systematic Literature Review (SLR) was performed to identify elements that compose the supporting approaches employed in software process improvement initiatives using agile methods, especially those related to Agile Project Management, in conjunction with

A. Mitasiunas et al. (Eds.): SPICE 2014, CCIS 477, pp. 177–189, 2014.

maturity models, and identify difficulties, lessons learned and recommendations about the joint application of these approaches. The SLR process undertaken in this work was driven by process guidelines specified by [3].

This paper is organized as follows. Section 2 presents the SRL process followed. Then, Section 3 presents the joint use characteristics of Agile Project Management with Maturity Models. After that, Section 4 presents threats to validity of this study. Finally, the last section, Section 5, presents conclusions and suggested future work.

2   Systematic Literature Review Planning and Execution

A SRL is a form of secondary study that uses a well-defined method to identify, analyze, evaluate and interpret all available evidence related to a particular research question seeking to reduce the bias of an informal review and make the process more repeatable [3]. The revision process utilized was divided into two main phases: Planning and Execution. Each phase is described in the sections 2.1 and 2.2. The StArt[1] tool was used to assist both phases of this study.

2.1   Planning

During the planning phase the SRL Protocol was defined and reviewed by the second author of this paper. The Protocol contains: the SRL objectives, the research questions, control publications, research sources, languages considered, the search expression, inclusion/exclusion criteria and data extraction procedures.

Research Objectives and Questions. The purpose of this SRL is to analyze scientific publications in order to identify the characteristics of agile project management in organizations using agile methods and maturity models; regarding support approaches employed; from the viewpoint of researchers; in academic and industrial context. To achieve this goal, this study aims to answer the questions in Table 1:

Table 1. Main Question (MQ) and Secondary Questions (SQ)

Code – Question
MQ - How does organizations that follow maturity models perform Agile Project Management?
SQ1 - What maturity models / standards / agile methods used?
SQ2 - What are the goals / reasons for using the agile method, the model / standard and for joint use?
SQ3 - What difficulties / recommendations / lessons learned about the joint use?
SQ4 - What are the characteristics of support approaches used to support joint application?

Control Publications. Control Publications are useful for an initial understanding about an area, help to define the search expression, and test and calibrate the searches on electronic databases. The control publications used in this work [P3, P4, P5, P6, P7, P8, P9, P10 – Appendix] were obtained during a prior informal literature review.

---

[1]   Available in: http://lapes.dc.ufscar.br/tools/start-tool

Data Sources and Search Expression. The search strategy included electronic databases presented in Table 2. These bases were chosen for allowing access to full-text papers and automatic searches in papers content.

Initially the search expression had three blocks. The 1st was related to "agile project management", the 2nd was related to "maturity models" and the 3rd was related to "support approaches" (environment, infrastructure, tools, approaches, methodology, technique). However, it was noticed that many publications reported some support for joint implementation, but it was not explicit in paper abstract. The third block was then removed from the final search expression. The Portuguese equivalent of the search expression and the plural of some terms did not influence the result, therefore were omitted from the final expression. The second author of this paper reviewed the search expression utilized.

It was necessary to make adjustments in the search expression for each database. The search expressions were executed on April 11, 2013, without start date restriction, therefore were returned papers published up to that date.

Table 2. Search Expressions for each Database

Database – Expression
Compendex - ((scrum OR "agile software" OR "agile methodology" OR "agile methodologies" OR "agile method" OR "agile methods" OR "agile management" OR "agile development" OR "agile project management" OR "extreme programming" OR xp) AND (cmm OR cmmi OR "maturity model" OR "process improvement" OR spi OR mps OR "plan driven" OR traditional OR conventional)) AND (72* wn CL)
IEEE Xplore - ((scrum OR "agile software" OR "agile methodology" OR "agile methodologies" OR "agile method" OR "agile methods" OR "agile management" OR "agile development" OR "agile project management" OR "extreme programming" OR xp) AND (cmm OR cmmi OR "maturity model" OR "process improvement" OR spi OR mps OR "plan driven" OR traditional OR conventional))
Scopus - TITLE-ABS-KEY((scrum OR "agile software" OR "agile methodology" OR "agile methodologies" OR "agile method" OR "agile methods" OR "agile management" OR "agile development" OR "agile project management" OR "extreme programming" OR xp) AND (cmm OR cmmi OR "maturity model" OR "process improvement" OR spi OR mps OR "plan driven" OR traditional OR conventional)) AND (LIMIT-TO(SUBJAREA,"COMP"))

Selection Procedures. The selection of studies was performed in 3 steps (Table 3):

Table 3. SRL steps

1.	Selection and preliminary cataloging of data collected. At this stage, the search expression was performed in selected databases, in order to identify potential publications. For each database, a BibText file was generated and imported in Start tool to catalog each of returned publications.
2.	Selection of relevant data - [1° filter]. After stage 1, title and abstract were read and analyzed in relation to the inclusion criteria (IC) and exclusion (EC) identified in Table 4.
3.	Selection of relevant data - [2° filter]. At this stage, full reading of publications accepted in the 1st filter was carried out and verification of those publications in relation to the criteria defined in Table 4 and Table 5. Publications accepted into this filter had their data extracted.

Table 4. Inclusion and Exclusion Criteria (1° Filter)

Code – Description
EC-01 - It is written in a different language from the selected for search (English and Portuguese).
EC-02 - Describes or presents keynote speeches, tutorials, courses, workshops and similar.
EC-03 – Presents the index of Congresses/Journal
EC-04 - Has no relationship with the joint application of maturity models/standards and agile project management.
EC-05 - Presents the use and/or recommendations on the use of some agile project management method, but not related to use in conjunction with maturity models/standards.
EC-06 - Presents the use of agile approaches and maturity models/ standards separately or treated as opposites.
IC-01 - Presents some improvement initiative using agile project management method in conjunction with maturity models/standards.

Table 5. Inclusion and Exclusion Criteria (additional do 2° Filtro)

Code – Description
EC-07 - Not available for download.
EC-08 - Not available without cost to the researcher.
EC-09 - Does not describe how occurred or how should occur agile project management in conjunction with maturity models/standard or the use of the approach AND gives no indication that there was actual execution of jontily application or that some supportive approach was utilized or proposed.
EC-10 – Presents support approach, but does not present subsidies that relate its application to real or hypothetical context where support for agile project management has been applied in conjunction with maturity models/standards.
IC-02 - Describes desirable characteristics for supportive approach related with agile project management in conjunction with maturity models / standards.
IC-03 - Describes problems/lessons learned/recommendations on the joint application of maturity models / standards and agile project management.
IC-04 - Presents the tool support / approach used to support the agile project management in conjunction with maturity models / standards.

Procedures for Data Extraction. A form has been created in the Start tool to extract data from the papers. Subsections 3.1, 3.2, 3.3 and 3.4 present part of data extracted.

2.2   Execution of the Systematic Literature Review

As result of Step 1 of papers selection, we got by the application of the expression for searching databases a total of 1724 papers (Compendex – 718, 42%; IEEE Xplore – 366, 21%; Scopus – 640, 37%).

During the application of Step 2 of papers selection (1° filter), the identification of duplicate papers (i.e., indexed by more than one base) was performed. Title and abstract of no duplicate papers were analyzed in relation to ICs and ECs identified in Table 4. When it was not possible to identify by reading the title and abstract if the paper should be accepted (go to next step), the paper was accepted. The second author of this paper was consulted whenever there was doubt about the acceptance of papers. During application of 1st filter, 295 (17%) studies were accepted, 754 (43%) classified as duplicated and 684 (40%) were rejected. Because of the low restriction of the search expression, there was a large workload during the application of the 1° filter and a high rate of rejected papers.

Afterwards we have conducted Step 3 of paper selection (2° filter). The purpose was to evaluate the papers approved in Step 2 both in relation to those criteria identified in Table 4 and Table 5. During the execution of the 2° filter 34 (11,5%) papers were accepted, 2 (0,7%) classified as duplicated and 259 (87,8%) rejected. For each paper approved for extraction, the following steps were followed: verified response for SQ1; verified whether the items of SQ2 could be answered; as the paper was read, categories to answer SQ3 emerged; new categories were added to the form to be collected for the other papers (including papers already extracted); then it was verified the answer to SQ4; A sample of the data extracted from the accepted papers was reviewed by the second author of this paper.

3   Characteristics of Agile Project Management in conjunction with Maturity Models/Standards

3.1   What are the Maturity Models/Standards/Agile Methods Utilized? (SQ1)

Fig. 1, – a) presents the utilized agile methods and the frequency of use in publications accepted for extraction. The distribution of agile methods for each year was collected but, due to the space constraints, will not be presented in this paper. Until 2004, papers accepted only cited the use of XP agile method or the use of XP in conjunction with Scrum. The use of Scrum isolated was cited since 2005. Scrum was the most cited method by the accepted publications. Fig. 1 - b) shows the maturity models/standards used and the frequency of use in the accepted publications.

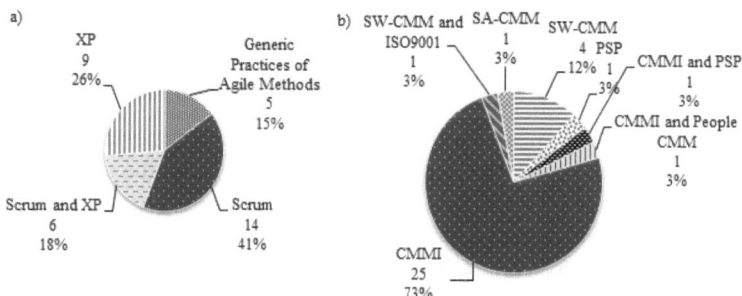

Fig. 1. Maturity Models / Standards utilized

3.2   What are the Goals/Reasons for Using the Agile Method, the Model/ Standard and Joint Use? (SQ2)

Only part of the accepted papers made clear the motivation for using agile method, model/ standard and joint use. The main motivation of the papers that made this information clear is presented in Table 6, Table 7 and Table 8.

Table 6. Motivation for Agile Method utilized

Motivation – References
Agile method used by adapting to changes. [P2], [P10, P11, P12]
Utilized the agile method to accelerate the development of its products. [P13]
Because the agile method used is effective in small and co-located teams. [P10]
Utilized the agile method to provide flexibility in the development process as a whole. [P3], [P15]
Because of the concentration of the method in Software Project Management. [P16]
Utilized the agile method seeking to improve product quality. [P17]
Utilized the agile method because it defines how, defines the process sequence. [P4], [P18]

Table 7. Motivation for Model/Standard utilized

Motivation – References
By focusing on discipline and continuous and systematic processes improvement. [P3], [P6], [P10]
Because of help and focus on processes institutionalizing. [P4], [P11, P12]
Position the department as an professional software development organization. [P12], [P16]
Participate in concurrence. [P6], [P17]
Due to the project size (Large Project). [P2]

Table 8. Motivation for joint use

Motivation – References
Considers that the model/standard can be improved with the application of agile method. [P16]
Considers that the agile method can be improved by applying the model/standard. [P1], [P18], [P20]
Utilized the joint approach considering that are complementary and that is beneficial joint use. [P3, P4], [P6, P7, P8], [P10]
Utilized the joint approach to meet needs that the use of only one approach can not supply (eg. minimize the number of lost and/or poorly implemented requirements, work with dynamic requirements, manage large and strategically important project). [P2], [P4], [P13], [P17], [P21]
The main goal was to professionalize the organization's development. [P19]

3.3   What difficulties/advice/lessons learned on the joint application? (SQ3)

The Table 9 presents the main contributions to this SRL of papers accepted for extraction (some studies had more than one contribution). Only 2 of the studies that contributed with "Experience on joint application" did this through Case Study [P2], [P9]. Despite the paper [P8] have considered the application of the proposed process as a Case Study, it was not possible from the data presented in the study to confirm that a rigorous process that requires a Case Study had been followed (e.g., as defined in [4]). The other papers reported industry experience.

Table 9. Contribution of accepted papers

Contribution – References
Experience on the joint application – [P2, P3, P4], [P6, P7, P8, P9], [P13, P14, P15], [P17], [P19, P21, P22, P23], [P26], [P33]
Mapping between Agile Method and Model/Standard - [P5], [P16], [P24, P25], [P34]
Difficulties/advice/lessons learned – [P1, P2, P3, P4, P5], [P7], [P9, P10], [P12, P13, P14, P15, P16, P17, P18, P19], [P21, P22, P23, P24, P25, P26], [P28], [P32, P33, P34]
Definition of Process/Parts of process – [P4], [P7, P8], [P11], [P20], [P27, P28, P29, P30], [P32]
Discussion of strengths/weaknesses of both approaches– [P8], [P10], [P20]
A method for configuring a hybrid process – [P28], [P31]

The difficulties/advice/lessons learned on the joint application, extracted from the accepted studies were divided into macro categories: Project Planning (PP), Project Monitoring and Control (PMC), Requirements Management (RM) (CMMI model process areas); and General Recommendations (categories that apply to the development cycle as a whole). Due to the space constraints, only categories related to PP and two General Recommendations are presented in this paper. The following categories of general recommendations were identified in addition to the presented: Plan the joint implementation, Perform experiments, Perform Training, Documentation, Greater Involvement of Management in agile way, Team, Client Close, Project Size, Processes Institutionalization, Involvement of everyone, Support of people involved and Communication.

Project Planning (PP). The papers [P1, P2, P3, P4, P5], [P10], [P12], [P15], [P21], [P26], [P28], [P33] consider that the practices related to PP area can be addressed by utilized agile methods by the planning phase defined by these methods and the inspection and adaptation that occurs in the execution of projects.

Table 10 presents specific goals and specific practices of the PP process area of CMMI. In Table 11 to Table 16 are gathered papers at which it was possible to make a clear mapping between recommendations/lessons learned and specific goals (SGs) and Specific Practices (SPs) of the PP process area. Recommendations/lessons learned about the PP process area untreated directly by agile method, but which were cited by papers were also collected, but omitted from this paper due to the space.

Table 10. Specific Goals and Practices - PP

SG – SPs
SG 1 Establish Estimates - SP 1.1 Estimate the Scope of the Project; SP 1.2 Establish Estimates of Work Product and Task Attributes; SP 1.3 Define Project Lifecycle Phases; SP 1.4 Estimate Effort and Cost.
SG 2 Develop a Project Plan - SP 2.1 Establish the Budget and Schedule; SP 2.2 Identify Project Risks; SP 2.3 Plan Data Management; SP 2.4 Plan the Project's Resources; SP 2.5 Plan Needed Knowledge and Skills; SP 2.6 Plan Stakeholder Involvement; SP 2.7 Establish the Project Plan.
SG 3 Obtain Commitment to the Plan - SP 3.1 Review Plans That Affect the Project; SP 3.2 Reconcile Work and Resource Levels; SP 3.3 Obtain Plan Commitment.

Table 11. SG1 – Satisfied practices

SP 1.1	According with [P16], [P23, P24, P25], in Scrum, the initial scope definition of the project occurs during the planning phase of the pre-game. The Work Breakdown Structure is composed of Product Backlog (PB) and predefined sprints. Detailed estimates are made at the beginning of each sprint, in the second part of the sprint planning meeting. In paper [P23], they fixed the time varied scope.
SP 1.3	According with [P16], [P24, P25] Scrum defines a life cycle. According to [P16], [P24], his cycle consists of four phases. In paper [P23], the project had an incremental life cycle, each iteration has formed a project phase.

Table 12. SG1 - Practices partially satisfied/unsatisfied

SP 1.2	According with [P16], [P24, P25], there is no explicit guidance on Scrum to establish size and/or complexity of items of PB and Sprint Backlog (SB). Some agile practices recommend the Planning Poker estimation technique. Organizations also use techniques such as function points, use case points, Wideband Delphi and story points. In paper [P23], estimates were based on expert opinion.
SP 1.4	According with [P16], [P24, P25], the Scrum team estimate is calculated by performance in previous sprints, the ability for the next sprint and complexity of the tasks necessary to deliver the sprint goal. However, the estimates do not follow a formal method and are not derived from the size or complexity. Scrum does not mention the use of a historical basis. The cost is not explicitly mentioned but is necessary for the Product Owner (PO) calculate budget and project financing. According to [P25], burndown and burnup charts facilitate the effort estimation. In paper [P23], the effort was estimated according to XP procedures in planning meetings.

Table 13. SG2 – Satisfied practices

SP 2.4	According with [P16], [P24, P25], in Scrum allocation of team and provision of infrastructure are made early in the project. During execution, the Scrum Master is responsible for providing new features when the current is not sufficient or if impediments related to insufficient resources are reported. In paper [P23], the planning team made rough estimate of people required and project duration. Resources were documented in the project plan.
SP 2.5	According with [P16], [P25] the definition of mechanisms to provide knowledge and skills are not clearly mentioned by Scrum. However can be easily achieved since, as identified in [P24], Scrum teams are cross-functional, self-managed and composed of skilled people to implement SB items. Senior members must manage, monitor and guide the other members. According to [P24, P25], if the project team is not able to implement SB, training and mentoring can be included in PB. According to [P25], the definition of mechanisms to provide knowledge and skills not found in the organization can be considered impediments and resolved during daily meetings and retrospectives.
SP 2.6	According with [P16], [P24, P25], Scrum defines roles, responsibilities and how actors will be involved during the execution of the project. This involvement should be monitored by the Scrum Master and registered in a communication plan.
SP 2.7	Accordig with [P16], [P24, P25], the minimum necessary to start a Scrum project consists of a vision and PB, which create a basis for the elaboration of a high level project plan. The vision describes why the project is being carried out and the desired end state. The PB, prioritized and estimated, defines functional and non-functional requirements that the system must fulfill to achieve the vision. In [P23], a written plan was established and updated after each iteration.

Table 14. SG2 – Practices partially satisfied/unsatisfied

SP 2.1	According with [P16], [P24, P25], in Scrum budget and schedule are obtained from PB and derived from estimated effort. PB is prioritized and divided into sprints. The schedule consists of the set of sprints. However, according to [P24], Scrum does not provide guidance on establishment of the budget. According to [P25], additional milestones or budget may be allocated to the project in each sprint during aprint planning. In [P23], the project had closed budget; the releases had fixed schedule. The schedule was established at planning meetings.
SP 2.2	According with [P16], [P24, P25], Scrum considers a risk as a possible impediment to the project. However, identification of risk does not occur in a systematic and parametrized way, using, for example, categories and sources of risk. According with [P25], impediments are reviewed in the retrospective meeting. In [P23], the project manager identified risks that were documented in the project plan and discussed. Actions originated from risks were discussed in post mortem meetings.
SP 2.3	According with [P16], [P24, P25], in Scrum all data generated by the project must be stored in public folders or whiteboard available to everyone, but there is not a formal data management plan or procedure to collect this data. Privacy and security are other weaknesses. During the pre-game, list of staffing and equipment needs are defined. In [P23], Configuration Management (CM) Plan identified configuration items and how to manage them, and the team made agreement on needed practices to manage other data.

Table 15. SG3 – Satisfied practices

SP 3.1	According with [P16], [P24, P25], in Scrum plans are revised at the beginning of each sprint and possible adaptations are carried out in accordance with changing requirements and technologies. According with [P25] this also occurs in retrospective.
SP 3.2	According with [P16], [P24, P25], reconciliation of paper occurs during the sprint planning meeting. Team, product owner and Scrum master define the functionalities to be developed in the sprint. According with [P25], the PB is dynamic and new estimates or schedules are possible. In [P23], scope was adjusted to resources.

Table 16. SG3 – Practices partially satisfied/unsatisfied

SP 3.3	According with [P16], [P23, P24, P25], commitment to the plan occurs at the beginning of each sprint, during the planning meeting. During sprint execution, the team must notify the PO if the workload is not sufficient to develop the agreed items, or if the workload of the team is greater than the effort required to implement the items, so that the Product Owner items to be removed (workload insufficient) or allocated (workload greater than the effort).

General Recommendations

Category	Lessons Learned/Recommendations
Process Support	The use of shared common processes makes it easy to share experiences and lessons learned between projects [P3]. In [P9], there was difficulty in the use of the process model. Often it is not possible to apply everything, and it was difficult to use the process because by the lack of tools to support the process. According with [P13], process manuals should show developers how to apply the light practices. According with [P21], the automation and documentation of the process is one of the most important factors for successful integration of CMMI and Agile. In [P26], a site has been used and has become an important way for processes and projects transparency. According with [P28], the team must have a shared vision of development workflow.
Process Tailoring	The paper [P3] adopted the agile mindset in the interpretation of existing processes. The paper [P19] considers that the model used (CMM) focuses primarily on large projects (a translation for the particular environment was performed). According with [P5, P6], [P22], organizations must not only put in place processes to pass in review, they should be evaluated about the value added and changed if benefits are offered. In the paper [P9], the agile method varied between the different types of projects. According with [P6], [P9], [P19] it is important that the organization define the use of the process in specific situations (customizations depending on the criticality, problem domain, technology, size and distribution of the time). According with [P2], [P15], [P26], it is important to allow adaptation of processes based on best practices found in projects. To [P28], the process should be adapted depending on the degree of flexibility that is desired for the project. A challenge found in [P17], was the fact that the considered client has rigid deadlines. For the implementation of urgent changes did not violate the company's processes, a working model to support the production was defined. This led to an initial frustration among developers, who had the perception that the processes were changing again.

3.4 What are the Characteristics of the Support Approach Used to Support the Joint Application? (SQ4)

Among the papers accepted, 20 mention or define support approach. For each study, were collected information as the type of addressed approach, overview of the approach and how agile project is addressed in conjunction with maturity model/standard. The Table 17 shows the publications and type of approach mentioned/defined. Due to space constraint has not been possible to present the details of the mentioned/defined approaches.

Table 17. Type of Approach

Type of Approach	Reference
Process/Parts of process Definition	[P4], [P8], [P11], [P20], [P27, P28, P29, P30], [P32]
Mentions/Proposes Approach to improve the process/choose process characteristics	[P9], [P14], [P28], [P31]
Mentions/Proposes use of tool support for PP/PMC/ RM	[P6], [P8], [P12], [P15], [P20, P21, P22], [P25, P26], [P28], [P33]
Mentions/Proposes use of process support tool	[P9], [P22], [P26], [P31]

4   Limitations and Threats to Validity

One threat to validity of this study is the fact of the word "agile" has always been combined with other terms, which reduced the papers covered by the search expression. On the other side, the removal of block of the string related to "support approaches" increased papers covered by the search expression.

Another threat to validity is that only the first author has executed data extraction (only samples of the extracted papers were reviewed by the second author). Moreover, by criteria EC-07 and EC-08, 47 papers were rejected (16% of the papers accepted in 1° filter). Part of these papers could contribute to the results of the SRL conducted. Finally, the addition of other electronic databases/digital libraries could also contribute to the results.

5   Conclusion

The SRL results help to better understanding how the joint approach occurs and what are the difficulties and lessons learned from this use. It was noticed that the area still lacks details on how to perform the software development activities, what techniques can be used to meet issues not directly addressed by agile methods without losing the desired agility, what tools can be used to facilitate the combination of approaches. Other challenges found refer to cultural changes and the lack of approaches to support the process.

It was possible to perceive that the joint application is possible and beneficial. The key to the combination is to adapt both approaches to projects and organizations characteristics. It is also important to adapt processes and tools to the organizational and project contexts. Furthermore, many studies recommend the use of tool support, on various levels, for the success of initiatives combining these approaches.

Although many studies present practical experience in joint application, the majority refers to industry reports. Therefore, the area needs more rigorous studies using, for example, case studies and / or experimental studies. This SRL can be extended by adding other research sources such as manual searches in conferences not indexed by electronic databases, besides the addition of other electronic databases.

One of the opportunities identified in this study was the need to adapt the processes used by organizations that combine agile methods with maturity models [P2, P3], [P5, P6], [P9], [P15], [P17], [P19], [P21, P22], [P26], [P28]. Based on practices, recommendations and difficulties identified in this study, is being defined an approach to processes tailoring and reuse that supports such characteristics and assists organizations in joint use [6].

References

1. Glazer, H., Dalton, J., Anderson, D., Konrad, M., Shrum, S.: CMMI or Agile: Why Not Embrace Both! Technical Note CMU/SEI-2008-TN-003, SEI of Carnegie Mellon University, Pittsburgh (2008)
2. Agile Manifesto for Software Development, http://www.agilemanifesto.org
3. Kitchenham, B.: Guidelines for performing Systematic Literature Reviews in Software Engineering. Technical Report EBSE 2007-001, Keele University and Durham University Joint Report (2007)
4. Wholin, C., Runeson, P., Höst, M., Ohlsson, M., Regnell, B., Wesslén, A.: Experimentation in Software Engineering. Springer (2012)
5. Batra, D., Xia, W., Vander Meer, D., Dutta, K.: Balancing agile and structured development approaches to successfully manage large distributed software projects: A case study from the cruise line industry. Communications of the Association for Information Systems 27, 379–394 (2010)
6. Carvalho, D., Chagas, L., Reis, C.: Definition of Software Process Lines for Integration of Scrum and CMMI. In: 50th Conferencia Latinoamericana en Informática (2014)

Appendix: Papers Accepted for Extraction (Code - Reference)

P1.	Martinsson, J.: Maturing XP through the CMM. In: Marchesi, M., Succi, G. (eds.) XP 2003. LNCS, vol. 2675, pp. 80–87. Springer, Heidelberg (2003)
P2.	Batra, D., Xia, W., Vander Meer, D., Dutta, K.: Balancing agile and structured development approaches to successfully manage large distributed software projects: A case study from the cruise line industry. Communications of the Association for Information Systems 27, 379–394 (2010)
P3.	Sutherland, J., Jakobsen, C., Johnson, K.: Scrum and CMMI Level 5: The Magic Potion for Code Warriors. In: Agile Conference 2007, pp. 272–278. IEEE, Washington (2007)
P4.	Jacobsen, C., Jonhson, K.: Mature Agile with a twist of CMMI. In: Agile Conference 2008, pp. 212–217. IEEE, Toronto (2008)
P5.	Omran, A.: AGILE CMMI from SMEs perspective. In: International Conference on Information and Communication Technologies, pp. 1–8. IEEE, Damascus (2008)
P6.	Cohan, S., Glazer, H.: An Agile Development Team's Quest for CMMI Maturity Level 5. In: Agile Conference 2009, pp. 201–206. IEEE, Chicago (2009)
P7.	Jakobsen, C., Sutherland, J.: Scrum and CMMI – Going from Good to Great. In: Agile Conference 2009, pp. 333–337. IEEE, Chicago (2009)
P8.	Rong, G., Shao, D., Zhang, H.: SCRUM-PSP Embracing Process Agility and Discipline. In: 17h Asia Pacific Software Engineering Conference, pp. 316–325. IEEE, Sydney (2010)
P9.	Pikkarainen, M., Salo, O., Kuusela, R., Abrahamsson, P.: Strengths and barriers behind the successful agile deployment - insights from the three software intensive companies in Finland. Empirical Software Engineering 17, 675–702 (2012)
P10.	Paulk, M.: Extreme programming from a CMM perspective. IEEE Software (18) (2001)
P11.	Lee, S., Kim, H., Lee, R.: Enterprise process model for extreme programming with CMMI framework. Computer and Information Science 131, 169–180 (2008)

P12.	Salinas, C., Escalona, M., Mejías, M.: A scrum-based approach to CMMI maturity level 2 in web development environments. In: 14th International Conference on Information Integration and Web-based Applications & Services, pp. 282–285. ACM, Bali (2012)
P13.	Reifer, D.: XP and the CMM. IEEE Software 20, 14–15 (2003)
P14.	Jakobsen, C., Poppendieck, T.: Lean as a Scrum Troubleshooter. In: Agile Conference 2011, pp. 168–174. IEEE, Salt Lake City (2011)
P15.	Babuscio, J.: How the FBI Learned to Catch Bad Guys One Iteration at a Time. In: Agile Conference 2009, pp. 96–100. IEEE, Chicago (2009)
P16.	Marcal, A., de Freitas, B., Furtado, F., Belchior, A.: Mapping CMMI Project Management Process Areas to SCRUM Practices. In: 31st IEEE Software Engineering Workshop, pp. 13–22 (2007)
P17.	Miller, J., Haddad, H.: Challenges Faced While Simultaneously Implementing CMMI and Scrum: A Case Study in the Tax Preparation Software Industry. In: 9th International Conference on Information Technology: New Generations, pp. 314–318. IEEE, Las Vegas (2012)
P18.	Dalton, J.: CMMI vs. Scrum? No - CMMI + Scrum! The Journal of Information Technology Management, Cutter IT Journal 25 (2012)
P19.	Vriens, C.: Certifying for CMM Level 2 and ISO9001 with XP@Scrum. In: Agile Development Conference (ADC) 2003, pp. 120–124. IEEE, Washington (2003)
P20.	Nawrocki, J., Jasinski, M., Walter, B., Wojciechowski, A.: Extreme programming modified: embrace requirements engineering practices. In: IEEE Joint International Conference on Requirements Engineering, pp. 303–310. IEEE, Germany (2002)
P21.	Kovacheva, T., Todorov, N.: Optimizing software development process: A case study for integrated Agile - CMMI process model. In: International Conference on Computer as a Tool, pp. 1–2. IEEE, Lisbon (2011)
P22.	Surdu, J., Parsons, D.J.: Army simulation program balances agile and traditional methods with success. The Journal of Defense Software Engineering, 4–8 (2006)
P23.	Kähkönen, T., Abrahamsson, P.: Achieving CMMI level 2 with enhanced extreme programming approach. In: Bomarius, F., Iida, H. (eds.) PROFES 2004. LNCS, vol. 3009, pp. 378–392. Springer, Heidelberg (2004)
P24.	Marcal, A., Freitas, B., Soares, F., Furtado, M., Maciel, T., Belchior, A.: Blending Scrum practices and CMMI project management process areas. Innovations in Systems and Software Engineering 4, 17–29 (2008)
P25.	Diaz, J., Garbajosa, J., Calvo-Manzano, J.: Mapping CMMI level 2 to scrum practices: An experience report. In: O'Connor, R.V., Baddoo, N., Cuadrago Gallego, J., Rejas Muslera, R., Smolander, K., Messnarz, R. (eds.) EuroSPI 2009. CCIS, vol. 42, pp. 93–104. Springer, Heidelberg (2009)
P26.	Bos, E., Vriens, C.: An agile CMM. In: Zannier, C., Erdogmus, H., Lindstrom, L. (eds.) XP/Agile Universe 2004. LNCS, vol. 3134, pp. 129–138. Springer, Heidelberg (2004)
P27.	Suwanya, S., Kurutach, W.: Applying Agility Framework in Small and Medium Enterprises. In: Ślęzak, D., Kim, T.-h., Kiumi, A., Jiang, T., Verner, J., Abrahão, S. (eds.) ASEA 2009. CCIS, vol. 59, pp. 102–110. Springer, Heidelberg (2009)
P28.	Geras, A., Smith, M., Miller, J.: Configuring hybrid agile-traditional software processes. In: Abrahamsson, P., Marchesi, M., Succi, G. (eds.) XP 2006. LNCS, vol. 4044, pp. 104–113. Springer, Heidelberg (2006)

P29.	Cintra, C., Price, R.: Experimenting a requirements engineering process based on rational unified process (RUP) reaching capability maturity model integration (CMMI) maturity level 3 and considering the use of agile methods practices. In: Workshop em Engenharia de Requisitos, pp. 153–159. Rio de Janeiro (2006)
P30.	Al-Allaf, O.: Hybrid web engineering process model for the development of large scale web applications. Journal of Theoretical and Applied Information Technology 53, 131–140 (2013)
P31.	Lukasiewicz, K., Miler, J.: Improving agility and discipline of software development with the Scrum and CMMI. IET Software 6, 416–422 (2012)
P32.	Navarrete, F., Botella, P., Franch, X.: Reconciling Agility and Discipline in COTS Selection Processes. In: 6th IEEE Conference on Commercial-off-the-Shelf-Based Software Systems 2007, pp. 103–113. IEEE, Banff (2007)
P33.	Anderson, D.: Stretching agile to fit CMMI level 3 - the story of creating MSF for CMMI process improvement at Microsoft corporation. In: Agile Conference 2005, pp. 193–201. IEEE (2005)
P34.	Zanatta, A., Vilain, P.: Uma analise do método ágil scrum conforme abordagem nas áreas de processo gerenciamento e desenvolvimento de requisitos do CMMI. In: Workshop em Engenharia de Requisitos, Porto, pp. 209–220 (2005)

An Agile Implementation within a Medical Device Software Organisation

Martin McHugh[1], Fergal McCaffery[1], and Garret Coady[2]

[1] Regulated Software Research Centre, Dundalk Institute of Technology, Dundalk, Ireland.
{Martin.McHugh,Fergal.McCaffery}@dkit.ie
[2] BlueBridge Technologies, Citywest, Dublin, Ireland
garretcoady@BlueBridgetech.com

Abstract. Three surveys conducted over a 6 year period revealed that medical device software organisations have difficulties in the area of requirements management, namely accommodating changes in requirements. Medical device software is traditionally developed in accordance with a plan driven software development lifecycle (SDLC). These SDLCs are rigid and inflexible to changes once the requirements management stage has been completed. Agile methods are gaining momentum in non-regulated industries but as of yet, the adoption of these methods in regulated industries such as the medical device software domain remains low. This study presents an implementation of agile methods within a medical device software development organisation based in Ireland. This implementation involved integrating agile practices with a traditional plan driven SDLC. Upon completing this implementation within a medical device software development project, the organisation identified cost savings and a reduction in the rework required when introducing a change in requirements.

Keywords: Agile, SDLC, Medical, AV-Model, Hybrid, IEC 62304.

1   Introduction

Three surveys, in 2007 [1], 2010 [2] and 2012 by the Regulated Software Research Centre at Dundalk Institute of Technology revealed that medical device software development organisations face challenges in managing requirements during development. Medical device software is typically developed in accordance with a plan driven Software Development Life Cycle (SDLC), such as the V-Model [3]. The V-Model appears to be the "best fit" with regulatory requirements as it produces the necessary deliverables required when seeking regulatory approval. However, use of the V-Model or any other SDLC is not mandated by international medical device software regulations or development standards [4]. Based upon this, an examination was performed of the software practices and methods in non-regulated domains to determine if lessons learned in these domains could be applied to the medical device software development industry.

A. Mitasiunas et al. (Eds.): SPICE 2014, CCIS 477, pp. 190–201, 2014.

This examination revealed that the adoption of agile practices within these non-regulated domains is increasing. A large scale survey of the software development industry revealed that 80% of respondents reported that they are following an agile approach [5]. These industries reported adopting agile methods for various reasons, one of which being the ability of agile practices to accommodate changes in requirements at any point in a development project.

Based upon this, the study focused on the medical device software development industry. An extensive mapping study was conducted to determine if agile practices have been used in regulated software domains and if so, how have they been adopted and to what success [6]. This mapping study revealed a very low adoption rate of agile practices within the medical device software development industry however, in instances where they have been adopted they have proved successful. For example, Rasmussen, Hughes, Jenks and Skach [7] reported that adopting agile practices in Abbott Diagnostics improved the process of requirements management during a medical device software development project. Further to this, where agile practices have been adopted successfully in the medical device software development industry, they have been integrated with a plan driven SDLC as no single agile method is sufficiently comprehensive in producing regulatory deliverables.

As a result of this research, a decision was taken to produce a hybrid SDLC incorporating agile practices with a plan driven SDLC in order to overcome the challenge of accommodating changes in requirements at any stage during development. This hybrid SDLC known as the AV-Model, was then implemented within a medical device software development organisation to validate its efficacy in practice.

The remainder of this paper is structured as follows; Section 2 presents the development of the AV-Model, Section 3 discuss the organisation and project in which the AV-Model was implemented, Section 4 presents the results produced as a result of the implementation of the AV-Model and Section 5 presents the conclusions of this research.

2   AV-Model Development

The process of developing the AV-Model was broken into clear distinct phases:

1.   Selection of foundation plan driven SDLC;
2.   Preparing for inclusion of agile practices into plan driven SDLC;
3.   Identification of applicable agile practices.

2.1   Selection of Foundation Plan Driven SDLC

When selecting the foundation of the hybrid SDLC, a number of plan driven SDLCs were examined. From performing a literature review we discovered that the V-Model is the most appropriate model on which to base the hybrid SDLC. The reasons for choosing the V-Model are:

- Medical device software organizations typically follow the V-Model. Consequently, they are already familiar with the structure and phases of the V-Model and would be more willing to adopt a hybrid model based upon a SDLC with which they are familiar [8].
- Medical device software organizations may have received regulatory approval to follow the V-Model when developing medical device software. If these organizations move to a completely different SDLC, they may need to re-apply for regulatory approval for the new SDLC. This may be a barrier as organizations could be reluctant to undergo the process of achieving regulatory approval again [9].
- Whilst none of the regulatory requirements or development standards mandate the use of the V-Model, it appears to be the best fit with regulatory requirements as it guides organizations through the process of producing the necessary deliverables required to achieve regulatory conformance [10].

2.2   Preparing for Inclusion of Agile Practices into Plan Driven SDLC

Each of the sequential plan driven SDLCs suffer the problem of being rigid and inflexible to change. All of the agile methodologies advocate iterative software development. Iterative techniques offer the ability to accommodate changes more easily than a plan driven approach [11]. However, to incorporate iterative techniques, the process of "Risk Identification" needs to be added to the model. Risk Identification involves analysing the project, dividing it into iterations and identifying the iterations which pose the most risk to the project and then creating a backlog as a result. The iterations identified as posing the most risk are then performed as early as possible in the project. Once risk identification is added, each of the stages of the V-Model is assessed to determine which of them could be performed iteratively. Consequently, all of the stages of the development lifecycle are divided into two categories: those that can be performed iteratively and stages that can only be performed in a single pass. For example, the Food and Drug Administration (FDA) requires medical device manufacturers to submit high level requirements prior to beginning development [12]. Therefore, this can only be done once. Also, the process of achieving regulatory approval can only be sought once a device is completed and the acceptance tests have all passed. Therefore, this can only be completed once. However, other stages such as including "Software Architecture Design" and "Unit Implementation" can be performed iteratively.

2.3   Identification of Applicable Agile Practices

As with selecting a foundation SDLC, a mechanism was required for the identification of suitable agile practices for inclusion into the hybrid SDLC. The primary objective of the hybrid SDLC is to assist medical device software organisations in the area of requirements management. As a result, an examination of the various agile methods revealed that the Scrum method is one of the only methods to provide complete guidance in all areas of development including requirements management. This finding was supported by the research conducted by Paetsch, et al. [13].

Based upon this, a decision was taken to establish which of the Scrum software development practices could be included into the hybrid SDLC. To discover which practices could be included, an examination of medical device software development regulations was performed to determine if any of the Scrum practices were contradictory with regulatory requirements. This examination revealed that none of the Scrum practices contradict regulatory requirements. To further reinforce the decision to adopt Scrum practices, the findings of the mapping study revealed that where agile practices have been adopted when developing medical device software, they have typically been Scrum practices [14-18].

The identification of suitable agile practices was not limited to the identification of a single agile method for integration with the V-Model. A review of empirically based research produced a list of agile practices from various agile methods which could successfully be adopted when developing medical device software. This review also included the extraction of practices from AAMI TIR45:2012 [19]. While these practices have not been adopted on a specific medical device software project, the authors of AAMI TIR45:2012 have extensive experience in both medical device software regulations and development. This places them as authorities as to which practices can be followed.

While the majority of the practices identified or followed when developing medical device software are typically Scrum practices, a number of other practices have been recognised such as Test Driven Development, Done is Done, Pair Programming and Self Organising Teams. As a result, a number of these practices were also included into the hybrid SDLC. It is expected that practices included from different agile methods will be complimentary [20].

Figure 1 shows the AV-Model which integrates agile practices with the V-Model. While the AV-Model may resemble the traditional V-Model, the approach taken is very different. The V-Model advocates fully completing a single stage before progressing to the next stage whereas with the AV-Model a number of stages are revisited during each iteration.

2.4   Iterative Approach Taken by AV-Model

A key component of the AV-Model is iterative software development. This iterative development facilitates changes in requirements at any point in the development life cycle, as no single stage of development is completed until the final requirement is passed through it. Figure 2 shows how a "Proposed System" is divided into a number of "Requirements", which are further sub divided into "Software Items" in accordance with the AV-Model. Once complete, these software items are combined to satisfy the requirement and then the requirements are joined to produce the finished system.

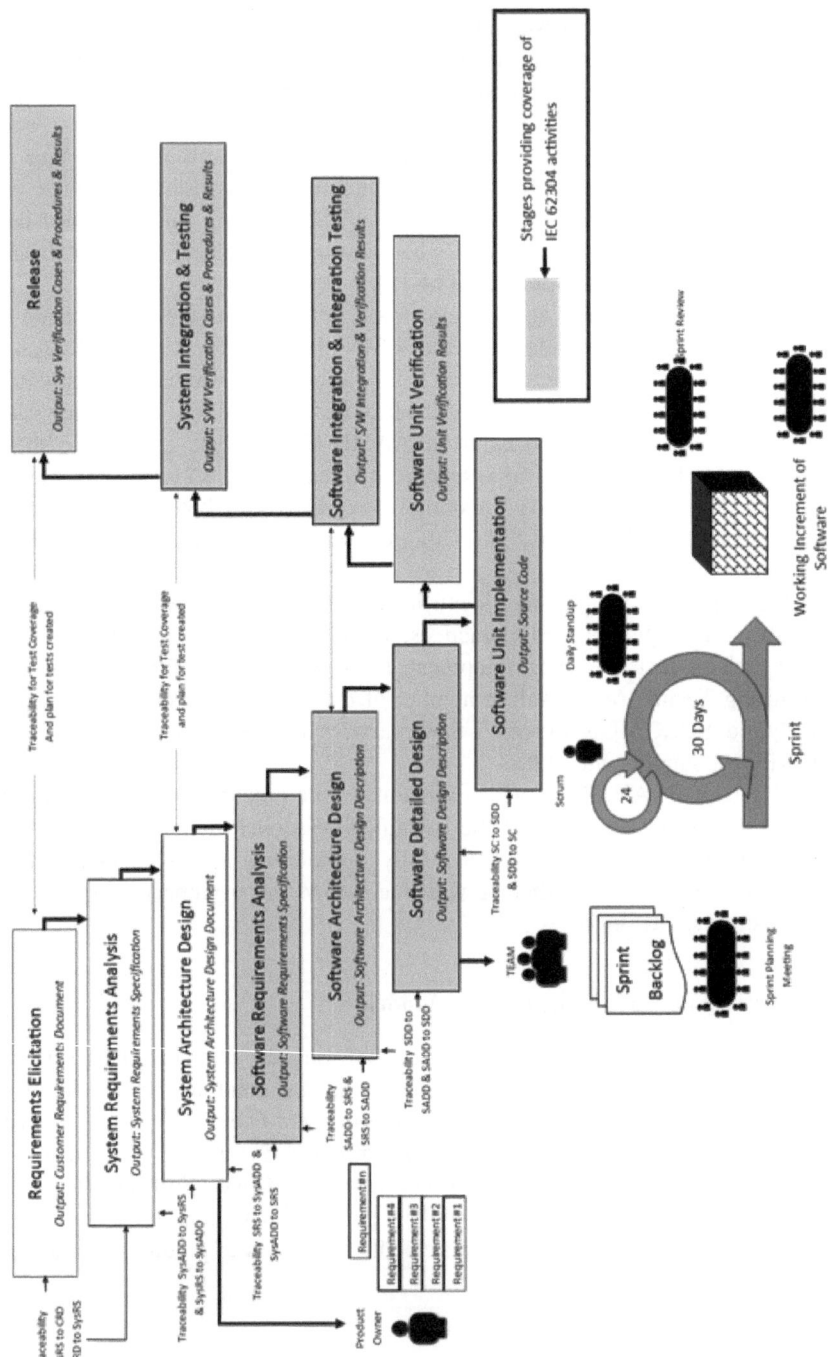

Fig. 1. AV-Model for Medical Device Software Development

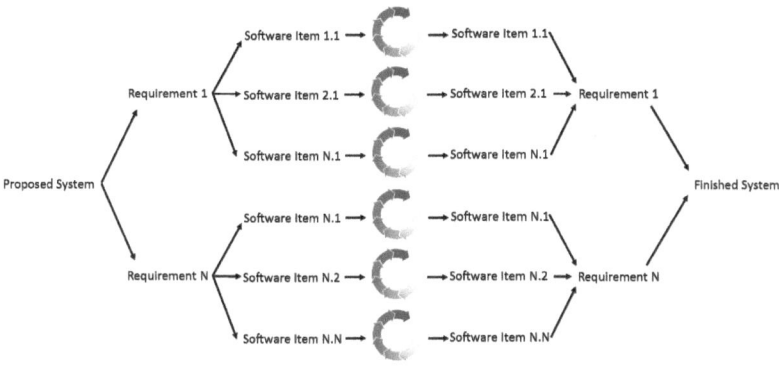

Fig. 2 Iterative Approach of AV-Model

Figure 2 would appear to suggest that Requirement 1 is to be developed concurrently with Requirement 2. However, this is not a requirement of the AV-Model. In smaller teams, it may not be possible to be developing a number of Requirements simultaneously. In smaller teams, when developing software in accordance with the AV-Model, once a software item is developed, it is frozen until another software item is finished and ready to be integrated. The same is true of the requirements of the system. Larger teams may be able to develop multiple software items and requirements concurrently. Either form of development is supported by the AV-Model. Figure 3, shows the relationship and activities to be performed at each stage of a development project when following the AV-Model.

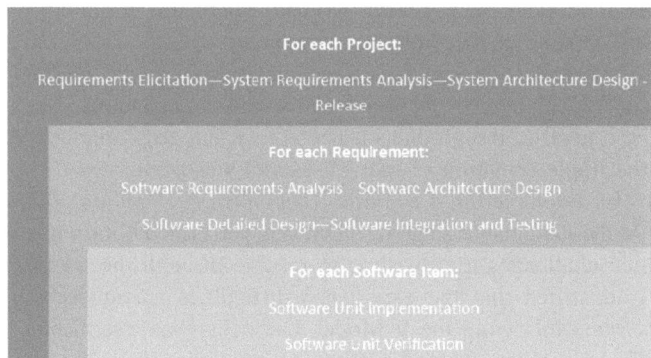

Fig. 3. Activities to be performed during AV-Model Implementation

3   Implementation and Validation

A key component of the development of the AV-Model was validation. This validation came in the form of implementation of the AV-Model within a medical device software organisation. This implementation was performed through the use of Action Research (AR). In AR, the researcher works closely with a group of people to establish an improvement path for a given situation. In AR, the researcher does not perform traditional research, instead the researcher acts as facilitator [21].

3.1   Organisation Profile

BlueBridge Technologies (BBT) offer a complete electronics and software development service including design, specification and procurement of the electronics and electro-mechanical systems. They are very strong in analogue and digital hardware and software design. They are highly experienced in design for scalable volume – from low to high volume manufacture. BBT has expertise in circuit design, from architecture, embedded firmware through to schematic capture and PCB layout design and test. BBT are experts in implementing a variety of communications protocols, as well as configuring device drivers. Their broad multidisciplinary team are well placed to develop sensors, both their deployment interfacing and integration and also test and evaluate performance.

3.2   AV-Model Implementation

BBT were awarded the contract to develop a "field use" diagnostics device for the detection and quantitation of antibodies using an enzyme linked immunoassay approach. The technology consists of an electrochemical biochip incorporated into a fluidics device which is covered by a deformable membrane. Upon depression of the membrane at specific loci, sample together with on-chip reagents are transported to a screen printed carbon electrode. A specific reaction then occurs producing an electrochemical signal (current) which is proportional to the concentration of analyte in the sample. The hand held "reader" component of this technology operates as a standalone unit capable of receiving and interfacing with the credit card size biochip. The product is designed for use by non-technically minded people and therefore the ergonomic considerations are important and a very light Human Machine Interface (HMI) will be critical to the products acceptability and error-free use in the field. As mentioned, the implementation of the AV-Model was performed through the use of AR. This involved completing 4 activities: *Diagnosing, Planning, Taking Action and Evaluating*. At the diagnosing stage research was performed within the organisation to establish which challenges they wished to resolve through the adoption of the AV-Model. BBT identified that the experience difficulties accommodating changes in requirements when following the V-Model. Once this was established, planning was performed. This planning involved performing training within the organisation. This involved two days of onsite training with the entire organisation. Once the organisation felt they had acquired the necessary skills, the AV-Model was implemented. During the implementation period the authors performed the role of consultants to the organisation. This involved partaking in the weekly Sprint Review and Retrospective meetings and also being available to answer any queries which arose during when implementation. Finally, at the diagnosing stage an evaluation was performed to establish if adopting the AV-Model, assisted the organisation in overcoming the challenges identified at the diagnosing stage. This evaluation was performed through the use of a Home Ground Analysis (HGA). Two HGA's were performed within the organisation, one prior to implementing the AV-Model [22] and one following implementation. The findings of the initial HGA served as a benchmark which were later used to establish the efficacy of the AV-Model implementation. The initial HGA also served the purpose of establishing whether or not BBT were suited to adopting agile methods. Should the initial HGA have revealed the organisation was rooted in a plan driven approach it may have been beyond the scope of this research to implement the AV-Model. Fortunately, the initial HGA revealed that BBT was equally suited to adopting either a plan driven or agile approach.

3.3   Findings

Figure 4 shows a radar chart plotting the results of the HGA conducted before and after implementing the AV-Model. Since the organisation has implemented the AV-Model, they have succeeded in becoming more agile. Through the process of learning how to adopt the AV-Model, a number of personnel became more familiar and comfortable with agile software development practices. During the implementation of the AV-Model there was a total of 6 requirement changes to be completed. This resulted in 33% of the final project consisting of requirements changes. Prior to implementing the AV-Model, the organisation was very reluctant to introduce any changes once development had begun as they experienced significant impacts on time and budget. Finally, following the development principles of the AV-Model, the percentage of the organisation which thrives on chaos increased significantly.

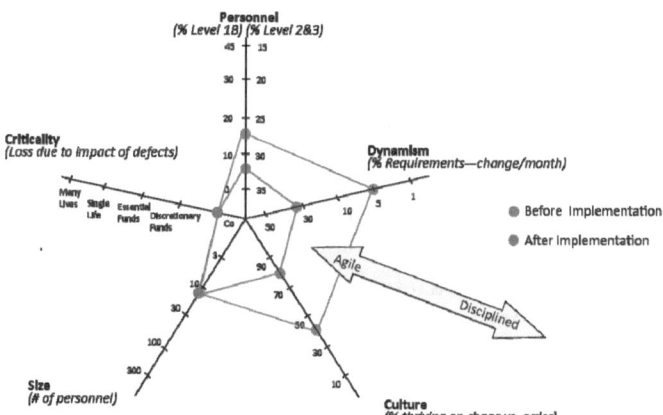

Fig. 4. Home Ground Analysis before and after implementation of the AV-Model

To accompany the HGA, key stakeholders within BBT were interviewed once the project was completed. The objective of this interview was to establish if the findings of the stakeholders reflected the statistical data gathered in the HGA. Those involved in the interview were the Marketing Director, the Product Owner and a Software

Developer. The interview took a focus group approach where the group was asked a number of questions and those that felt they had relevant input responded.

Q1. Did you perform the same amount of up-front planning when following the AV-Model as you would have when following the V-Model?

Historically, when following the V-Model we would have added an incubation period prior to beginning development. We had this incubation to allow the customer time to fully consider all potential changes in requirements as we know it can be very difficult to introduce a change in requirements when following the V-Model. When following the AV-Model we did not include this incubation period as the AV-Model was advertised as being able to accommodate changes at any point during development.

Q2. Without this incubation period did you miss any potential requirements changes?

The participants confirmed that they did miss three of the changes in requirements i.e. Configure Debugging, Configure Project in IDE and Battery Level Detection. The other three requirements changes i.e. Set/Verify Clocks, Low Power Mode and Flip LCD direction were more subtle changes which would have only been identified once development had begun, regardless of SDLC being followed. However, they did acknowledge that even though they had missed the changes, they found them easy to integrate when following the AV-Model.

Q3. If these changes had been introduced when following the V-Model what the implications would be, with regards to time, rework and cost?

Firstly, the participants noted that while there was 6 requirements changes when following the AV-Model, there would only have been 3 requirements changes when following the V-Model as the other 3 would have been identified during the incubation period which historically precedes implementing the V-Model.

Based upon this, the participants confirmed that if they had been following the V-Model and that the changes were identified at week 5 of a 14 week project, they would have been identified at either the "Software Detailed Design" stage or during the "Implementation" stage. As a result, the System Requirements Specification and Software Requirements Analysis documents would be completed. Consequently, to implement the changes identified, all of the preceding stages would need to be revisited and the work completed at each stage updated accordingly. They further explained that this rework would have taken 2 weeks to complete. When considering the implementation of the AV-Model, six requirements changes were introduced. Despite this, the project schedule was not impacted negatively, as the team originally overestimated the amount of time it would take to address each requirement. Should these 6 requirements changes not have been identified and introduced, the project would have finished approximately 1 week earlier than expected. Therefore, the time spent on introducing the requirements changes as part of this project, when following the AV-Model, was halved compared to following the V-Model. These times solely relate to the development time and do not include the incubation period which would have been included when following the V-Model.

With regards to the cost implications of introducing these changes when following the V-Model, the participants acknowledged that it is hard to quantify however they estimate 15% of the budget would be spent on the necessary rework. As discussed, had there been no changes in requirements, the project would have taken 1 less week to complete with an estimated cost of 7% of the budget being spent on accommodating these changes in requirements.

Q4. Did your testing process change when following the AV-Model when compared to that of the V-Model?
They confirmed that their testing process had changed, as they had to do more testing as each software item and software requirement had to be tested when it was integrated to ensure compatibility with the other software items and requirements completed previously. However, they did note that even though their testing process changed, there was no time implications as the process of continuous integration ensure all of the integration testing was performed. This continuous integration would not have been performed when following the V-Model as the software system would be developed as a single entity. As a result, they predicted that the time spent testing when following the AV-Model would be very similar to the testing that would have been performed if following the V-Model i.e. testing during continuous integration would take the same amount of time as single phase testing.

Q5. Did following the AV-Model produce the necessary deliverables required as part of IEC 62304?
The participants noted that they were not contractually obliged to followed IEC 62304 on this project however, they did expect at some point the customer would seek regulatory approval for the device in the future, therefore BBT ensured that they produced the requirements as part of IEC 62304. The participants identified that they expected this device to be deemed a Class I device, this meaning they did not need to fully follow IEC 62304. Despite not needing to produce all of the requirements as part of IEC 62304, the AV-Model did provide guidance to meet the requirements which they needed as part of this project

Q6. Was there any business value obtained from implementing the AV-Model?
Historically, when following the V-Model, BBT did not want to see the customer after development began, as this would typically lead to changes in requirements. They also noted that it can be very hard to impress on the customer the impact these changes can have on budget and time. However, with following the AV-Model, they can now advertise to customers that they can accommodate changes at any point in a software development project at a reduced cost when compared to following the V-Model, feeling this would give them a business advantage over competitors.

4   Conclusions

The AV-Model was developed in response to the recognition that medical device software development organisations are experiencing difficulties when accommodating changes in requirements once the requirements management stage is completed. The AV-Model incorporates agile practices with a traditional plan driven SDLC as a combination of both approaches reaps the benefits associated with adopting agile practices while producing the necessary regulatory deliverables. Once developed, the AV-Model was implemented through AR within a medical device software development organisation to validate its efficacy and to determine if it meets its primary objective i.e. assist medical device software organisations in handling changes in requirements when compared to following a traditional plan driven SDLC. The organisation in which the AV-Model was implemented reported reductions in cost and rework in accommodating changes in requirements when developing medical device software in accordance with the AV-Model, when compared to if they had of been following the traditional V-Model on the same project. In spite of these results, further adoption and analysis of the AV-Model would be useful in determining it's overall effectiveness at assisting medical device software organisations in overcoming the challenges associated with accommodating changes in requirements.

Acknowledgments. This research is supported by the Science Foundation Ireland (SFI) Stokes Lectureship Programme, grant number 07/SK/I1299, the SFI Principal Investigator Programme, grant number 08/IN.1/I2030 (the funding of this project was awarded by Science Foundation Ireland under a co-funding initiative by the Irish Government and European Regional Development Fund), and supported in part by Lero - the Irish Software Engineering Research Centre (*http://www.lero.ie*) grant 10/CE/I1855.

References

[1]   Denger, C., Feldman, R.L., Host, M., Lindholm, C., Schull, F.: A Snapshot of the State of Practice in Software Development for Medical Devices. Presented at the First International Symposium on Empirical Software Engineering and Measurement, ESEM 2007, Madrid (2007)

[2]   Embedded Forecasters, Embedded Market Forecasters Survey Ashland, MA (2010)

[3]   McCaffery, F., McFall, D., Donnelly, P., Wilkie, F.G., Sterritt, R.: A Software Process Improvement Lifecycle Framework for the Medical Device Industry. Presented at the Proceedings of the 12th IEEE International Conference and Workshops on the Engineering of Computer-Based Systems, ECBS 2005 (2005)

[4]   McHugh, M., McCaffery, F., Casey, V.: Barriers to Adopting Agile Practices when Developing Medical Device Software. In: Mas, A., Mesquida, A., Rout, T., O'Connor, R.V., Dorling, A. (eds.) SPICE 2012. CCIS, vol. 290, pp. 141–147. Springer, Heidelberg (2012)

[5]   VersionOne, 6th Annual State of Agile Survey (2011)

[6]   McHugh, M., Cawley, O., McCaffery, F., Richardson, I., Wang, X.: An Agile V-Model for Medical Device Software Development to Overcome the Challenges with Plan-Driven Software Development Lifecycles. In: Software Engineering in Healthcare (SEHC) Workshop at the 35th International Confernence on Software Engineering (ICSE), San Francisco CA (2013)

[7]   Rasmussen, R., Hughes, T., Jenks, J.R., Skach, J.: Adopting Agile in an FDA Regulated Environment. In: Agile Conference, AGILE 2009 (2009)

[8]   Faris, T.H.: Safe And Sound Software: Creating an Efficient and Effective Quality System for Software Medical Device Organizations. Asq Press (2006)

[9]   McHugh, M., Ali, A.-R., McCaffery, F.: Challeneges experieced by medical device software development organisations when following a plan driven Software Development Lifecycle. Presented at the European Systems and Software Process Improvement and Innovation Conference (EuroSPI), Dundalk, Ireland (2013)

[10]   Heeager, L.T., Nielsen, P.A.: Agile Software Development and its Compatibility with a Document-Driven Approach? A Case Study. Presented at the 20th Australasian Conference on Information Systems Compatibility of Agile and Document-Driven Approaches, Melbourne (2009)

[11]   Nerur, S., Mahapatra, R., Mangalaraj, G.: Challenges of migrating to agile methodologies. ACM Communications 48, 72–78 (2005)

[12]   U. Food and D. Administration,Premarket notification (510k), ed. (2010)

[13]   Paetsch, F., Eberlein, A., Maurer, F.: Requirements engineering and agile software development. Presented at the Proceedings of Enabling Technologies: Infrastructure for Collaborative Enterprises, WET ICE 2003 (2003)

[14]   Vogel, D.: Agile Methods: Most are not ready for prime time in medical device software design and development. DesignFax Online 2006 (2006)

[15]   Spence, J.W.: There has to be a better way! (software development). In: Agile Conference, 2005, Denver (2005)

[16]   Weyrauch, K.: What Are We Arguing About? A Framework for Defining Agile in our Organization. Presented at the Proceedings of the Conference on AGILE 2006 (2006)

[17]   Rottier, P.A., Rodrigues, V.: Agile Development in a Medical Device Company. Presented at the Proceedings of the 11th AGILE Conference, AGILE 2008 (2008)

[18]   Ge, X., Paige, R.F., McDermid, J.A.: An Iterative Approach for Development of Safety-Critical Software and Safety Arguments. In: Agile 2010 (2010)

[19]   AAMI, AAMI TIR45:2012 – Guidance on the use of agile practices in the development of medical device software. In: Association for the Advancement of Medical Instrumentation, Arlington, VA (2012)

[20]   Fitzgerald, B., Hartnett, G., Conboy, K.: Customising agile methods software practices intel shannon. European Journal of Infornation Systems 15, 200–213 (2006)

[21]   Dawson, C.: Introduction to Research Methods: A Practical Guide for Anyone Undertaking a Research Project. Constable & Robinson, London (2009)

[22]   McHugh, M., McCaffery, F., Fitzgerald, B., Stol, K.J., Casey, V., Coady, G.: Balancing Agility and Discipline in a Medical Device Software Organisation. Presented at the 13th International Conference Process Improvement and Capability Determination, Bremen (2013)

Assessing Software Agility: An Exploratory Case Study[*]

Özden Özcan Top and Onur Demirörs

Informatics Institute, Middle East Technical University, Ankara, Turkey
ozdentop@gmail.com, demirors@metu.edu.tr

Abstract. In this paper, we present an exploratory study towards developing a Software Agility Assessment Model, to fill the gap of a structured assessment model in the field. The purpose of the model is to assess organizations' or projects' agility and provide roadmaps to organizations in the continuous improvement path. The model has two dimensions with a similar structure to ISO/IEC 15504: agility dimension and aspect dimension. We performed an exploratory case study to identify the improvement opportunities for the draft model and discussed the results.

Keywords: Agile, Agility Assessment, Agile Capability, Agile Maturity, Software Agility Assessment Model, AgilityMOD.

1 Introduction

There are many reasons why an organization fails to deliver software products rapidly and with the desired quality [1]. Low response capability to changes, heavy and formal processes, late feedback mechanisms and lack of communication are some of these reasons. Methods that enhance agility are seen as solutions to these major problems of failures by software community. However, not every organization that tries to adopt agile methods succeeds, that is mostly because practitioners see a single agile method as a complete solution to all problems or misinterpret the agile principles, practices during the adoption and transformation. Moreover, agility is frequently confused with being undisciplined for ad-hoc development [2].

Agile maturity and agility assessment are brought as new concepts into the field because of unsuccessful adaptation of agile principles/practices. Sufficiency and usability of the current maturity models for organization to be agile is subject to research studies and none of which are defined as a well-established solution [3, 4]. There is still a fundamental need to assist organizations in assessing their agile capability and introducing roadmaps in adopting agile principles/practices. [5].

In this paper, we describe the first version of the Software Agility Assessment Model (AgilityMOD) that we developed to assess organizations' agility level with its well-defined structure and help them to draw roadmaps in improving their agile capability. AgilityMOD is developed with a similar structure of ISO/IEC 15504 [6]. It has

---

[*] This study has been supported by Turkish Scientific and Technological Research Council of Turkey (TUBITAK), Project 113E528 in 2014.

A. Mitasiunas et al. (Eds.): SPICE 2014, CCIS 477, pp. 202–213, 2014.

two dimensions named "agility dimension" and "aspect dimension". In order to identify AgilityMOD's applicability and suitability in agility assessment, we performed an exploratory case study and presented the results.

In the rest of the paper, the literature survey on current agile maturity models, AgilityMOD, the case study and conclusions are described in section 2, 3, 4 and 5 respectively.

2   Literature Review

In 2001, a group of people from different disciplines published the agile manifesto and started the agile software development movement [7]. Since then, various methods have been developed in conformance to the agile manifesto and agile principles [8-12].

In the meantime to answer the questions of organizations on how agile they are and how they can reach a better agility level; agile maturity models have been developed. In the current state, there are about forty models related to maturity, including both academic publications and Internet publications [4, 13]. Schweigert *et al.* conducted an analysis on the level naming conventions of these models. Based on their classification the models are grouped into three: those which are influenced by the structure of CMMI, those which have a specific leveling structure and those which do not use an explicit leveling structure. They also argue that these models do not measure the real agility. Instead, they check for the implementation of some specific agile practices [4].

In one of our previous studies [3] five of the most frequently referenced agile maturity models are applied in an organization and evaluated (Table 1). The evaluation is based on six quality criteria: fitness for purpose, completeness, definition of agile levels, objectivity, correctness and consistency.

Table 1. List of the Agile Maturity Models/Frameworks Evaluated

ID	Model Owner[8]	Name of the Model/Framework
M1	Patel and Ramachandran	Agile Maturity Model [14]
M2	Yin	Scrum Maturity Model [15]
M3	Sidky	Agile Adoption Framework [5]
M4	Benefield	Benefield's Model [16]
M5	Ambler	Agile Scaling Model [2]

The results of the study indicated that none of these models satisfies all the expected criteria and need to be improved in terms of scope, definitions of agility levels and objectivity. The most obvious deficiency of the models is that they do not support an agile process architecture holistically. Each model focus on different parts of the software development life cycle. None of the models has a well-defined structure with process inputs, practices and outputs forms.

Among this model quagmire, there is no commonly accepted agile maturity/assessment model. The need for a structured agility assessment model or agile or to be agile organizations remains valid.

3   Software Agility Assessment Model

We defined the Software Agility Assessment Model's (AgilityMOD) structure in accordance with ISO/IEC 15504 Software Process Improvement and Capability Determination (SPICE) Model [6]. Our purpose was to create a common basis for performing assessments of agility and present the assessment results using a common rating scale. However, instead of capability dimension and process dimension of SPICE Model, we defined Agility Dimension and Aspect Dimension as can be seen from Fig. 1.

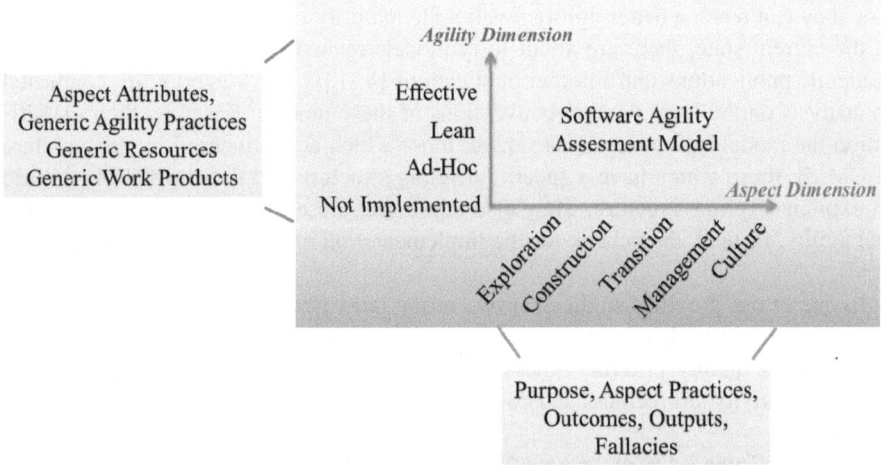

Fig. 1. Structure of the Agility Assessment Model

Formal process layers of traditional software development are intertwined to each other in agile software development. It is difficult to realize boundaries of the processes. Therefore, we performed a new modulation of agile processes and practices in order to integrate them under meaningful and agile compatible abstract definitions, and called them as "Aspects". In the aspect dimension, aspects are defined and classified into aspect categories as *Exploration, Construction, Transition, Management and Culture.*

Exploration aspect covers activities of capturing customer needs, elaborating and managing requirements artifacts, detecting and resolving issues and specifying dependencies. Construction aspect includes architecture, design, coding and unit testing activities. Transition aspect covers build, integration, testing and deployment activities. Management aspect deals with planning, estimating, monitoring activities in an agile manner. Culture aspect includes activities to align and adopt environmental conditions and people behavior in accordance with agile values.

In the other dimension, a set of aspect attributes grouped into agility levels is defined. Each attribute describes a major part of agility. All attributes are directly derived from twelve agile principles [7]. We defined the attributes "Performing Aspect Practices" for the 1st level; "Simple" and "Iterative" for the 2nd level and "Technically Excellent" and "Learning" for the 3rd level. The mapping of agile principles and aspect attributes are given in the following table. There is many to many relationship in this mapping.

Table 2. Mapping of Agile Principles and Aspect Attributes

Number of the Agile Principle	Name of the Aspect Attribute
1-3-4-6-7	Iterative Attribute
2-4-10	Simple Attribute
9-12	Technical Excellence Attribute
5-8-11-12	Learning Attribute

Aspect attribute is an indicator of the aspect performance. They define the characteristics of the aspects and they are applicable to all aspect practices. "Iterative" attribute specifies that the work products related to an aspect are delivered in an iterative and incremental way. The purposes of "simple" attribute are to support aspects to eliminate any kind of activity that does not add value and cause waste in software development process, to achieve the balance between the just-in-time works and upfront works and to manage the incoming and outgoing workflows. "Technical excellence attribute ensures that agile engineering methods and tools are integrated into aspects to improve productivity and lower defects. "Learning" attribute ensures that the aspects serve for the purpose of organizational learning and improvement.

Agility of an aspect is described with a four-point ordinal scale which enables the agility to be assessed at "Not Implemented", "Ad-Hoc", "Lean" and "Effective" levels. When an aspect progresses from the bottom level: "Not Implemented" to the top level: "Effective", its conformance to agile values and principles increases.

Achievement of an agility level is assessed upon the two types of indicators: Agility indicators and aspect performance indicators. Aspect practices and generic agility practices ensure the achievement of outcomes and outputs which are produced as a result of successfully realizing the aspect.

Agility Indicators:

— Generic Agility Practices
— Generic Resources
— Generic Work Products (Outputs)

Aspect Performance Indicators:

— Aspect Practices
— Work Products (Outputs)

Details of the model are explained in the technical report and can be provided on demand. [17].

4   The Case Study

We aim to conduct a single exploratory case study prior to the final version of the Software Agility Assessment Model (AgilityMOD). Exploratory characteristic of the case study will not only enables us to answer the research questions given below, but also it will provide flexibility during the conduct of the case study.

This section is described in three sub-sections including the case study design, conduct and findings.

4.1   Case Study Design

Two of the objectives of this study are to investigate the applicability of the Agility-MOD in assessing the aspect's agility at different levels in an organization and identifying if the agility assessment model could be used as a roadmap for organizations to improve aspects' agility. Another objective is to reveal improvement opportunities related to the AgilityMOD.

Considering these objectives we identified the following research questions (RQ):

RQ1: How suitable the "Software Agility Assessment Model" to be used with the purpose of identifying aspects' agility?

RQ2: What are the improvement opportunities for the first version of Agility-MOD?

Case Selection Strategy: Our strategy is to select the same organization that has been subject to one of our previous studies where we assessed the strengths and weaknesses of five agile maturity model/framework from agile process assessment perspective [3]. The reason of this selection is that we already had an idea about the agile maturity of the organization and knew the specific problems. From these perspectives, the organization will enable us better to observe if the model capable of revealing these problems and indicating the agility level of the organization.

Data Collection Strategy: In the selected organization, we aim to perform gap analyses through interviews and evidence collection and review. Interviews are planned to be performed with people from different roles/positions in accordance with five aspects of the model. These roles are planned to include at least one product owner, one business analyst, one developer, one configuration manager and one tester. We planned to record the interviews for further analyses. We also planned to perform gap analyses with two projects since the processes performed in the projects may differentiate, and the generalization of the assessment results through the organization is possible.

Validation Strategy: After the gap analyses, we planned to prepare an assessment report and discuss it with the interviewees to obtain their opinion on the assessment results.

4.2   Conduct of the Case Study

We performed the agility assessment in a government organization which is developing various management information systems related with the digitization of the procurement procedures for government purchases and health management and law tracking systems. It is a small sized company with sixty employees. The organization had been formerly assessed with other agile maturity models in 2013 by us in [3].

Prior to the assessment, we prepared the assessment questions for each aspect practices and generic agility practices.

We performed interviews with the product owner, the architect who has been formerly software development team leader and developer, the business analyst team leader and the test manager separately. Interviews took 13 person-hours in total.

During the assessment, we observed that people tend to describe positive sides of their job and positive practices; therefore, contradictory questions or failure scenarios also need to be asked related to practices. Direct evidences were also collected and reviewed in the scope of the assessment.

We used a four-level scale to express the achievement of the aspect attributes: "not achieved (0), partially achieved (1), largely achieved (2) and fully achieved (3) and not applicable (NA)"

4.3   Findings

Findings Related to Agility of the Organization
We assessed the agility level of the organization over two types of projects: one maintenance and one new development. Fig. 2 gives the colored schema of the assessment rating to capture the results at a glance.

Aspects/Practices	1. AD-HOC						2. LEAN					3. EFFECTIVE					
							Iterative		Simple			Technically Excellent		Learning			
	AP1	AP2	AP3	AP4	AP5	AP6	GP 2.1.1	GP 2.1.2	GP 2.2.1	GP 2.2.2	GP 2.2.3	GP 3.1.1	GP 3.1.2	GP 3.2.1	GP 3.2.2	GP 3.2.3	GP 3.2.4
EXPLORATION	2	2	2	2	2	2	1	2	0	2	1	1	2	1	2	3	2
CONSTRUCTION	2	2	2	1	NA	NA	1	2	1	2	2	0	2	1	2	1	1
TRANSITION	2	2	2	2	2	NA	1	2	1	2	3	1	1	1	2	1	1
CULTURE	2	1	0	2	3	1	0	2	XX	XX	1	XX	XX	1	1	1	1
MANAGEMENT	2	1	1	1	1	NA	1	2	0	0	1	1	0	1	2	1	1

Fig. 2. Colored schema for the assessment ratings based on each practice

The numbers and the colors in each cell display the ratings given: "0" and "red" means that the practice is not achieved. "1" and "yellow" means that the practice is partially achieved. "2" and "orange" means that the practice is largely achieved. "3" and "green" means that the practice is fully achieved. For the achievement of an agility level, assessed attributes must be rated as either largely achieved or fully achieved. The result of the assessment indicates that the exploration aspect is at ad-hoc level, the construction aspect is at not implemented level, the transition aspect is at ad-hoc level, the management aspect is at "not implemented" level, and the culture aspect is at "not implemented" level.

Fig. 3 displays the comparison between the current situation of the organization (inner pentagon) and the ideal case (outer pentagon) in the form of a radar chart. The data to draw the radar chart is obtained by adding the rating values given on Fig. 2 for each aspect.

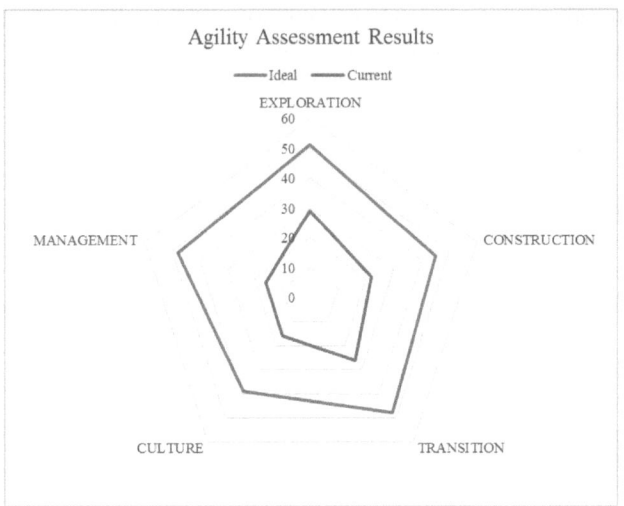

Fig. 3. Comparison of the Current Situation of the Organization and Ideal Situation

Below, we briefly present the major findings for each aspect. Each aspect is questioned based on both the aspect practices belong to the level 1 and the generic agile practices belong to the level 2 and 3.

Exploration Aspect: Major findings and improvement areas identified related to exploration aspect are as follows:

- Customers do not regularly involve in the exploration activities which limits the feedback obtained at an early phase.
- There is no consistency in transforming user needs into simple requirements artifacts (user requirements, business process models, detailed use case descriptions are developed all together or not at all)
- Formal review and approval procedures are applied for scope and requirements documents which may even take the same amount of time of the analysis process.
- Detailed specifications are preventing the development team to wait for a long time before the development activities start. On the other hand, in most cases test team need to explore and learn what is going to be tested since there is nothing exist in written form after the development is completed.
- All employees work in the same open-office which enhances communication. However, lack of continuous and regular communication channels cause cases where a developer made a change on a requirement item without notification to test team or analysts until the last moment.
- The organization maintains two large systems interacting with each other. Even if the internal and external dependencies partially known, there is a significant need to identify all dependencies since the numbers of hotfixes continue growing because of the lack of knowledge on change impact.

- This is an organization where requests of customers continuously flowing to analysts or technical leads. All the requests obtained from the customers at different sizes are entered to Team Foundation Server (TFS) tool. TFS is used maintaining the requests obtained from customers at different sizes such as a backlog. However, backlog items are not differentiated based on their types and regularly groomed by the product owner.
- Collaborative working changes from the team to team and team members do not share the full responsibility.

Construction Aspect: Major findings and improvement areas identified related to construction aspect are as follows:

- Developers elaborate the items with business analysts and/or customer one by one. The testers are not involved in these activities and remain unaware of the items and solution approach especially for small and medium sized requests. If the developer does not provide enough information about the item, it may be released without testing.
- Architectural elaboration meetings are performed weekly among architects and technical leaders. However, alternative solutions are not evaluated consistently, and there are cases where redevelopment occurred.
- Static code analyses are performed if the capacity of the development environment is sufficient. Code reviews are not performed except for the changes on critical modules.
- Physical configuration audits on source code are not performed. Therefore, it is not an unusual thing to deliver items without notice of test team or technical leads.
- Developers do not write unit tests except for mobile applications, even though, unit tests are the backbone for fast feedback.
- Experiences of the people in certain cases remain as tacit knowledge, there is no such a knowledge platform for sharing experiences in the organization.

Transition Aspect: Major findings and improvement areas identified related to transition aspect are as follows:

- Source code may be waiting for a long time in developers' branch before check-in to the mainline. Build time also varies based on the length of the code that is expected to be short in agile environments. The systems are lack of continuous integration.
- The systems are not supported with automated regression test suite. Only 6% of the whole system can be automatically tested (start-up tests).
- Functional black-box tests and regression tests are performed manually.
- It approximately takes 2-2.5 months to deploy the solution to the real system. After deployment, automated start-up tests are run. However, unknown errors may be sent to real system which is not in the scope of start-up tests causes high numbers of hot-fixes.

- Status of the integration and deployment processes are followed through e-mails. However, monitoring the progress through dashboards and making the progress visible to everyone is a better option.
- Even if the teams agree that necessary documentation needs to be produced to maintain the software, current documentation types do not help them in maintaining software since they are not continuously updated. It is obvious that the organization needs to rethink how efficiently document the product.

Management Aspect: Major findings and improvement areas identified related to management aspect are as follows:

- Before the initiation of the projects feasibility studies are performed. Scope is defined for new development type projects. A formal approval procedure and long waiting times are also valid for management type documents. Our suggestion is to use simpler forms such as one page "project data sheets" for scope and vision.
- There is not an accepted and applied estimation approach in maintenance type projects. Bottom-up estimation technique was applied in a few new development projects where every team member is involved. Estimation techniques should be reviewed considering the overall approach.
- Tracking is truly based on communication among team members and technical leaders. Such major metrics to identify team velocity is not gathered since there is no planned and actual effort.
- High-level strategic plans exist for maintenance type projects. However, there is no high level or level plans developed dynamically. Tasks are assigned people in a just-in time fashion. Teams dynamically adapt the conditions by quickly modifying resources. This practice is useful in rush times however idle resources cannot be identified.

Culture Aspect: Major findings and improvement areas identified related to culture aspect are as follows:

- One of the major problems of the organization is that there is no common "Agile" perception and understanding among the people. Some believe that they are developing according to agile principles, some do not have an idea about the agile concepts.
- Most of the customers are also unaware of agile software methodologies and how and when they are going to involve the processes.
- Even though the roles are not specialized according to agile principles, teams are constructed based on a matrix structure with people from different areas and different experiences.
- Domain trainings are given by business analysts to other team members. Process trainings and technological trainings are also provided by third party consultants. There is a need to focus on agile process and practice trainings.
- Teams and projects are managed by technical leaders and project managers respectively. Resource management and leveling are performed by technical leaders whereas project managers work as administrators mostly. They are seen as non-value

adding people to processes. Tasks are also assigned by technical leaders. Therefore, we cannot talk about self-organizing teams.

- Teams care about working collaboratively, however, there are examples where redevelopment is needed since the opinion of the experienced developers were not asked. Personal issues may also go upfront of the business.

Findings Related to the Software Agility Assessment Model

We met the purpose of this exploratory case study and identified the improvement opportunities and problems related to the first version of AgilityMOD.

First of all, we observed that the model can be used for assessing organizations' agility level. Improvement suggestions given based on the model can be utilized as a roadmap for improving organizations' agility. It is also noticeable that the assessment based on AgilityMOD can be performed with a reasonable effort.

We identified three types of internal problems: redundancies, missing practices, and excess of practices.

Redundancy: Aspect practices belong to the culture aspect and generic agility practices belong to 2nd and 3rd level of agility level questions the similar practices and principles. When we performed an assessment based on the generic agility practices, there is no need to assess the organization with practices of culture aspect.

While we design the Model's structure, we aimed that the generic agility practices will be applicable to and valid for all aspect practices. However, it seems that the practices of culture aspect and 2nd and 3rd level generic agility practices do not comply in this sense (marked with XXs in Fig. 2.).

Missing practice: We observed that we do not question if the applied practices such as elicitation is project specific or applied at organization-wide in the Model.

Excess of practices: Practices of learning attribute, GP 3.2.3 and 3.2.4, are very close to each other in terms of their meaning and can be combined for a better structure.

One of the defined practices of learning attribute is "Obtain frequent feedback" which belong to 3rd level, however it more conforms to 2nd level since the purpose of 2nd level is providing feedback about progress.

Validity Threads

We designed the case study as a single exploratory case study. Assessing one organization limited us to observe the applicability of the Model for different levels of agility apart from "not implemented" and "ad-hoc".

5   Conclusions

In this paper, we briefly present the AgilityMOD that we built to assess agility levels of organizations and close the gap of a structural assessment model need in the field. The structure of the Model has been influenced from the SPICE Model.

The assessment is performed through the practices and the work products that are linked to the attributes. However, instead of process and capability dimensions of the SPICE Model, the AgilityMOD has aspect and agility dimensions.

In the scope of this study, we performed an exploratory case study with the first version of AgilityMOD as a prelude to the multiple case study to be conducted with the final version of it. The case study included a gap analysis to identify the organization's agility level and the improvement opportunities related to the Model.

The case study revealed that the proposed Model's structure is applicable for the agility assessment of software organizations. However, the internal integrity of the Model could be improved by eliminating redundancies, adding missing practices, and providing separation of concerns between the agility level and aspect level. Together with these improvements, it will meet the criteria (fitness for purpose, completeness, definition of agile levels, objectivity, correctness and consistency) that we had defined before building this solution and reach a ready to be applied maturity.

References

[1] Schwaber, K.: The enterprise and scrum. Microsoft Press (2011)
[2] Ambler, S.W., Lines, M.: Disciplined Agile Delivery: A Practitioner's Guide to Agile Software Delivery in the Enterprise. IBM Press (2012)
[3] Özcan Top, Ö., Demirörs, O.: Assessment of Agile Maturity Models: A Multiple Case Study. In: Software Process Improvement and Capability Determination, Bremen, Germany, pp. 130–141 (2013)
[4] Schweigert, T., Vohwinkel, D., Korsaa, M., Nevalainen, R., Biro, M.: Agile Maturity Model: A Synopsis as a First Step to Synthesis. In: McCaffery, F., O'Connor, R.V., Messnarz, R. (eds.) EuroSPI 2013. CCIS, vol. 364, pp. 214–227. Springer, Heidelberg (2013)
[5] Sidky, A.: A structured approach to adopting agile practices: The agile adoption framework. Virginia Polytechnic Institute and State University (2007)
[6] I. O. f. Standardization. ISO/IEC 15504-2:2003 Information technology – Process assessment – Part 2: Performing an assessment (2003)
[7] Agile Manifesto (2001), http://www.agilemanifesto.org
[8] Beck, K.: Extreme programming explained: Embrace change: Addison-Wesley Professional (2000)
[9] Schwaber, K.: Scrum development process. In: Business Object Design and Implementation, pp. 117–134. Springer (1997)
[10] Highsmith, J.A., Orr, K.: Adaptive software development: A collaborative approach to managing complex systems. Dorset House Pub. (2000)
[11] Cockburn, A.: Crystal clear: A human-powered methodology for small teams. Addison-Wesley Professional (2004)
[12] Poppendieck, M., Poppendieck, T.: Lean software development: An agile toolkit. Addison-Wesley Professional (2003)
[13] Schweigert, T., Vohwinkel, D., Korsaa, M., Nevalainen, R., Biro, M.: Agile maturity model: Analysing agile maturity characteristics from the SPICE perspective. Journal of Software: Evolution and Process (2013)

[14] Patel, C., Ramachandran, M.: Agile Maturity Model (AMM): A Software Process Improvement framework for Agile Software Development Practices. International Journal of Software Engineering 2, 3–28 (2009)

[15] Yin, A., Figueiredo, S., Mira da Silva, M.: Scrum Maturity Model: Validation for IT organizations' roadmap to develop software centered on the client role. In: The Sixth International Conference on Software Engineering Advances, ICSEA 2011, pp. 20–29 (2011)

[16] Benefield, R.: Seven Dimensions of Agile Maturity in the Global Enterprise: A Case Study. In: 2010 43rd Hawaii International Conference on System Sciences (HICSS), pp. 1–7 (2010)

[17] Özcan Top, Ö.: Agility Assessment Model v1.0. Informatics Institute, METU/II-TR-2014-37

Modeling SPI Sustainment in Software-Developing Organizations: A Research Framework

Nazrina Khurshid and Paul L. Bannerman

NICTA, Australian Technology Park, Sydney, Australia
UNSW, The University of New South Wales, Sydney, Australia
{nazrina.khurshid,paul.bannerman}@nicta.com.au

Abstract. While software process improvement is well established as a practice, it still presents challenges for some adopters. Drop-outs from SPI programs are not uncommon. The paper argues that SPI sustainment is a function of the organizational context of the program, not just of the program (or SPI 'product') itself. Critical in this context is the organization's operational capabilities and capacity for change, as well as key external factors that, together, can influence SPI outcomes. SPI sustainment is not an established topic of research. To foster interest and progress is responding to the problem, the paper makes a theoretical contribution by developing and proposing a research model of SPI sustainment, called SUSTAIN, from published research on process improvement. Four testable propositions are developed from the model. Implications of the model and plans for future work are also discussed.

Keywords: Software process improvement, sustainment, SPI, reference model.

1 Introduction

Software Process Improvement (SPI) has emerged as the preferred approach in the software engineering industry to improve software product quality and reliability and increase employee and customer satisfaction, resulting in a positive return on investment. Improvement frameworks, models, methodologies and standards such as Software Process Improvement Capability dEtermination (SPICE or ISO/IEC 15504) [12], Bootstrap [22], Capability Maturity Model Integration (CMMI) [42] and ISO 9004:2000 have been widely adopted in practice. SPI adoption, however, still presents challenges for software-developing organizations [38]. While many organizations successfully adopt and experience the benefits of SPI [18][10], others abandon the effort before realizing SPI's potential [21][4].

Motivated by the aim of bridging the sustainment gap (the gap between SPI goals and actual SPI outcomes), this paper investigates the issue of SPI sustainment. As used in this study, SPI sustainment is defined as the enablement of SPI activities, efforts and outcomes to continuously improve software development processes. The paper contributes a research model, developed from the literature, of contextual factors that influence SPI sustainment that can be used to manage SPI implementation and utilization, and sustain ongoing improvements. The model is based on the assumption that SPI sustainment is

A. Mitasiunas et al. (Eds.): SPICE 2014, CCIS 477, pp. 214–225, 2014.

dependent upon more than the SPI framework itself. Having the right skills (individuals and team operational capabilities), organizational support (capacity for change), and the leverage of external stakeholders and experts are critical in influencing software-developing organizations to sustain their commitment to SPI [12][30]. This requires close alignment and integration of SPI with organizational infrastructures that can add survival value to SPI as an organizational initiative and/or software engineering function.

While sustainment of improvement initiatives is broadly discussed in the management literature, SPI sustainment has attracted little focused attention. Drawing widely from the literature on sustaining process improvement, this paper makes a theoretical contribution by developing a proposed research model, SUSTAIN, in response to two research questions:

> RQ1:   What factors influence SPI sustainment?
> RQ2:   How do these factors relate to SPI sustainment?

The literature on sustaining process improvement is overviewed in the next section (Section 2). Section 3 describes the research method used to generate the proposed model. Section 4 then presents the SUSTAIN research model and develops formal propositions. Finally, Section 5 discusses the implications and planned future work before conclusions are drawn.

2   Prior Research

While no existing SPI sustainment model has been found in the literature, the notion is discussed or implied in some SPI frameworks. Concepts of software sustainment are also discussed in software-intensive systems literature.

2.1   Sustaining Process Improvement in Existing SPI Frameworks

Most existing SPI frameworks contain references to process improvement sustainment if not, also, some form of actual enabler(s). However, the focus of these frameworks tends to be more on specific process-related improvements than sustainment of an improvement initiative. In SPICE [19] and CMMI [42], for example, SPI sustainment appears to be aligned with institutionalization, which is reflected in the process maturity level, reaching optimization at Level 5. This implies that SPI sustainment may only be achieved at the highest level of maturity while organizations with lower levels of maturity certification and/or those that choose to remain at lower levels may not be able to sustain their process improvements.

In support of existing SPI frameworks, some conceptual frameworks also imply sustainment; most notably, the *SPI Manifesto* [33] and the *ImprovAbility*[TM] model [7]. The SPI Manifesto aims to give expression to SPI knowledge via three values and ten principles clustered intro three action categories: people, business and change. By contrast, ImprovAbility[TM] is used to assess an organization's process improvement ability and likelihood of project success, focusing on four groups of parameters: foundation; initiation; project and; in-use. Conceptually, these frameworks share some factors in common with the proposed SUSTAIN model.

SUSTAIN does not seek to resolve issues within specific SPI frameworks. Rather, its focus is the organizational context in which SPI frameworks are implemented and the potential influencers in these contexts that might enable sustainment of SPI. It reflects alignment and integration of SPI initiatives with organizational infrastructure contexts, which can influence SPI adoption, implementation, and sustainment.

Research to assess process improvement sustainability is more prevalent within the manufacturing industry, especially through continuous improvement (CI) approaches such as statistical process control [6] and lean measurement programs [27]. For example, Bateman and David [5] use a manufacturing organization case study to outline a model for assessing the sustainability of process improvement programs. Whilst CI approaches are beginning to take shape in the software industry, research is yet to provide clear guidance for policy and practice on how to implement and optimize CI methods in software development settings [16]. Evidence of important effects and the factors that modify effects in different contexts remains limited [8].

While CI approaches within the Total Quality Management field address software quality through customer satisfaction and the work environment, software maturity models such as CMMI deal with software system and development issues. The proposed SUSTAIN model adopts an integrated approach whereby sustainment is observed through influential critical success factors and their contextual relationship with the implementing organization, regardless of the SPI framework adopted.

2.2   Software Sustainment in Evolving Critical Systems

Another form of 'software sustainment' that is discussed extensively in software-development lifecycle and evolution literature is 'software maintenance'. Indeed, the terms 'software sustainment' and 'software maintenance' are often used interchangeably. Consistent with this approach, the SEI's working definition of software sustainment is "The processes, procedures, people, materiel, and information required to support, maintain, and operate the software aspects of a system" [23]. However, SPI sustainment comprises more than the usage and upkeep of SPI processes and practices. It also takes into account the skills of the SPI team, the support of the organization, and the attitude of customers and influence of industry bodies and experts. This recognizes that the individual/team, organizational and external contexts in which SPI frameworks are applied are also key determinants of SPI sustainment.

2.3   Sustainable Software Process

An alternative approach found in the literature defines a Sustainable Software Process as one that meets its (realistic) sustainability objectives, expressed in terms of direct and indirect impacts on the economy, society, human beings, and environment that result from its definition and deployment [28]. Some recent research has sought to consider eco-sustainability (also known as Green-IT) within software engineering [36][39]. For example, sustainability is defined during the initial system development (with responsible use of ecological, human, and financial resources – leveraging green business processes) and maintenance processes (with continuous monitoring of quality, knowledge management) [29]. The research model developed here is limited to software process improvement sustainment rather than eco-sustainability.

3   Research Method

The proposed SPI sustainment research model was developed in three main steps as summarized in Fig. 1. First, the literature was reviewed to identify variables that may influence SPI sustainment (that is, the relationship may or may not have been empirically validated). Second, the variables were clustered into related topics to identify potential sustainment constructs. Third, the findings were synthesized into an integrated sustainment model. Each step is further discussed following.

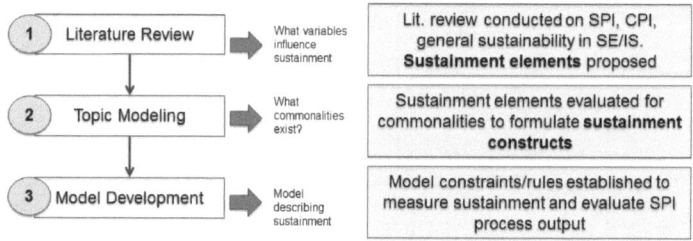

Fig. 1. Research process steps

3.1   Literature Review

The first step searched and reviewed the literature to answer *RQ1: What factors influence SPI sustainment?* The search focused on Software Process Improvement (SPI), Continuous Process Improvement (CPI), and general sustainment. Automated searches were made of the IEEE and ACM digital libraries, ScienceDirect, ABI-INFORM, Google Scholar, and Google. Further, articles identified in a published systematic literature review on the sustainability of software engineering were also included [29]. Fig. 2 summarizes the literature search process and results.

The search strategy was based on keywords derived from the research questions in the form of *population* AND *intervention*, as in Table 1. The selection criteria were applied to the title and abstract, and introduction and conclusion, if necessary.

Table 1. Keyword search strategy

Population	Intervention
"process improvement" OR "software process improvement" OR "SPI"	sustain* OR maintain* OR continuous* OR institutionalization*

First, the following exclusion criteria were applied: contains no obvious theoretical or industrial empirical basis; comprises an opinion piece or general discussion on improvement methods and model evaluation; focuses on "Green IT" (environmental sustainment) concepts [28] or long-living systems (software maintenance); and/or is a duplicate of another paper.

Then, the following inclusion criteria were applied: contains an existing research model relating to process improvement sustainability; contains an implementation of SPI focusing on motivation, challenges and outcomes; or contains framework/model application and assessment methods and results in software-developing organizations or other domains.

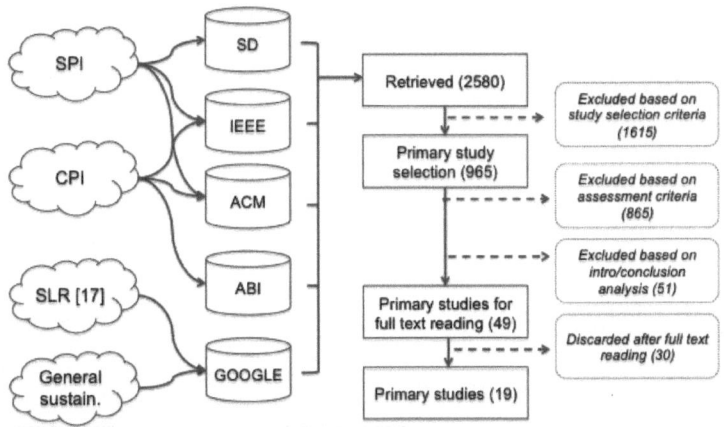

Fig. 2. Literature Review Process

This filtering resulted in selection of 19 primary papers for detailed analysis. Table 2 lists the data extracted from each paper for use in the next step.

Table 2. Data extraction structure used as input for Step 2

Data Extraction	Details
Metadata	Title, authors, abstract, publication details, keywords
Sustainment take away	Findings/discussions relating to sustainment and process improvement
Sustainment Constructs	Factors relating to process improvement and its sustainability
Sustainment Dimensions	Individual/program level, organizational and others (external forces)

3.2   Topic Clustering

The second step analyzed and clustered [45] the keyword data extracted from the previous step to answer *RQ2: How do these factors relate to SPI sustainment?* First, a set of factors that the literature suggests might influence SPI sustainment were identified. Second, to illustrate any overlap with existing SPI frameworks, the identified sustainment factors were mapped to each of three established SPI approaches that show some recognition of the factor: SPICE (ISO/IEC 15504); CMMI; and ISO 9004. This indicates that the factor may also have some role within SPI models. Third, affinity analysis was used to cluster factors into related variables based on logic presented in the primary papers. Finally, affinity analysis was used to cluster variables into related constructs based on their apparent positioning in the context of SPI initiatives. Constructs were identified in three contextual categories: individual/team (Operational Capabilities); organizational (Capacity for Change); and external/industry influencers (External Stakeholders). These analyses are summarized in Table 3.

Table 3. Identified SPI sustainment factors

Sustainment Factors	Variables	Construct	Lit review	CMMI	SPICE	ISO 9004
Assessment			[11][31]			
Change management			[26][1][24]			
Configuration Management				✓		
Data Analysis			[3] [31] [11]			
Implementation			[32][3][17][37][24]		✓	✓
Implement & measure					✓	
Measurement	Implementation		[9][41][3][17][24][35]	✓	✓	✓
Monitor					✓	
Monitor and Control		Operational Capabilities		✓		
Op. management			[35]			
Planning					✓	
Process Analysis			[31]			
Process management			[3]	✓	✓	✓
Systems Assessment			[31]			
Results			[9][32][24]	✓	✓	✓
Resource engagement	Competencies		[32]			
Team engagement			[17]			
Reward	Reward System					
Reward System			[37][13][34]			
Culture			[37][14]			
Policy				✓		
Strategy	Strategy & Policy		[44][15]			
Strategy & Policy						✓
Adoption			[35]			
Goal			[9][1][17][24][44]		✓	
Origin			[32]			
Commitment			[26][2][17]	✓		
Commitment & Leadership			[24]			
Leadership	Leadership & Commitment	Capacity for Change	[1][37][35][44][14]			
Leadership/Management						✓
Top management			[32]			
Op. Resource involvement			[17]			
Resource management	Resourcing		[3][37][24][13]	✓		✓
Resources			[1][17][44][14][15]	✓		
Teaming			[11][2][17][44]			
Education & training			[9]			
HRD & training			[24]			
Learning	Education & Training		[37]			
PIR			[9][1][32][3]			
Tools			[31][2][44]			
Training			[2][35][13]	✓		
Compliance	Compliance			✓		
Ref Model		External Stakeholders	[20][17][13]			
Customer feedback	External Feedback		[31][13]			
Experts			[32]			
Feedback					✓	

3.3 Model Development

The final step comprised the formation of a research model based on the findings of the previous two steps and the formulation of theoretical propositions based on that model. These are detailed in the next section.

4 SUSTAIN: SPI Sustainment Research Model

Based on the research process described in the previous Section, factors influencing SPI sustainment were found to cluster into three primary contextual dimensions: individual/team influences (Operational Capabilities); organizational influences (Capacity for Change); and external/industry influences (External Stakeholders). Together, the literature suggests that these factors influence SPI sustainment as shown in the theoretical model in Fig. 3.

The intent is for the model to be used to assess and predict SPI outcomes based on organizational SPI goals and influencing contextual factors. Given an organization's goal(s) to adopt, implement and/or continuously improve its software processes through an SPI program, the model enables analysis of influential factors that can impact the success of the SPI program and predict its likely outcome. This is independent of the internal effectiveness of the SPI model itself (i.e., SPICE, CMMI or something else).

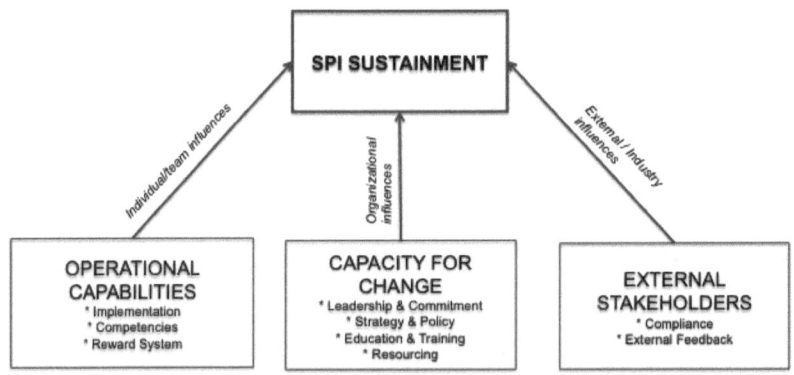

Fig. 3. SUSTAIN SPI Sustainment Research Model

Following, first, the model is described, focusing on the three clusters of influencing SPI sustainment factors; second, theoretical propositions are formulated; and, finally, model validation is discussed.

4.1 SPI Sustainment Factors

Operational Capabilities. Fundamental in the sustainment of SPI initiatives are the organization's operational capabilities around the individuals and teams who implement improvements, use the improved software processes, and sustain their ongoing improvement. These particularly relate to the application of relevant principles, behaviors and practices in adopting and implementing process improvements (Implementation); engagement of appropriate skills to enact SPI initiatives (Competencies); and incentive and reinforcement mechanisms to encourage and promote improvement of the organization's software processes (Reward System).

Capacity for Change. Other organizational factors are also critical in successfully adopting, implementing, and sustaining software process improvements. The literature suggests that organizations that can align and institutionalize SPI sustainment with their existing organizational infrastructure are more likely to achieve or exceed their goals [40]. Particularly relevant here is the organization's strategic intent, goals, governance and policies that motivate and frame SPI initiatives (Strategy & Policy); the engagement, support and commitment of senior executives to signal the relevance and importance of SPI to the organization (Leadership & Commitment); allocation, empowerment and management of appropriate resources to achieve the SPI goals (Resourcing); and provisioning of suitable training programs and tools to equip individuals and teams for SPI activities (Education & Training).

External Stakeholders. Sustainment of an organization's software process improvement can also be influenced by external factors, mostly related to regulatory, industry and vendor stakeholders. In particular, these influences include vendors' SPI program offerings and the importance that industries places on SPI (Adoption); conformance with customer- and industry-based process quality assurance expectations, reference models and standards (Compliance); and process and product quality feedback from customers and SPI assessors, as well as the influences of industry experts and stories about competitors' SPI activities (External Feedback).

4.2   Theoretical Propositions

Our literature-based research suggests that the difficulties some organizations experience in sustaining software process improvements and reaping the full benefits from their SPI frameworks extends beyond the specific reference model and/or tools selected to how SPI is introduced and integrated with the organizational infrastructures in which the software processes operate. Consequently, as outlined above, the SUSTAIN research model identifies individual/team, organizational and external sources of influence on SPI sustainment, as reflected in the following proposition.

P1: SPI sustainment is a function of operational capabilities, capacity for change and external influencers.

More specifically, the organizational context comprises contingent factors that are as critical to SPI sustainment success as the effectiveness of the SPI framework itself. Beginning with the individuals and teams who apply the software processes, that is, with the organization's operational capabilities, the SUSTAIN model recognizes that SPI sustainment will be difficult without applying the right skills in adopting, implementing and managing SPI, supported by suitable reward mechanisms. Hence,

P2: SPI sustainment is influenced by the operational capabilities used to support the adoption, implementation, and utilization of SPI

Further, enablement of the organization through its capacity for change is recognized in the literature as fundamental to sustained SPI success. In particular, influential support such as alignment of SPI initiatives with organizational goals and strategies, visible support and commitment from senior executives, allocation of suitable resources, as well as funding and provisioning of staff education and training to maintain required software process knowledge, skills and tools are recognized as significant determinants of SPI program and ongoing software process management outcomes. Therefore, the SUSTAIN model proposes that:

P3: SPI sustainment is influenced by the organization's capacity for change in ensuring continued utilization of SPI and extended adoption of SPI framework offerings

Finally, the external environment can exert significant influence over software-developing organizations, particularly through stakeholders, the perceived behavior of competitors, industry and subject matter experts, and general market and economic conditions. The SUSTAIN model recognizes three key influencing factors in the external environment – adoption, compliance and stakeholder feedback. Adoption and utilization of SPI is often influenced by what others are doing or what is expected in the industry context (why go through the expense and pain of process assessments if it does not help to attract new work?). Similarly, is compliance with a process standard necessary or beneficial in my industry to assure or highlight product quality? Finally, feedback from customers, competitors and industry analysts can be influential in determining the continuation or discontinuation of an SPI program. Therefore, a final proposition from the SUSTAIN model is that:

P4: SPI sustainment may be influenced by external stakeholders who can leverage organizational behaviors for resilience.

4.3   Model Validation

As this research is exploratory in nature and time is a fundamental dimension in sustaining any activity, the SUSTAIN model lends itself to validation via a longitudinal case study analysis design. Accordingly, work is underway to operationalize and evaluate the model against multiple longitudinal case studies of organizations that participated in a government program to subsidize CMMI Level 2 adoption in Malaysia. By applying the model to measure the influence of factors from the three contextual dimensions at staged points throughout and after participation in the program (such as before adoption, after implementation, and after the program ended), the veracity of the factors identified in influencing SPI sustainment and the ability of the model to predict future outcomes based on those influences can be evaluated. Other within-case cross-sectional time series field studies could also be used.

5   Discussion and Conclusions

To our knowledge, this is the first attempt to develop an SPI sustainment model. We argue that sustaining software process improvement requires more than good implementation of a good SPI framework. It requires integration of SPI initiatives into the fabric of the adopting software-developing organization to foster favorable influences from key enabling contextual factors. In particular, these include the resources applied to the SPI initiative or function; the capacity of the organization to support change and ongoing process improvement; and influential external stakeholders and specialists. In the absence of an established knowledge base on SPI sustainment, the contribution of the paper is theoretical, vested in the proposed SUSTAIN research model. Work is underway by the authors to validate the model using longitudinal case studies.

For research, the paper highlights the potential contribution of factors outside of the adopted SPI framework to influence SPI outcomes, and identifies an initial set of factors that the literature suggests may help sustain process improvement. Theoretical and empirical contributions on this topic are also encouraged from other researchers.

For practice, the SUSTAIN model offers the foundations of a mechanism that can be used as a health check of the sustainability of current SPI programs and functions. Analyzing the organization's position against each variable in the context clusters can highlight areas of exposure in the program and predict ('red flag') the likelihood of an adverse outcome.

The SUSTAIN model proposes that SPI sustainment is contingent upon congruence between SPI initiatives and the organizational and external contexts of the effort. This essentially opens up an additional front for research in improving the effectiveness and longevity of software process improvement.

Acknowledgements. NICTA is funded by the Australian Government through the Department of Communications and the Australian Research Council through the ICT Centre of Excellence Program.

References

1. Allison, I.: Organizational Factors Shaping Software Process Improvement in Small-Medium Sized Software Teams: A Multi-Case Analysis. In: 7th Int. Conference on the Quality of Information and Communications Technology (QUATIC), pp. 418–423. IEEE (2010)
2. Arent, J., Iversen, J.H., Andersen, C.V., Bang, S.: Project Assessments: Supporting Commitment, Participation, and Learning in Software Process Improvement. In: Proceedings of the 33rd Hawaii International Conference on System Sciences (HICSS), pp. 1–10. IEEE (2000)
3. Assessment of Organizational XYZ company, a.s., http://dae-projects.cz/2012/assessment-of-organizational-maturity-of-xyz-company-a-s/
4. Baldwin, L.P., Tillal, E., Ray, J.P.: Business Process Design: Flexible Modelling with Multiple Levels of Detail. Bus. Proc. Manage. J. 11(1), 22–36 (2005)
5. Bateman, N., David, A.: Process Improvement Programmes: A Model for Assessing Sus-tainability. Int. J. Oper. Prod. Man. 22(5), 515–526 (2002)
6. Caivano, D.: Continuous Software Process Improvement through Statistical Process Control. In: 9th European Conference on Software Maintenance and Reengineering (CSMR), pp. 288–293. IEEE (2005)
7. Christiansen, M., Jørn, J.: ImprovAbility™ Guidelines for Low Maturity Organizations. Soft. Proc. Improv. Pract. 13(4), 319–325 (2008)

8. Comparing Total Quality Management and the Capability Maturity Model (CMM) in an Organizational Change Perspective, http://asq.org/qic/display-item/?item=11247
9. Durdik, Z., Klatt, B., Koziolek, H., Krogmann, K., Stammel, J., Weiss, R.: Sustainability Guidelines for Long-living Software Systems. In: 28th International Conference on Software Maintenance (ICSM), pp. 517–526. IEEE (2012)
10. Dyba, T.: An Empirical Investigation of the Key Factors for Success in Software Process Improvement. IEEE T. Software Eng. 31(5), 410–424 (2005)
11. Ekdahl, F., Larsson, S.: Experience Report: Using Internal CMMI Appraisals to Institution-alize Software Development Performance Improvement. In: 32nd EUROMICRO Conference on Software Engineering and Advanced Applications (SEAA), pp. 216–223. IEEE (2006)
12. Emam, K.E., Drouin, J.-N., Melo, W.: SPICE: The Theory and Practice of Software Process Improvement and Capability Determination. IEEE Computer Society, Los Alamitos (1998)
13. Ferguson, P., Leman, G., Perini, P., Renner, S., Seshagiri, G.: Software Process Improvement Works! Carnegie Mellon, Software Engineering Institute, CMU/SEI-99-TR-027 (1999)
14. Foster, R., Wright, L., McRae, P.: Leading and Sustaining School Improvement Initiatives: A Review of Site-based Research from AISI Cycles 1, 2, and 3. Alberta Education, Edmonton (2008)
15. Glover, W.J., Farris, J.A., Van Aken, E.M., Doolen, T.L.: Critical Success Factors for the Sustainability of Kaizen Event Human Resource Outcomes: An Empirical Study. Int. J. Prod. Econ. 132(2), 197–213 (2011)
16. Halvorsen, C.P., Conradi, R.: A Taxonomy to Compare SPI Frameworks. In: Ambriola, V. (ed.) EWSPT 2001. LNCS, vol. 2077, pp. 217–235. Springer, Heidelberg (2001)
17. Hardgrave, B.C., Armstrong, D.J.: Software Process Improvement: It's a Journey, Not a Destination. Commun. ACM 48(11), 93–96 (2005)
18. Herbsleb, J., Zubrow, D., Goldenson, D., Hayes, W., Paulk, M.: Software Quality and the Capability Maturity Model. Commun. ACM 47, 30–40 (1997)
19. ISO/IEC: ISO/IEC 15504-1 Information Technology – Process Assessment – Part 1: Con-cepts and Vocabulary. ISO, Geneva (2004)
20. Jha, A.: Beyond CMMI, KPMG Business Excellence Report, http://www.kpmg.com/in/en/services/advisory/performance-technology/itas/spi_docs/beyond%20cmmi.pdf
21. Krasner, H.: Accumulating the Body of Evidence for the Payoff of Software Process Improvement (1997), http://www.utexas.edu/coe/sqi/archive/krasner/spi.pdf
22. Kuvaja, P., Similä, J., Krzanik, L., Bicego, A., Saukkonen, S., Koch, G.: Software Process Assessment & Improvement – The Bootstrap Approach. Blackwell, Oxford (1994)
23. Lapham, M.A., Woody, C.: Sustaining Software-Intensive Systems. Carnegie Mellon, Software Engineering Institute, CMU/SEI-2006-TN-007 (2006)
24. Liesener, T.: Why Do Continuous Improvement Fail to Sustain, http://www.kaizen-factory.com/2013/05/19/why-do-continuous-improvement-initiatives-fail-to-sustain/
25. Lepmets, M., Ras, E., Renault, A.: Organizational Support for Process Improvement – Results of an International Survey. In: O'Connor, R.V., Rout, T., McCaffery, F., Dorling, A. (eds.) SPICE 2011. CCIS, vol. 155, pp. 133–144. Springer, Heidelberg (2011)

26. Mathiassen, L., Pries-Heje, J., Ngwenyama, O. (eds.): Improving Software Organizations: From Principles to Practice. Addison-Wesley, Reading (2002)
27. Näslund, D.: Lean, Six Sigma and Lean Sigma: Fads or Real Process Improvement Methods? Bus. Proc. Manage. J. 14(3), 269–287 (2008)
28. Naumann, S., Dick, M., Kern, E., Johann, T.: The Greensoft Model: A Reference Model for Green and Sustainable Software and its Engineering. Sust. Comp.: Informatics and Systems 1(4), 294–304 (2011)
29. Penzenstadler, B., Bauer, V., Calero, C., Franch, X.: Sustainability in Software Engineering: A Systematic Literature Review. In: Evaluation & Assessment in Software Engineering (EASE), pp. 32–41 (2012)
30. Persse, J.R.: Process Improvement Essentials: CMMI, Six Sigma, and ISO 9001. O'Reilly, Sebastopol (2006)
31. Phalpher, R.: Sustaining Organisational Change, http://peo.on.ca/index.php/ci_id/20846/la_id/1.htm
32. Pillet, M., Maire, J.L.: How to Sustain Improvement at High Level: Application in the Field of Statistical Process Control. TQM J. 20(6), 570–587 (2008)
33. Pries-Heje, J., Johansen, J.: SPI Manifesto (2010), http://www.iscn.com/Images/SPI_Manifesto_A.1.2.2010.pdf
34. Pries-Heje, J., Johansen, J.: Change Strategy for ISO/IEC 33014: A Multi-case Study on Which Change Strategies Were Chosen. In: Barafort, B., O'Connor, R.V., Poth, A., Messnarz, R. (eds.) EuroSPI 2014. CCIS, vol. 425, pp. 317–330. Springer, Heidelberg (2014)
35. Quesada-Pineda, H.J., Madrigal, J.: Sustaining Continuous Improvement: A Longitudinal and Regional Study. Int. J. Eng. Bus. Manag. 5(43), 1–153 (2013)
36. Ray, S.: Green Software Engineering Process: Moving Towards Sustainable Software Product Design. J. Global Res. Comp. Sc. 4(1), 25–29 (2013)
37. Repenning, N.P., Sterman, J.D.: Nobody Ever Gets Credit for Fixing Problems that Never Happened. Calif. Manage. Rev. 43(4), 64–88 (2001)
38. Ross, N.C., Haddad, H.M.: Software Process Improvement and Metrics Adoption in Small Organizations. J. Inf. Syst. Technol. Plan. 3(6), 6 (2010)
39. Sara, S., Mahmoud, S.S.M., Imtiaz Ahmad, I.A.: A Green Model for Sustainable Software Engineering. Int. J. Softw. Eng. Ap. 7(4), 55–74 (2013)
40. Scott, L., Jeffery, R.: Practical Software Process Improvement - The IMPACT Project. In: Proceedings of the Australian Software Engineering Conference, pp. 182–189 (2001)
41. Seacord, R.C., Elm, J., Goethert, W., Lewis, G.A., Plakosh, D., Robert, J., Wrage, L., Lindvall, M.: Measuring Software Sustainability. In: International Conference on Software Maintenance (ICSM), pp. 450–459. IEEE (2003)
42. SEI: Capability Maturity Model Integration for Development, Version 1.3: Improving Processes for Developing Better Products and Services (CMMI-DEV, V1.3), Carnegie Mellon, Software Engineering Institute, CMU/SEI-2010-TR-033 (2010)
43. Sihvonen, H., Jantti, M.: How Does Training Support Software Process Improvement in Organizational Changes? In: Proceedings of 5th International Conference on New Trends in Information Science and Service Science (NISS), vol. 1, pp. 8–15. IEEE (2011)
44. Smith, L., Ahern, J.: Sustaining e-Learning Innovations: Literature Review - Australian Flexible Learning Framework (2002)
45. Wartena, C., Brussee, R.: Topic Detection by Clustering Keywords. In: 19th International Workshop on Database and Expert Systems Application (DEXA), pp. 54–58. IEEE (2008)

Early Stage Adoption of ISO/IEC 29110 Software Project Management Practices: A Case Study

Rory V. O'Connor[1,2]

[1] Lero, the Irish Software Engineering Research Centre, Ireland
[2] Dublin City University, Dublin, Ireland
Rory.OConnor@computing.dcu.ie

Abstract. The ISO/IEC 29110 standard has at its core a Management and Engineering Guide [1] which are targeted at very small entities (enterprises, organizations, departments or projects) having up to 25 people [2], to assist them unlock the potential benefits of using standards which are specifically designed to address their needs. This paper discusses the role and structure of Project Management in the ISO/IEC 29110 standard and the design and development of project management support documentation. In particular this paper describes a case study of an early adopter of ISO/IEC 29110 project management practices and their experiences with implementing these in an industrial context.

Keywords: VSE, ISO/IEC 29110, ISO, Standards, Project Management.

1   Introduction

There are multiple approaches to organizing the software development process and multiple factors influencing the software development process [3], with two major ones being the traditional (or plan based), which rely primarily on managing explicit knowledge, and agile methods, which primarily rely on managing tacit knowledge and recognises the importance of human interaction in the software process [4, 5]. Due to the rich variety of software development settings (for example: the nature of the application being developed, team size, requirements volatility), the implementation of a set of practices for software development may be quite different from one setting to another [6].

Projects are the cornerstone of all business activities in small and very small companies. Firms must complete various projects to achieve their financial goals and obtain information. Business owners and managers have only one attempt executing a project successfully. Hence, the process must be carefully thought out and planned. In their study into why software projects fail [7] have shown that software specialists spend about 40 to 50 percent of their time on avoidable rework rather than on what they call value-added work, which is basically work that's done right the first time.

Administering software development is usually achieved through the introduction of a software project management process. However, implementing software project management controls in very small software companies is a major challenge. This paper introduces the project management practices in the newly published ISO/IEC 29110 [1]

A. Mitasiunas et al. (Eds.): SPICE 2014, CCIS 477, pp. 226–237, 2014.

standard Software Process Lifecycles for Very Small Entities. The following sections discuss the role of project management in general, the structure of ISO/IEC standard and its project management practices. Finally the paper focuses on the design and development of project management support documentation and their associated usage in early trials of ISO/IEC 29110.

2   ISO/IEC 29110 Standard

The ISO/IEC 29110 standard "Lifecycle profiles for Very Small Entities" [1] is aimed at addressing the issues identified above and addresses the specific needs of VSEs [8, 9, 10] and to tackle the issues of poor standards adoption by small companies [11, 12, 13]. The approach [14, 15] used to develop ISO/IEC 29110 started with the pre-existing international standard ISO/IEC 12207 dedicated to software process lifecycles. The overall approach consisted of three steps: (1) Selecting ISO/IEC 12207 [16] process subset applicable to VSEs of up to 25 employees; (2) Tailor the subset to fit VSE needs; and (3) Develop guidelines for VSEs.

The basic requirements of a software development process are that it should fit the needs of the project and aid project success [10]. And this need should be informed by the situational context where in the project must operate and therefore, the most suitable software development process is contingent on the context [5, 17]. The core situational characteristic of the entities targeted by ISO/IEC 29110 is size, however there are other aspects and characteristics of VSEs that may affect profile preparation or selection, such as: Business Models (commercial, contracting, in-house development, etc.); Situational factors (such as criticality, uncertainty environment, etc.); and Risk Levels. Creating one profile for each possible combination of values of the various dimensions introduced above would result in an unmanageable set of profiles. Accordingly VSE's profiles are grouped in such a way as to be applicable to more than one category. Table 1 illustrates a Profile Group which contains three profiles (labeled A, B and C) that are mapped to nine combinations of business models and situational factors.

Table 1. Allocating VSE characteristics to profile groups

Business Models	Profile Situational Factors		
	Critical	User Uncertainty	Environment Change
Contract	*Profile A*	*Profile A*	*Profile A*
In-House	*Profile C*	*Profile B*	*Profile A*
Commercial	*Profile B*	*Profile A*	*Profile A*

Profile Groups are a collection of profiles which are related either by composition of processes (i.e. activities, tasks), or by capability level, or both. The "Generic" profile group has been defined [18] as applicable to a vast majority of VSEs that do not develop critical software and have typical situational factors. This profile group does not imply any specific application domain, however, it is envisaged that in the future new domain-specific sub-profiles may be developed in the future. Table 2 illustrates this profile group as a collection of four profiles, providing a progressive approach to satisfying the requirements of profile group.

Table 2. Graduated profile of the Generic profile group

	Generic Profile Group		
Entry	Basic	Intermediate	Advanced

To date the Basic Profile [1] has been published, the purpose of which is to define a software development and project management guide for performing one project at a time.

2.1   Engineering and Management Guide

At the core of this standard is a Management and Engineering Guide (ISO/IEC 29110-5) [1] focusing on *Project Management* and *Software Implementation* as illustrated in figure 1. The purpose of the *Project Management* process is to establish and carry out in a systematic way the tasks of a software implementation project, which complies with the project's objectives in terms of quality, time and cost. *Project Management* generates a *Project Plan* to direct the software project. During the execution of the project *Change Requests* may cause revisions to the *Project Plan*. The project is the subject of *Project Assessment and Control* during the lifetimes of the project until the *Software Implementation* is complete and *Project Closure* occurs.

Software Implementation (SI) produces a specified software system implemented as a software product or service. This process starts with the establishment of *Software Requirements*, after which *Architectural and Detailed Design* are produced. Software is the *Constructed* and verified using *Integration and Test* procedures. The final staged being *product d*elivery to the customer.

Within ISO/IEC 29110, the purpose of the Project Management process is to establish and carry out in a systematic way the Tasks of the software implementation project, which allows complying with the project's Objectives in the expected quality, time and costs. It is intended to be used by the VSE to establish processes to implement any development approach or methodology including, e.g., agile, evolutionary, incremental, test driven development, etc. based on the VSE organization or project needs.

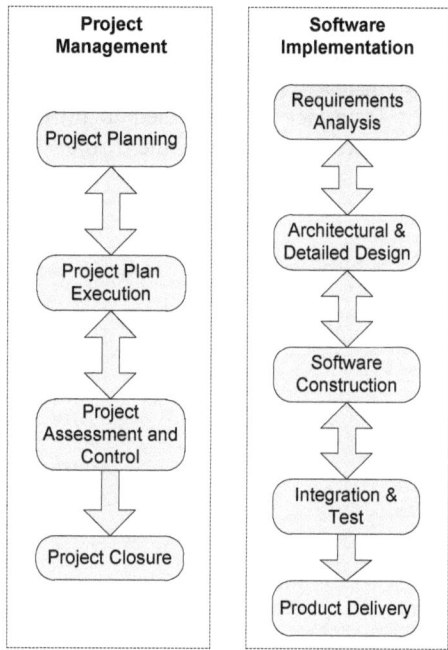

Fig. 1. ISO/IEC 29110 Basic profile Process Diagrams

2.2   ISO/IEC 2910 Project Management Objectives Practices

Figure 2 shows the flow of information between the Project Management Process activities of the Basic profile including the most relevant work products and their relationship.

The objectives of the ISO/IEC 29110-5-1-2 Project Management Process are:

- The *Project Plan* for the execution of the project is developed according to the *Statement of Work* and reviewed and accepted by the *Customer* and the *Tasks and Resources* necessary to complete the work are sized and estimated.
- Progress of the project is monitored against the *Project Plan* and recorded in the *Progress Status Record*. Corrections to remediate problems and deviations from the plan are taken when project targets are not achieved. Closure of the project is performed to get the *Customer* acceptance documented in the *Acceptance Record*.
- The *Change Requests* are addressed through their reception and analysis. Changes to software requirements are evaluated for cost, schedule and technical impact.
- Review meetings with the *Work Team* and the *Customer* are held and agreements are registered and tracked.
- Risks are identified as they develop and during the conduct of the project.

- A software *Version Control Strategy* is developed, where items of *Software Configuration* are identified, defined and baselined, and releases of the items are controlled and made available to the *Customer* and *Work Team*.
- *Software Quality Assurance* is performed to provide assurance that work products and processes comply with the *Project Plan* and *Requirements Specification*.

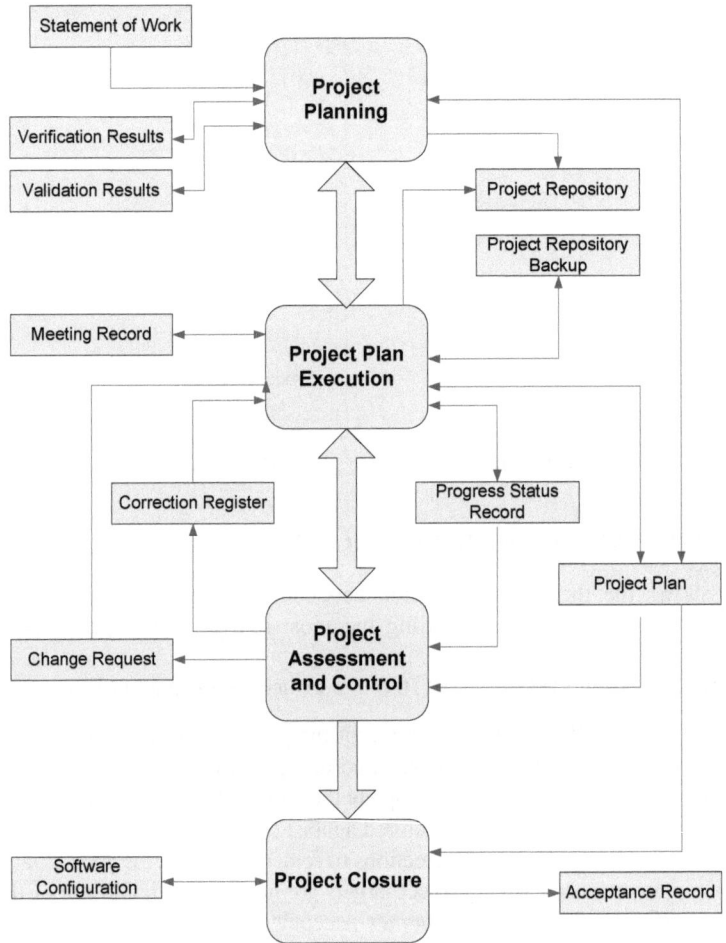

Fig. 2. Overview of ISO/IEC 29110 Project Management Practices

The four activities of the Project Management Process of ISO/IEC 29110-5-1-2 are:

- **Project Planning** - The primary objective of this process is to produce and communicate effective and workable project plans. This process determines the scope of the project management and technical activities, identifies process outputs, project tasks and deliverables, establishes schedules for project task conduct, including achievement criteria, and required resources to accomplish project tasks".

- **Project Plan Execution** - To implement the actual work tasks of the project in accordance with the project plan. Ideally when the project plan has been agreed and communicated to all teams members, work of the development of the product, which is the subject of the project, should commence.
- **Project Assessment and Control** - purpose is to determine the status of the project and ensure that the project performs according to plans and schedules, within projected budgets and it satisfies technical objectives. This process includes redirecting the project activities, as appropriate, to correct identified deviations and variations from other project management or technical processes. Redirection may include re-planning as appropriate.
- **Project Closure** - typically involves releasing the final deliverables to the customer, handing over project documentation to the business, terminating supplier contracts, releasing project resources and communicating project closure to all stakeholders. Often a final step is to undertake a Post Implementation Review (post-mortem) to identify the level of project success and note any lessons learned for future projects.

2.3   Deployment and Implementation Assistance

In order to assist with the deployment of ISO/IEC 29110 and to provide guidance on the actual implementation of ISO/IEC 29110-5 in VSEs a series of *Deployment Packages* and *Implementation Guides* have been developed to define guidelines and explain in more detail the processes defined in the ISO/IEC 29110 profiles [19].

A set of *Deployment Packages* (DP) (which are freely available from [20]) are a set of artifacts developed to facilitate the implementation of a set of practices, of the selected framework, in a VSE. A DP is not a process reference model (i.e. it is not prescriptive). The elements of a typical DP are: description of processes, activities, tasks, roles and products, template, checklist, example, reference and mapping to standards and models, and a list of tools. Packages are designed such that a VSE can implement its content, without having to implement the complete framework at the same time. The table of content of the project management deployment package is illustrated in figure 3.

In addition a series of *Implementation Guides* have been developed to help implement a specific process supported by a tool and are freely available from [20]. To date a small number of implementation guides have been developed. These include:

- Version Control with CVS
- Version Control with SVN
- Project Management with GForge
- Issue tracking with GForge
- Software Process Improvement with OpenOffice Calc.

---

1. Technical description

    Importance of project management

    Project management success and failure

2. Definitions (generic and specific definitions)

3. Relationships with ISO/IEC 29110

    Project management process

    Tasks and roles

4. Detailed description

    Roles, products and artifacts

5. Templates

    WBS, Project status template, etc.

6. Examples

    Project management lifecycle practices, etc.

7. Checklists

    Project plan review checklist, etc.

8. Tools

9. Reference to other standards and models

    ISO 9000, ISO/IEC 12207 and CMMI for Development

10. References

11. Deployment package evaluation form

Fig. 3. Table of Content of a Project Management deployment package

3   The Case Study

To date a series of pilot projects have been completed in several countries utilizing some of the deployment packages developed [21]. For example in France, a pilot study [22] was conducted with a 14-people VSE that builds and sells counting systems about the frequenting of natural spaces and public sites.

Furthermore a series of studies have been conducted to understand the perceptions [23] and potential commitment [24] of VSE management towards ISO.IEC 29110 [25]. In this section we describe the adoption of ISO/IEC 29110 Project Management practices by an Irish based VSE.

3.1   Case Study Company

An Irish based VSE, henceforth referred to using the pseudonym 'Emerald Island Software' expressed an interest in the adoption of ISO/IEC 29110 Project Management. Emerald Island Software has been in existence for 8 years and employs

9 people, 8 of which are involved directly in software development. Their primary market is financial services and insurance market sectors, where they have a single software product line and undertake bespoke software development for a variety of private clients. The CEO (and founder) of the company approached the researcher as part of an Irish governmental sponsored publicity launch of ISO/IEC 29110 and expressed an interest in exploring the potential benefits from partial or full standards practice adoption. After an initial series of briefing meetings with the CEO, CTO and two project manager in the company, where the ISO/IEC 29110 standard was presented and explained, the company agreed to adopt ISO/IEC 2910 Project Management practices as an initial starting point for exploring the potential of full practice adoption of ISO/IEC 29110.

The company already had an informal project management practices which varied depending on the specific project. Tools such as Microsoft Excel were generally used for project planning and scheduling purposes with 2 large whiteboards in the office used for open tracking of tasks and task allocation. The company used a modified waterfall approach to development, with some use of agile story cards as part of the requirements gathering phase. However, no formal project management practices were common to all projects and project managers were allowed significant amounts of discretion is managing projects under their control. However the company founders (who are the CTO and CEO) were becoming increasingly concerned about slippage on recent projects and issues of project velocity due to recent staff changes and a new project manager hire. The primary motivation for exploring ISO/ISC 29110 Project Management practices was to being some visibility and certainty to projects control. Accordingly 2 pilot projects were launched within the company.

3.2   Pilot Projects

Emerald Island Software agreed to implement all ISO/IEC 29110 Project Management Practices (as outlined above) for 2 new bespoke projects being undertaken. The first project (project Alpha) was 4 months in duration and was a totally new software package for an existing client delivering assistance with customer profiling in a financial institution. The second project (project Beta) was a 3-month project to add additional functionality to an existing bespoke package to a difference existing financial institution client. Table 3 illustrates some basic project information.

Table 3. Projects Alpha and Beta

	Project Alpha	**Project Beta**
Duration	4 months	3 months
Team	3 developers and project manager	2 developers and project manager
Client	Existing financial institution	Existing financial institution
Project risk	Medium	Low
Project type	New bespoke	Maintenance (new functionality) existing system

The pilot project was initiated by the researcher facilitates a series of round table 'Town Hall' style meetings where the role and purpose of ISO/IEC 29110 Project Management practices was explored in detail and discussions had on how the gap between existing practices and the tasks in ISO/IEC 29110. A 'standards champion' was appointed from the experienced staff and with assistance from the researcher he formulated a project management process guide for the company based on the published Project Management Deployment Package [26], which included the implemented of all the mandated lifecycle practices for the four 29110 Project Management Practices. This process guide was subject to review and enhancing by the researcher and was subject to further review and change at two further open 'town hall' style meetings within the VSE. The final outcome of this was a completed project management process guide for which Emerald Island Software would use to manage projects Alpha and Beta. For reasons of pre-agreed confidentiality none of the contents of the process guide can be disclosed in this paper.

3.3   Post-Mortem Interviews

A series of post-mortem interviews were conducted at the end of projects Alpha and Beta. These interviews were unstructured open interviews [27] and involved the project manager for each project. In addition the CEO and CTO were interviewed regarding both projects. The interviews lasted 2 hours in duration and were audio recorded and transcribed. The Grounded Theory [28] coding mechanisms was used to analyze interview data. Due to pre-agreed confidentiality reasons none of the empirical data collected regarding these pilot projects can be discussed in this paper.

Overall the experience of adoption ISO/IEC 29110 project management practices was regarded as a positive one by the company, with few reservations. The primary reservation – in particular as expressed by management – was the significant amount of time and resources consumed during the creation of the internal project management process guide. An interview extract illustrating this point from the CEO was *"Is they [ISO] want us [VSEs in general] to adopt standards then they should make it easier for us... they should give us complete how to guides and not just a list of task criteria... its too long and too difficult to create all these processes "*. Furthermore company management noted the lack of requirement from the market in general and their customer in relation to the need to have or follow a recognized standard. Examples of interviewee opinion illustrating these would be: *"In a company of our size they [standards] would not necessarily add value... we would only need more sophisticated process if we were a larger company"* and *"Our developers are busy with coding, we don't have resources to do that [standards compliance]"*. Furthermore as noted by one project manager there customer base did not require standards, saying, *"we had never had a problem selling our stuff or not selling our stuff because we don't follow an ISO standard"*.

By contrast interviews with project managers were generally supportive, however both questioned the need to change from existing practices, indicating, *"Nothing was really that wrong"* and *"we didn't really need to be this heavyweight in changing the way we work"*.

In order to understand more about the needs of VSEs in general regarding lifecycle standards, we asked all of the interviewees what criteria they considered important in a software lifecycle standard and for project management aspects in particular. The main criteria elicited were:

- Align with current development process style and working style
- Provide detailed guidelines and assistances
- Provide clear templates and example documentation
- Provision of mentorship and detailed guidance on how to actually apply practices in every day working situations
- Align with company existing business and development process.
- Align with others specific software technical standard and process.

4   Discussion

The relationship between the success of a software company and the software process it utilized has been investigated [29, 30, 31] showing the need for all organizations, not just VSEs to pay attention to software process practices such as ISO standards. As ISO/IEC 29110 is an emerging standard there is much work yet to be completed. The main remaining work item is to finalize the development of the remaining three profiles: (a) Entry – a six person-months effort project or a start-up VSEs; (b) Intermediate - Management of more than one project and (c) Advanced - business management and portfolio management practices. In addition the development of additional Profile Groups for other domains such as critical software, game industry, scientific software development are being studied

Recently, the ISO working group was mandated to develop a standard for VSEs developing systems. A system may include material, computer programs, firmware and technical documentation. The new standard for VSEs will use ISO/IEC 15288 System life cycle processes standard as the main framework. The objective of the working group is to develop a systems engineering basic profile which will match the software engineering basic profile. The working group will use the actual project management process of the software basic profile as the baseline to modify or add new tasks required by systems engineers. As an example, since most systems have material components, the project manager of a VSE must decide if the material components will be developed and built internally or subcontracted. This 'make or buy' task was not a task of the software project management process, it will therefore be added to the systems basic profile [32].

Acknowledgments. This work is supported, in part, by Science Foundation Ireland grant 03/CE2/I303_1 to Lero, the Irish Software Engineering Research Centre (www.lero.ie).

References

1. International Organization for Standardization (ISO): ISO/IEC TR 29110-5-1-2 Software engineering - Lifecycle profiles for Very Small Entities (VSEs) Part 5-1-2: Management and engineering guide: Generic profile group: Basic profile, Geneva (2011)

2. Laporte, C.Y., Alexandre, S., O'Connor, R.V.: A Software Engineering Lifecycle Standard for Very Small Enterprises. In: O'Connor, R., Baddoo, N., Smolander, K., Messnarz, R. (eds.) EuroSPI 2008, 129–141. CCIS, vol. 16, pp. 129–141. Springer, Heidelberg (2008)

3. Ryan, S., O'Connor, R.V.: Acquiring and sharing tacit knowledge in software development teams: An empirical study. Information and Software Technology 55(9), 1614–1624 (2013)

4. Ryan, S., O'Connor, R.V.: Development of a team measure for tacit knowledge in software development teams. Journal of Systems and Software 82, 229–240 (2009)

5. Clarke, P., O'Connor, R.V.: The situational factors that affect the software development process: Towards a comprehensive reference framework. Journal of Information and Software Technology 54(5), 433–447 (2012)

6. Jeners, S., Clarke, P., O'Connor, R.V., Buglione, L., Lepmets, M.: Harmonizing Software Development Processes with Software Development Settings – A Systematic Approach. In: McCaffery, F., O'Connor, R.V., Messnarz, R. (eds.) EuroSPI 2013. CCIS, vol. 364, pp. 167–178. Springer, Heidelberg (2013)

7. Charette, R.N.: Why Software Fails. IEEE Computer Society, Spectrum (2005)

8. O'Connor, R.V., Laporte, C.Y.: Deploying Lifecycle Profiles for Very Small Entities: An Early Stage Industry View. In: O'Connor, R.V., Rout, T., McCaffery, F., Dorling, A. (eds.) SPICE 2011. CCIS, vol. 155, pp. 227–230. Springer, Heidelberg (2011)

9. O'Connor, R.V., Laporte, C.Y.: Using ISO/IEC 29110 to Harness Process Improvement in Very Small Entities. In: O'Connor, R.V., Pries-Heje, J., Messnarz, R. (eds.) EuroSPI 2011. CCIS, vol. 172, pp. 225–235. Springer, Heidelberg (2011)

10. O'Connor, R.V., Laporte, C.Y.: Towards the provision of assistance for very small entities in deploying software lifecycle standards. In: Proceedings of the 11th International Conference on Product Focused Software (PROFES 2010). ACM (2010)

11. Coleman, G., O'Connor, R.V.: Investigating Software Process in Practice: A Grounded Theory Perspective. Journal of Systems and Software 81(5), 772–784 (2008)

12. O'Connor, R.V., Coleman, G.: Ignoring 'Best Practice': Why Irish Software SMEs are rejecting CMMI and ISO 9000. Australasian Journal of Information Systems 16(1) (2009)

13. O'Connor, R.V.: Evaluating Management Sentiment towards ISO/IEC 29110 in Very Small Software Development Companies. In: Mas, A., Mesquida, A., Rout, T., O'Connor, R.V., Dorling, A. (eds.) SPICE 2012. CCIS, vol. 290, pp. 277–281. Springer, Heidelberg (2012)

14. O'Connor, R.V., Laporte, C.Y.: An Innovative Approach to the Development of an International Software Process Lifecycle Standard for Very Small Entities. International Journal of Information Technology Systems Approach 7(1), 1–22 (2014)

15. Laporte, C.Y., O'Connor, R.V., Fanmuy, G.: International Systems and Software Engineering Standards for Very Small Entities. CrossTalk - The Journal of Defense Software Engineering 26(3), 28–33 (2013)

16. Clarke, P., O'Connor, R.V.: Harnessing ISO/IEC 12207 to Examine the Extent of SPI Activity in an Organisation. In: Riel, A., O'Connor, R.V., Tichkiewitch, S., Messnarz, R. (eds.) EuroSPI 2010. CCIS, vol. 99, pp. 25–36. Springer, Heidelberg (2010)

17. Jeners, S., O'Connor, R.V., Clarke, P., Lichter, H., Lepmets, M., Buglione, L.: Harnessing software development contexts to inform software process selection decisions. Software Quality Professional 16(1), 35–36 (2013)

18. O'Connor, R.V., Laporte, C.Y.: Towards the provision of assistance for very small entities in deploying software lifecycle standards. In: Proceedings of the 11th International Conference on Product Focused Software, PROFES 2010. ACM (2010)

19. Laporte, C.Y.: Contributions to Software Engineering and the Development and Deployment of International Software Engineering Standards for Very Small Entities. PhD thesis of the Université de Bretagne Occidentale, Brest (2009)
20. ISO/IEC JCT1/SC7 Working Group 24 Deployment Packages repository, http://profs.logti.etsmtl.ca/claporte/English/VSE/index.html
21. O'Connor, R.V., Sanders, M.: Lessons from a Pilot Implementation of ISO/IEC 29110 in a Group of Very Small Irish Companies. In: Woronowicz, T., Rout, T., O'Connor, R.V., Dorling, A. (eds.) SPICE 2013. CCIS, vol. 349, pp. 243–246. Springer, Heidelberg (2013)
22. Ribaud, V., Saliou, P., O'Connor, R.V., Laporte, C.Y.: Software Engineering Support Activities for Very Small Entities. In: Riel, A., O'Connor, R.V., Tichkiewitch, S., Messnarz, R. (eds.) EuroSPI 2010. CCIS, vol. 99, pp. 165–176. Springer, Heidelberg (2010)
23. Basri, S., O'Connor, R.V.: Understanding the Perception of Very Small Software Companies towards the Adoption of Process Standards. In: Riel, A., O'Connor, R.V., Tichkiewitch, S., Messnarz, R. (eds.) EuroSPI 2010. CCIS, vol. 99, pp. 153–164. Springer, Heidelberg (2010)
24. O'Connor, R.V., Basri, S., Coleman, G.: Exploring Managerial Commitment towards SPI in Small and Very Small Enterprises. In: Riel, A., O'Connor, R.V., Tichkiewitch, S., Messnarz, R. (eds.) EuroSPI 2010. CCIS, vol. 99, pp. 268–279. Springer, Heidelberg (2010)
25. Basri, S., O'Connor, R.V.: Organizational Commitment Towards Software Process Improvement An Irish Software VSEs Case Study. In: Proceedings of 4th International Symposium on Information Technology (ITSim 2010), Malaysia (June 2010)
26. O'Connor, R.V., Laporte, C.Y.: Software Project Management in Very Small Entities with ISO/IEC 29110. In: Winkler, D., O'Connor, R.V., Messnarz, R. (eds.) EuroSPI 2012. CCIS, vol. 301, pp. 330–341. Springer, Heidelberg (2012)
27. O'Connor, R.V.: Using grounded theory coding mechanisms to analyze case study and focus group data in the context of software process research. In: Mora, M., Gelman, O., Steenkamp, A., Raisinghani, M. (eds.) Research Methodologies, Innovations and Philosophies in Software Systems Engineering and Information Systems, ch. 13, pp. 1627–1645. IGI Global (2012)
28. Coleman, G., O'Connor, R.V.: Using grounded theory to understand software process improvement: A study of Irish software product companies. Journal of Information and Software Technology 49(6), 531–694 (2007)
29. Clarke, P., O'Connor, R.V.: The influence of SPI on business success in software SMEs: An empirical study. Journal of Systems and Software 85(10), 2356–2367 (2012)
30. Clarke, P., O'Connor, R.V.: Business success in software sMEs: Recommendations for future SPI studies. In: Winkler, D., O'Connor, R.V., Messnarz, R. (eds.) EuroSPI 2012. CCIS, vol. 301, pp. 1–12. Springer, Heidelberg (2012)
31. O'Connor, R.V., Basri, S.: Understanding the role of knowledge management in software development: a case study in very small companies. International Journal of Systems and Service-Oriented Engineering 4(1), 39–52 (2014)
32. Laporte, C.Y., O'Connor, R.V.: A Systems Process Lifecycle Standard for Very Small Entities: Development and Pilot Trials. In: Barafort, B., O'Connor, R.V., Poth, A., Messnarz, R. (eds.) EuroSPI 2014. CCIS, vol. 425, pp. 13–24. Springer, Heidelberg (2014)

Issues in Applying Model Based Process Improvement in the Cloud Computing Domain

Jeremy Cade[1], Lian Wen[2,3], and Terry Rout[2]

[1] Machine Intelligence and Pattern Analysis Laboratory (MiPAL),
Griffith University
jeremy.cade@griffithuni.edu.au
[2] Institute of Integrated and Intelligent Systems (IIIS),
Griffith University
l.wen@griffith.edu.au
[3] School of Information and Communication Technology (ICT),
Griffith University 170 Kessels Rd, Qld 4111, Australia
t.rout@griffith.edu.au

Abstract. Cloud Computing offers organisations a range of benefits, both economic and technological. However the decision to deploy an application or service to the cloud is a not a trivial one. Organisations need to be fully aware of not only the business requirements for a given application or service, but also the technological requirements and or constraints of the cloud. Model-based process assessment and improvement has been shown to support organisational change in different domains of application, but there are few reports of application in cloud computing. As a first step in defining suitable models to support process management, the impact of working with cloud resources on existing standard processes has been examined using the techniques of behavior engineering. A path for future work is proposed.

Keywords: Process Model, Software Process, Behavior Engineering, Cloud Computing.

1 Introduction

Organisations of all sizes are trending towards the Cloud Computing model as the preferred means of provisioning new, or migrating existing Information Technology (IT) systems. Cloud Computing offers organisations a greater degree of IT flexibility through access to inexpensive on-demand IT resources that are able to meet high levels of availability, reliability and scalability. This paradigm shifts the responsibility of maintenance and ownership of IT infrastructure and computing services from the organisation to Cloud Computing provides, who in turn make these services available as pay-per-use commodities.

The primary push to adopt Cloud Computing has historically come from organisations such as IBM, Amazon and Microsoft as a way to reduce the cost of IT infrastructure, application development and deployment [14][25]. A 2013 Forrester Research report found organisations were able to obtain a *Risk-Adjusted*

A. Mitasiunas et al. (Eds.): SPICE 2014, CCIS 477, pp. 238–249, 2014.

Return On Investment (ROI) of 349%, along with sizeable improvement in development/test environment setup and configuration by leveraging Microsoft's Azure Cloud Computing infrastructure[9]. While there are potential economic benefits, software and services engineered specifically for the paradigm are required if organisations wish to take full advantage of the possibilities offered by Cloud Computing.

It has been clearly demonstrated[13] that model-based process improvement provides a firm basis for defining productive approaches to development and operation of IT systems, specifically addressing the needs of particular domains; application to defence, aerospace, automotive and medical device systems have been documented. However, there are few (if any) reports on adaptation of common processes to working with cloud infrastructure. Our aim in this paper is to provide an initial evaluation of the issues and potential for process definition and improvement in relation to cloud computing.

In exploring potential process improvement strategies, it is useful to distinguish between the "basic" systems development processes, dealing with the specific engineering activities involved in developing the system, and the "infrastructure" processes concerned with managing and controlling the system development. The collection of infrastructure processes can commonly be represented by a "quality management system", and it is not unusual for process improvement in different domains to focus on the tailoring of the infrastructure, while leaving the basic processes largely unaffected. This can, however, result in significant problems and inefficiencies if the domain requires modification of the basic processes. The first step in applying process improvement in the cloud computing domain should be to determine whether specific tailoring of the basic processes is required, or whether improvement to the infrastructure processes alone is sufficient.

The set of basic processes are defined in International Standards such as ISO/IEC 12207 and ISO/IEC 15288; these also provide definitions of the bulk of the infrastructure processes. The distinction between the two classes of process is made clearer in process assessment models such as ISO/IEC 15504-5 and related organisational maturity models (ISO/IEC 15504-7).

In this paper we asses the current set of Software Engineering standards in relation to Cloud Computing. The Behavior Engineering technique, which has been demonstrated to be useful in verifying consistency in process definitions is applied to the common Process Reference Model (PRM) of ISO/IEC 12207 and ISO/IEC 15288, specifically looking at the Stakeholder Needs and Requirements Definition Process.

The rest of this paper is organised as follows. Section 2 provides background information on Cloud Computing, Process Management and Improvement, and Behavior Engineering. Section 3 describes the issues with the current Software Engineering approaches and provides a case study. Finally the paper is concluded and we set forth future research in Section 4.

2   Background

2.1   Cloud Computing

The Cloud Computing paradigm is a significant shift from traditional in-house IT infrastructure, allowing organisations to effectively deliver a wide range of services to consumers at lower cost[1]. The US Institute of Standards and Technology (NIST) provides the following definition[20]: *Cloud computing is a model for enabling ubiquitous, convenient, on-demand network access to a shared pool of configurable computing resources (e.g., networks, servers, storage, applications, and services) that can be rapidly provisioned and released with minimal management effort or service provider interaction.*

The Cloud Computing paradigm is comprised of four deployment models and three service models. The deployment models, Community Cloud, Hybrid Cloud, Public Cloud and Private Cloud all provides varying levels of tenancy of the underlying Cloud Computing infrastructure. At one end of the scale, Private Cloud provides resources for a single tenant, it may be provided offsite and managed by a Cloud Computing provider, or on-site and managed in a way similar to traditional IT infrastructure. At the other end of the scale is the Public Cloud, where resources are shared between multiple tenants. Community Cloud is similar to Private in that infrastructure is provisioned for a single community of tenants from multiple organisations that share a common concern. The Hybrid Cloud model is a combination of one or more of the three previous Cloud deployment models. The three service models Software as a Service (SaaS), Platform as a Service (PaaS) and Infrastructure as Service (IaaS) provide varying levels of control and management over the underlying cloud infrastructure. In the SaaS model software is delivered as a service on cloud infrastructure and is provided to a consumer or user through the use of a thin-client (e.g. a web-browser) or an Application Programming Interface (API). SaaS services are often consumer focused, but may also be enterprise services. PaaS provides a development platform and services that assist developers in deploying applications or software in a controlled manner. The developer has no responsibility for the underlying operating system configuration or infrastructure. IaaS capabilities are provided for the virtualisation of entire data-centres, providing Consumers with the ability to control infrastructure from the operating system up.

Cloud Computing providers may offer one of more deployment models, combined with one or more service models as part of a wider product offering, e.g. Both Amazon and Microsoft[1] offer both Infrastructure as a Service (IaaS) and Platform as a Service (PaaS), where as Google only provides a PaaS solution[2].

Previous research[6][11][10][23][29] in the Cloud Computing domain have identified a range of Software Engineering issues, though all agree that Requirements Engineering (RE) to be of significant importance.

RE has said to be the single hardest part of building a software system[4]. Requirements are often poorly defined in ambiguous language or exist within a

---

[1] Microsoft Azure: http://azure.microsoft.com/en-us/

[2] https://developers.google.com/appengine/training/intro/whatisgae#paas

large problem space. The traditional RE approaches can be broken down into five broad groups (Elicitation, Modelling, Requirements Analysis, Validation & Verification and Requirements Management)[5]. The traditional RE approach focuses on the elicitation and verification of requirements from the users and organisations that will make use of a software system. The different deployment and service models all have a slightly different set of requirements, particularly in relation to the required Software Engineering and/or developer skill sets[22]. These requirements may or may not be communicated by a Cloud Computing. Additional non-functional requirements also need to be considered by those tasked with RE when considering Cloud Computing deployments. These include:

- Quality of Service (QoS)
- Concurrency
- Storage
- Scalability
- Performance
- Portability
- Stability
- Security
- Regulatory Compliance
- Service Level Agreements (SLA)

Cloud Computing providers, as a supplier of infrastructure also need to be aware of an organisations requirements. This somewhat complicates the process of selecting acceptable Cloud Computing providers.

Service Management is of critical importance to successful implementation of Cloud Computing deployments. However there are a number of areas that may be affected by either the choice of Cloud Computing deployment model or the proposed workload. For example; A data and application based workload such as data-mining may be better suited to a private cloud, which may present additional service management requirements in relation to the cost of the infrastructure and organisation expertise deployment. IBM has suggested that Service Management Maturity Level Four processes are likely needed in order for a Cloud Computing deployment to be successful[15].

2.2   Process Management and Improvement

In addressing concerns with the deployment of a new infrastructure such as Cloud Computing, process management and improvement approaches offer much that is of benefit. As demonstrated by Humphrey[13], traditional approaches of process improvement can have significant impact in the IT environment. Following the model of ISO/IEC 24774, processes can be described in terms of their purpose and the outcomes of implementation; these descriptions can then be used as the basis for identifying strengths, weaknesses and improvement opportunities in the operations of the processes.

In order to apply this approach to Cloud Computing, the nature of the processes involved in working in a Cloud environment needs to be examined in more depth. A starting point for this can be found in the international standards for software and system life cycle processes, ISO/IEC 12207 and ISO/IEC 15288. These two core standards are currently under revision, and the new releases will be based around a set of core processes common to both standards. Following the framework of ISO/IEC 33001 and ISO/IEC 33004, we can say that the two standards have a common Process Reference Model (PRM), and we can extract process definitions generally applicable for software and systems development from this PRM.

As noted above, a key issue in Cloud Computing is the issues associated with Requirements Engineering. In the common PRM, the relevant process is the Stakeholder Needs and Requirements Definition process, defined as follows:

Purpose: The purpose of the Stakeholder Needs and Requirements Definition process is to define the stakeholder requirements for a system that can provide the capabilities needed by users and other stakeholders in a defined environment.

It identifies stakeholders, or stakeholder classes, involved with the system throughout its life cycle, and their needs. It analyses and transforms these needs into a common set of stakeholder requirements that express the intended interaction the system will have with its operational environment and that are the reference against which each resulting operational capability is validated. The stakeholder requirements are defined considering the context of the system of interest with the interoperating systems and enabling systems.

Outcomes: As a result of the successful implementation of the Stakeholder Needs and Requirements Definition process:

a) Stakeholders of the system are identified.
b) Required characteristics and context of use of capabilities and concepts in the life cycle stages, including operational concepts, are defined.
c) Constraints on a system are identified.
d) Stakeholder needs are defined.
e) Stakeholder needs are prioritised and transformed into clearly defined stakeholder requirements.
f) Critical performance measures are defined.
g) Stakeholder agreement that their needs and expectations are reflected adequately in the requirements is achieved.
h) Inputs for requirements of any enabling systems or system elements that serve the stakeholder needs and requirements activities are identified.
i) Any enabling systems or services needed for stakeholder needs and requirements are available.
j) Traceability of stakeholder requirements to stakeholders and their needs is established.

2.3   Behavior Engineering

Initially described in 2003, Behavior Engineering (BE)[8][7][3] is a formalised process allowing Software Engineers to translate natural language software requirements into a complete and consistent requirements specifications [3]. Behavior Engineering consists of the Behavior Modelling Process (BMP) and the Behavior Modelling Language (BML) notation [fig. 1], a formally grounded graphical notation consisting of Behavior Trees (BT) and Component or Composition Trees (CT) [3].

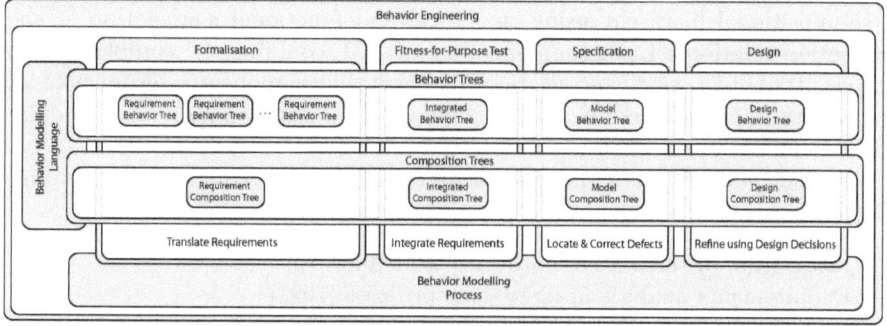

Fig. 1. Overview of Behavior Engineering

2.4   Behavior Modelling Process

The Behavior Modelling Process (BMP) consists of four distinct stages, Formalisation, Fitness for Purpose Test, Specification and Design. At each stage the process makes use of BML to address problems of scale, complexity and ambiguous language within natural language requirements.

Formalisation requirements are modelled one a time to for a Requirement Behavior Tree (RBT) and a corresponding Requirements Composition Tree (CBT) whilst trying to capture the original intent of the natural language requirement while removing ambiguity.

Fitness for Purpose RBTs are integrated together to form a Integrated Behavior Tree (IBT), while CBTs are integrated into Integrated Composition Tree (ICT) further reducing the number of errors and ambiguity in the natural language requirements.

Specification an executable specification called a Model Behavior Tree (MBT) is created by addressing the issues of incompleteness, inconsistency and redundancy within the IBT.

Design system boundary decisions are applied to the MBT

2.5   Behavior Modelling Language

As mentioned above the Behavior Modelling Language is a formally-grounded graphical notation.

BT are a formal, tree-like graphical form that represents behaviour of individual or networks of entities which realise or change states, make decisions, respond-to/cause events, and interact by exchanging information and/or passing control [8].

CT contain the complete system vocabulary, which by definition is consistent with the vocabulary used in BT as they both originate from the same natural language requirements. CT are a tree of components arranged into a compositional hierarchy using structural and functional aggregation or specialisation relations. Each component in the CT contains the complete set of states, attributes, events and relations in which the component is responsible for. CT are an important tool in resolving defects not visible in individual Requirement Behavior Trees, such as aliases.

Previous research has shown that aspects of BE may be of use in a wide range of applications including:

- Integration of software & hardware modelling [19]
- Requirements analysis in large scale projects [7][21]
- Risk-based testing [28]
- Semi-automated hazard analysis [12]
- Process modelling, comparison and validation [24][26][27]

2.6   Using Composition Trees to Model Software Processes

According to ISO/IEC 24774:2007 [18], the standard elements to describe a process include the title, the purpose, outcomes, activities and tasks. Apart from the title, which is only the name of a process, purpose and outcomes are more static elements, so they may be more suitable to be modelled by composition trees.

The benefit to model process in a composition tree is that the graph presentation provides a overall view of the process. The graphic presentation is less ambiguous, and formal verification such as comparing two processes can be performed by using automated tools[26].

Details about how to construct a Composition Tree from a process's purpose and/or outcomes can be found in our previous papers [26][27]. Here we only use one simple example to illustrate the composition tree constructed from the purpose of Configuration Management process defined in ISO/IEC 12207, AMD 1 / 2, 2000 [16].

Process Name. Configuration management.

Process Purpose. The purpose of the Configuration management process is to establish and maintain the integrity of the work products/items of a process or project and make them available to concerned parties.

In order to model this process, the first step is to identify and list all the components:

CMP Configuration Management Process

WPI Work product or work item
CPT Concerned Party

The composition tree translated from the process purpose is presented in fig.2, which shows that there are two different types of components under CMP, WPI and CPT; the * sign indicates that the component may have more than one instance. The WPI has an attribute called integrity and the integrity needs to be established and maintained. There is also a relationship for WPI; the relationship is that WPIs should be available to CPTs. The tag P in each box means this piece of compositional information is translated from the purpose of the process.

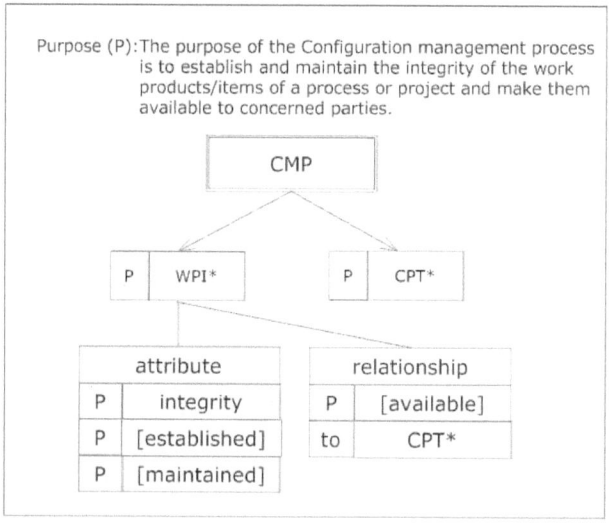

Fig. 2. The CT constructed from the purpose of the Configuration Management process

3   A Case Study

As identified, the impact from Cloud Computing on Software Engineering is all-dimensional and significant [10], ranging from requirement definition, requirement analysis, design and implementation to testing, deployment and maintenance. Therefore, in order to provide cloud computing based high quality software systems economically, the entire spectrum of software processes in the software life-cycle might need to be reviewed to address the impact from the cloud computing.

In this paper, we examine the Stakeholder Need and Requirement Definition Process defined in the latest version of Systems and software engineering - software life cycle process [17]. All the outcomes of this process are listed in the previous section; here we modelled the outcomes in a composition tree [fig. 3].

In this composition tree, CPM stands for critical performance measure and ESSE means enabling system or system element.

The difference between a traditional software project and a software project with Cloud Computing involved is that the later introduces an important stakeholder, the Cloud Computing service provider, who has dramatic influence on the project during the entire project life cycle. As this paper focus on the requirement definition stage, we only discuss the impact from the cloud service provider on the requirement definition stage.

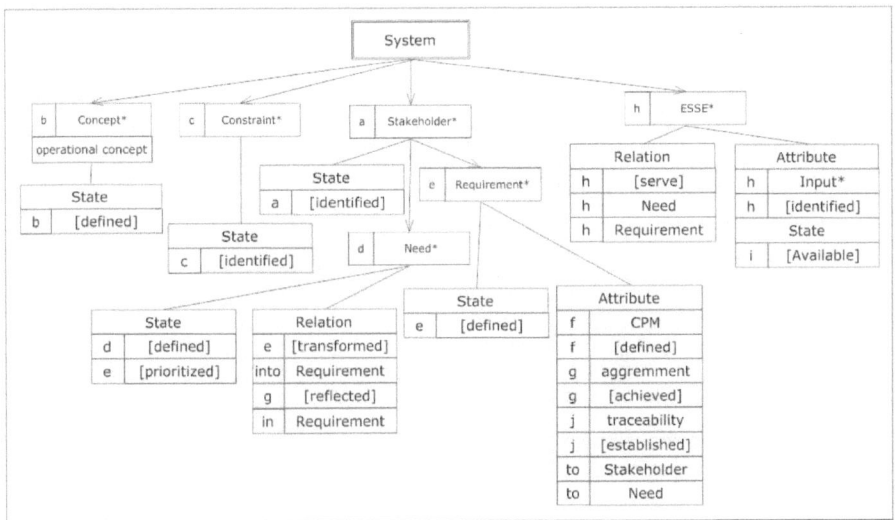

Fig. 3. Stakeholder Needs and Requirements Definition, modelled as a Composition Tree

For Cloud Computing enabled software systems, they usually confront following issues. Firstly, as a Cloud Computing enabled software system will have its data and services hosted and maintained in a third party Cloud Computing environment, security is always a concern, though is often demonstrated, many organisations are not knowledgeable of their own security needs nor they can state their security requirements properly [2]. Secondly, different Cloud Computing service providers might have different delivery capabilities. To match the customer's needs to the service provided by different Cloud Computing service providers and identify the most suitable one is not a trivial task [10]. Thirdly, due to the capability of the Cloud Computing service provider and budget, the customer needs to negotiate the requirements with the Cloud Computing service provider[29] and sometimes sacrifice the customer's requirements or policy. To illustrate those issues, we will introduce a real case study, the Griffith University Staff Email system, which had encountered a number of the issues.

Griffith University has a comprehensive on-line system called Griffith Portal, which integrates many subsystems covering nearly all the management aspects in the university. The university policy is that there should be only one authentication server for valid users to access all the different subsystems, and the authentication server must be hosted and fully controlled by the university. The university had evaluated a few cloud service providers including Microsoft and Google and finally selected Google to provide the staff email system. However, Google has its own account authentication server and its own privacy policy, which is inconsistent to with Griffith University's privacy policy. Under this situation, Griffith University and Google had to negotiate in order to find a solution that was acceptable for both parties. Eventually, a dedicated adapter is introduced to solve the policy conflicts. Under this arrangement, a user may feel that he/she is still using the ID and password assigned with their University account to login into the email service, however a second secret password is generated in the back-end to satisfy the authentication requirements of a Google account. This adapted solution is made slightly more transparent when a user tires to use a mobile device to access the email account. The user has to retrieve the second secret password and use it on the mobile device directly.

4   Conclusions and Future Research Topics

The case study above indicates that for a cloud involved software system, some important practices such as evaluating different cloud service providers, finding out the best match service provider, negotiating with the service provider regarding to the requirements, adjusting and even sacrificing some requirements are critical to the success of the system. However, those practices and their expected outcomes have not been adequately addressed in the traditional software process. At least the current stakeholder needs and requirement definition process does not explicitly state them in its outcomes. People may argue that even though the process outcomes do not address those issues directly, the given outcomes are actually abstract and high-level enough to cover nearly every practices discussed above. However, as those practices are so critical, they should be addressed explicitly to maximum the chance for a project to succeed.

At this stage the research is still in its preliminary stages. Future research will look to complete empirical studies within industry to confirm our initial findings while aiming to specify in detail the basic process model for the Cloud Computing domain. Long term research will be aimed at developing a suite of standards and processes for improving process models within the Cloud Computing domain; it is clear that the results of this research will impact on standards specific to the Cloud Computing domain, within the scope of JTC1 SC38/WG3, as well as to the work of WG10 and WG7 in JTC1 SC7, dealing with the definition, assessment and improvement of relevant processes.

References

1. Armbrust, M., Fox, A., Griffith, R., Joseph, A., Katz, R., Konwinski, A., Zaharia, M.: A view of cloud computing. Communications of the ACM 53(4), 50–58 (2010), doi:10.1145/1721654.1721672

2. Beckers, K., Heisel, M.: Structured Pattern-Based Security Requirements Elicitation for Clouds. In: Eighth International Conference on Availability, Reliability and Security (ARES), pp. 465–474 (2013)

3. Behavior Engineering Web Site, http://www.beworld.org/BE/

4. Brooks, F.: No Silver Bullet: Essence and Accidents of Software Engineering. IEEE Computer 20(4), 10–19 (1987)

5. Cheng, B.H.C., Atlee, J.M.: Research Directions in Requirements Engineering. In: Future of Software Engineering (FOSE 2007), pp. 285–303 (2007)

6. da Silva, E.A.N., Lucredio, D.: Software Engineering for the Cloud: A Research Roadmap. In: 26th Brazilian Symposium on Software Engineering (SBES), pp. 71–78 (2012), doi:10.1109/SBES.2012.12

7. Dromey, R.G.: Climbing Over the 'No Silver Bullet' Brick Wall. IEEE Software 23(2), 118–120 (2006)

8. Dromey, R.G.: From Requirements to Design: Formalising the Key Steps. In: IEEE International Conference on Software Engineering and Formal Methods (SEFM 2003), pp. 2–11 (2003)

9. Forrester Research: The Total Economic Impact of Windows Azure (2013), http://info.windowsazure.com/rs/microsoft/images/WhitePaper_The_Total_Economic_Impact_Of_Microsoft_Windows_Azure_Forrester.pdf (retrieved)

10. Guha, R., Al-Dabass, D.: Impact of Web 2.0 and Cloud Computing Platform on Software Engineering. In: 2010 International Symposium on Electronic System Design, pp. 213–218 (2010), doi:10.1109/ISED.2010.48

11. Grundy, J., Kaefer, K., Keong, J., Liu, A.: Software Engineering for the Cloud. IEEE Software 29(2), 23–29 (2012)

12. Grunske, L.: An Automated Failure Mode and Effect Analysis based on High-Level Design Specification with Behavior Trees. In: Proceedings of International Conference on Integrated Formal Methods (IFM), pp. 129–149 (2005)

13. Humphrey, W.S.: Managing the Software Process (Hardcover). Addison-Wesley Professional (1989)

14. IBM : IBM Perspective on Cloud Computing (2008), ftp://ftp.software.ibm.com/software/tivoli/brochures/IBM_Perspective_on_Cloud_Computing.pdf (retrieved)

15. IBM : Integrated service management and cloud computing. (2010), http://www.ibm.com/ibm/files/E955200R99025N70/5Integrated_service_management_and_cloud_computing_644KB.pdf (retrieved)

16. ISO/IEC 12207:1988, AMD 1 / 2:2000 Information technology Software engineering & Software life cycle processes (2000)

17. ISO/IEC IEEE 12207 CD1 - revision of 12207:2008 Systems and software engineering Software life cycle processes (2014)

18. ISO/IEC TR 24774. Software and systems engineering – Life cycle management – Guidelines for process description (2007)

19. Myers, T., Fristzon, P., Dromey, R.G.: Seamlessly Integrating Software & Hardware Modelling for Large-Scale Systems. In: 2nd International Workshop on Equation-Based Object-Oriented, pp. 5–15 (2008)

20. National Institute of Standards and Technology: The NIST Definition of Cloud Computing (2011)
21. Powell, D.: Requirements evaluations using Behavior Trees - findings from industry. In: Australian Software Engineering Conference (ASWEC 2007) (2007)
22. Ranger, S.: How cloud computing changes (almost) everything about the skills you need. ZDNet (2013),
    http://www.zdnet.com/how-cloud-computing-changes-almost-everything-about-the-skills-you-need-7000020163/ (retrieved)
23. Rimal, B.P., Jukan, A., Katsaros, D., Goeleven, Y.: Architectural Requirements for Cloud Computing Systems: An Enterprise Cloud Approach. Journal of Grid Computing 9(1), 3–26 (2012)
24. Tuffley, D., Rout, T.: Behavior Engineering as a Process Model Verification Tool. In: Proceedings of the 10th International SPICE Conference (2010)
25. Varia, J., Mathew, S.: Overview of Amazon Web Services. Amazon (2014), http://media.amazonwebservices.com/AWS_Overview.pdf (retrieved)
26. Wen, L., Tuffley, D., Rout, T.: Using Composition Trees to Model and Compare Software Process. In: O'Connor, R.V., Rout, T., McCaffery, F., Dorling, A. (eds.) SPICE 2011. CCIS, vol. 155, pp. 1–15. Springer, Heidelberg (2011)
27. Wen, L., Rout, T.: Using Composition Trees to Validate an Entry Profile of Software Engineering Lifecycle Profiles for Very Small Entities (VSEs). In: Mas, A., Mesquida, A., Rout, T., O'Connor, R.V., Dorling, A. (eds.) SPICE 2012. CCIS, vol. 290, pp. 38–50. Springer, Heidelberg (2012)
28. Wendland, M., Kranz, M., Schienferdecker, I.: A Systematic Approach to Risk-Based Testing Using Risk-annotated Requirements Models. In: CSEA 2012: The Seventh International Conference on Software Engineering Advances, pp. 636–642 (2012)
29. Zardari, S., Bahsoon, R.: Cloud Adoption: A Goal-Oriented Requirements Engineering Approach. In: Proceedings of the 2nd International Workshop on Software Engineering for Cloud Computing, pp. 29–35 (2011)

An Assessment Framework for Engineering Education Systems

Siegfried Rouvrais[1,2] and Claire Lassudrie[1]

[1] Telecom Bretagne, Institut Mines Télécom, France
[2] IRISA, CNRS UMR 6074
{Siegfried.Rouvrais,Claire.Lassudrie}@telecom-bretagne.eu

Abstract. Based on a return on experience, this paper describes and analyzes the application of a model-based assessment taking inspiration from ISO 15504 Process Assessment Models and Measurement Framework to the domain of higher educational systems. The context of the analysis is a medium higher educational institution in engineering. A worldwide used educational framework for engineering education quality is first described. By analyzing its underlying assessment model and measurement framework, the authors propose some improvements inspired by ISO 15504 series thanks to assessment experiences to highlight further research and development to move towards a Higher Education-15504 model.

Keywords: Assessment model, educational systems, engineering education, CDIO, SPICE.

1 Introduction

It is essential for higher educational institutions (HEI) to strengthen their educational programmes and better align them with new requirements by improving their quality. In particular, improving education and training system quality has been set as a key target in European strategy to become a smart, sustainable and inclusive economy by 2020. In higher education, several frameworks are defined for quality assurance, including accreditation systems (e.g. the Accreditation Board for Engineering and Technology in the USA or European Accreditation of Engineering Programmes, a.k.a. EUR-ACE framework standards). Lacking shared examples of evidence or best practices among HEIs, these frameworks are not well suited to continuous quality enhancement and are often informal. For HEIs, flexible and innovative models and processes are welcomed to support quality enhancement on a more continuous basis, as a complement to accreditations.

It is now recognized that software quality is largely dependent on the quality of the software design, development and maintenance processes. Computer Science and Software Engineering methods can contribute to an educational programme lifecycle. For example, the field of software engineering has experienced a crisis several years ago: software products were too often far from quality criteria. How can the assessment of quality in the industry, e.g. software industry, inspire the assessment of quality in higher

A. Mitasiunas et al. (Eds.): SPICE 2014, CCIS 477, pp. 250–255, 2014.

education in a flexible manner? An opportunity for educational programme designers might be to map capability maturity models to development [1, 2].

In the context of HEI in engineering, the CDIO (Conceive, Design, Implement, and Operate) framework [3] is often used as a continuous complement to meet accreditation expectations. In 2014, more than 100 HEI worldwide are members of the CDIO initiative, among which many apply an educational programme self-assessment process [4]. This experience paper reports the application of such frameworks including maturity models specific to HEIs in engineering [5,6]. However, these frameworks have some limitations concerning assessment reliability, repeatability and accuracy. By making an analogy between the various elements of the CDIO models and the generic SPICE assessment models and measurement framework, the broad lines of a new assessment model and measurement framework based on CDIO Standards can be proposed.

2   The CDIO Framework for Quality Enhancement

The international CDIO initiative [3] defines its vision as providing students with an education that stresses engineering fundamentals set, in a context of *Conceive, Design, Implement, and Operate* real-world systems, processes and products. It identifies three overall goals:

- Master a deeper working knowledge of technical fundamentals;
- Lead in the creation and operation of new products, processes and systems;
- Understand the importance and strategic impact of research and technological development on society.

To meet these goals, the initiative has created a set of resources that support the achievement of proper curricula. In order to help different key stakeholders of engineering education to assess and improve the quality of undergraduate engineering education, the initiative has developed a reference model of best practices that includes twelve Standards:

- Programme Philosophy (Standard 1),
- Curriculum Development (Standards 2, 3 and 4),
- Design-implement Experiences and Workspaces (Standards 5 and 6),
- Teaching and Learning Methods (Standards 7 and 8),
- Learning assessment (Standard 11),
- Faculty Competence (Standards 9 and 10),
- Programme Assessment (Standard 12).

Each Standard is defined by a description, a rationale, and a rubric, which is a six-point rating scale for assessing levels of compliance with a Standard. The CDIO Standards, with the associated rubrics can be considered as an Assessment Model in the context of Engineering Education systems. To help performing an assessment, some samples of evidence are provided per level for each Standard. As a measurement framework, the levels seek to indicate progress towards the planning, implementation and adoption of each Standard based on evidence gathered:

   0.   There is no documented plan or activity related to the Standard;

1. There is an awareness of need to adopt the Standard and a process is in place to address it;
2. There is a plan in place to address the Standard;
3. Implementation of the plan to address the Standard is underway across the programme components and constituents;
4. There is documented evidence of the full implementation and impact of the Standard across programme components and constituents;
5. Evidence related to the Standard is regularly reviewed and used to make improvements.

Compared to maturity scales defined for example in CMMI (Capability Maturity Model Integration) or ISO 15504-2, this is a very progressive approach, since full implementation of the Standards is only considered from level 4.

Each Standard is assessed individually; the final result is a radar profile of the educational system. The CDIO Assessment Process is defined in Standard 12: "A CDIO programme should be evaluated relative to the twelve CDIO Standards. Evidence of overall programme value can be collected with course evaluations, instructor reflections, entry and exit interviews, reports of external reviewers, and follow-up studies with graduates and employers [...]. This feedback forms the basis of decisions about the programme and its plans for continuous improvement."

3   Improving the CDIO Assessment Model Thanks to Experiences

3.1   Some Limits and Weaknesses

The CDIO framework provides useful guidance for continuous improvement of an educational system on aspects such as strategy, curriculum development, pedagogical activities, learning experiences and workspaces. The CDIO approach is implemented since 2008 at Telecom Bretagne, a French graduate engineering school. Several CDIO self-assessments have been carried out [5], by deans, teachers, and a group of students. However, the rating results are to be taken with caution: because it is non normative, the CDIO assessment model is sometimes informal and subject to confusion. During these assessments, several weaknesses of the CDIO model were identified:

- **Poor repeatability**: different assessors often produce different scorings due to lack of guidance (samples of evidence are not sufficient and may have an anecdotic character). Ratings of engineering education programme quality may thus differ depending on assessors [7]. HEI programme assessments are to be repeatable, as stated in SPICE-ISO 15504-2 [8] standard for process assessment;
- Difficulty to produce a scoring because of the **duality of some rubrics** (for example, level 1 involves both awareness and process implementation);
- **Lack of accuracy** in the scoring: one cannot express that a level is only partially satisfied (e.g. satisfied only in some departments of the institution). As an example, CDIO Standard 1 contains the criteria "CDIO is adopted as the context for the engineering programme [...]" at a given compliance level.

But, the assessor is left with the question of what would be "adopted as the context" (e.g. adopted by Management and/or programme leaders, or even fully understood and adopted by the whole educational system and staff);

- The CDIO framework does not provide a complete quality management model, as it does not address aspects such as learners support, relationships between research and education, or human resource management.

3.2   Towards an HEI-15504 Model

The main strength of the CDIO framework is its usability. Practical experiences led us now to propose an improved CDIO assessment model inspired by the ISO 15504 assessment model requirements.

- First, the definition of the **measurement scale should be improved** by introducing the concept of Standard Attribute (SA). Each Standard Attribute defines a specific aspect of Standard compliance. For example, level 1 of the Generic Rubric, "Awareness about the Standard" corresponds to two Standard Attributes:

  o   SA 1.1: The stakeholders concerned by the Standard are aware of the importance of its adoption;
  o   SA 1.2: A process is in place to address the Standard and implement it.

- The second improvement concerns the **introduction of the N-P-L-F attribute rating scale** defined in ISO 15504-2, 2003, to measure the extent of achievement of each Standard Attribute. This allows a more accurate scoring of each Standard.
- Finally, the **introduction of indicators** associated with each Standard Attribute categorized as practices, work products (e.g., curriculum, course supports, questionnaires, interview reports) and resources (e.g., pedagogical resources, rooms, human resources) will permit to build a complete CDIO assessment framework and allow repeatable assessments and benchmarking among different institutions. This work is still in progress.

The resulting assessment model has not yet been used, but its implementation will probably improve the reliability of assessments. However, the usability criteria, which was the main strength of CDIO model could be somewhat reduced because using a more formal model will involve some training.

4   Conclusion and Perspectives

A need for more flexible assessment models and processes is identified in HEI to reduce the inertia of heavy accreditations. In this experience report, we have analyzed the limits and weaknesses of the CDIO framework, considered as a more flexible and usable educational assessment model than the quality assurance systems encouraged by accreditation systems. Frameworks based on capability maturity models have overcome some of the identified limitations, with the potential of taking into account specific processes for educational systems. The SPICE approach extends its applications in various domains, sometimes with non SPICE compliant Process Reference Models or Process Assessment Models. Some improvements inspired by ISO 15504 were thus proposed in this short paper to improve repeatability and accuracy of CDIO assessments for HEIs. The proposed assessment model builds on CDIO standards to lead to a potential new HEI-15504 model dedicated to educational systems continuous improvement.

The new assessment model proposed has not been used yet. Future work will involve the development of a complete process reference model and assessment model specific to Engineering Education by establishing a correspondence between the CDIO Standards and related process and practices derived from generic process reference models. It would then be interesting to analyze whether the positive aspects of the initial CDIO model can be confirmed and see whether the educational system can be improved by implementing the new model on a continuous basis. Following an approach similar to Team SPICE [9], processes related to the implementation of each Standard could be identified.

In addition, and in line with the new series of standards ISO 330xx, different quality characteristics in educational systems assessment, such as flexibility, evolution, reliability, or scalability could be investigated and a new rating scale may be proposed. These new characteristics may be relevant for educational systems in engineering, which need to adapt to fast technological or societal evolutions.

Acknowledgments. This work has been initiated in the context of the 2014-2016 QAEMarketPlace4HEI project under the Erasmus+ European Programme on cooperation for innovation and the exchange of good practices. The consortium members in this project are committed to develop the quality of education in their strategies, but also to study assessment models and processes so as to propose more continuous, objective, and constructive evaluation procedures for European HEIs in engineering.

The authors express their gratitude towards *Ing. Samia Ech-Chantoufi* and *Soukaina Bakrim*, both senior engineering students at Telecom Bretagne in 2014. In the perspective of the 2015 educational programme renewal in their institution, they analyzed models and processes for quality enhancement during a joint semester project, proposed to enhance the in place assessment models and processes, and implemented a software prototype to support multi-role assessment.

References

1. Lister, R.: What If We Approached Teaching Like Software Engineering? ACM InRoads. Computing Education Research 2(1) (2011)
2. Larrondo Petrie, M.M.: Towards an Engineering Education Capability Maturity Model. In: Proceedings of the American Society for Engineering Education Annual Conference & Expositions (2004)
3. Crawley, E., Malmqvist, J., Ostlund, S., Brodeur, D., Edström, K.: Rethinking Engineering Education: The CDIO Approach, 2nd edn., p. 311. Springer (2014)

4. Kontio, J., Granholm, P., Valmu, H., Mäntykoski, J., Kruusamäe, K., Aukstuoliene, M., Savulionienes, L., Munkebo Hussmann, P., Edström, K.: Supporting Programmeme Development with Self- and Cross-evaluations – Results from an International Quality Assurance Project. In: Intl. Conference on Engineering Education, pp. 816–823 (2012)
5. Lassudrie, C., Kontio, J., Rouvrais, S.: Managing the Continuous Improvement Loop of Educational Systems: Students as key actors in programme evaluation. In: Proc. of the 9th Intl. CDIO Conference. MIT & Harvard School of Engineering and Applied Sciences (2013)
6. Rouvrais, S., Le Locat, C., Flament, S.: Return on Experience from Sustainability Audits in European Engineering Educational Institutions. In: Proceedings of the 41st Intl. SEFI Conference: "Engineering Education Fast Forward", KU Leuven, Belgium (2013)
7. Bennedsen, J., Georgsson, F., Kontio, J.: Evaluating the CDIO Self-Evaluation. In: Electronic Proc. of the 10th Intl. CDIO Conference. Universitat Politècnica de Catalunya, Barcelona (2014)
8. ISO/IEC 15504-2: Information technology - Process assessment - Part 2: Performing an assessment (2003)
9. Amengual, E., Mas, A.: Teamwork Best Practices in ISO/IEC 15504. In: Proc. of the 9th Intl. Conference on Software Process Improvement and Capability Determination, pp. 106–112 (2009)

Improving the Hardware/Software Culture

Joanne Schell and Paul Schwann

NXP Semiconductors Austria GmbH, Gratkorn, Austria
{joanne.schell,paul.schwann}@nxp.com

Abstract. In the automotive industry, hardware development has been solidly in place for about 130 years while software has contributed only progressively in the last 37 years [1, 2]. In spite of its recent appearance, software innovation becomes more and more critical for maintaining a competitive edge within semiconductor design, due to its relatively low cost and high flexibility. A stumbling block for many companies however is the persistence of a hardware design culture around software development. From our experience in multiple semiconductor companies, we present in this paper a pro-active approach towards improving the hardware/software collaboration and capitalizing on the strengths of both cultures.

Keywords: Software, hardware, automotive, process improvement, culture.

1 Problem, Root Cause and Impact

Software development within the automotive industry continues to be, in many instances, a secondary consideration to hardware. This status becomes apparent not infrequently, in various formats and scenarios, for example:

- A customer requirement specification for a complex product contains approximately 2000 hardware requirements. There is only one requirement related to software: "The product shall have software."
- A new product development is started; everyone meets for a week discussing the project but the software group is not invited.
- The software project manager is not invited to customer meetings.
- A company-wide innovation summit is held. Not a single software paper is presented.
- The upper management doesn't understand software problems.
- The standardized hardware development environment, including these elements:

  - automatic set up of tool versions, libraries, paths, environment variables for hardware engineers and support of environment tailoring
  - standardization, maintenance and archiving of hardware development environment

  ....is developed and maintained by a dedicated group. The software development environment is not.

A. Mitasiunas et al. (Eds.): SPICE 2014, CCIS 477, pp. 256–260, 2014.

- A simulation error persists for months because the hardware engineers seek a hardware bug when in fact the problem was in the software.

Software is an afterthought. It is not fundamentally in the automotive corporate culture.

Why do we have this situation? It is likely due, in part, to the abstract nature of software compared to hardware; you can touch hardware but you can't touch software. When the latest microchip is showcased in the automotive world, the schematic or layout view is generally presented and such a view doesn't contain software – so it's tempting to forget software.

Another reason is certainly the limited presence of pure software engineers on all levels within semiconductor companies. The software perspective is simply often lacking in discussions of company strategy and direction.

Of course, additionally, the hardware culture was established over decades and software is a relatively recent and gradual addition to the development space. It's natural, then, that software would be less integrated in the development process.

This notable lack of software craftsmanship leads to a misunderstanding of software complexity by both supplier and customer. The impact is multi-fold and significant:

- Quality suffers. Quality practice specific to software for requirements capturing, design, implementation, testing and documentation is not optimal and therefore the quality of the end product is not optimal.
- Planning is poor. Misconceptions about software generally result in underestimation by marketing and upper management. This is likely related to the inability to account for all the tasks in a software implementation.
- Reuse is limited. Poor architecture makes software components unstable and reduces application.
- There are missed business opportunities because of an inadequate understanding of the software potential.

Generally, the lack of software expertise means we are not exploiting the full power from the software/hardware system.

2   Solution

A cultural shift is necessary to capitalize on the tremendous potential of the hardware/software mix. We discuss in this section three broad practices for affecting that shift: 1) strengthening the software community 2) a procedural refresh 3) setting a price tag on software.

1. Strengthen the Software Community. In the past, hardware engineers wrote the software on a "Friday afternoon". Gradually that team and effort has grown but there has been no recognition that a different way of working is necessary. An awareness of a distinctive software community, requiring a different way of working, is vital. A consciousness/cohesiveness in the software development team *itself* is a first step.

One move towards this goal is to improve the software staff. Add pure computer scientists to the team, where possible. Ensure that software engineers have the same available career path as hardware engineers and that there are visible software persons with the highest title (e.g., "Fellow") in the organization.

Training the software engineers is, of course, also a necessary component of staff improvement. Take advantage of on-line software courses, like coursera [3] and MIT open courseware [4]. Develop internal software experts through the creation of internal trainings, led by software team members themselves. Introduce a yearly software summit to bring together software engineers from different units. A world-wide invitation helps to merge local communities into one virtual team. Possible agenda topics could include:

- overview of software sites, projects
- pre-summit software survey on tool use, challenges, wish lists; results presented at summit
- external speaker, for example, customer
- key note from internal upper management on software
- pre-summit call for papers; paper presentation at summit

A software summit not only strengthens the software community itself but it also brings software awareness to the rest of the organization, which should be supplemented with direct training.

This training is crucial (and often overlooked) for the non-software community as many members have limited understanding of software as a component of the hardware chip. Set up mini-seminars on high-level software topics especially for marketing, field application experts, hardware architects and management – persons who interface with the customer more and, hence, influence system design. Training topics should include:

- Explain the common elements in a software system and how the software interacts with the hardware.
- Highlight the potential of software for the product and customer.
- Encourage customer discussion of software requirements from marketing.
- Promote continuous exchange with the software team.

Implementing these practices was prompted in part by results from internal surveys across research and development departments. Software engineers rated trainings and software awareness in the hardware community highest on their improvement wish list.

2. Procedural Refresh. Many semiconductor companies developed their Quality Management System with hardware design in mind. Try this exercise – count the number of hits in your corporate QMS for the word "hardware" versus "software". If software is not being adequately represented, consider introducing a systematic assessment and update of the development procedures for software applicability.

The authors have observed two particularly effective techniques for improving software awareness through procedural edits. One is the introduction of software-specific slides into (management) presentation templates (where applicable.) The second technique is the inclusion of the software perspective earlier in the product development: make it part of the road mapping process and the review of early requirements. Checklists can help here to ensure attention to essential software topics, for example, with a software requirements checklist.

Additionally, we have taken procedures from either software or hardware and introduced it to the counterpart. Some significant hardware methodologies that we have seen successfully applied to software development include systematic risk management as defined by the FMEA procedure [5] and continuous process improvement – Kaizen [6]. We have also applied software methodologies to our hardware environment, for instance, the use of Scrum [7] in hardware design projects.

3. Set a Price Tag on Software. How much is software worth? This is clearly not an easy question to answer for software in the semiconductor space. However, developing a systematic method for determining software value can stimulate necessary attention to the existence and importance of software and help justify software improvements. (We have seen counterpart benefits of detailed price determination demonstrated in the hardware environment.) In determining value, one should cover at least costs in the price calculation. Consider not only what you think your software is worth, but also what your customers think. Some questions to aid the assessment:

- What are the competing products?
- What is the demand?
- Who needs this solution, and how unique is it?
- How hard would it be to develop the product from scratch? How much does the customer save?
- How much do your competitors charge?

Get help from the marketing department and use on-line sites, like StackExchange [8]. As the values will likely contain some qualitative aspects, ensure that the method is clear in communications. And also that the communications go to the software team itself. The exercise of price tag determination may be imprecise in the end, but it is, in itself, an excellent method to broaden the understanding of the customer's perspective and the software impact on the product.

The three solutions above have the advantage of being low effort and low cost but effective. Other approaches may be less attractive. For example, implementing a standard software development environment at a corporate level would have many benefits. However, the authors found the attempt in the short run overly expensive in terms of time and effort. (The compromise the we executed was to define a standardized software development environment at a local level.)

3 Experiences and Summary

Almost all recommendations in this presentation were implemented in our past experiences. We have seen many benefits including:

- Substantial software involvement begins earlier, before the start of the development project.
- Software groups are automatically invited to important events.
- The impact of software is articulated in management meetings by hardware team members.

- Because of management awareness, it is easier and faster to make decisions and get resources.
- Other disciplines adopt the software way of working.

In summary, software is relatively new in the automotive industry and the full potential of the hardware/software mix is still to be uncovered. Introducing the right software practices and extending the best practices of hardware can help you drive a leading-edge development culture.

References

1. History of the automobile, Wikipedia (June 5, 2014),
   http://en.wikipedia.org/wiki/History_of_cars (accessed June 20, 2014)
2. Charette, R.N.: This Car Runs on Code. IEEE Spectrum (February 1, 2009),
   http://spectrum.ieee.org/transportation/systems/this-car-runs-on-code (accessed January 20, 2014)
3. coursera, https://www.coursera.org/
4. MIT Open Courseware, http://ocw.mit.edu/courses/
5. Failure mode and effects analysis, Wikipedia (August 21, 2014),
   http://en.wikipedia.org/wiki/Failure_mode_and_effects_analysis (accessed August 23, 2014)
6. Kaizen, Wikipedia (August 6, 2014),
   http://en.wikipedia.org/wiki/Kai_Zen (accessed August 23, 2014)
7. Scrum (software development), Wikipedia (August 22, 2014),
   http://en.wikipedia.org/wiki/Scrum_%28software_development%29 (accessed August 23, 2014)
8. INC202721 How do you decide how much your software will cost? StackExchange,
   http://programmers.stackexchange.com/questions/8956/how-do-you-decide-how-much-your-software-will-cost/9552 (accessed June 20, 2014)

Learning Process Maturity Model

Justinas Marcinka, Oleg Mirzianov, and Antanas Mitasiunas

Vilnius University, 3 Universiteto Street, Vilnius, LT-01315, Lithuania
{justinas.marcinka,oleg.mirzianov}@gmail.com,
antanas.mitasiunas@maf.vu.lt

Abstract. Process capability maturity modeling elaborated by the Software Engineering community became applicable for any process oriented activity assessment and improvement. The purpose of this paper is to contribute to the solution of learning improvement problem based on the process capability maturity modeling approach. Learning process maturity model is developed based on R. Marzano taxonomy of learning objectives. Partial validation of the model developed is performed for the case of two groups of students. Preliminary conclusion: learning process maturity model can be used for learning activity assessment and improvement.

Keywords: Learning process, maturity model, SPICE, process assessment.

1   Introduction

Process capability maturity modeling elaborated by the Software Engineering community became applicable for any process oriented activity assessment and improvement. Is learning a process oriented or a creative activity? Furthermore, process capability maturity modeling typically is applied for processes performed by organizations, except PSP [5], which is performed by individuals. For instance, education process is performed by higher education institution. The results of such processes are quite tangible.

Contrary, learning is performed by a single human mentally. The results of the learning are intangible. Is it possible to express learning activity in process oriented terms? The way to find answers to these questions is to develop a learning process model and to prove the adequacy of this model based on the inspiring experience of innoSPICE – innovation, knowledge and technology transfer process capability model [1]. Such process model can be seen as a systematization and codification of the Body of Knowledge in the area of learning.

The state of the art in learning process capability maturity modeling is provided in the section 2. The sections 3 and 4 contain authors' contribution to learning process maturity modeling: development and validation of the learning process maturity model. The last section concludes results achieved and provides future work to be done to complete the solution of the problem addressed.

A. Mitasiunas et al. (Eds.): SPICE 2014, CCIS 477, pp. 261–267, 2014.

2   Learning Process Capability Maturity Modeling

Capability maturity modeling at organizational learning level is well elaborated [12]. Even process capability or organizational maturity improvement is understood as an organizational learning. There are few more or less direct attempts to touch capability maturity modeling at individual learning level. Personal software process [5] can be treated as learning how to improve personal performance based on planning, measurement and tracking, i.e., understanding the process performed.

Capability maturity modeling in e-Learning area [8] attracts bigger attention of researchers. E-Learning is situated in between of education as organizational activity and learning as individual activity. E-Learning creates conditions for learner centric education. Education process itself is an organizational process [11] and can be modelled by ISO/IEC 15504 [6] conformant and Enterprise SPICE based model [4].

Learning process maturity model [13, 14] is oriented to software development learning and is based on the idea that learning improvement can be achieved using the same concepts as software development improvement. The learning as an education area stresses on mental process of a learner. This area first of all is represented by the Bloom's Taxonomy [3] and the following learning models and approaches, including [2].

Particular place among them takes Marzano's New Taxonomy [9, 10] because of its process orientation. According to Marzano's Taxonomy learning is conditioned by three systems of mental activity: ego system, metacognitive system, and cognitive system. Ego system is responsible for decision making concerning learning. Metacognitive system defines the goals and strategy for goals achievement. Cognitive system is responsible for effective performance of the tasks related to information processing: comparison, classification, conclusion, etc. All these systems use knowledge possessed by a learner. Cognitive system consists of processes grouped into four levels of knowledge processing: retrieve, understanding, analysis and use. Hierarchical structure of learning process proposed by Marzano corresponds to authors' experience of learning and teaching gained during 40 years.

3   New Approach to Learning Process Capability Maturity Modeling

The main idea of this work is to take an attempt to decompose the learning activity into a set of processes and their performance descriptions, i.e., to create learning process as a "white box", instead of external behavior description of traditional "black box". The creative aspect of learning is often provided as an argument against such approach. Of course, creativity cannot be modeled by process based notions. The question is whether learning is really a completely creative activity. If yes, then a process oriented approach is indeed not suitable. Further, we will argue that this is not the case. Consider that software engineering is also an extremely creative activity, however it has been expressed in process oriented terms [7]. Developed and validated enhanced innovation and technology transfer process capability maturity model [1] is another successful confirmation of the possibility to express in process oriented terms such creative activity as innovation. Introduced here, the learning process maturity model consists of 7 processes to be performed by a learner. The descriptions of these processes satisfying ISO/IEC 15504-2 requirements for Process Reference Model [6] are provided in Table 1. The extended descriptions of learning processes for Process Assessment Model are developed and used for model validation that is provided in Section 4.

Table 1. Learning Process Reference Model

LEAR.1. Motivation Assessment	
Purpose	**Outcomes**
To assess motivation to learn and identify reasons for motivation	1) The importance of knowledge to be acquired is assessed by a learner. 2) Learner's opinion about his own ability to acquire identified knowledge and skills is self-evaluated. 3) Emotions related to knowledge and skills to be acquired and their acquisition are identified. 4) The reasons that condition learner's motivation to learn are identified.

LEAR.2. Learning Goals Definition	
Purpose	**Outcomes**
To define learning goals, level of knowledge acquisition and to select suitable strategy to reach learning goals, and to develop learning plan	1) Based on motivation target the knowledge level to be achieved (knowledge retrieve, synthesis, analysis or application ability) is identified by the learner. 2) Learning goals are defined. 3) Strategy to achieve learning goals is selected. 4) Learning plan is developed. 5) Learning sources are selected.

LEAR.3. Knowledge Retrieve Ability Development	
Purpose	**Outcomes**
To acquire ability to recognize and reproduce target knowledge	1) Learner is able to identify and recognize knowledge items. 2) Learner is able to reproduce and perform a procedure.

LEAR.4. Knowledge Synthesis Ability Development	
Purpose	**Outcomes**
To develop ability to abstract and aggregate knowledge	1) Learner is able to recognize essential and non-essential features of a knowledge item. 2) Learner is able to generalize a set of knowledge items with identic essential features by a single abstract notion. 3) Learner is able to represent, recognize and operate with abstract notions. 4) Learner is able to aggregate knowledge items and structures.

Table 1. *(Continued)*

LEAR.5. Knowledge Analysis Ability Development	
Purpose	**Outcomes**
To develop ability to verify consistency of aggregated knowledge and matching of new knowledge item to aggregate created.	1) Learner is able to identify similarities and differences of knowledge items. 2) Learner is able to identify knowledge items subsets and supersets. 3) Learner is able to identify mistakes in knowledge presentation. 4) Learner is able to identify special cases and derive related conclusions. 5) Learner is able to forecast possible circumstances.
LEAR.6. Knowledge Application Ability Development	
Purpose	**Outcomes**
To develop ability to apply aggregated knowledge for new tasks solution.	1) Learner is able to derive task solution based on knowledge aggregate possessed. 2) Learner is able to identify and assess solution's alternatives. 3) Learner is able to use knowledge and skills acquired as a tool for hypothesis investigation. 4) Ability to verify trustworthy of external information is acquired.
LEAR.7. Learning Results Tracking	
Purpose	**Outcomes**
To assess acquired knowledge and skills, and to compare learning achievements with learning goals.	1) Learner is able to track acquisition efficiency (to assess learning actions for learning goals achievement) of knowledge and skills being learned. 2) Learner is able to track consistency and precision of knowledge and skills being learned. 3) Learner is able to track trustworthiness of knowledge and skills being learned.

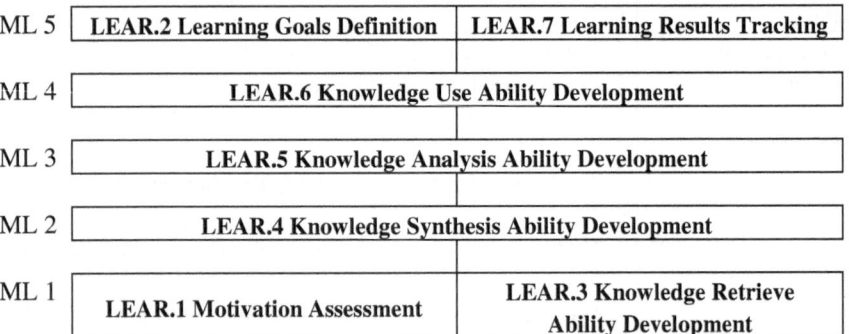

Fig. 1. Learning process maturity model

Learning process improvement path is defined by the five Maturity Levels (ML) of the learning process maturity model provided in Figure 1.The starting point for learning activity is motivation self-assessment and decision making for learning. When a decision to learn is made, the first step in learning process is Knowledge retrieve ability development. These two processes successfully performed ensure maturity level 1. Learning maturity levels 2, 3, and 4 are achieved by successful performance of knowledge synthesis, knowledge analysis and knowledge use processes. Maturity level 5 is ensured by learning process management oriented processes Learning Goals Definition and Learning Results Tracking.

4   Learning Process Maturity Model Validation

In order to partially validate the developed learning process maturity model, the experiments with participation of two groups of university students were performed. One group consisted of 10 students with the highest grades of one subject and other group – of 10 students with the lowest grades of the same subject.

Learning capability assessment was performed for all participants of the experiment using learning process assessment model not published yet. The participants of the highest grades (Group 1) achieved maturity level 3. The participants of the lowest grades (Group 2) failed to achieve maturity level 1.

Figure 2 displays assessment results in percent of performance of all seven processes for each group respectively. Process performance assessment for each group is calculated as the average of individual assessments for the same process of all participants of the group. The extent of student process performance assessment is evaluated in the scale from 0 to 100 percent. Maturity levels 1-3 are composed by processes LEAR.1, LEAR.3, LEAR.4 and LEAR.5. These processes are performed by the Group 1 at the extent 82, 89, 95 and 92 percent correspondingly, i.e., fully within assessment allowed deviation.

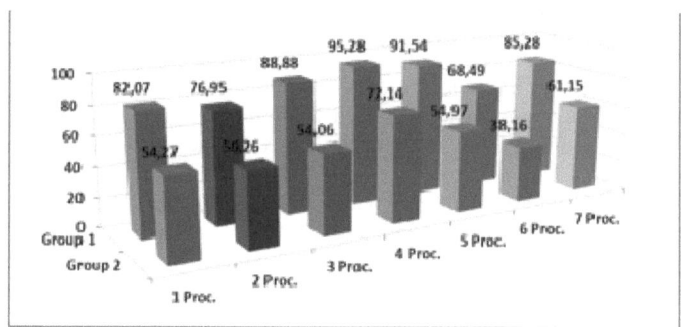

Fig. 2. Learning process maturity model validation experiment

5   Conclusions and Future Work

The paper provides the following new results in learning process modeling for its capability assessment and improvement:

1) Learning process maturity model based on R. Marzano taxonomy of learning objectives is developed;
2) The developed model is partially validated;
3) Learning process maturity model can be used for the development of learning improvement methodology.

To address the problem of learning improvement based on the process capability maturity modeling approach remaining future work should be done:

1) To develop learning methodology based on Learning process maturity model;
2) To perform learning improvement experiment in order to validate applicability of Learning process maturity model to the learning improvement;
3) To collect data to prove the correlation between the learning process maturity level and the learning success assessed by independent means.

References

1. Besson, J., Woronowicz, T., Mitasiunas, A., Boronowsky, M.: Innovation, Knowledge- and Technology Transfer Process Capability Model – innoSPICE®. In: Mas, A., Mesquida, A., Rout, T., O'Connor, R.V., Dorling, A. (eds.) SPICE 2012. CCIS, vol. 290, pp. 75–84. Springer, Heidelberg (2012)
2. Biggs, J.B., Collis, K.F.: Evaluating the quality of learning: The SOLO taxonomy (structure of the observed learning outcome). Academic Press, New York (1982)
3. Bloom, B.S., Engelhart, M.D., Frust, E.J., Hill, W.H., Krathwohl, D.R. (eds.): Taxonomy of educational objectives: The Classification of Educational Goals. Handbook I: Cognitive Domain (1956)
4. Enterprise SPICE An Integrated Model for Enterprise-wide Assessment and Improvement. Technical Report - Issue 1. The Enterprise SPICE Project Team, p.184 (September 2010), http://www.enterprisespice.com/page/publication-1
5. Humphrey, W.S.: Introduction to the personal software process (1997)
6. ISO/IEC 15504-2, Information Technology – Process Assessment – Part 2: Performing an Assessment (2003)
7. ISO/IEC 15504-5, Information Technology – Process Assessment – Part 5: An exemplar software life cycle process assessment model (2012)
8. Marshall, S., Mitchell, G.: Applying SPICE to e-Learning: An e-Learning Maturity Model. In: ACE 2004: Proceedings of the Sixth Conference of Australasian Computing Education, pp. 185–191. Australian Computer Society (2004)
9. Marzano, R.J.: Designing a New Taxonomy of Educational Objectives (2001)
10. Marzano, R.J., Kendall, J.S.: Designing & Assessing Educational Objectives: Applying the new taxonomy. Thousand Oaks, CA 91320, USA Designing (2008)
11. Mitasiunas, A., Novickis, L.: Enterprise SPICE based education capability maturity model. In: Niedrite, L., Strazdina, R., Wangler, B. (eds.) BIR Workshops 2011. LNBIP, vol. 106, pp. 102–116. Springer, Heidelberg (2012)

12. People Capability Maturity Model (P-CMM), Version 2.0, Second Edition, SEI CMU, 2009. CMU/SEI-2009-TR-003, ESC-TR-2009-003 (2009)
13. Thompson, E.: Towards a learning process maturity model. In: Freyberg, C., Hartmann, S., Kaschek, R., Kinshuk, Schewe, K.-D. & Turull Torres, J. M (Eds.) PhD Workshop. Palmerston North, Department of Information Systems, Massey University (2004)
14. Thompson, E.: Using a Subject Area Model as a Learning Improvement Model. In: The Eighth Australasian Computing Education Conference (ACE 2006) (2006)

Designing Systems Engineering Profiles
for Very Small Entities

Claude Y. Laporte[1] and Rory V. O'Connor[2,3]

[1] École de technologie supérieure, Montréal, Canada
claude.laporte@etsmtl.ca
[2] Lero, the Irish Software Engineering Research Centre, Ireland
[3] Dublin City University, Dublin, Ireland
roconnor@computing.dcu.ie

Abstract. To address the systems lifecycle needs of Very small entities, a set of standards and guides have been recently developed using the systems engineering lifecycle standard ISO/IEC/IEEE 15288 as the main framework. The systems engineering handbook, developed by the International Council on Systems Engineering (INCOSE), is used as the reference for the development of a set of systems engineering deployment packages. This short paper presents an overview of this new systems engineering standard and discusses certification scheme needs and future developments.

Keywords: VSE, ISO/IEC 29110, ISO, System Engineering Standards, ISO/IEC/IEEE 15288.

1 Introduction

A wide variety of approaches exist to guide software and systems engineering development with a significant number of situational factors [1] influencing the decision of which approach to use. For example, some approaches emphasize the importance of human interaction [2] and the transfer of tacit knowledge [3] between team members and others champion the meticulous execution of a systematic process. However, it is commonly agreed that no single approach is universally implemented and it seems likely that no single approach can be universally useful [4], primarily as no two settings are identical [5].

To assist very mall companies in tackling this problem, relatively new software and systems engineering lifecycle standards has been introduced, known as ISO/IEC 29110 Lifecycle profiles for Very Small Entities [6]. The approach [7, 8] used to develop ISO/IEC 29110 started with the pre-existing international standard ISO/IEC/IEEE 12207 [22] dedicated to software process lifecycles [9]. The overall approach consisted of three steps: (1) Selecting ISO/IEC/IEEE 12207 process subset applicable to VSEs of up to 25 people; (2) Tailor the subset to fit VSE needs; and (3) Develop guidelines for VSEs. There has been numerous papers written about the design and introduction of the ISO/IEC 29110 Lifecycle profiles for Very Small Entities standard [10, 11, 12] which specifically addresses the software lifecycle needs of Very Small Entities (VSEs) has been defined as being *"an enterprise,*

A. Mitasiunas et al. (Eds.): SPICE 2014, CCIS 477, pp. 268–273, 2014.
© Springer International Publishing Switzerland 2014

organization, department or project having up to 25 people" [13]. Furthermore several publications have presented the results of early stage evaluations and pilot projects to implement this standard in software development companies in several [14, 15, 16]. This short paper concentrates on the design and development of the next major stage of this standard, which is an extension to specifically address the Systems Engineering (as opposed to software engineering) needs of VSEs and the development of the ISO/IEC TR 29110-5-6-2:2014 - Systems Engineering Lifecycle Profiles for Very Small Entities (VSEs)' [18].

At the SC7 Plenary meeting in France in May 2011, the ISO/IEC 29110 project editor submitted, on behalf of Canada, a formal project proposal to develop a set of systems engineering standards for VSEs similar to the set developed for software VSEs. A draft systems engineering Management and Engineering guide for the Basic profile was attached to the formal proposal. The scope of this work includes the current scope of ISO/IEC/IEEE 15288, the associated guidance documents and other relevant SC7 Standards such as ISO/IEC/IEEE 15289 and ISO/IEC 29110. The project will produce Standards and Technical Reports (Guides), similar to the ISO/IEC 29110 set of Software documents for the Generic profile group (i.e. for VSEs developing non critical system), which establishes a common framework for describing assessable system engineering life cycle profiles for Very Small Entities (VSEs). The generic profile group is a collection of four profiles (Entry, Basic, Intermediate, Advanced) and is applicable to VSEs that do not develop critical systems. VSEs targeted by the Entry profile are those working on small projects (e.g., at most six person-months of effort) and for start-ups. The Basic profile describes the development practices of a single application by a single project team with no special risk or situational factors. The Intermediate profile is targeted at VSEs developing multiple projects within the organization. The Advanced profile is targeted at VSEs wishing to sustain and grow as independent competitive businesses.

2   The Systems Engineering Basic Profile

The Basic profile, as illustrated in Figure 1, as for the software engineering Basic profile which was used to develop the systems engineering Basic profile, is composed of two processes: a Project Management (PM) process and a System definition and Realization (SR) process. As defined in ISO/IEC 29110, the purpose of the Project Management (PM) process is to establish and carry out in a systematic way the tasks of the system development, which allows complying with the project's objectives in the expected quality, time and cost. The objectives of the ISO/IEC TR 29110-5-6-2 Project Management Process of the Basic profile are [18]:

- **PM.O1.** The Project Plan, the Statement of Work (SOW) and commitments are reviewed and accepted by both the Acquirer and the Project Manager. The Tasks and Resources necessary to complete the work are sized and estimated.
- **PM.O2.** Progress of the project is monitored against the Project Plan and recorded in the Progress Status Record. Corrections to remediate problems and deviations from the plan are taken when project targets are not achieved.

Closure of the project is performed to get the Acquirer acceptance documented in the Acceptance Record.

- **PM.O3.** Change Requests are addressed through their reception and analysis. Changes to system requirements are evaluated by the project team for cost, schedule, risks and technical impact.
- **PM.O4.** Review meetings with the Work Team and the Acquirer, suppliers are held. Agreements are registered and tracked.
- **PM.O5.** Risk Management Approach is developed. Risks are identified, analyzed, prioritized, and monitored as they develop and during the conduct of the project. Resources to manage the risks are determined.
- **PM.O6.** A Product Management Strategy is developed. Items of Product are identified, defined and baselined. Modifications and releases of the items are controlled and made available to the Acquirer and Work Team. The storage, handling and delivery of the items are controlled.
- **PM.O7.** Quality Assurance is performed to provide assurance that work products and processes comply with the Project Plan and System Requirements Specifications.
- **PM.O8.** A Disposal Management Approach is developed to end the existence of a system entity.

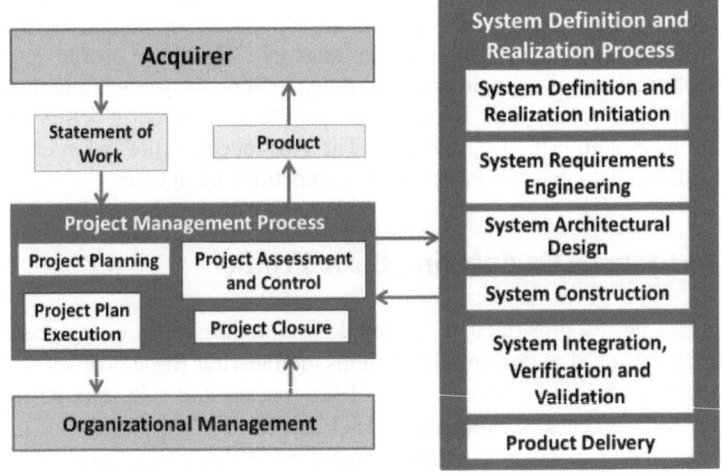

Fig. 1. Processes of the systems engineering Basic Profile

The purpose of the System Definition and Realization (SR) process is the systematic performance of the analysis, design, construction, integration, verification, and validation activities for new or modified system according to the specified requirements. The seven objectives of the SR process are [18]:

- **SR.O1.** Tasks of the activities are performed through the accomplishment of the current Project Plan.
- **SR.O2.** System requirements are defined, analyzed for correctness and testability, approved by the Acquirer, baselined and communicated.

- **SR.O3.** The System architectural design is developed and baselined. It describes the System elements and internal and external interfaces of them. Consistency and traceability to system requirements are established.
- **SR.O4.** System elements defined by the design are produced or acquired. Acceptance tests are defined and performed to verify the consistency with requirements and the design. Traceability to the requirements and design are established.
- **SR.O5.** System elements are integrated. Defects encountered during integration are corrected and consistency and traceability to System Architecture are established.
- **SR.O6.** A System Configuration, as agreed in the Project Plan, and that includes the engineering artifacts is integrated, baselined and stored at the Project Repository. Needs for changes to the Product are detected and related change requests are initiated.
- **SR.O7.** Verification and Validation Tasks of all required work products are performed using a defined criteria to achieve consistency among output and input products in each activity. Defects are identified, and corrected; records are stored in the Verification/Validation Reports.

Each objective of ISO/IEC 29110 is linked to processes of a standard. For example, objective SR.O5 is linked to ISO/IEC 15288:2008, 6.4.5 Integration Process, with just 2 of the 4 outcomes, of the integration process of ISO/IEC/IEEE 15288 being selected for the Basic profile.

So far, two Canadian systems engineering organizations have implemented the ISO/IEC 29110: a 4-person start-up VSE in the transportation field [23] and a large engineering firm. In the engineering firm, a cost and benefit study, using the ISO methodology to assess and communicate the economic benefits of standards [24], has showed significant savings from the implementation of ISO/IEC 29110 [20].

3   Future Work

Having developed ISs and TRs for VSEs involved in the development of software, WG24 developed the ISO/IEC 29110 systems engineering Basic profile management and engineering guide. Then members of the INCOSE VSE WG developed a set of Deployment Packages to help implement the Basic profile. WG24 started the development of the Entry profile for systems engineering. Once a stable version of the SE Entry profile is available [17], the INCOSE VSE working group will be able to start the development of the deployment packages to support the Systems Engineering Entry Profile. Once the ISO/IEC 29110 software Intermediate and Advanced profiles are ready, the development of the two matching systems engineering profiles for VSEs will start. Since many VSEs developing systems are also involved in the development of critical systems, WG24 and the INCOSE VSE Working Group will conduct an analysis to determine if a set of systems/software engineering standards for VSEs developing critical systems should be developed [19, 20]. Finally, the ISO/IEC 29110 SE profile specifications [21] should be published in 2015. This document, ISO/IEC 29110-4-6, will be an international standard and will be required by the auditors when they perform a systems engineering ISO/IEC 29110 audit. The certification scheme is based on ISO Standards on Conformity Assessment.

References

1. Clarke, P., O'Connor, R.V.: The situational factors that affect the software development process: Towards a comprehensive reference framework. Journal of Information and Software Technology 54(5), 433–447 (2012)
2. Ryan, S., O'Connor, R.V.: Acquiring and sharing tacit knowledge in software development teams: An empirical study. Information and Software Technology 55(9), 1614–1624 (2013)
3. Ryan, S., O'Connor, R.V.: Development of a team measure for tacit knowledge in software development teams. Journal of Systems and Software 82, 229–240 (2009)
4. Jeners, S., O'Connor, R.V., Clarke, P., Lichter, H., Lepmets, M., Buglione, L.: Harnessing software development contexts to inform software process selection decisions. Software Quality Professional 16(1), 35–36 (2013)
5. Jeners, S., Clarke, P., O'Connor, R.V., Buglione, L., Lepmets, M.: Harmonizing Software Development Processes with Software Development Settings – A Systematic Approach. In: McCaffery, F., O'Connor, R.V., Messnarz, R. (eds.) EuroSPI 2013. CCIS, vol. 364, pp. 167–178. Springer, Heidelberg (2013)
6. International Organization for Standardization (ISO): ISO/IEC TR 29110-5-1-2 Software engineering - Lifecycle profiles for Very Small Entities (VSEs) Part 5-1-2: Management and engineering guide: Generic profile group: Basic profile, Geneva (2011)
7. O'Connor, R.V., Laporte, C.Y.: An Innovative Approach to the Development of an International Software Process Lifecycle Standard for Very Small Entities. International Journal of Information Technology Systems Approach 7(1), 1–22 (2014)
8. Laporte, C.Y., O'Connor, R.V., Fanmuy, G.: International Systems and Software Engineering Standards for Very Small Entities. CrossTalk - The Journal of Defense Software Engineering 26(3), 28–33 (2013)
9. Clarke, P., O'Connor, R.V.: Harnessing ISO/IEC 12207 to Examine the Extent of SPI Activity in an Organisation. In: Riel, A., O'Connor, R., Tichkiewitch, S., Messnarz, R. (eds.) EuroSPI 2010. CCIS, vol. 99, pp. 25–36. Springer, Heidelberg (2010)
10. O'Connor, R.V., Basri, S., Coleman, G.: Exploring Managerial Commitment towards SPI in Small and Very Small Enterprises. In: Riel, A., O'Connor, R.V., Tichkiewitch, S., Messnarz, R. (eds.) EuroSPI 2010. CCIS, vol. 99, pp. 268–279. Springer, Heidelberg (2010)
11. O'Connor, R.V., Sanders, M.: Lessons from a Pilot Implementation of ISO/IEC 29110 in a Group of Very Small Irish Companies. In: Woronowicz, T., Rout, T., O'Connor, R.V., Dorling, A. (eds.) SPICE 2013. CCIS, vol. 349, pp. 243–246. Springer, Heidelberg (2013)
12. O'Connor, R.V.: Evaluating Management Sentiment Towards ISO/IEC 29110 in Very Small Software Development Companies. In: Mas, A., Mesquida, A., Rout, T., O'Connor, R.V., Dorling, A. (eds.) SPICE 2012. CCIS, vol. 290, pp. 277–281. Springer, Heidelberg (2012)
13. Laporte, C.Y., Alexandre, S., O'Connor, R.: Software Engineering Lifecycle Standard for Very Small Enterprises. In: O'Connor, R.V., Baddoo, N., Smolander, K., Messnarz, R. (eds.) EuropeComm 2009. CCIS, vol. 16, pp. 129–141. Springer, Heidelberg (2009)
14. O'Connor, R.V., Laporte, C.Y.: Deploying Lifecycle profiles for Very Small Entities: An Early Stage Industry View. In: O'Connor, R.V., Rout, T., McCaffery, F., Dorling, A. (eds.) SPICE 2011. CCIS, vol. 155, pp. 227–230. Springer, Heidelberg (2011)
15. O'Connor, R.V., Laporte, C.Y.: Using ISO/IEC 29110 to Harness Process Improvement in Very Small Entities. In: O'Connor, R.V., Pries-Heje, J., Messnarz, R. (eds.) EuroSPI 2011. CCIS, vol. 172, pp. 225–235. Springer, Heidelberg (2011)

16. O'Connor, R., Laporte, C.Y.: Towards the provision of assistance for very small entities in deploying software lifecycle standards. In: Proceedings of the 11th International Conference on Product Focused Software (PROFES 2010). ACM (2010)
17. ISO/IEC DTR 29110-5-6-1:2014 - Systems and Software Engineering – Lifecycle Profiles for Very Small Entities (VSEs) - Systems Engineering Management and engineering guide: Generic profile group: Entry profile, Geneva, Switzerland: International Organization for Standardization/International Electrotechnical Commission
18. ISO/IEC TR 29110-5-6-2:2014 - Systems and Software Engineering –Lifecycle Profiles for Very Small Entities (VSEs) – Part 5-6-2 - Systems Engineering - Management and engineering guide: Generic profile group: Basic profile, International Organization for Standardization/International Electrotechnical Commission: Geneva, Switzerland
19. Laporte, C.Y., Houde, R., Marvin, J.: Systems Engineering International Standards and Support Tools for Very Small Enterprises. In: 24th Annual International Symposium of INCOSE (International Council on Systems Engineering), Las Vegas, US, June 30-July 3 (2014)
20. Laporte, C.Y., O'Connor, R.V.: A Systems Process Lifecycle Standard for Very Small Entities: Development and Pilot Trials. In: Barafort, B., O'Connor, R.V., Poth, A., Messnarz, R. (eds.) EuroSPI 2014. CCIS, vol. 425, pp. 13–24. Springer, Heidelberg (2014)
21. ISO/IEC CD 29110-4-6:2014 Systems and software engineering — Lifecycle Profiles for Very Small Entities (VSEs) — Part 4-6: Systems Engineering profile specifications: Generic Profile Group, Geneva, Switzerland: International Organization for Standardization/International Electrotechnical Commission
22. ISO/IEC/IEEE 12207:2008, Systems and software engineering - Software life cycle processes, Geneva, Switzerland: International Organization for Standardization/ International Electrotechnical Commission (2008)
23. Laporte, C.Y., O'Connor, R., Garcia Paucar, L.H., Gerançon, B.: An Innovative Approach in Developing Standard Professionals by Involving Software Engineering Students in Implementing and Improving International Standards. In: International Cooperation for Education about Standardization Conference, Ottawa, Canada (August 14, 2014)
24. Economic benefits of Standards - ISO Methodology 2.0, International Organization for Standardization, Geneva, Switzerland (2010)

MDevSPICE - A Comprehensive Solution for Manufacturers and Assessors of Safety-Critical Medical Device Software

Paul Clarke, Marion Lepmets, Fergal McCaffery, Anita Finnegan,
Alec Dorling, and Derek Flood

Regulated Software Research Centre, Dundalk Institute of Technology,
Dundalk, Ireland
{paul.clarke,marion.lepmets,fergal.mccaffery,
anita.finnegan,alec.dorling,derek.flood}@dkit.ie

Abstract. Software development is frequently challenged with quality concerns. One of the primary reasons for such issues is the very nature of the software development process. First, it can be difficult to accurately and completely identify the requirements for a software development product. Also, the implementation on various platforms and the need to integrate with sometimes unforeseeable additional systems adds complexity. For safety critical domains, such as the medical device and healthcare sectors, these hurdles are amplified. Whereas a failure in a desktop application may be resolved through a restart with no harm incurred, a failure in a medical device can have life threatening consequences. Our work in the Regulated Software Research Centre (RSRC) aims to support medical device producers in the production of safer medical device software. In this paper, we describe the MDevSPICE framework and how it addresses the safety concerns faced by medical device producers.

Keywords: Medical Device Software, Software Process Improvement, Medical Device Software Process Assessment and Improvement, MDevSPICE.

1 Introduction

As software is increasingly incorporated into medical devices, so too is there a growing need to address the potential harm that can be caused by faulty software. As recently as 2011, "software failures were behind 24% of all the medical device recalls" FDA [1]. While the medical device domain is controlled by regulations that are designed to promote safety, the regulation is in practice satisfied through the implementation of appropriate process and quality standards. In recent years, a significant number of new or extended medical device software standards and guidance has emerged, with the result that we now have a large body of often disparate information on how best to implement medical device software. This circumstance gives rise to a number of issues. Firstly, with the information originating from different sources, it is expensive and difficult for manufacturers to determine the scope of each source, and more difficult still to accurately determine

A. Mitasiunas et al. (Eds.): SPICE 2014, CCIS 477, pp. 274–278, 2014.

the overlap and distinction between the sources. Secondly, competent authorities are also challenged to stay in tune with the emerging standards and guidelines in a domain that traditionally had a much smaller software footprint. Thirdly, the task of both manufacturers and competent authorities is further complicated by the absence of a consistent, internationally recognized and authoritative framework for assessing the manufacturers to deliver robust and reliable software to the medical device sector.

To address these issues, researchers in the RSRC have developed an internationally recognized framework hand-in-hand with the international standards organisations that consolidates the disparate medical device best practices into a single framework: MDevSPICE (formerly known as MediSPICE). Furthermore, the MDevSPICE framework is leveraged on leading generic software engineering best practice frameworks, and provides for a consistent and repeatable method for evaluating the competency of medical device software developers.

2   Medical Device Regulation and Standards

A medical device can consist wholly of software or have software as a component of the overall device [2]. In order to market a medical device within a given jurisdiction, it is necessary that the device complies with the regulatory demands of that region. The two largest global bodies involved in the development and evolution of medical device regulation are the Food and Drug Administration (FDA) and the European Commission (EC).

In the case of the US, the FDA issues the relevant regulation through a series of formal channels, including the Code of Federal Regulation (CFR) Title 21, Chapter I, Subchapter H, Part 820 [3] (ref. Figure 1). In the EU, the regulation is outlined in a number of sources: Medical Device Directive (MDD) 93/42/EEC [2], Active Implantable Medical Device Directive (AIMDD) 90/385/EEC [4], and *In-vitro* Diagnostic (IVD) Medical Device Directive 98/79/EC [5] – with all of these being amended by MDD 2007/47/EC [6]. Both the US and EU regulations outline varying degrees of safety concerns dependent on the medical device classification, which is broadly similar in both jurisdictions, ranging from Class I devices that are not intended to support or sustain human life, to Class III devices which have a critical role to play in supporting life.

The regulation outlined in the previous paragraphs may be satisfied through the implementation of medical device guidance and standards. ISO 13485:2003 (ISO 13485 from hereon) [7] outlines the requirements for regulatory purposes from a Quality Management System (QMS) perspective. ISO 13485, which is based on ISO 9001 [8], can be used to evaluate an organisation's ability to meet both customer and regulatory requirements. However, ISO 13485 does not offer specific guidance on software development, a role that is filled by IEC 62304:2006 (IEC 62304 from hereon) [9] which outlines the lifecycle processes necessary for the safe design and maintenance of medical device software. Beyond IEC 62340, numerous additional standards and guidance documents exist, such as ISO/IEC 12207:2008 and ISO/IEC 15504-5:2012 (ref. Figure 1) and these have been integrated into the MDevSPICE framework. In Figure 2, we provide an overview of the primary standards and sources of best practice that have been incorporated into the MDevSPICE solution. With all of the acknowledged best practice and guidance for medical device software development now housed within a single framework, it is possible to assess medical device software development to the most rigourous level. This MDevSPICE framework can be adapted and extended as the underlying standards and guidance evolve, thus ensuring that by adopting the MDevSPICE solution, organisations and assessment bodies can be confident that no key items have been overlooked.

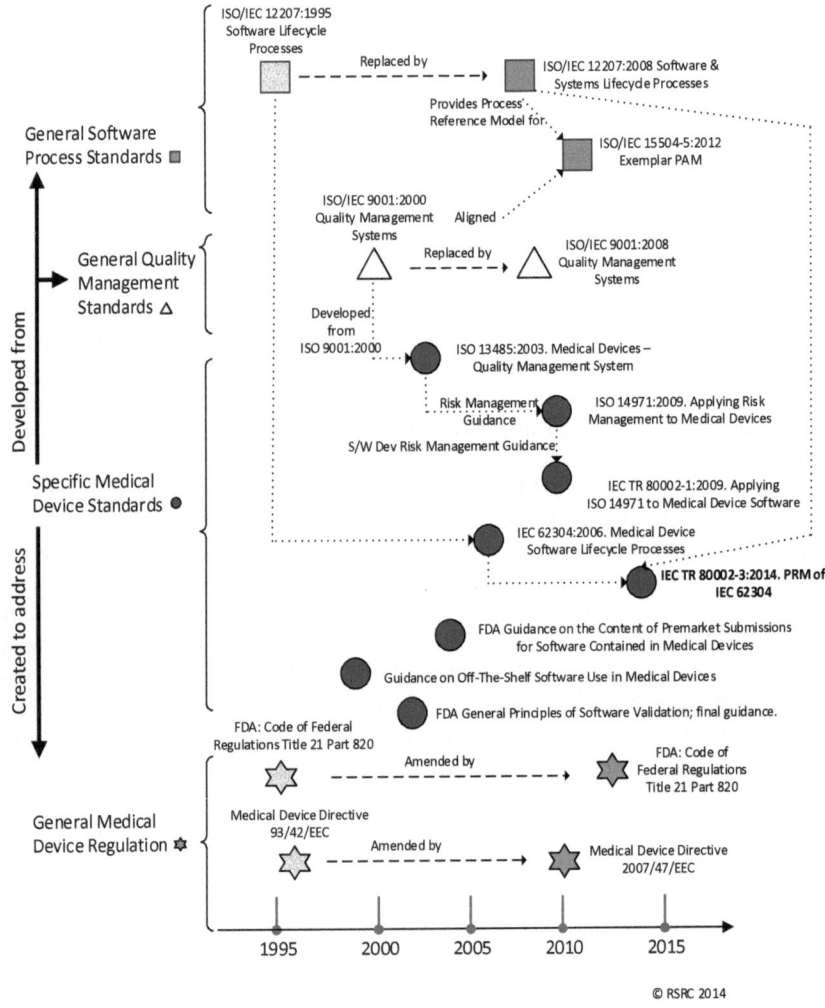

Fig. 1. Medical Device Regulations and Standards

In developing MDevSPICE significant international standards engagement has been required, with IEC TR 80002-3 (Process Reference Model for IEC 62304) now published [10]. IEC TR 80002-3 represents the culmination of many years of dedicated work by the RSRC, creating important new standards within the working groups of both the ISO and the IEC. Work of this nature also established a solid international agreement on the contributions made by the RSRC. Through working with international standards working groups such as IEC SC62A/ JWG3, IEC SC62A/JWG7 and ISO/IEC JTC1 SC7 WG10, the RSRC has advanced other standards, including IEC 80001-1-7 (Process Assessment Model for IEC 80001-1) and IEC 80001-2-8 (Guidance on standards for establishing Security Capabilities identified in IEC/TR 80001-2-2).

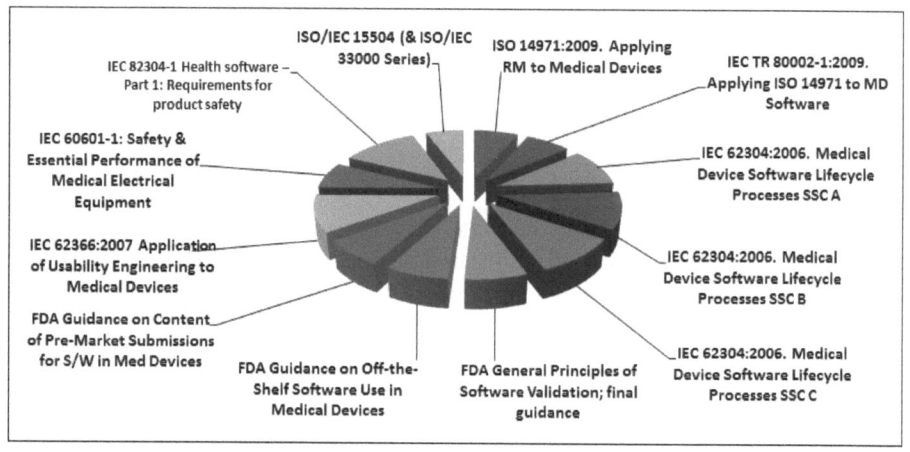

Fig. 2. MDevSPICE Process Assessment.

MDevSPICE itself is scheduled to be brought to the global market in Q4.2014 and it will for the first time concentrate the accumulated medical device best practices from all leading sources, while also supporting the industry and regulators in consistently and accurately evaluating software process implementation. This is good news for regulators, as a robust and thorough framework grounded in international standards will exist for assessing medical device software producers. And it is good news for the producers too, as all the medical device know-how will for the first time be assembled in a single, authoritative framework.

Acknowledgments. This research is supported by Enterprise Ireland and the European Regional Development Fund (ERDF) under the National Strategic Reference Framework (NSRF) 2007-2013, grant number CF/2012/2631, and in part by the Science Foundation Ireland (SFI) Stokes Lectureship Programme, grant number 07/SK/I1299, and the SFI Principal Investigator Programme, grant number 08/IN.1/I2030 (the funding of this project was awarded by Science Foundation Ireland under a co-funding initiative by the Irish Government and European Regional Development Fund).

References

1. FDA. FDA News on Software Failures Responsible for 24% of all Medical Device Recalls (2012),
   `http://www.fdanews.com/newsletter/article?articleId=147391&i ssueId=15890` (cited April 12, 2013)
2. European Commission, Directive 93/42/EEC of the European Parliament and of the Council concerning medical devices, in OJ o L 247 of 2007-09-21. 1993: European Commission, Brussels, Belgium
3. FDA. Chapter I - Food and drug administration, department of health and human services subchapter H - Medical devices, Part 820 - Quality system regulation,
   `http://www.accessdata.fda.gov/scripts/cdrh/cfdocs/cfcfr/ CFRSearch.cfm?CFRPart=820` (cited May 15, 2013)
4. European Commission, Council directive 90/385/EEC on active implantable medical devices (AIMDD). 1990: Brussels, Belgium
5. European Commission, Directive 98/79/EC of the European parliament and of the council of 27 October 1998 on in vitro diagnostic medical devices. 1998: Brussels, Belgium
6. European Commission, Directive 2007/47/EC of the European Parliament and of the Council concerning medical devices, in OJ no L 247 of 2007-09-21. 2007, EC: Brussels, Belgium
7. ISO, ISO 13485: Medical Devices - Quality Management Systems - Requirements for Regulatory Purposes. 2003, ISO: Geneva, Switzerland
8. ISO, ISO 9001:2000 - Quality Management Systems - Requirements, Geneva, Switzerland (2000)
9. IEC, IEC 62304: Medical Device Software - Software Life-Cycle Processes. 2006, IEC: Geneva, Switzerland
10. IEC, IEC TR 80002-3:2014: Medical device software – Part 3: Process reference model of medical device software life cycle processes (IEC 62304)

Enterprise SPICE Export Extension

Jeremy Besson, Antanas Mitasiunas, and Saulius Ragaisis

Vilnius University, Universiteto Str. 24, LT-01513 Vilnius, Lithuania
jeremy.besson@gmail.com,
{antanas.mitasiunas,saulius.ragaisis}@mif.vu.lt

Abstract. The process capability modeling became a tool for systematization and codifying knowledge of process oriented activities. Enterprise SPICE defines a domain independent integrated model for enterprise-wide assessment and continuous improvement. This paper presents employment of SPICE conformant application dependent process modeling to export activities and the resulting export process assessment model designed as Enterprise SPICE extension.

Keywords: Enterprise SPICE, application dependent process modeling, export, process assessment model.

1   Introduction

The process capability modeling became a tool for systematization and codifying knowledge of process oriented activities. By introducing the process capability concept it enables to assess the predictability of activity and to improve the quality of its results. Enterprise SPICE [1] defines a domain independent integrated model for enterprise-wide assessment and continuous improvement. But application domains contain application specific knowledge that cannot be covered in width and depth needed by domain independent process model.

This paper presents employment of SPICE conformant application dependent process modeling to export activities and the resulting export process assessment model designed as Enterprise SPICE extension.

2   Design Approach

The methodology for SPICE conformant application domain dependent process capability modeling based on the ISO/IEC 15504 capability framework and Enterprise SPICE domain independent external process model has been proposed in [2]. But it should be noted that applying this methodology for different application areas the resulting models differ in the processes of Application process category only, i.e. all such models contain the Enterprise SPICE processes. So, it is preferable to define this application dependent model as extension of Enterprise SPICE.

Enterprise SPICE has the concept of Special Applications that is also targeted to "re-use of the model without recreating processes that are already well established" [1].

A. Mitasiunas et al. (Eds.): SPICE 2014, CCIS 477, pp. 279–282, 2014.

But application practices are implemented by using other Enterprise SPICE processes in the particular context. This approach is suitable for Safety and Security because it express some specific point of view on the main company's business. But in the case of export, the situation is different: as a rule the products or services are created by the life cycle processes and they should be exported, i.e. there is a need to have separate processes for the export. So, the export process assessment model has been developed as Enterprise SPICE extension (not as special application area).

The purpose of Export process category introduced here is to reflect directly the body of knowledge in terms of essential processes and base practices of application satisfying requirements of ISO/IEC 15504-2 for process reference models (PRM) and process assessment models (PAM). The official US government resource for small and medium-sized business [3] has been taken as the main source of domain body of knowledge.

3   Export Process Category

All export related activities could be distributed into two stages: preparation for export and exporting itself. Therefore, two relative subcategories of processes have been introduced. Processes of Export Preparation and Exporting subcategories are listed in Table 1 and 2 correspondingly. Columns "O" contain the number of process outcomes, and "BP" – the number of process base practices.

Table 1. Processes of Export Preparation Subcategory (PRM level)

Process	O	BP
EXP.1. Export Conception. Purpose: to prepare conception of export of company's products or services.	6	6
EXP.2. Determining Export Potential. Purpose: to identify and evaluate internal and external obstacles, interferences and opportunities for products or services export that could prevent or significantly influence move to foreign markets.	6	9
EXP.3. Developing Export Strategy. Purpose: based on export goals and current constraints, to update the company's business strategy so that export goals will be achieved.	7	8
EXP.4. Export Decision Making. Purpose: according to company's goals and export strategy to evaluate internal and external factors determining products and/or services export and to take decision concerning export plan development and implementation.	7	7
EXP.5. Market Research. Purpose: to select countries and their regions having greatest potential for products and/or services export.	6	7
EXP.6. Distribution Channels Selection. Purpose: to identify the set of distribution channels and to select the most suitable distribution channels based on established criteria.	5	8
EXP.7. Finding Qualified Buyers. Purpose: to find qualified buyers for products and/or services and business partners abroad.	6	8
EXP.8. Export Planning. Purpose: to develop actions, measures and deadlines for products and/or services export goals achievement.	6	11

Table 2. Processes of Exporting Subcategory (PRM level)

Process	O	BP
EXO.1. Export Agreement Management. Purpose: to tune up and approve agreement for product and/or services export defining clearly and unequivocally expectations, rights, duties, and responsibilities of both parties, specifying products and/or services delivered, their price and payment conditions.	7	7
EXO.2. Delivery Terms Negotiation. Purpose: to reconcile commitments of seller and buyer and to submit them for approval by export agreement.	7	7
EXO.3. Pricing. Purpose: to create pricing policy of products and/or services, to reconcile price and payment conditions with buyer and to submit them for approval by export agreement.	7	8
EXO.4. Delivery Preparation. Purpose: to ensure availability of products and/or services for their recipient.	6	6
EXO.5. Shipping Management. Purpose: to select the most suitable shipping method and carrier or dispatcher for products export and conclude agreement for products transportation.	6	7
EXO.6. Exporting Services. Purpose: to provides the services that meet the contractual requirements.	6	6
EXO.7. Export Documentation. Purpose: to prepare documents of products and/or services export for cross border and/or at destination export transactions.	5	6
EXO.8. Export Insurance. Purpose: to mitigate the risk of damage or loss of products carried by international routes.	3	4
EXO.9.Payment Processing. Purpose: to ensure a smooth exchange of goods and/or services and to minimize the risk of failure to comply commitments.	10	14
EXO.10. Financing Export. Purpose: to ensure circulating assets for export of products and/or services.	7	8
EXO.11. Importer Satisfaction Survey. Purpose: to receive ongoing assessment of export by customers and partners.	5	6

The PAM level definition of a process consists of process identifier (formed from subcategory abbreviation and the sequential process number in the subcategory), process name, process outcomes, and base practices related to outcomes achievement of which they support. Example of complete process definition is provided in Table 3.

As a rule companies starting with process assessment models complain that it is not clear how models practices should be implemented. Therefore, the export processes are complemented with their implementation guidelines and examples of recognized business activities.

Table 3. Example of PAM level process definition

EXP.1. Export Conception
Purpose: to prepare conception of export of company's products or services.
Outcomes
1. Export goals are defined.
2. Export goals are consistent with company's goals.
3. Export potential of company's products and/or services is determined.
4. Suitability for export or adaptation possibilities of products and/or services is evaluated.
5. Resources required for export goals to be reached are determined and available.
6. Export priority is defined.
Base Practices
BP.1: Define export goals. [Outcome: 1]
BP.2: Align export goals with company's goals. [O.: 2]
BP.3: Determine export potential of company's products and/or services. [O.: 3]
BP.4: Estimate resources for products and/or services preparation for export. [O.: 4 and 5]
BP.5: Evaluate the changes in company's business will be caused by export. [O.: 2 and 5]
BP.6: Define export priority among all company's activities. [O: 6]

4   Conclusions and Future Work

SPICE conformant application dependent process modeling methodology has been applied for modeling of export activities. Approach for Enterprise SPICE extending by inclusion of application dependent PAMs has been proposed. The process assessment model for export processes has been developed as Enterprise SPICE extension.

The first trial of the model developed has been started by Lithuanian company exporting medical products. More extensive trials in different business sectors are needed for the appropriate validation of the model.

References

1. Enterprise SPICE. An Integrated Model for Enterprise-wide Assessment and Improvement. Technical Report - Issue 1. The Enterprise SPICE Project Team, 184 p. (September 2010), http://www.enterprisespice.com/page/publication-1
2. Boronowsky, M., Mitasiunas, A., Ragaisis, J., Woronowicz, T.: An Approach to Development of an Application Dependent SPICE Conformant Process Capability Model. In: Woronowicz, T., Rout, T., O'Connor, R.V., Dorling, A. (eds.) SPICE 2013. CCIS, vol. 349, pp. 61–72. Springer, Heidelberg (2013)
3. A Basic Guide to Exporting. U. S. Department of Commerce, 2012 edition, 246 p., http://www.export.gov/basicguide/

Author Index

Alves, Angela M.   48

Bannerman, Paul L.   214
Barafort, Béatrix   36
Besson, Jeremy   279

Cade, Jeremy   238
Cater-Steel, Aileen   165
Chagas, Larissa Fernandes   118, 177
Clarke, Paul   144, 274
Coady, Garret   190
Cortina, Stéphane   36

Dávila, Abraham   84
de Carvalho, Daniel Dias   118, 177
Demirörs, Onur   94, 202
Dorling, Alec   274

Figueiredo, Adriana M.C.M.   12
Finnegan, Anita   274
Flood, Derek   72, 274

Garcia, Cecilia   84
Gökalp, Ebru   94

Jung, Ho-Won   1

Khurshid, Nazrina   214

Laporte, Claude Y.   268
Lassudrie, Claire   250
Lepmets, Marion   60, 144, 274
Lima, Adailton Magalhães   118, 177

Maintinguer, Sonia T.   48
Marcinka, Justinas   261
Mas, Antònia   60
Mattos, Carolina V.   48
Mayer, Nicolas   36
McBride, Tom   1

McCaffery, Fergal   72, 144, 190, 274
McDaid, Kevin   72
McHugh, Martin   190
Mesquida, Antoni-Lluís   60
Mirzianov, Oleg   261
Mitasiunas, Antanas   261, 279

Neumann, Robert   131
Nevalainen, Risto   157

O'Connor, Rory V.   226, 268

Peldzius, Stasys   106
Pessoa, Marcelo   84
Plösch, Reinhold   24

Ragaisis, Saulius   106, 279
Regan, Gilbert   72
Reis, Carla Alessandra Lima   118, 177
Renault, Alain   36, 60
Rout, Terry   165, 238
Rouvrais, Siegfried   250

Salviano, Clenio F.   12, 48
Schell, Joanne   256
Schossleitner, Robert   131
Schwann, Paul   256
Shrestha, Anup   165
Stallinger, Fritz   24, 131
Stefanuto, Giancarlo N.   48

Toleman, Mark   165
Top, Özden Özcan   202

Varkoi, Timo   1, 157

Wen, Lian   238

Zeitoum, Camila   48